British Romantic Poetry

박병희 편주

UUP.

British Romantic Poetry

2010년 3월 2일 초판 인쇄
2010년 3월 7일 초판 발행

지은이 | 박병희
발행인 | 김도연
발행처 | UUP (울산대학교출판부)

출판등록 | 제370-1996-000001호(1996.3.13)
주소 | 680-749 울산광역시 남구 대학로 102
전화 | (052) 259-2488
팩스 | (052) 277-3011
홈페이지 | http://uup.ulsan.ac.kr
e-mai | press@mail.ulsan.ac.kr

값 15,000원

ISBN 978-89-7868-209-1 93840

Introduction

영문학사에서 낭만주의 시대는 워즈워스와 콜리지의 합작시집인 『서정담시집(Lyrical Ballads)』의 초판이 발간된 1798년부터 스코트(Sir Walter Scott)가 사망한 해인 1832년까지의 기간이다. 그 이전은 신고전주의 시대(Neo-classical Age)이고 그 이후는 빅토리아조 시대(Victorian Age)이다. 영문학사에서 낭만주의 시대에 작품 활동을 한 시인들로는 낭만주의 제1세대인 워즈워스(William Words- worth)와 콜리지(Samuel Taylor Coleridge), 그리고 낭만주의 제2세대인 바이런(George Gordon, Lord Byron), 셸리(Percy Bysshe Shelley), 키츠(John Keats)가 있다. 그러나 문학사의 시대구분은 다분히 자의적인 측면이 없지 않다. 게다가 문예사조의 변화는 어느 순간에 갑자기 일어나는 것이 아니라 장기간에 걸쳐서 서서히 일어난 것이다. 신고전주의 시대 중에서 문학에서 고전적인 기운이 쇠퇴한 시기인 존슨(Samuel Johnson)의 시대 혹은 그 이전부터 낭만주의적 기운이 일어나기 시작했다. 이러한 기운은 James Thomson (1700-48), William Collins (1721-59), Thomas Gray (1716-71), William Cooper (1731-1800), Robert Burns (1759-96), William Blake (1757-1827) 등 소위 "전 낭만파(preromantics)"로 분류되는 시인들의 작품에서 이미 감지되거나 상당히 발전되어 오고 있었다. 이들 중에서 특히 블레이크는 주요 작품인 『순수의 노래』를 1789년에 발표하였으므로, 시기적으로는 신고전주의 시대와 낭만주의 시대에 걸쳐 있지만, 그의 시는 다른 어느 시인 못지않게 낭만주의적 특질을 가지고 있으므로 이 책에서는 본격적인 낭만주의 시인으로 낭만주의 제1세대에 포함시켰다.

낭만주의 시를 공부하기 위해서는 먼저 그러한 시를 낳은 시대의 역사적 배경을 알아둘 필요가 있다. 낭만주의 문학을 탄생시킨 배경에는 두 가지 중요한 역사적 사건이 자리 잡고 있는데, 그것은 산업혁명과 프랑스혁명이다.

산업혁명은 경제구조를 농업과 상업 중심에서 산업 중심으로 탈바꿈시킨 역사적 사건이며, 영국에서는 1767년 James Watt의 증기기관 발명으로부터 시작되었다. 이것은 일련의 기계 및 기술혁명을 촉발시켜 섬유, 기계, 석탄, 제철공업 등의 비약적 발전을 이루게 하였고, 이 과정에서 새롭게 형성된 노동자계급은 정치·사회적 평등과 경제활동의 자유를 요구하게 된다. 이와 아울러 산업화의 과정의 부산물로 생긴 환경오염과 자연파괴는 오늘날 인간의 생존을 위협하는 갖가지 생태계 및 환경 문제의 원인을 제공했다.

프랑스혁명은 1789년 7월 14일 절대군주에 의한 압제의 상징인 바스티유 감옥의 파괴로부터 시작되어 왕정을 폐지하고 공화제를 수립하려고 한 정치적 사건이었다. 프랑스혁명의 정신은 라파예트(Lafayette)가 기초한 "인권선언"에 담겨 있으며, 자유, 평등, 주권재민, 언론자유, 사유재산의 불가침 등을 강조하였다. 그 후 1793년에 소집된 국민공회(National Convention)는 루이16세를 처형하고 왕정을 폐지하고 공화제를 수립하였다. 그러나 로베스피에르(Robespierre)의 공포정치(Reign of Terror)와 나폴레옹 황제의 등장으로 말미암아 프랑스혁명은 결국 실패로 끝나고 말았다. 이 두 가지 역사적 사건은 낭만주의 시를 이해하는 데에 직접적인 관련은 많지 않지만 시대정신을 이해하는 데 도움이 된다.

시대적 배경 다음으로 시를 보는 관점의 변화를 알아두는 것이 낭만주의 시를 읽는 데에 도움이 될 것이다. 낭만주의 시의 특징은 그 직전 시대인 신고전주의 시대의 시와 시론과의 대비를 통해서만 뚜렷이 나타나게 될 것이다. 신고전주의 시대에는 "자연을 비추는 거울(a mirror help up to nature)"처럼 인간의 삶을 모방한 것이 시라는 모방론(mimetic theory)과, 모방의 목적은 독자에서 즐거움과 교훈을 주는 데에 있다는 실용론(pragmatic theory)이

지배하였다. 그러나 낭만주의 시인들은 시를 외부세계의 모방이 아니라 시인의 내면적 감정의 표현으로 봄으로써 시의 원천을 내부세계에서 찾았다. M. H. Abrams는 낭만주의 시론을 이전의 모방론이나 실용론과 구별하여 "표현론(expressive theory)이라 명명하였다.

낭만주의 시론은 워즈워스(Wordsworth)와 콜리지(Coleridge)의 『서정담시집』(Lyrical Ballads) 서문(1800), 콜리지의 『문학평전』(Biographia Literaria), 셸리의 『시의 옹호』(A Defence of Poetry), 키츠의 『서간집』(Letters) 등에 담겨 있다. 이 중에서 특히 『서정담시집』 제2판에 수록된 워즈워스의 서문은 낭만주의 성명서라 불릴 정도로 중요한 문학사적 의의를 갖는다. 이 서문에서 워즈워스는 시를 "강한 감정의 자연발생적인 넘쳐흐름"(the spontaneous overflow of powerful feelings)이라 정의하였다. 이 정의는 시의 원천이 외부세계가 아니라 시인의 내부에 있음을 의미한다. 즉 시는 시인의 내면적 정서의 표현이다. 그 밖의 시인들도 비록 표현은 달라도 핵심적인 내용은 대동소이하다. 셸리는 『시의 옹호』에서 시를 "상상력의 표현"이라 정의했다.

낭만주의 영시를 공부하는 궁극적 목표는 낭만주의 영시의 본질을 파악하는 데에 있겠으나, 학부 과정에서는 추상적인 이론에 앞서 개별 작가의 작품을 읽고 그 작가의 작품 경향을 이해하는 것이 무엇보다도 중요하다. 작품을 제대로 읽고 이해할 수 있어야 개별 작가의 작품 경향과 낭만주의 영시의 보편적 특성을 유추해 볼 수 있을 것이다. 편저자는 이 책에서 각 시인의 작품 경향을 파악하는 데에 꼭 필요한 작품을 선정하여 가능한 한 자세하게 주석을 붙여 개별 작품을 이해하는 데에 도움을 주려고 노력하였다. 그리고 각 시인들의 작품 말미에 최소한의 참고문헌 목록을 첨부하였다. 개별 작품을 읽어나가면서 각 시인에 대한 기초적인 비평서를 함께 읽는다면 낭만주의 영시를 이해하는 데에 도움이 될 것이다.

2010년 2월 편저자 씀

Contents

John Keats (1795-1821) / 321

William Blake
(1757~1827)

William Blake in an 1807;
portrait by Thomas Phillips

Title Page, *The Book of Urizen* (1794)

블레이크의 생애와 작품

블레이크(William Blake)는 1757년 11월 28일 런던에서 잡화상의 3남으로 태어났다. 정규교육은 받지 못하였고, 10세 때까지 어머니에게 가정교육을 받았다. 10세에 미술학교(drawing school)에 보내졌고, 15세 때부터 7년 동안 판화가 제임스 버자이어(James Basire)의 도제가 되어 미술공부를 하였고, 1779년에 왕립미술학교(Royal Academy of Art)에 입학했다.

블레이크는 1778년에 다수의 이단자들과 교제했고, 그들 중 판화가인 John Flaxman 같은 친구들은 스베덴보리 추종자들의 신비적 종파에 가담했다. 1782년에 정원사의 딸 캐서린 바우처(Catherine Boucher)와 결혼했다. 결혼 당시에 그녀는 문맹자였으나 블레이크는 캐서린에게 글을 가르쳐주었고 그의 판화제작을 돕게 하였다. 초기 전기에는 캐서린이 가난한 천재를 내조한 이상적인 아내로 그려져 있었으나, 실은 그녀가 소유욕이 강하고 질투심이 많아 가정불화가 잦았다. 그들 사이에는 자녀가 없었다.

블레이크는 한동안 회화교습을 하고 책에 삽화도 그리고 판화도 제작하면서 꽤 여유 있게 살았다. 그러나 일거리의 주문이 줄어들게 되자 1800년에 아마추어 화가인 윌리엄 헤일리(William Hayley)의 후원으로 서섹스 해안의 펠펌에 있는 시골집으로 이사했다. 헤일리가 그를 인습적인 화가로 만들려고 하자, 블레이크는 이에 반발하여 펠펌에서 3년을 보낸 후 런던으로 돌아갔다. 1809년에 개인전을 열었으나 완전히 실패로 돌아가자 그는 초야에 묻히는 신세가 되었다. 육십 대에 들어서서 그는 미술에만 전념하기 위하여 시작을 그만두었다. 그는 일생동안 수백 점의 작품을 남겼는데, 그중에서 많은 것들은 다른 시인들의 작품을 도해한 것이었다. 이를테면 초서(Geoffrey Chaucer)의 캔터베리 순례객의 묘사, 욥기를 위한 도안, 단테의 작품 도해 등이 그것이다. 세상을 떠날 당시 그는 세상에 별로 알려지지 않은 화가였으며, 시인으로서도 거의 무명의 존재였다. 19세기 중반에 라파엘 전파들(Pre-Raphaelites) 간에 일단의 숭배자들이 생겼고, 1920년대 중반 이후 마침내 시와 그림에서 독창적인 예술가로 평가받게 되었다. 블레이크는 70세가 되던 해에 세상을 떠났다.

블레이크의 첫 시집 『시적 소묘』(Poetical Sketches)는 그가 26세 되던 해인 1783년에 인쇄된 것으로 당대의 시적 관습에 대한 불만과 새 형식과 기법에 대한 주구를 보여준다. 그는 신고전주의 시의 전통에서 벗어나 엘리자베스조와 17세기 시인들, 그리고 콜린즈(William Collins), 토마스 채터튼(Thomas Chatterton) 등에서 서정시의 모델을 찾았다. 블레이크는 특유의 리듬과 비유법을 사용하여 근대 상징시의 선구가 되었다. 어릴 때부터 비상한 상상력을 지녔으며, 창가에서 천사와 이야기하고 언덕 위에 올라 하늘을 만진 체험이 있다고 하지만, 그러한 신비로운 체험을 최초로 표현한 것이 『순수의 노래』(Songs of Innocence)이다. 이 시집을 제작할 때 그는 동판으로 한 페이지를 몇 장씩 찍은 후 손으로 수채물감을 칠하여 텍스트와 그림과 장식이 앙상블을 이루는 특이한 시집을 만들었다. 이 시집은 자연과 인간의 세계에 순수한 사랑과 아름다움으로 가득 차 있다는 사상이 기조가 되어 있는데, 『셀의 서』(The Book of Thel)(1789)는 그 속편이라 할 수 있다. 『천국과 지옥의 결혼』(The Marriage of Heaven and Hell)(1790)에서는, 스웨덴의 신비주의 신학자 스베덴보리(Swedenborg)의 영향을 받으면서도 그의 사상을 비판하여, 인간의 근원에 있는 두 개의 대립된 상태, 즉 이성과 에너지(活力)의 조화가 새로운 도덕이 되어야 한다고 주장하였다. 그리하여 『순수의 노래』에 그려진 목가적 동심의 세계는 『경험의 노래』(Songs of Experience)(1794)에서 일단 부정되고, 분열되고 투쟁하는 현실 세계의 어두운 면이 강조된다. 전자에서는 양(羊)의 순진함을 노래하였으나, 후자에서는 밤의 숲속에서 빛을 내는 호랑이에 시선을 돌린다. 이러한 인간관과 이에 입각한 사회비판은 이윽고 몇 권의 예언서를 낳았다. 미국의 독립을 노래한 『아메리카』(America)(1793)이외에 『유럽』(Europe)(1794), 『유리젠 기』(The Book of Urizen)(1794), 『네 개의 분신』(The Four Zoas) 등 서사적 신화가 식각(蝕刻)되었고, 나아가서 죄의 용서를 중심사상으로 하는 『밀턴』(Milton)(1804~1808)과 『예루살렘』(Jerusalem)(1804~1820)이 완성되었다. 인간정신에는 언어를 매개로 하지 않고 상징에 의하여 생각하는 영역이 있는데, 블레이크의 신화적 상징은 바로 그러한 원초적 체험을 표현하려고 한 것으로, 그런 의미에서 시대를 앞선 시인이었다.

블레이크의 예언서는 인간의 창조와 타락, 인류의 역사와 구원 그리고 에덴동산 및 새로운 예루살렘 회복의 약속으로 이어지는 성경 줄거리의 몇몇 대목을 다룬 것이다. 그는 성경의 사건들을 정신적 의미로 해석하였다. 그는 예언서에서 워즈워스, 콜리지, 사우디, 그리고 수많은 영국의 급진적 신학자들과 마찬가지로 당시의 혁명을 성서의 예언에 따라 인류와 세상의 구원이 임박하였음을 알리는 전조로 설명하였다. 그의 후기 시에서 혁명정신을 상징하는 오크(Orc)가 상상력을 상징하는 로스(Los)에게 중심인물의 자리를 내어주게 되었는데, 이것은 그가 초기 신념을 철회한 것이기보다는 오히려 혁명에 대한 계시에서 상상력에 의한 계시로 역점이 바뀐 것으로 보아야 한다.

From *Songs of Innocence* (1789)[1)]

Introduction

Piping down the valleys wild
Piping songs of pleasant glee
On a cloud I saw a child.
And he laughing said to me.

Pipe a song about a Lamb!
So I piped with merry chear.
Piper, pipe that song again—
So I piped, he wept to hear.

Drop thy pipe, thy happy pipe
Sing thy songs of happy chear,
So I sung the same again,
While he wept with joy to hear.

Piper, sit thee down and write
In a book, that all may read—
So he vanish'd from my sight,
And I pluck'd a hollow reed.

And I made a rural pen,
And I stain'd the water clear,
And I wrote my happy songs,
Every child may joy to hear.

---

1) 블레이크는 이 시집에서 18세기 시의 틀을 깨고 동요 형식과 무구한 어린 아이의 어조를 사용하여 원형적인 사상을 표현하는 독특한 방법을 창안했다. 그는 작품 하나하나에 그림을 그리고 색칠을 하여 특이한 시집을 만들어냈다. 이 서시에서 어린아이가 곡을 불러주고 Piper가 받아 적는다. 어린아이는 곡을 연주하는 것을 듣고 기뻐서 운다. 그는 그 곡을 노래로 불러 달라고 요구한다. 그리고 글로 적어 달라고 말한다. 불러주는 어린아이—어른—듣는 어린아이로 이어지는 단순한 과정에는 복잡하고 심오한 진리가 숨어 있다. 어린아이는 다른 아이들에게 직접적으로 소박하게 말을 한다. 어른은 전달자요 보존자로서의 관계를 맺고 있다. 그러나 이 시를 읽는 어른은 단순히 엿듣는 사람에 머문다. 어른이 듣는 내용은 어린아이의 지혜요, 가식에 물들지 않은 순수한 어린아이의 목소리이다.

Ecchoing Green

The Sun does arise,
And make happy the skies.
The merry bells ring,
To welcome the Spring.
The sky-lark and thrush,
The birds of the bush,
Sing louder around,
To the bells' chearful sound,
While our sports shall be seen
On the Ecchoing Green.

Old John, with white hair.
Does laugh away care,
Sitting under the oak,
Among the old folk.
They laugh at our play,
And soon they all say,
Such, such were the joys,
When we all girls & boys,
In our youth time were seen,
On the Ecchoing Green.

Till the little ones weary
No more can be merry
The sun does descend,
And our sports have an end:
Round the laps of their mothers,
Many sisters and brothers,
Like birds in their nest,
Are ready for rest:
And sport no more seen,
On the darkening Green.

The Lamb

Little Lamb, who made thee
Dost thou know who made thee
Gave thee life & bid thee feed,
By the stream & o'er the mead;
Gave thee clothing of delight,
Softest clothing, wooly, bright;
Gave thee such a tender voice,
Making all the vales rejoice:
Little Lamb, who made thee
Dost thou know who made thee

Little Lamb, I'll tell thee,
Little Lamb, I'll tell thee;
He is called by thy name,
For he calls himself a Lamb:[1]
He is meek & he is mild;
He became a little child:[2]
I a child & thou a lamb,
We are called by his name.
Little Lamb, God bless thee,
Little Lamb, God bless thee.

---

* 양에 대한 즐거운 묘사와 어린아이의 양에 대한 본능적 사랑 그리고 신에 대한 소박하고 순수한 이해를 표현하고 있다. 단순한 리듬과 율격과 반복을 통해 어린아이의 말투를 재생해낸다. 양은 부드러운 털 외투와 계곡에 울려 퍼지는 울음소리, '개울가 풀밭에서 풀을 뜯는' 것으로 묘사되고 있다. 좀 더 자세히 읽어보면, 이 시는 기독교 신학을 훌륭하게 표현하고 있음을 알 수 있다. 제1연에서 어린아이는 조물주에 대해 질문하고, 제2연에서 자신의 질문에 답한다. 양을 창조하신 하느님은 그 자신이 양이라 불린다. 그는 십자가에 못 박혀 죽었다("He called Himself a Lamb"). 그리고 부활하여 어린아이로 다시 태어났다(He became a little child). 어린아이와 양이 둘 다 하느님의 이름으로 불리는 것은 신의 두 가지 속성이 부활(Incarnation)과 수난(Passion)이기 때문이다. 이 시에는 블레이크가 말한 "threefold vision"이 나타나 있다. 이 시는 동물과 인간이 자비로운 신의 보호 아래 완전한 사랑과 조화 속에 살고 있는 지상의 낙원(Beulah)의 모습을 보여준다. (Watson 80)

1) *a Lamb*: 양은 속죄양을 의미하여 십자가에 못 박혀 죽은 그리스도의 수난을 암시한다.

2) *a little child*: 하나님이 아기 예수의 모습으로 탄생한 것과 그리스도의 부활을 암시한다.

The Little Black Boy

My mother bore me in the southern wild,
And I am black. but O! my soul is white;
White as an angel is the English child:
But I am black as if bereav'd of light.

My mother taught me underneath a tree
And, sitting down before the heat of day,
She took me on her lap and kissed me,
And pointing to the east began to say:

Look on the rising sun: there God does live
And gives his light, and gives his heat away.
And flowers and trees and beasts and men recieve
Comfort in morning, joy in the noonday.

And we are put on earth a little space,
That we may learn to bear the beams of love.
And these black bodies and this sunburnt face
Is but a cloud, and like a shady grove.

For when our souls have learn'd the heat to bear
The cloud will vanish: we shall hear his voice,
Saying: 'Come out from lhe grove, my love & care,
And round my golden tent like lambs rejoice..

Thus did my mother say, and kissed me.
And thus I say to little English boy.
When I from black and he from white cloud free,
And round the tent of God like lambs we joy:

I'll shade him from the heat, till he can bear,
To lean in joy upon our father's knee.
And then I'll stand and stroke his silver hair,
And be like him, and he will then love me.

The Chimney Sweeper

When my mother died I was very young,
And my father sold me while yet my tongue
Could scarcely cry weep weep weep weep.
So your chimneys I sweep & in soot I sleep.

Theres little Tom Dacre, who cried when his head
That curl'd like a lamb's back, was shav'd, so I said,
Hush. Tom never mind it, for when your head's bare,
You know that the soot cannot spoil your white hair.

And so he was quiet, & that very night,
As Tom was a sleeping he had such a sight,
That thousands of sweepers Dick, Joe, Ned & Jack
Were all of them lock'd up in coffins of black,

And by came an Angel who had a bright key,
And he open'd the coffins & set them all free.
Then down a green plain leaping, laughing, they run
And wash in a river. and shine in the Sun.

Then naked & white, all their bags left behind,
They rise upon clouds, and sport in the wind.
And the Angel told Tom, if he'd be a good boy,
He'd have God for his father & never want joy.[1)]

And so Tom awoke and we rose in the dark
And got with our bags & our brushes to work.
Tho' the morning was cold, Tom was happy & warm.
So if all do their duty, they need not fear harm.[2)]

---

1) "착하게 굴면 하나님을 아버지로 모시고 행복하게 살 수 있다"는 말은 주일학교 선생님의 말씀이다.

2) "의무를 다하면 해를 입을까 두려워할 필요가 없다": 어른들 말씀을 잘 들으면 매는 맞지 않을 것이다. 성인의 관점에서 보면 이 말이 암시하는 노예상태는 끔찍하게 여겨질 것이다.

The Divine Image

To Mercy Pity Peace and Love,[1]
All pray in their distress:
And to these virtues of delight
Return their thankfulness.

For Mercy Pity Peace and Love,
Is God our father dear:
And Mercy Pity Peace and Love,
Is Man his child and care.

For Mercy has a human heart
Pity, a human face:
And Love, the human form divine,
And Peace, the human dress.

Then every man of every clime,
That prays in his distress,
Prays to the human form divine
Love Mercy Pity Peace.

And all must love the human form,
In heathen, turk or jew.
Where Mercy, Love & Pity dwell,
There God is dwelling too.

---

* 인간의 내부에 있는 신의 속성은 "자비, 연민, 평화, 사랑"이며, 그 중 으뜸이 "사랑"이다. 제4연에서 이 네 가지 속성은 "the human form divine"과 동격으로 되어 있다. 블레이크는 "살아 있는 것은 모두 신성하다(everything that lives is holy)"고 했다. 그는 당대의 이신론(Deism)을 타파하는 것을 필생의 과업으로 삼았으며, 초월자가 아니라 그리스도를 신성의 전형으로 보았다. "신성한 인간성"은 모든 인간의 내면에 있는 신이다. 블레이크의 그리스도는 한 인간이 태어날 때마다 다시 태어나며, 한 인간의 몸 안에서 출생과 삶과 죽음을 경험하는 인간성 그 자체이다. 그는 또한 그리스도의 본질은 상상력(Imagination)이라 생각했다.

1) *Mercy Pity Peace and Love*: 자비와 연민과 평화와 사랑, "신성한 인간성"과 동일시된다.

Holy Thursday

'Twas on a Holy Thursday[1] their innocent faces clean
The children walking two & two in red & blue & green
Grey headed beadles[2] walkd before with wands[3] as white as snow
Till into the high dome of Paul's[4] they like Thames waters flow.

O what a multitude they seemd these flowers of London town
Seated in companies they sit with radiance all their own
The hum of multitudes was there, but multitudes of lambs
Thousands of little boys & girls raising their innocent hands.

Now like a mighty wind they raise to heaven the voice of song
Or like harmonious thunderings the seats of heaven among
Beneath them[5] sit the aged men wise guardians of the poor
Then cherish pity; lest you drive an angel from your door.[6]

---

* 그리스도 승천일에 예배 보러 세인트 폴 대성당으로 가고 있는 자선시설의 어린이들이 깨끗한 얼굴과 형형색색의 제복(uniforms)을 입고 있어서 아름다워 보인다. 이 장면은 솔직하고 편견 없는 눈으로 보여주기 때문에 마치 구경꾼은 이 장면의 매력에만 관심을 갖고 있는 듯하다. "이들은 어떤 아이들인가?", "왜 이렇게 많은 아이들이 자선시설에 수용되어 있는가?" 등의 질문은 독자의 몫이다. 이 시의 순수는 상처받기 쉬운 순수이다. 양들과 어린 아이들은 부모의 사랑과 가정의 보살핌을 모르고 있다. (Watson 87)

1) *Holy Thursday*: 그리스도 승천일 (부활절 이후 40일째 되는 목요일)

2) *beedle*: 교구(敎區) 직원 (a parish officer)

3) *wand*: 관장(官杖), 직표(職標) (a rod or staff carried as a sign of office)

4) *St. Paul's*: 세인트 폴 대성당 (런던에 있으며, Christopher Wren이 설계하였음)

5) *Beneath them*: 그들(어린이들) 아래에; 세인트 폴 대성당의 좌석은 계단식으로 되어 있지 않기 때문에 좌석의 위치를 의미하는 것이 아니다. 이 말은 어린이들은 찬송가를 부르면서 승천하여 천사가 되는 반면에, 늙은 교구직원들은 "현명"하지만 세속에 발이 묶여 있음을 암시한다.

6) 성서의 인유이다. "손님 대접하기를 잊지 말라: 이로써 부지중에 천사들을 대접한 이들이 있었느니라"(Be not forgetful to entertain strangers: for thereby some have entertained angels unawares-Hebrews 13:2); 입으로는 "가난한 사람들의 보호자"를 자처하면서 자선을 실천하지 않는 어른들의 위선을 비판하는 의미를 함축하고 있다.

Nurse's Song

When the voices of children are heard on the green
And laughing is heard on the hill,
My heart is at rest within my breast
And everything else is still.

Then come home my children, the sun is gone down
And the dews of night arise
Come come leave off play, and let us away
Till the morning appears in the skies.

No no let us play, for it is yet nay
And we cannot go to sleep
Besides in the sky, the little birds fly
And the hills are all coverd with sheep.

Well well go & play till the light fades away
And then go home to bed
The little ones leaped & shouted & laugh'd
And all the hills ecchoed.

A Dream

Once a dream did weave a shade,
O'er my Angel-guarded bed,
That an Emmet[1)] lost it's way
Where on grass methought I lay.

Troubled wilderd[2)] and folorn
Dark benighted travel-worn,
Over many a tangled spray,
All heart-broke I heard her say.

O my children! do they cry,
Do they hear their father sigh.
Now they look abroad to see,
Now return and weep for me.

Pitying I drop'd a tear:
But I saw a glow-worn near:
Who replied, What wailing wight[3)]
Calls the watchman of the night.

I am set to light the ground,
While the beetle goes his round[4)]:
Follow now the beetles hum,
Little wanderer hie thee home.

---

* 이 시에서 블레이크는 가장 하찮은 동물로써 인간의 상황을 나타내는 우화를 만들어냈다. 화자는 꿈속에서 풀밭에서 길을 잃고 자식 걱정을 하는 개미를 본다. 그 개미가 자신의 운명을 슬퍼하며 눈물을 흘리려 할 때, "밤의 파수꾼"인 개똥벌레가 나타나 풍뎅이의 도움을 받아 개미를 집으로 데려다 준다. 블레이크는 이 시에서 가장 하찮은 미물에게 닥친 슬픔을 그린 우화로써 "밤의 숲"에서 길을 잃은 인간의 영혼을 묘사하고 있다. 신은 개미와 같은 미물마저도 사랑과 연민으로 보살피며, 개똥벌레를 사자로 보내 안전하게 보호한다.

1) *emmet*: 개미
2) *wilder*: 길을 잃게 하다 (cause to lose one's way)
3) *wight*: (癈) 생물 (a living being, a creature); 인간 (a human being)
4) *go his round*: 순찰하다 (take one's customary route for delivery, inspection, etc.)

From *Songs of Experience*

Introduction[1)]

Hear the voice of the Bard![2)]
Who Present, Past, & Future sees
Whose ears have heard,
The Holy Word,
That walk'd among the ancient trees.[3)]

Calling the lapsed Soul
And weeping in the evening dew:
That might controll
The starry pole:
And fallen fallen light renew!

O Earth O Earth return!
Arise from out the dewy grass;[4)]
Night is worn,
And the morn
Rises from the slumberous mass.

Turn away no more:
Why wilt thou turn away
The starry floor
The watry shore
Is giv'n thee till the break of day.

---

1) "순수의 노래"는 "경험의 노래"와 대조를 통해서 그 의미가 완전하게 드러난다. 경험에 대한 의식이 있을 때, 순수의 상태는 사악하고 타락한 세상에서 추구해야 할 하나의 이상이 된다.

2) *bard*: (고대 켈트족의) 음유시인; 여기서는 현재와 과거와 미래를 보고, 하나님의 말씀을 들을 줄 아는 예언자(Ezekiel 또는 Isaiah와 같은)의 성격을 가진 시인이다.

3) 성서의 인유. "And they heard the voice of the Lord God walking in the garden in the cool of the say: and Adam and his wife hid themselves from the presence of the Lord God amongst the trees."(Genesis 3:8)

4) 성서의 인유: "Arise, shine, for thy light is come, and the glory of the Lord is risen upon thee."(Isaiah 60:1)

Earth's Answer[1)]

Earth rais'd up her head,
From the darkness dread & drear.
Her light fled:
Stony dread!
And her locks cover'd with grey despair.

Prison'd on watry shore
Starry Jealousy does keep my den
Cold and hoar
Weeping o'er
I hear the Father of the ancient men

Selfish father of men
Cruel jealous selfish fear
Can delight
Chain'd in night
The virgins of youth and morning bear.

Does spring hide its joy
When buds and blossoms grow?
Does the sower?
Sow by night?
Or the plowman in darkness plow?

Break this heavy chain,
That does freeze my bones around
Selfish! vain!
Eternal bane!
That free Love with bondage bound.

---

1) 시인의 부름에 대지는 자신이 이성과 질투심 많은 물질세계의 창조자(Urizen)의 포로가 되었다고 대답한다. 대지는 에덴에서 인간이 타락함으로써 상실해버린 자유로운 사랑(free love)을 달라고 요구한다.

The Clod & the Pebble

Love seeketh not Itself to please,
Nor for itself hath any care;
But for another gives its ease,
And builds a Heaven in Hells despair.

So sang a little Clod of Clay[1],
Trodden with the cattles feet;
But a Pebble[2] of the brook,
Warbled out these metres meet.

Love seeketh only Self to please,
To bind another to Its delight:
Joys in anothers loss of ease,
And builds a Hell in Heavens despite.

---

1) *a little Clod of Clay*: 작은 흙덩이; 흙덩이는 조약돌에 비해 부드럽고 유연하다. 흙덩이는 이타적인 사랑의 노래(즉 순수의 노래)를 부르며, 천국을 만들어 이기적인 지옥을 절망에 빠뜨린다.

2) *the Pebble*: 조약돌: 물질주의를 상징하는 개울 바닥에 고정된 조약돌은 경험의 상태를 상징하며, 이기적 사랑의 노래를 부르며, 지옥을 만든다.

Holy Thursday

Is this a holy thing to see,
In a rich and fruitful land,
Babes reducd to misery,
Fed with cold and usurous[1)] hand?

Is that trembling cry a song?
Can it be a song of joy?
And so many children poor?
It is a land of poverty!

And their sun does never shine.
And their fields are bleak[2)] & bare.
And their ways are fill'd with thorns
It is eternal winter there.

For where-e'er the sun does shine,
And where-e'er the rain does fall:
Babe can never hunger there,
Nor poverty the mind appall[3)].

---

* 『순수의 노래』에서 아름다운 장면 묘사의 이면에 암시되어 있던 자선시설 어린이들의 실상과 어른들의 위선이 이 시에서는 적나라하게 노출되어 있다. 블레이크는 "부유하고 풍요로운 나라"에서 가난이 존재한다는 수치스러운 현실을 직설적으로 고발한다. 이 나라의 영적인 상태는 햇빛이 비치지도 비가 내지지도 않는 "영원한 겨울"과 같다.

1) *usurous*: usurious: 고리대금업을 하는; 착취하는
2) *bleak*: 삭막한 (bare, exposed, wind-swept)
3) *appall*: 오싹하게 하다 (dismay, terrify)

The Chimney Sweeper

A little black thing among the snow:
Crying weep, weep, in notes of woe!
Where are thy father & mother? say?
They are both gone up to the church to pray.

Because I was happy upon the heath,
And smil'd among the winters snow:
They clothed me in the clothes of death,
And taught me to sing the notes of woe.

And because I am happy, & dance & sing,
They think they have done me no injury:
And are gone to praise God & his Priest & King[1)]
Who make up a heaven of our misery.

Nurses Song

When the voices of children, are heard on the green
And whisprings are in the dale:
The days of my youth rise fresh in my mind,
My face turns green and pale.

Then come home my children, the sun is gone down
And the dews of night arise
Your spring & your day, are wasted in play
And your winter and night in disguise.

---

* 시인은 이 작품에서 경험의 세계에 속한 어른들의 위선을 직접적으로 드러내고 있다. 부모들은 어린 자식을 굴뚝소제부로 팔아먹고도 그들의 잘못을 깨닫지 못하고 있다. 교회는 순수한 어린이들에게 잔인한 행위를 저지르는 것을 묵과하기 때문에, 이들은 교회에 가서 기도를 한다.

1) *God & his priest & King*: 신과 사제와 왕; 이들은 모두 이성과 물질주의가 만들어낸 종교와 정치 제도를 대표하는 인물들이다.

The Sick Rose

O Rose thou art sick.
The invisible worm,
That flies in the night
In the howling storm:

Has found out thy bed
Of crimson joy:
And his dark secret love
Does thy life destroy.

Ah! Sun-flower

Ah Sun-flower! weary of time,
Who countest the steps of the Sun:
Seeking after that sweet golden clime,
Where the travellers journey is done.

Where the Youth[1] pined away with desire,
And the pale Virgin[2] shrouded in snow:
Arise from their graves and aspire,
Where my Sun-flower wishes to go.

---

1) *the Youth*: 나르시스(Narcissus)를 연상시킨다: 나르시스는 Echo의 사랑을 거부한 벌로 물속의 제 그림자를 사랑해야 하는 운명에 처한다. 그는 자신의 운명을 비관하여 물에 빠져 죽는다. 그가 죽은 자리에 수선화가 피었다고 한다.

2) *the pale Virgin*: Persephone를 연상시킨다: Persephone는 Enna에서 꽃을 꺾다가 Pluto에게 들켜 하계로 끌려가서 하계의 여왕이 된다. 그녀는 일 년 중 한 철만 지상에 나와 살다가 나머지 기간은 Pluto와 살게 된다. 그녀가 하계로 끌려갈 때 흰 꽃(asphodel)이 길을 덮었다 한다.

The Tyger

Tyger Tyger, burning bright,
In the forests of the night;
What immortal hand or eye,
Could frame thy fearful symmetry?

In what distant deeps or skies.
Burnt the fire of thine eyes?
On what wings dare he aspire?
What the hand, dare sieze the fire?

And what shoulder, & what art.
Could twist the sinews of thy heart?
And when thy heart began to beat,
What dread hand! & what dread feet?

What the hammer? what the chain,
In what furnace was thy brain?
What the anvil? what dread grasp,
Dare its deadly terrors clasp?

When the stars threw down their spears
And water'd heaven with their tears:[1]
Did he smile his work to see?
Did he who made the Lamb make thee?

---

* 호랑이는 양의 유순(柔順)과 반대되는 에너지를 상징한다. 에너지는 활력과 분노와 연관된 것이다. 분노는 도덕적 미덕으로 간주된다. 『천국과 지옥의 결혼』에는 "The tigers of wrath are wiser than the horses of instruction"이라는 말이 나온다. 호랑이의 힘과 분노가 없으면 타락한 세상을 변화시킬 수가 없다. 호랑이의 힘은 열려 있고 불타는 것이 눈에 보이기 때문에 속임수나 감춰진 분노 또는 신비와 정반대이다.

1) 천국의 전쟁에 관한 묘사이다. 밀턴의 *Paradise Lost*에는 천국의 전쟁 다음에 천지창조가 이어진 것으로 되어 있다. 이 부분은 전쟁이 끝나고 호랑이가 처음 등장하는 순간에 관하여 언급한 것이다. 창세기에는 "하나님이 보시기에 좋았더라(God saw that it was good)" (1:4, 10, 12, 18, 21, 25, 31)라는 말이 반복해서 나온다. 이것은 하나님이 자신이 창조한 것에 만족했음을 의미한다.

Tyger Tyger burning bright,
In the forests of the night:
What immortal hand or eye,
Dare frame thy fearful symmetry?

The Garden of Love

I went to the Garden of Love.
And saw what I never had seen:
A Chapel was built in the midst,
Where I used to play on the green.

And the gates of this Chapel were shut,
And Thou shalt not[1]. writ over the door;
So I turn'd to the Garden of Love,
That so many sweet Bowers bore,

And I saw it was filled with graves,
And tomb-stones where flowers should be:
And Priests in black gowns, were walking their rounds,
And binding with briars, my joys & desires.

---

* 꽃은 사랑을 상징한다. 화자가 사랑을 찾아 어릴 적에 뛰놀았던 "사랑의 화원"에 가보니, 그곳에는 제도화된 종교를 상징하는 교회가 세워져 있다. 교회 문은 닫혀 있고, 문 위에는 십계명이 새겨져 있다. 교회 뜰에는 꽃이 피어있던 곳에 무덤의 묘석들이 서 있고, 인간의 본능적 감정을 억압하는 "검은 제복의 사제들"이 걸어 다니고 있다.

1) *Thou shalt not*: 십계명 (Exodus 20;3-17; Deuteronomy 5: 7-21); "하지 말라"는 말로 일관하는 억압적 종교를 가리킨다. "Thou shalt have no other gods before me. Thou shalt not make unto thee any graven image....Thou shalt not take the name of the Lord thy God in vain....Thou shalt not kill. Thou shalt not commit adultry. Thou shalt not steal. Thou shalt not bear false witness against thy neighbour. Thou shalt not covet thy neighbour's house...."

London

I wander thro' each charter'd[1] street.
Near where the charter'd Thames does flow
And mark[2] in every face I meet
Marks[3] of weakness, marks of woe.

In every cry of every Man,
In every Infants cry of fear,
In every voice; in every ban,
The mind-forg'd manacles[4] I hear

How the Chimney-sweepers cry
Every blackning[5] Church appalls,
And the hapless[6] Soldiers sigh
Runs in blood down Palace walls

But most thro' midnight streets I hear
How the youthful Harlots curse
Blasts[7] the new-born Infants tear
And blights[8] with plagues the Marriage hearse[9]

---

1) *charter'd*: 임대한 (hired); 인간이 자연으로부터 잠시 빌린
2) *mark*: 보다 (notice, observe, watch)
3) *mark*: 표시 (a sign, an indication); 흔적 (a trace)
4) *mind-forged manacles*: 마음이 만든 수갑; 인간이 만든 온갖 제도를 의미하는 은유임.
5) *blackning*: making or becoming dark
6) *hapless*: 불행한, 불운한 (unlucky)
7) *blast*: 시들게 하다, 마르게 하다 (wither, shrivel)
8) *blight*: 병들게 하다 (affect with diseases)
9) *hearse*: 영구차 (a vehicle for carrying coffins)

The Human Abstract

Pity would be no more,
If we did not make somebody Poor:
And Mercy no more could be,
If all were as happy as we:

And mutual fear brings peace:
Till the selfish loves increase.
Then Cruelty knits a snare,
And spreads his baits with care.

He sits down with holy fears,
And waters the ground with tears:
Then Humility takes its root
Underneath his foot.

Soon spreads the dismal shade
Of Mystery[1] over his head;
And the Catterpiller and Fly,
Feed on the Mystery.

And it bears the fruit of Deceit,
Ruddy and sweet to eat:

---

* 아름다운 신의 이미지가 회의적이고 냉소적인 "인간적 추상"으로 뒤틀려 있다. 이처럼 비뚤어진 시각은 어디서 오는 것일까? 이것은 자비, 연민, 평화, 사랑을 전적으로 인간적인 시각에서 보기 때문이다. 이것들은 신의 자질이 아니라 타락한 악의 세계의 결괴이다. 연민(Pity)은 가난의 결과요, 자비는 불평등한 행복의 결과요, 평화는 서로에 대한 공포의 결과요, 사랑은 이기적 사랑(self-love)의 결과다. Blake는 그 다음 연들에서 이러한 무시무시한 변화의 원인을 추적한다. 그 원인은 종교가 실천적 신성의 자질로서의 mercy, pity, peace, love에 관심을 갖지 않고 humility, mystery와 같은 전통적 종교적 추상개념에 관심을 갖기 때문이다. 비하(卑下)는 잔인의 눈물로 젖은 땅에 뿌리를 내린다. 신비의 나무(the tree of mystery)는 모충(毛蟲)이 잎을 갉아먹으면 더 자란다. 즉 이 나무는 기생충의 힘으로 번성하는 나무다. 이 나무에는 기만(欺瞞: Deceit)의 열매가 열린다. 지상의 신들이 이 나무를 찾아봐도 어디에도 없다. 그 나무는 인간의 두뇌 속에서 자라는 나무다. 잘못은 인간에게 있다: 사회가 부패하게 되는 것은 인간의 사고 습관 때문이다. 인간은 종교를 지상에 신의 왕국을 창조하는 것이 아니라 신비를 숭배하는 것으로 보기 때문이다. (Watson 95)

1) Mystery: 신비의 나무 (the Tree of Mystery)

And the Raven his nest has made
In its thickest shade.

The Gods of the earth and sea,
Sought thro' Nature to find this Tree
But their search was all in vain;
There grows one in the Human Brain

A Poison Tree

I was angry with my friend:
I told my wrath, my wrath did end.
I was angry with my foe:
I told it not, my wrath did grow.

And I waterd it in fears,
Night & morning with my tears:
And I sunned it with smiles,
And with soft deceitful wiles.

And it grew both day and night,
Till it bore an apple bright.
And my foe beheld it shine,
And he knew that it was mine.

And into my garden stole,
When the night had veild the pole;
In the morning glad I see;
My foe outstretchd beneath the tree.

From *The Marriage of Heaven and Hell*[1)]

THE VOICE OF THE DEVIL

All Bibles or sacred codes, have been the causes of the following Errors.

1. That Man has two real existing principles Viz: a Body & a Soul.
2. That Energy, call'd Evil, is alone from the Body, & that Reason, call'd Good, is alone from the Soul.
3. That God will torment Man in Eternity for following his Energies.

But the following Contraries to these are True.

1. Man has no Body distinct from his Soul; for that call'd Body is a portion of Soul discern'd by the five Senses, the chief inlets of Soul in this age.
2. Energy is the only life and is from the Body and Reason is the bound or outward circumference of Energy.
3. Energy is Eternal Delight.

Those who restrain desire, do so because theirs is weak enough to be restrained;

1) 이 작품은 전통적 종교이론과 스베덴보리(Swedenborg)의 신비주의 종교이론을 비판한 풍자시이다. 이 작품은 첫 부분인 "요약"(Argument)과 마지막의 "자유의 노래"(The Song of Liberty)만 운문으로 되어 있고, 그 나머지는 모두 산문으로 되어 있다. 본문은 6개의 장으로 구성되어 있고, 각 장은 설명 부분과 삽화 그리고 "A Memorable Fancy"로 이루어져 있다. 먼저 "악마의 음성"(The Voice of the Devil)이 혁명적 윤리의 원리를 제시한다. 그리고 첫번째 "A Memorable Fancy" 다음에 70개의 "지옥의 속담"(Proverbs of Hell)이 이어진다. 블레이크는 이 작품에서 전통적 기독교의 "선"과 "악"의 개념을 뒤엎는다. 전통적인 악은 육체 및 육체적 욕망과 관련된 일체의 것을 의미하며, 에너지, 풍요, 행동, 자유 등으로 이루어진다. 전통적 선은 영혼과 관련된 이성, 속박, 복종 및 금지 등으로 이루어진 것을 의미한다. 블레이크는 스스로 "악마의 목소리"의 역할을 맡아서 "지옥의 격언들"을 만들어낸다. 이러한 전통적 가치의 전도는 표준적 도덕의 허실을 인식시키고자 고안한 블레이크의 복합적 아이러니의 첫 단계이다. 그는 "요약"에서 "상반된 것이 없으면 진전이 없다. 끌어당김과 밀어냄, 이성과 에너지, 사랑과 증오는 모두 인간 생존에 필요하다. 이 상반된 상태에서 소위 종교에서 선과 악이라 부르는 것이 나온다. 선은 이성에 복종하는 수동적인 상태이고 악은 에너지에서 나오는 능동적인 상태이다(Without Contraries is no progression. Attraction and Repulsion, Reason and Energy, Love and Hate, are necessary to Human existence. From these contraries spring what the religious call Good and Evil. Good is the passive that obeys Reason. Evil is the active springing from Energy.)"라고 말하면서 "이성과 에너지"는 둘 다 인간의 생존에 필수적인 것이라 주장한다. 그는 욕망과 억압, 에너지와 이성, 천국과 지옥, 등과 같이 극단적으로 상반된 상태들은 서로 적대적인 상태에 있어야 하며, 이 둘을 화해시키려고 기도하는 것은 존재를 파괴하려고 하는 것이라 말한다. 이러한 관점에서 볼 때, 진정한 삶은 상반된 상태들이 서로 승리도 억압도 없이 공존하는 끝없는 갈등이다.

and the restrainer of reason usurps its place & governs the unwilling.

And being restrain'd it by degrees becomes passive till it is only the shadow of desire.

The history of this written in Paradise Lost, & the Governor of Reason is call'd Messiah.

And the original Archangel or possessor of the command of the heavenly host, is call'd the Devil or Satan and his children are call'd Sin & Death.

But in the Book of Job Milton's Messiah is call'd Satan.

For this history has been adopted by both parties.

It indeed appear'd to Reason as if Desire was cast out, but the Devils account is that the Messiah (Plate 6) fell, & formed a heaven of what he stole from the Abyss.

This is shewn in the Gospel, where he prays to the Father to send the comforter or Desire that Reason may have Ideas to build on, the Jehovah of the Bible being no other than he who dwells in flaming fire. Know that after Christs death, he became Jehovah.

But in Milton' the Father is Destiny, the Son, a Raio of the five senses, & the Holy-ghost, Vacuum!

Note: The reason Milton wrote in fetters when he wrote of Angels & God, and at liberty when of Devils & Hell, is because he was a true Poet and of the Devils party without knowing it.

A Memorable Fancy

As I was walking among the fires of hell, delighted with the enjoyments of Genius; which to Angels look like torment and insanity, I collected some of their Proverbs; thinking that as the sayings used in a nation, mark its character, so the Proverbs of Hell, shew the nature in Infernal wisdom better than any description of buildings or garments,

When I came home: on the abyss of the five senses, where a flat sided steep frowns over the present world, I saw a mighty Devil folded in black clouds, hovering on the sides of the rock, with corroding fires (Plate 7) he wrote the following sentence now percieved by the minds of men, & read by them on earth.

How do you know but ev'ry Bird that cuts the airy way,
Is an immense world of delight, clos'd by your senses five?

Proverbs of Hell

In seed time learn, in harvest teach, in winter enjoy.
Drive your cart and your plow over the bones of the dead.
The road of excess leads to the palace of wisdom.
Prudence is a rich ugly old maid courted by Incapacity.
He who desires but acts not, breeds pestilence.
The cut worm forgives the plow.
Dip him in the river who loves water.

A fool sees not the same tree that a wise man sees.
He whose face gives no light, shall never become a star.
Eternity is in love with the productions of time.
The busy bee has no time for sorrow.
The hours of folly are measur'd by the clock, but of wisdom: no clock can measure.

All wholsom food is caught without a net or a trap.
Bring out number weight & measure in a year of dearth.
No bird soars too high, if he soars with his own wings.
A dead body, revenges not injuries.
The most sublime act is to set another before you.
If the fool would persist in his folly he would become wise.
Folly is the cloke of knavery.
Shame is Pride's cloke.

Prisons are built with stones of Law, Brothels with bricks of Religion.
The pride of the peacock is the glory of God.

The lust of the goat is the bounty of God.

The wrath of the lion is the wisdom of God.

The nakedness of woman is the work of God.

Excess of sorrow laughs. Excess of joy weeps.

The roaring of lions, the howling of wolves, the raging of the stormy sea, and the destructive sword, are portions of eternity too great for the eye of man.

The fox condemns the trap, not himself.

Joys impregnate. Sorrows bring forth.

Let man wear the fell of the lion, woman the fleece of the sheep.

The bird a nest, the spider a web, man friendship.

The selfish smiling fool, & the sullen frowning fool, shall be both thought wise, that they may be a rod.

What is now proved was once, only imagin'd.

The rat, the mouse, the fox, the rabbit: watch the roots; the lion, the tyger, the horse, the elephant, watch the fruits.

The cistern contains; the fountain overflows.

One thought, fills immensity.

Always be ready to speak your mind, and a base man will avoid you.

Every thing possible to be believ'd is an image of truth.

The eagle never lost so much time, as when he submitted to learn of the crow.

The fox provides for himself, but God provides for the lion.

Think in the morning. Act in the noon. Eat in the evening. Sleep in the night.

He who has suffer'd you to impose on him knows you.

As the plow follows words, so God rewards prayers.

The tygers of wrath are wiser than the horses of instruction.

Expect poison from the standing water.

You never know what is enough unless you know what is more than enough.

Listen to the fools reproach! it is a kingly title!

The eyes of fire, the nostrils of air, the mouth of water, the beard of earth.

The weak in courage is strong in cunning.

The apple tree never asks the beech how he shall grow, nor the lion, the horse, how he shall take his prey.

The thankful reciever bears a plentiful harvest.

If others had not been foolish, we should be so.

The soul of sweet delight, can never be defil'd.

When thou seest an Eagle, thou seest a portion of Genius, lift up thy head!

As the catterpiller chooses the fairest leaves to lay her eggs on, so the priest lays his curse on the fairest joys.

To create a little flower is the labour of ages.

Damn, braces: Bless relaxes.

The best wine is the oldest, the best water the newest.

Prayers plow not! Praises reap not!

Joys laugh not! Sorrows weep not!

The head Sublime, the heart Pathos, the genitals Beauty, the hands & feet Proportion.

As the air to a bird of the sea to a fish, so is contempt to the contemptible.

The crow wish'd every thing was black, the owl, that every thing was white.

Exuberance is Beauty.

If the lion was advised by the fox, he would be cunning.

Improvement makes strait roads, but the crooked roads without Improvement, are roads of Genius.

Sooner murder an infant in its cradle than nurse unacted desires.

Where man is not nature is barren.

Truth can never be told so as to be understood, and not be believ'd.

Enough! or Too much!

The Book of Urizen[1)]

Lambeth. Printed by Will Blake 1794.

Plate 2

Preludium to The First Book of Urizen[2)]

Of the primeval Priest's[3)] assum'd power,
When Eternals spurn'd back[4)] his religion;
And gave him place in the north,
Obscure, shadowy, void, solitary.

Eternals I hear your call gladly,
Dictate swift winged words, & fear not
To unfold your dark visions of torment.

Plate 3

Chap: I[5)]

1. Lo, a shadow of horror[6)] is risen
   In Eternity! Unknown, unprolific![7)]

---

1) 이 작품은 Blake의 『創世記』(Genesis)에 해당한다. Blake는 자신의 예언서(Prophetic Books)에서 성서를 다시 쓰고 있다. 그는 성서를 패러디하면서 독자적인 신화체계를 만들어냈다. 그의 신화의 출발점은 우주적 인간(Universal Man), 또는 "the Human Form Divine"이다. 그는 타락하기 이전의 완전한 인간(Man)을 "Albion"이라 부른다. 이 인간은 창조의 과정에서 그 구성요소인 네 개의 분신들(four Zoas), 즉 Urizen(reason), Los(imagination), Orc(passion), 그리고 Tharmas(unity of perception)로 분리된다. 따라서 그의 천지창조(creation)는 물질세계의 창조인 동시에 분리(division)에 의한 타락(Fall)을 의미한다. 이 작품에서는 Urizen, Los, Orc가 영원의 세계(Eternity)로부터 분리되는 과정이 묘사되어 있으나, Albion과 Tharmas에 관한 언급은 나오지 않는다. "Urizen"은 "your reason" 또는 "horizon"에서 유래하며, "Orc"는 Orcum(Hell)에서 유래한다. (Blake의 신화체계에 관해서는 Paananen의 William Blake, pp. 45-7과 Bloom의 The Visionary Company, pp27-29를 참조할 것.)

2) 서시(Preludium)는 서사시의 표현 양식에 따라 주제를 요약하고 시신들(여기서는 "Eternals" 즉 영원의 존재들)에게 기원하는 내용을 담고 있다.

3) *the primeval Priest*: "태고의 사제"는 Urizen을 가리킨다.

4) *spurn back*: refuse to accept

5) 제1장의 제목은 "Urizen Divides Eternity and Infinity"라 할 수 있다.

6) *a shadow of horror*: Urizen의 그림자를 의미한다. 물리적 세계가 존재하기 이전의 영적인 상태이기 때문에 그림자로 묘사되어 있다. 그는 영원의 세계에서 떨어져 나와 한계를 설정하기 시작한다.

7) *unprolific*: unproductive

Self-closed, all-repelling: what Demon
Hath form'd this abominable void
This soul-shudd'ring vacuum?–Some said
"It is Urizen," But unknown, abstracted[1],
Brooding secret, the dark power hid.

2. Times on times he divided, & measur'd
Space by space in his ninefold darkness,
Unseen, unknown! changes appeard
In his desolate mountains rifted furious
By the black winds of perturbation,[2]

3. For he strove in battles dire
In unseen conflictions with shapes
Bred from his forsaken wilderness,
Of beast, bird, fish, serpent & element,[3]
Combustion, blast, vapour and cloud.

4. Dark revolving in silent activity:
Unseen in tormenting passions;
An activity unknown and horrible;
A self-contemplating shadow,
In enormous labours occupied.

5. But Eternals[4] beheld his vast forests.
Age on ages[5] he lay, clos'd, unknown,
Brooding shut in the deep; all avoid
The petrific[6] abominable chaos.

6. His cold[7] horrors silent, dark Urizen

---

1) *abstracted*: separated
2) *perturbation*: agitation; disturbance
3) *element*: 자연계를 구성하고 있다고 생각되었던 earth, water, air, fire 등의 원소.
4) *Eternals*: 영원의 존재들
5) *Age on ages:* for ages
6) *petrific*: 석화되어가는(having the quality of turning into stone)
7) *cold*: Urizen의 전형은 창조적 능력이 없는 겨울의 영(spirit)이다.

Prepar'd: his ten thousands of thunders
Rang'd in gloom'd array[1] stretch out across
The dread world, & the rolling of wheels
As of swelling seas, sound in his clouds
In his hills of stor'd snows, in his mountains
Of hail & ice; voices of terror,
Are heard, like thunders of autumn,
When the cloud blazes over the harvests.

Chap: II[2]

1. Earth was not: nor globes of attraction[3]
The will of the Immortal expanded
Or contracted his all flexible senses.
Death was not, but eternal life sprung.

2. The sound of a trumpet the heavens
Awoke & vast clouds of blood roll'd
Round the dim rocks of Urizen,[4] so nam'd
That solitary one in Immensity.

3. Shrill the trumpet: & myriads of Eternity,
Plate 4 Muster around the bleak desarts[5]
Now fill'd with clouds, darkness & waters
That roll'd perplex'd labring, & utter'd
Words articulate, bursting in thunders

---

1) *Ranged in gloomed array*: arranged in dark group
2) 제2장의 제목은 "Urizen's Promulgation of His Laws"이다.
3) 타락 이후에는 Newton의 역학이 작용한다. "Immortal"이라는 형용사는 제4장에서도 반복해서 나오는데, Urizen이 타락하기 이전에 속했던 세계를 강조하기 위해 사용되고 있다. "불멸의 존재들(Immortals)"의 특징은 그들의 감각이 "flexible"하다는 것이다.
4) *the dim rocks of Urizen*: Urizen의 세계는 "유연한 감각"이 아니라 고정된 바위의 세계이다. Urizen은 "무한한 공간(Immensity)의 고독한 자"라 불린다.
5) *the bleak desarts*: 구름과 암흑과 물로 가득 찬 "황량한 사막"은 Urizen의 세계를 의미한다. 이것은 그 다음에 나오는 관계대명사 "that"의 선행사이며 동사 "utter'd"의 주어이다. Urizen은 아직 실체가 없기 때문에 그의 연설 즉 "분명한 말(Words articulate)"은 사막에서 우레처럼 울려나온다. Urizen은 Milton의 Satan, 성경의 Moses나 Jehovah의 성격을 두루 갖추고 있다. 타락한 이후 Urizen의 이름은 Satan이다.

That roll'd on the tops of his mountains.

4. "From the depths of dark solitude, From
The eternal abode in my holiness,
Hidden set apart in my stern counsels[1])
Reserv'd for the days of futurity,
I have sought for a joy without pain,
For a solid without fluctuation.
Why will you die O Eternals?
Why live in unquenchable burnings?[2])

5. "First I fought with the fire; consum'd
Inwards, into a deep world within:
A void immense,[3]) wild dark & deep,
Where nothing was; Nature's wide womb
And self balanc'd, stretch'd o'er the void,
I alone, even I! the winds merciless
Bound; but condensing, in torrents
They fall & fall; strong I repell'd
The vast waves, & arose on the waters
A wide world of solid obstruction.

6. "Here alone I in books formd of metals
Have written the secrets of wisdom

---

1) *counsels*: 은밀한 목적(secret purpose) 또는 계획(plan)

2) Urizen의 인식의 오류를 보여주는 부분이다. 그의 계획 또는 목표는 "변동이 없는 고체"를 찾는 것이다. 블레이크는 영원의 세계를 불(fire)의 세계로 묘사한다. Blake의 신화에서 네 가지 존재의 상태는 Beulah(unorganized innocence), Generation(experience), Eden(organized innocence), 그리고 Ulro(Hell)인데, Eden은 불의 도시로, Beulah는 Eden을 둘러싸고 있는 화원으로, Generation은 Beulah의 주위에 있는 밤의 숲으로, Ulro는 물의 세계로 묘사되어 있다.(Bloom, *The Visionary Company*, p. 22.) 따라서 영원의 존재들이 사는 불의 세계는 Urizen의 관점에서 보면 죽음의 세계로 보인다. 그러나 죽음을 선택한 것은 Urizen 자신이다.

3) *a void immense*: 거대한 허공; Urizen은 불과 싸우다가 "깊은 내면의 세계"로 쫓겨 간다. 이 "허공"은 이 작품에서 11번 반복되어 사용되고 있는데 "chaos"와 같은 의미를 갖는다. 이 허공은 지옥과 창조된 우주 사이에 있는 지역인데, 세 가지 원소인 불, 바람, 물을 제압한 다음 네 번째 원소인 "earth", 즉 그가 추구하는 단단한 물질의 세계가 솟아오른다. Urizen은 먼저 불과 싸워 자신의 내면의 "허공"으로 들어가서 바람("the merciless winds")을 묶고, 그 바람을 응축시켜 물을 만든다. 그 다음 "거대한 파도"를 밀어내자 "단단하게 가로막는 넓은 세계" 즉 육중한 대지가 솟아오른다.

The secrets of dark contemplation
By fightings and conflicts dire,
With terrible monsters Sin-bred:[1)]
Which the bosoms of all inhabit;
Seven deadly Sins of the soul.

7. "Lo! I unfold my darkness: and on
This rock, place with strong hand the Book
Of eternal brass, written in my solitude.

8. "Laws of peace, of love, of unity:
Of pity, compassion, forgiveness.
Let each chuse one habitation:
His ancient infinite mansion:
One command, one joy, one desire,
One curse, one weight, one measure
One King, one God, one Law."[2)]

Chap: III[3)]

1. The voice ended, they saw his pale visage
Emerge from the darkness; his hand
On the rock of eternity unclasping
The Book of brass. Rage siez'd the strong.[4)]
2. Rage, fury, intense indignation
In cataracts of fire blood & gall
In whirlwinds of sulphurous smoke:
And enormons forms of energy;

---

1) Urizen은 자신의 심리적 갈등으로부터 보편적 도덕률을 창조한다. "영혼의 일곱 가지 큰 죄"는 오만(pride), 탐욕(covetousness), 음욕(lust), 분노(anger), 탐식(gluttony), 시기(envy), 나태(sloth)이다. 이것들은 "만인의 가슴 속에 사는 무서운 괴물들"이다.

2) *Laws*: "The Human Abstract"에 묘사된 법이다. 연민은 가난의 결과요, 자비는 불평등한 행복의 결과요, 평화는 서로에 대한 공포의 결과요, 사랑은 이기심의 결과이다. Blake는 *The Marriage of Heaven and Hell*에서 "One Law for the Lion & Ox is Oppression"이라고 했다.

3) 제3장의 주제는 "Urizen Cast out of Eternity"이다.

4) the strong: "강한 자들"은 영원의 존재들을 의미한다. 영원의 존재들의 분노가 Urizen을 영원의 세계로부터 추방한다.

All the seven deadly sins of the soul
Plate 5 In living creations appear'd[1)]
In the flames of eternal fury.

3. Sund'ring, dark'ning, thund'ring!
Rent away with a terrible crash,
Eternity roll'd wide apart,
Wide asunder rolling
Mountainous all around
Departing; departing; departing:
Leaving ruinous fragments of life,
Hanging, frowning cliffs, & all between
An ocean of voidness unfathomable.

4. The roaring fires ran o'er the heav'ns
In whirlwinds & cataracts of blood
And o'er the dark desarts of Urizen
Fires pour thro' the void on all sides
On Urizens self-begotten armies.[2)]

5. But no light from the fires. All was darkness
In the flames of Eternal fury.

6. In fierce anguish & quenchless flames
To the desarts and rocks he ran raging
To hide, but he could not: combining
He dug mountains & hills in vast strength,
He piled them in incessant labour,
In howlings & pangs & fierce madness
Long periods in burning fires labouring
Till hoary, and age-broke, and aged,
In despair and the shadows of death.

---

1) 법은 그 법이 금지하는 죄를 만든다. 그리고 Urizen은 영원의 세계로부터 분리된다.
2) armies: "무리들"; 영원의 존재는 하나인 동시에 다수이다. Urizen은 영원과 분리되면서 다수가 된다.

7. And a roof, vast petrific around,
On all sides he fram'd: like a womb;[1]
Where thousands of rivers in veins
Of blood pour down the mountains to cool
The eternal fires beating without
From Eternals; & like a black globe
View'd by sons of Eternity, standing
On the shore of the infinite ocean,
Like a human heart strugling & beating
The vast world of Urizen appear'd.

8. And Los round the dark globe of Urizen,
Kept watch for Eternals to confine
The obscure separation alone;
For Eternity stood wide apart,
Plate 6 As the stars are apart from the earth.

9. Los wept howling around the dark Demon:[2]
And cursing his lot; for in anguish,
Urizen was rent from his side;
And a fathomless void for his feet;[3]
And intense fires for his dwelling.

10. But Urizen laid[4] in a stony sleep
Unorganiz'd, rent from Eternity.

11. The Eternals said: "What is this? Death.
Urizen is a clod of clay."

Plate 7 12: Los howld in a dismal stupor,
Groaning! gnashing! groaning!
Till the wrenching apart was healed.

---

1) *a womb*: Urizen의 세계는 tomb 즉 죽음의 세계이며, 또한 숙명적 생명을 잉태하는 자궁(womb)이 된다.

2) *the dark Demon*: Urizen

3) (Los had), 또는 (With)를 보충해서 해석해보라.

4) *laid*: (was) laid.

13: But the wrenching of Urizen[1] heal'd not
Cold, featureless, flesh or clay,
Rifted with direful changes
He lay in a dreamless night

14: Till Los rouz'd his fires,[2] affrighted
At the formless unmeasurable death.

Plate 8

Chap: IV[a][3]

1: Los smitten with astonishment,
Frightend at the hurding bones

2: And at the surging sulphureous
Perturbed Immortal, mad raging

3: In whirlwinds & pitch & nitre
Round the furious limbs of Los;

4: And Los formed nets & gins
And threw the nets round about

5: He watch'd in shuddring fear
The dark changes & bound every change
With rivets of iron & brass;

6. And these were the changes of Urizen.

Plate 10

Chap: IV[b]

1. Ages on ages roll'd over him!
In stony sleep ages roll'd over him!

---

1) *the wrenching of Urizen*: Urizen이 찢겨져 나간 상처
2) "로스가 불을 일으켰다." 그의 동기는 훌륭하지만, 그의 전략은 소용이 없다. 그는 다만 Urizen의 분리를 심화시킬 뿐이다.
3) 제4장의 주제는 "The Attempts of Los to Control Urizen"이다. 그는 쇠사슬과 못으로 Urizen의 변화를 중지시키려고 노력한다.

Like a dark waste stretching chang'able
By earthquakes riv'n, belching sullen fires.
On ages roll'd ages in ghastly
Sick torment; around him in whirlwinds
Of darkness the eternal Prophet howl'd
Beating still on his rivets of iron
Pouring sodor[1] of iron; dividing
The horrible night into watches.[2]

2. And Urizen (so his eternal name[3])
His prolific delight obscurd more & more
In dark secresy, hiding in surgeing
Sulphureous fluid his phantasies.
The Eternal Prophet[4] heavd the dark bellows,[5]
And turn'd restless the tongs; and the hammer
Incessant beat; forging chains new & new,
Numb'ring with links. hours, days & years.

3 The eternal mind,[6] bounded, began to roll
Eddies of wrath ceaseless round & round,
And the sulphureous foam surgeing thick
Settled, a lake, bright, & shining dear:
White as the snow on the mountains cold.

4. Forgetfulness, dumbness, necessity!
In chains of the mind locked up,
Like fetters of ice shrinking together
Disorganiz'd, rent from Eternity,[7]

---

1) *sodor*: 땜납(sodder, 또는 solder)
2) *watches*: 고대인들의 밤 시간 구분; 초경(初更: first watch), 이경(二更), 삼경(三更), 사경(四更)으로 나누었다. Los도 시간을 창조한다.
3) 영원의 세계에서 Urizen이라 불리며, 타락한 세계에서는 Satan이라 불린다.
4) *The Eternal Prophet*: Los를 가리킨다.
5) *bellows*: 풀무(a contrivance used for driving air into a fire); "The Tyger"에 나오는 조물주처럼 Los는 대장장이에 비유되어 있다.
6) *The eternal mind*: Urizen
7) Los도 영원의 세계에서 분리된다.

Los beat on his fetters[1] of iron;
And heated his furnaces & pour'd
Iron sodor and sodor of brass.

5. Restless turnd the immortal,[2] inchain'd
Heaving dolorous! anguish'd! unbearable,
Till a roof shaggy wild inclos'd
In an orb, his fountain of thought.[3]

6. In a horrible dreamful slumber;
Like the linked infernal chain;
A vast Spine writh'd in torment
Upon the winds; shooting pain'd
Ribs, like a bending cavern
And bones of solidness, froze
Over all his nerves of joy.
And a first Age passed over,
And a state of dismal woe.

7. From the caverns of his jointed Spine,
Down sunk with fright a red
Round globe[4] hot burning deep
Deep down into the Abyss:
Panting: Conglobing, Trembling
Shooting out ten thousand branches
Around his solid bones.
And a second Age passed over,
And a state of dismal woe.

8. In harrowing fear rolling round;
His nervous brain shot branches

---

1) *fetters*: 쇠못(nails)
2) *the immortal*: Urizen
3) *a roof shaggy... his fountain of thought*: 털복숭이 지붕이... 그의 생각의 샘을 가두었다. 일곱 시대에 걸쳐서 Urizen의 육신이 창조된다. 첫째 시대에는 그의 머리("a roof shaggy"), 척추("A vast Spine") 그리고 늑골("Ribs")이 나타난다.
4) *a red / Round globe*: 심장(heart); 둘째 시대에는 심장과 혈관이 나타난다.

Round the branches of his heart.
On high into two little orbs
And fixed in two little caves
Hiding carefully from the wind,
His Eyes beheld the deep,
And a third Age passed over:[1]
And a state of dismal woe.

9. The pangs of hope began,
In heavy pain striving, struggling.
Two Ears in close volutions.
From beneath his orbs of vision
Shot spiring out and petrified
As they grew. And a fourth Age passed[2]
And a state of dismal woe.

10. In ghastly torment sick;
Hanging upon the wind;
Plate 13 Two Nostrils bent down to the deep.
And a fifth Age passed over;[3]
And a state of dismal woe.

11. In ghastly torment sick;
Within his ribs bloated round,
A craving Hungry Cavern;[4]
Thence arose his channeld Throat,
And like a red flame a Tongue
Of thirst & of hunger appeard.
And a sixth Age passed over:
And a state of dismal woe.

12. Enraged & stifled with torment

---

1) 셋째 시대에는 뇌(brain), 신경조직(nervous system), 그리고 두 눈(Eyes)이 나타난다.
2) 넷째 시대에는 두 귀(Ears)가 나타난다.
3) 다섯째 시대에는 코(Nostrils)가 나타난다.
4) *A craving Hungry Cavern*: 위(stomach); 여섯째 시대에는 위와 목구멍(Throat)과 혀(Tongue)가 나타난다.

He threw his right Arm to the north
His left Arm to the south
Shooting out in anguish deep,
And his Feet stampd the nether Abyss
In trembling & howling & dismay.
And a seventh Age passed over:[1)]
And a state of dismal woe.

Chap: V[2)]

1. In terrors Los shrunk from his task:
His great hammer fell from his hand:
His fires beheld, and sickening,
Hid[3)] their strong limbs in smoke.
For with noises ruinous loud;
With hurtlings & clashings & groans
The Immortal[4)] endur'd his chains,
Tho' bound in a deadly sleep.
2. All the myriads of Eternity:
All the wisdom & joy of life:
Roll like a sea around him,
Except what his little orbs
Of sight by degrees unfold.

3. And now his eternal life
Like a dream was obliterated.

4. Shudd'ring, the Eternal Prophet[5)] smote
With a stroke, from his north to south region.
The bellows & hammer are silent now.
A nerveless silence, his prophetic voice

1) 일곱째 시대에는 팔과 발이 창조된다.
2) 제5장의 제목은 "The Creation of Pity: The Separation of Woman from Humanity"이다.
3) "Hid"의 주어는 "His fires"이다. "Los의 불이 약해지면서("sickening") 연기 속에 강한 사지(불꽃)를 감춘다." 즉 Los의 불이 꺼진다.
4) *The Immortal*: Urizen; "his"는 "Los's"이다.
5) *the Eternal Prophet*: Los

Siez'd;[1] a cold solitude & dark void
The Eternal Prophet & Urizen clos'd[2].

5. Ages on ages rolld over them
Cut off from life & light, frozen
Into horrible forms of deformity.
Los suffer'd his fires to decay
Then he look'd back with anxious desire
But the space undivided by existence[3]
Struck horror into his soul.

6. Los wept obscur'd with mourning[4]:
His bosom earthquak'd with sighs;
He saw Urizen deadly black,
In his chains bound, & Pity began,

7. In anguish dividing & dividing
(For pity divides the soul)[5]
In pangs eternity on eternity[6].
Life in cataracts pourd down his cliffs
The void shrunk the lymph[7] into Nerves
Wand'ring wide on the bosom of night
And left a round globe of blood
Trembling upon the Void.

Plate 15 Thus the Eternal Prophet was divided
Before the death-image of Urizen

---

1) *A nerveless silence... /Seiz'd*: "무기력한 침묵이 그의 예언의 목소리를 사로잡았다." 즉, Los의 예언의 목소리도 이제 침묵한다.
2) *clos'd*: enclosed; Urizen을 속박하면서 Los 자신도 속박 당한다. 그의 창조적 에너지가 소진되고 예언의 목소리가 침묵함에 따라, Los도 Urizen의 허공 속으로 들어간다.
3) *the space...by existence*: "존재로 나누어지지 않은 공간" 즉 영원의 세계를 의미한다.
4) *boscur'd with mourning*: 눈물이 앞을 가린 채(=dimmed with tears).
5) 사랑(Love)은 우애이지만, 연민(pity)은 자기비하(condescension)의 의미를 함축한다. "만약 우리가 누군가를 가난하게 만들지 않는다면, 연민을 없을 것이다"(Pity would be no more / If we did not make somebody Poor). ("The Human Abstract")
6) *eternity on eternity*: 오랜 세월 동안(=for ages)
7) the lymph: 체액; 생명(Life), 체액(lymph), 신경(Nerves), 심장(globe of blood)이 차례로 나타나는 과정이 마치 진화의 과정처럼 묘사되어 있다.

For in changeable clouds and darkness
In a winterly night beneath,
The Abyss of Los stretch'd immense:
And now seen, now obscur'd, to the eyes
Of Eternals, the visions remote
Of the dark seperation appear'd.
As glasses discover Worlds
In the endless Abyss of space,
So the expanding eyes of Immortals
Beheld the dark visions of Los,
And the globe of life blood trembling.

Plate 18

8. The globe of life blood trembled
Branching out into roots;
Fibrous, writhing upon the winds;
Fibres of blood, milk and tears;
In pangs, eternity on eternity.
At length in tears & cries imbodied
A female form trembling and pale
Waves before his deathly face.

9. All Eternity shudderd at sight
Of the first female[1)] now separate
Pale as a cloud of snow
Waving before the face of Los

10. Wonder, awe, fear, astonishment,
Petrify the eternal myriads;
At the first female form now separate
Plate 19 They call'd her Pity, and fled.
11. "Spread a Tent, with strong curtains around them
"Let cords & stakes bind in the Void
That Eternals may no more behold them."

---

1) *the first female*: 최초의 여자 이름은 Enitharmon이다 (VI, 3 참조); 이 여성은 고전 신화의 Pandora를 연상시킨다. 남녀가 성적인 역할을 하거나, 인간 공동체를 보지 못하게 될 때, 그들을 서로를 고문한다. 제6장에서 Los와 Enitharmon은 서로를 성적인 대상으로 보고 구애놀이를 한다.

12. They began to weave curtains of darkness
They erected large pillars round the Void
With golden hooks fastend in the pillars
With infinite labour the Eternals
A woof[1]) wove, and called it Science.

Chap: VI[2])

1. But Los saw the Female & pitied
He embrac'd her, she wept, she refus'd
In perverse[3]) and cruel delight
She fled from his arms, yet he followd

2. Eternity shudder'd when they saw,
Man begetting his likeness,
On his own divided image.

3. A time passed over, the Eternals
Began to erect a tent;
When Enitharmon, sick,
Felt a Worm within her womb.

4. Yet helpless it lay like a Worm
In the trembling womb
To be moulded into existence.

5. All day the worm lay on her bosom
All night within her womb
The worm lay till it grew to a serpent
With dolorous hissings & poisons
Round Enitharmons loins folding,

---

1) A woof: 천(=woven fabric); 이 천은 과학의 천막(Tent of Science)이 되어 지상의 삶을 덮는 새로운 천정이 된다. 사랑과 질투의 광경은 영원의 존재들이 보기에는 너무나 고통스러운 광경이므로, 과학의 천막으로 덮어버린다.

2) 제6장의 제목은 "The Birth of Orc"이다.

3) *perverse*: 사악한(=wicked)

6. Coild within Enitharmons womb
The serpent grew casting its seales;
With sharp pangs the hissings began
To change to a grating cry.
Many sorrows and dismal throes,
Many forms of fish, bird & beast,
Brought forth an Infant form
Where was a worm before.[1)]

7. The Eternals their tent finished
Alarm'd with these gloomy visions
When Enitharmon groaning
Produc'd a man Child to the light.

8. A shriek ran thro' Eternity:
And a paralytic stroke;
At the birth of the Human shadow.

9. Delving earth in his resistless way;
Howling, the Child with fierce flames
Issu'd from Enitharmon.

10. The Eternals, closed the tent:
They beat down the stakes, the cords
Stretch'd for a work of eternity;
No more Los beheld Eternity.

11. In his hands he siez'd the infant
He bathed him in springs of sorrow
He gave him to Enitharmon.

---

1) 진화과정에 대한 발생학적 반복설에 관한 연구는 Carmen S. Kreiter의 논문을 참조할 것: *Studies in Romanticism* 4 (1965), 110-18).

Chap: VII[1]

1. They named the child Orc, he grew
   Fed with milk of Enitharmon.

2. Los awoke her; O sorrow & pain!
   A tight'ning girdle grew,
   Around his bosom. In sobbings
   He burst the girdle in twain,
   But still another girdle
   Oppressd his bosom. In sobbings
   Again he burst it. Again
   Another girdle succeeds
   The girdle was form'd by day;
   By night was burst in twain.

3. These falling down on the rock
   Into an iron Chain
   In each other link by link lock'd

4. They took Orc to the top of a mountain.
   O how Enitharmon wept!
   They chain'd his young limbs to the rock
   With the Chain of Jealousy
   Beneath Urizens deathful shadow.

5. The dead[2] heard the voice of the child
   And began to awake from sleep.
   All things. heard the voice of the child
   And began to awake to life.

6. And Urizen craving with hunger

---

1) 제7장의 제목은 "The Sacrifice of Orc and the Awakening of Urizen"이다.
2) the dead: "죽은 자들"; 영원의 관점에서는 죽은 자들이지만, 소위 우리가 말하는 "산 자들"을 의미한다. Orc의 음성을 듣고 만물이 소생한다.

Stung with the odours of Nature
Explor'd his dens around.[1]

7. He form'd a line & a plummet
To divide the Abyss beneath.
He form'd a dividing rule:

8. He formed sceales to weigh;
He formed massy weights;
He formed a brazen quadrant[2];
He formed golden compasses
And began to explore the Abyss
And he planted a garden of Fruits.[3]

9. But Los encircled Enitharmon
With fires of Prophecy
From the sight of Urizen & Orc.

10. And she bore an enormous race.

Chap: VIII[4]

1. Urizen explor'd his dens,
Mountain, moor, & wilderness,
With a globe of fire[5] lighting his journey:
A fearful journey, annoy'd
By cruel enormities[6]: forms
Of life on his forsaken mountains.

---

1) Orc의 저항은 Urizen을 포함하여 만물을 소생시킨다.
2) quadrant: 사분의(四分儀): 각도 눈금이 새겨진 사분원을 달아 놓은 도구로서, 천문이나 항해에서 고도를 측정하는 데에 사용되었다.
3) *a garden of Fruits*: Urizen의 정원은 "The Poison Tree"에 묘사된 지옥의 정원이다.
4) 이 장의 제목은 "Urizen's Suppression of his Progeny"이다.
5) *a globe of fire*: 그리스 견유학파(the cynic) Diogenes의 등불을 연상시킨다. Urizen은 계속해서 측정 도구를 만들고 그의 유한한 세계를 측정한다.
6) *enormities*: 비정상적인 사물들(abnormal or irregular things), 악행, 범죄(crime)

2. And his world teemd vast enormities:
Frightning; faithless; fawning[1)]
Portions of life; similitudes
Of a foot, or a hand, or a head
Or a heart, or an eye; they swam mischevous[2)]
Dread terrors! delighting in blood.[3)]

3. Most Urizen sicken'd to see
His eternal creations appear.
Sons & daughters of sorrow[4)] on mountains.
Weeping! wailing! first Thiriel appear'd,
Astonish'd at his own existence
Like a man from a cloud born; & Utha
From the waters emerging, laments!
Grodna rent the deep earth howling,
Amaz'd! his heavens immense cracks
Like the ground parch'd with heat; then Fuzon
Flam'd out! first begotten, last born.
All his eternal sons in like manner:
His daughters from green herbs & cattle
From monsters, & worms of the pit.

4. He, in darkness clos'd, view'd all his race,
And his soul sicken'd! he curs'd
Both sons & daughters; for he saw
That no flesh nor spirit could keep
His iron laws one moment.

---

1) *fawning*: 두 가지 의미를 갖는다: "꼬리를 흔들며 아양 부리는," "새끼를 낳는"

2) *mischevous*: mischievous(=having harmful effects)

3) 현실 세계는 이상 세계의 모방이라는 플라톤의 학설에 따라, 생명체의 부분들이 존재할 수 있는 것으로 받아들여진다. 분석적 이성을 상징하는 Urizen의 세계에는 토막 난 사지들이 우글거리고 있어서 전쟁터나 외과수술실을 방불케 한다.

4) Sons & daughters of sorrow: Urizen의 자손들을 의미한다; 이들의 어머니 즉 Urizen의 배우자인 Ahania는 이 작품의 속편인 The Book of Ahania에 자세히 묘사되어 있다. 그의 자손들은 4원소를 의인화한 Thiriel(air), Utha(water), Grodna(earth), Fuzon(fire) 또는 초목, 가축, 괴물, 벌레 등과 같은 자연물들이다. 그는 자손들이 그의 법을 따르지 않는다고 해서 핍박한다.

5. For he saw that life liv'd upon death:
The Ox in the slaughter house moans
The Dog at the wintry door,
And he wept, & he called it Pity,
And his tears flowed down on the winds.

6. Cold he wander'd on high, over their cities
In weeping & pain & woe!
And where-ever he wanderd in sorrows
Upon the aged heavens
A cold shadow follow'd behind him
Like a spiders web, moist, cold, & dim
Drawing out from his sorrowing soul
The dungeon-like heaven, dividing
Where ever the footsteps of Urizen
Walk'd over the cities in sorrow.

7. Till a Web dark & cold, throughout all
The tormented element, stretch'd
From the sorrows of Urizen's soul
And the Web is a Female in embrio.
None could break the Web, no wings of fire.

8. So twisted the cords, & so knotted
The meshes: twisted like to the human brain.

9. And all calld it, The Net of Religion.

Chap: IX[1)]

1. Then the Inhabitants of those Cities:
Felt their Nerves change into Marrow[2)]

---

1) 제9장의 제목은 "Degeneration and Rebellion"이다.
2) 신경이 굳어지고 "질병"에 감염되어 무감각해짐에 따라 감각이 수축되기 시작한다.

And hardening Bones began
In swift diseases and torments,
In throbbings & shootings & grindings
Thro' all the coasts; till weaken'd
The Senses inward rush'd, shrinking,
Beneath the dark net of infection.

2. Till the shrunken eyes clouded over
Discernd not the woven hipocrisy
But the streaky slime in their heavens
Brought together by narrowing perceptions
Appeard transparent air[1]; for their eyes
Grew small like the eyes of a man
And in reptile forms shrinking together[2]
Of seven feet stature they remaind.

3. Six days they shrunk up from existence
And on the seventh day they rested[3],
And they bless'd the seventh day, in sick hope:
And forgot their eternal life.
4. And their thirty cities divided
In form of a human heart
No more could they rise at will
In the infinite void, but bound down
To earth by their narrowing perceptions,
They lived a period of years
Then left a noisom[4] body
To the jaws of devouring darkness.

5. And their children wept, & built

---

1) Urizen의 눈은 위선을 식별하지 못하고, "줄무늬 진창(streaky slime)"을 "투명한 공기(transparent air)로 착각할 정도로 그이 지각능력이 축소된다.
2) *Paradise Lost* (X, 504-84)에서 뱀으로 변신한 악마들의 운명을 연상케 한다.
3) Genesis (2:2-3)를 패러디한 것이다. 여기서 신의 창조의 시대는 인간 타락의 시대가 되어 있다.
4) *noisom*: extremely unpleasant

Tombs in the desolate places,
And form'd laws of prudence[1]), and call'd them
The eternal laws of God.

6. And the thirty cities remaind
Surrounded by salt floods, now call'd
Africa: its name was then Egypt.[2])

7. The remaining sons of Urizen
Beheld their brethren shrink together
Beneath the Net of Urizen;
Perswasion was in vain;
For the ears of the inhabitants
Were wither'd, & deafen'd, & cold.
And their eyes could not discern
Their brethren of other cities[3]).

8. So Fuzon call'd all together
The remaining children of Urizen:
And they left the pendulous earth:
They called it Egypt, & left it[4]).

9. And the salt ocean rolled englob'd[5]).

The End of the [first] book of Urizen.

---

1) laws of prudence: "신중의 법"은 "Thou shalt not"로 일관된 모세의 율법을 의미한다.
2) Egypt: 성경에서 타락한 도시로 묘사되어 있다. 이스라엘 민족이 이집트를 탈출한 것이 Exodus이다. 앞에서(X, 5)묘사된 바와 같이 무덤을 만든 것이 이집트의 주요 업적이다.
3) 감각 능력이 수축된 결과로 영원의 세계뿐만 아니라 인간에 대한 공동체 의식마저 상실해버렸다.
4) *the pendulous earth*: *Paradise Lost* (Ⅳ, 1000)에 나오는 "the pendulous round earth"의 인유이다.
5) englobed: 지구가 둥글다는 것을 강조한 표현이다. 텅 빈 허공에 고립된 둥근 지구는 Blake의 우주에서 타락의 특징을 잘 나타내고 있다. 그리고 "salt Ocean"은 Noah의 홍수를 연상시킨다. 밀려오는 파도는 홍해(the Red Sea)의 파도를 연상시킨다. 이리하여 Fuzon을 따른 자들은 Moses와 Noah를 따른 자들처럼 파멸로부터 구원을 받는다.

Selected Bibliography

1. Primary Sources

Keynes, Geoffrey (ed.). *Blake: Complete Writings*. London: Oxford UP, 1966.

Johnson, Marylynn and John E. Grant (ed.). *Blake's Poetry and Designs*. New York: Norton, 1970.

2. Secondary Sources:

Bloom, Harold. *The Visionary Company: A Reading of English Romantic Poetry*. Garden City, N. Y.: Doubleday, 1961..

______ (ed.). *William Blake's Songs of Innocence and of Experience*. New York: Chelsea House Publishers, 1987.

______ (ed.). *William Blake: Modern Critical Views 66*. New York: Chelsea House Publishers, 1985.

Bottrall, Margaret (ed.). *William Blake: Songs of Innocence and Experience: A Casebook*. London and Basingstoke: Macmillan, 1970.

Damon, S. Foster. *A Blake Dictionary: The Ideas and Symbols of William Blake*. Colorado: Shambhala Publications, 1965.

Ferber, Michael. *The Social Vision of William Blake*. Princeton, N. J.: Princeton UP, 1985.

Fry, Northrop. *Fearful Symmetry*. Princeton, N. J.: Princeton UP, 1947.

Gardner, Stanley. *Blake*. New York: Arco Publishing Co., 1968, 1969.

Keynes, Geoffrey. *Blake Studies: Essays on his Life and Work*. Oxford: Clarendon P, 1971.

O'Neill, Judith (ed.). *Critics on Blake: Readings in Literary Criticism*. London: George Allen and Unwin Ltd., 1970.

Paananen, Victoria N. *William Blake*. Boston: Twayne Publishers, 1977.

Raine, Kathleen. *Blake and the New Age*. London: George Allen & Unwin, 1979.

William Wordsworth
(1770~1850)

Wordsworth in 1798, about the time he began The Prelude

Hawkshead Grammar School

Dove Cottage

워즈워스의 생애와 작품

워즈워스(William Wordsworth)는 잉글랜드 북부, 컴벌랜드의 코커마우스(Cockermouth)에서 변호사의 아들로 태어나 소년시절을 호수지방에서 보냈다. 그는 8세 때 어머니를 여의고 난 후 Esthwaite 호수 근처의 마을에 있는 학교(Hawkshead Grammar School)에 다녔다. 윌리엄과 그의 3형제는 앤 타이슨(Ann Tyson)의 시골집에 기숙하였다. 타이슨은 어린 형제들에게 따뜻한 애정을 베풀었고, 아름다운 호수지방의 자연 속에서 마음껏 뛰놀게 하였다. 또한 그 학교의 교장 윌리엄 테일러(William Taylor)는 어린 소년에게 자신이 소장하고 있던 장서를 읽게 하고 시를 쓰도록 용기를 주었다. 이때의 경험은 『서곡』 첫 두 권에 묘사된 바와 같이 그가 시인으로 성장하는 데에 중요한 밑거름이 되었다. 부친 존 워즈워스(John Wordsworth)는 그가 13세 되던 해에 세상을 떠나면서 자신이 법정 대리인으로 봉직했던 론즈데일(Londsdale) 경의 부채를 고스란히 자식들에게 물려주었다. 이처럼 어려운 여건 속에서도 그는 1787년 케임브리지 대학의 St. John's College에 입학하였고, 대학 공부에 별로 흥미를 느끼지 못한 탓에 1791년에 평범한 성적으로 대학을 졸업했다.

워즈워스는 대학 3학년 때(1790년) 친구 로버트 존즈(Robert Jones)와 함께 프랑스와 알프스 지방을 도보로 여행했다. 그 무렵 프랑스는 바스티유 감옥 파괴 1주년을 경축하고 있었다. 1791년 대학을 졸업하고 또 다시 존즈와 함께 웨일즈를 도보로 여행했다. 이때의 경험은 『서곡』제13권에 스노든(Snowdon) 등반으로 기록되어 있다. 그 후 불어를 공부하기 위해 혼자 다시 프랑스로 건너갔다. 때마침 절정기에 이른 프랑스혁명의 이상에서 깊은 감명을 받고 열렬한 프랑스혁명 지지자가 되었다. 오를레앙(Orleans)에 머무는 동안 아네트 발롱(Annette Vallon)과 사랑에 깊이 빠져 결혼을 계획하고 있었으나, 딸 캐롤라인(Caroline)이 태어난 직후 수중에 돈이 떨어져 하는 수 없이 1792년 12월에 영국으로 돌아갔다. 그러나 영국과 프랑스 사이에 전쟁이 발발하자 아네트와의 재회는 불가능해졌다. 그는 아네트에 대한 죄의식, 영국과 프랑스에 대한 애국심의 갈등, 프랑스 혁명의 과정에 대한 환멸 등으로 인하여 거의 신경쇠약 증세까지 보였다.

1793년에 『저녁산책』(*An Evening Walk*)과 『풍경소묘』(*Descriptive Sketches*)를 출판하였는데, 시형은 상투적인 영웅대련(heroic couplet)이지만, 곳곳에 생생한 자연묘사가 돋보였다. 콜리지는 케임브리지 대학 시절에 알프스 여행을 소재로 한 『풍경소묘』를 읽고 워즈워스의 천재성을 간파하고서 그들 당대 최고의 시인이라 칭찬했다.

1795년 친구 캘버트(Raisley Calvert)가 그에게 상당한 유산을 남겨주어 Dorsetshire의 Racedown에 있는 시골집에 누이(Dorothy)와 함께 정착할 수 있게 되었다. 그는 조용한 자연과 누이의 자상한 애정으로 인하여 마음의 안정을 되찾아갔다. 1797년 여름에는 다시 Alfoxden으로 이사하여 가까운 곳에 살고 있던 콜리지와 친교를 맺었고, 그들은 거의 매일 만나서 시에 관하여 토론하고 많은 시를 지었다. 1798년 이 두 시인은 공동으로 『서정담시집』(*Lyrical Ballads, With a Few Other Poems*)을 출판하였다. 이 시집에서 콜리지는 초자연의 세계를, 워즈워스는 일상의 비근한 사건을 각각 다룸으로써 새로운 시경(詩境)을 개척, 영문학 사상 낭만주의 부활의 한 시기를 결정짓는 시집이 되었다. 이 시집에는 그의 초기 대표 시 「틴턴 수도원」과 콜리지의 「노수부송」이 포함되어 있다. 초판이 발간된 지 얼마 안 되어 워즈워스 남매와 콜리지는 독일 여행을 떠났고, 워즈워스 남매는 Goslar에서 겨울을 보냈다. 그는 그곳에서 한 영국 소녀를 주제로 한 Lucy 시편들을 지었고, 또한 자신의 시심이 성장해온 발자취를 내면적으로 더듬은 『서곡』(*The Prelude*)을 집필하기 시작하였다.

1799년 독일에서 귀국한 뒤 워즈워스는 누이와 함께 그라스미어 호반의

비둘기 집(Dove Cottage)에 정착하여 1808년까지 그 집에서 살았다. 『서정담시집』은 2년 만에 매진되어 1800년에 개정판을 냈다. 이 개정판에는 영국에서의 최초의 낭만주의 문학 선언이라고 볼 수 있는 유명한 서문이 실렸다. 이 서문에는 새로운 시의 정의, 시의 소재, 언어, 및 시인에 관한 이론이 담겨 있다. 그는 이 서문에서 특히 가난한 시골 사람들의 감정의 발로만이 진실한 것이며, 그들이 사용하는 소박하고 친근한 언어야말로 시에 알맞은 언어라고 주장하여 18세기의 장식적 시어를 배척하였다.

1802년 워즈워스는 누이와 함께 프랑스로 건너가 아네트와 그의 딸 캐롤라인을 만났고, 귀국하여 유년시절부터 알고 지낸 호수지방의 처녀 메리 허친슨(Mary Hutchinson)과 결혼하였다. 1803년에는 누이와 함께 스코틀랜드를 여행하고 나서 여러 편의 소네트를 지었다. 그리고 그해 Sir George Beaumont를 만났고, 그들의 우정은 1827년 Sir George Beaumont가 죽기까지 계속되었다. 1805년에 동생 John이 난파 사고로 익사하고, 1810년에는 콜리지와의 언쟁으로 둘 사이가 최악의 상태에 이르러 그로부터 근 20년간 화해가 이루어지지 않았다.

워즈워스의 생애에서 창작활동이 가장 왕성했던 시기는 『서정담시집』 이후의 10년간이었다. 그는 이 시기에 늙은 양치기와 그의 아들의 운명을 그린 "Michael"을 썼고, 대표작 『서곡』을 완성하였으며, 그 밖에 *Poems in Two Volumes* (1807)을 출간했다. 이 시집에는 "I wandered lonely," "The Solitary Reaper," "My heart leaps up," "Ode: Intimations of Immortality" 등 주옥같은 명시가 수록되어 있다.

1813년 그는 Rydal Mount로 이사하여 죽을 때까지 그곳에서 살았다. 1814년 장시 『소요(逍遙)』(The Excursion)을 완성하였으나, 이 무렵부터 그의 작품은 도덕적, 보수적 색채가 농후해져 갔다. 시인으로서의 명성은 1820년경부터 점차 높아져 1843년에는 R. Southey의 뒤를 이어 계관시인이 되었다. 워즈워스는 1850년 4월 23일에 세상을 떠났고, 그의 유해는 그라스미어 교회 묘지에 묻혀 있다. 그의 자서전적 걸작인 『서곡』은 1850년 그의 사후에 출판되었다.

Goody Blake and Harry Gill[1]

A True Story

Oh! what's the matter? what's the matter?
What is't that ails young Harry Gill?
That evermore his teeth they chatter,
Chatter, chatter, chatter still.
Of waistcoats Harry has no lack,
Good duffle[2] grey, and flannel fine;
He has a blanket on his back,
And coats enough to smother nine.

In March, December, and in July,
'Tis all the same with Harry Gill;
The neighbours tell, and tell you truly,
His teeth they chatter, chatter still.
At night, at morning, and at noon,
'Tis all the same with Harry Gill;
Beneath the sun, beneath the moon,
His teeth they chatter, chatter still.

Young Harry was a lusty drover,
And who so stout of limb as he?
His cheeks were red as ruddy clover,
His voice was like the voice of three.
Auld Goody Blake was old and poor,
Ill fed she was, and thinly clad;
And any man who pass'd her door,
Might see how poor a hut she had.

All day she spun in her poor dwelling,
And then her three hours' work at night!
Alas! 'twas hardly worth the telling,

---

1) Written at Alfoxden. The incident from Dr. Darwin's *Zoonomia*.
2) duffle: rough heavy cloth

It would not pay for candle-light.
—This woman dwelt in Dorsetshire,
Her hut was on a cold hill-side,
And in that country coals are dear,
For they come far by wind and tide.

By the same fire to boil their pottage,
Two poor old dames as I have known,
Will often live in one small cottage,
But she, poor woman, dwelt alone.
'Twas well enough when summer came,
The long, warm, lightsome summer-day,
Then at her door the canty[1] dame
Would sit, as any linnet gay.

But when the ice our streams did fetter,
Oh! then how her old bones would shake!
You would have said, if you had met her,
'Twas a hard time for Goody Blake.
Her evenings then were dull and dead;
Sad case it was, as you may think,
For very cold to go to bed,
And then for cold not sleep a wink.

Oh joy for her! whene'er in winter
The winds at night had made a rout,
And scatter'd many a lusty splinter,
And many a rotten bough about.
Yet never had she, well or sick,
As every man who knew her says,
A pile before hand, wood or stick,
Enough to warm her for three days.

Now when the frost was past enduring,

---

1) canty: 쾌활한(lively)

And made her poor old bones to ache,
Could any thing be more alluring,
Than an old hedge to Goody Blake?
And now and then, it must be said,
When her old bones were cold and chill,
She left her fire, or left her bed,
To seek the hedge of Harry Gill.

Now Harry he had long suspected
This trespass of old Goody Blake,
And vow'd that she should be detected,
And he on her would vengeance take.
And oft from his warm fire he'd go,
And to the fields his road would take,
And there, at night, in frost and snow,
He watch'd to seize old Goody Blake.

And once, behind a rick of barley,
Thus looking out did Harry stand;
The moon was full and shining clearly,
And crisp with frost the stubble land.
—He hears a noise—he's all awake—
Again?—on tip-toe down the hill
He softly creeps—'Tis Goody Blake,
She's at the hedge of Harry Gill.

Right glad was he when he beheld her;
Stick after stick did Goody pull,
He stood behind a bush of elder,
Till she had filled her apron full.
When with her load she turned about,
The bye-road back again to take,
He started forward with a shout,
And sprang upon poor Goody Blake.

And fiercely by the arm he took her,
And by the arm he held her fast,
And fiercely by the arm he shook her,
And cried, "I've caught you then at last!"
Then Goody, who had nothing said,
Her bundle from her lap let fall;
And kneeling on the sticks, she pray'd
To God that is the judge of all.

She pray'd, her wither'd hand uprearing,
While Harry held her by the arm-
"God! who art never out of hearing,
O may he never more be warm!"
The cold, cold moon above her head,
Thus on her knees did Goody pray,
Young Harry heard what she had said;
And icy-cold he turned away.

He went complaining all the morrow
That he was cold and very chill:
His face was gloom, his heart was sorrow,
Alas! that day for Harry Gill!
That day he wore a riding-coat,
But not a whit the warmer he:
Another was on Thursday brought,
And ere the Sabbath he had three.

'Twas all in vain, a useless matter,
And blankets were about him pinn'd;
Yet still his jaws and teeth they clatter,
Like a loose casement in the wind.
And Harry's flesh it fell away;
And all who see him say 'tis plain,
That, live as long as live he may,
He never will be warm again.

No word to any man he utters,
A-bed or up, to young or old;
But ever to himself he mutters,
"Poor Harry Gill is very cold."
A-bed or up, by night or day;
His teeth they chatter, chatter still.
Now think, ye farmers all, I pray,
Of Goody Blake and Harry Gill.

Simon Lee,

the Old Huntsman, with an incident
in which he was concerned

In the sweet shire of Cardigan,[1)]
Not far from pleasant Ivor-hall,[2)]
An old man dwells, a little man,-
'Tis said he once was tall.
Full five-and-thirty years he lived
A running huntsman merry;
And still the centre of his cheek
Is red as a ripe cherry.

No man like him the horn could sound,
And hill and valley rang with glee
When Echo bandied, round and round,
The halloo of Simon Lee.
In those proud days, he little cared
For husbandry or tillage;
To blither tasks did Simon rouse
The sleepers of the village.

He all the country could outrun,
Could leave both man and horse behind;
And often, ere the chase was done,
He reeled, and was stone-blind.
And still there's something in the world
At which his heart rejoices;
For when the chiming hounds are out,
He dearly loves their voices!

But, Oh the heavy change! -bereft
Of health, strength, friends, and kindred, see!

---

1) *the shire of Cardigan*: 카디건셔(Cardiganshire): 영국 웨일즈 서부의 주; 주도는 Cardigan.
2) *Ivor-hall*: 영주의 저택

Old Simon to the world is left
In liveried poverty.
His Master's dead, and no one now
Dwells in the Hall of Ivor;
Men, dogs, and horses, all are dead;
He is the sole survivor.

And he is lean and he is sick;
His body, dwindled and awry,
Rests upon ankles swoll'n and thick;
His legs are thin and dry.
One prop he has, and only one,
His wife, an aged woman,
Lives with him, near the waterfall,
Upon the village Common.

Beside their moss-grown hut of clay,
Not twenty paces from the door,
A scrap of land they have, but they
Are poorest of the poor.
This scrap of land he from the heath
Enclosed when he was stronger;
But what to them avails the land
Which he can till no longer?

Oft, working by her Husband's side,
Ruth does what Simon cannot do;
For she, with scanty cause for pride,
Is stouter of the two.
And, though you with your utmost skill
From labour could not wean them,
'Tis little, very little -all
That they can do between them.

Few months of life has he in store

As he to you will tell,
For still, the more he works, the more
Do his weak ankles swell.
My gentle Reader, I perceive
How patiently you've waited,
And now I fear that you expect
Some tale will be related.

O Reader! had you in your mind
Such stores as silent thought can bring,
O gentle Reader! you would find
A tale in every thing.
What more I have to say is short,
And you must kindly take it:
It is no tale; but, should you think,
Perhaps a tale you'll make it.

One summer-day I chanced to see
This old Man doing all he could
To unearth the root of an old tree,
A stump of rotten wood.
The mattock tottered in his hand;
So vain was his endeavour,
That at the root of the old tree
He might have worked for ever.

"You're overtasked, good Simon Lee,
Give me your tool," to him I said;
And at the word right gladly he
Received my proffered aid.
I struck, and with a single blow
The tangled root I severed,
At which the poor old Man so long
And vainly had endeavoured.
The tears into his eyes were brought,

And thanks and praises seemed to run
So fast out of his heart, I thought
They never would have done.
—I've heard of hearts unkind, kind deeds
With coldness still returning;
Alas! the gratitude of men
Hath oftener left me mourning.

Anecdote for Fathers

I have a boy of five years old,
His face is fair and fresh to see;
His limbs are cast in beauty's mould,
And dearly he loves me.

One morn we strolled on our dry walk,
Our quiet home all full in view,
And held such intermitted talk
As we are wont to do.

My thoughts on former pleasures ran;
I thought of Kilve's[1)] delightful shore,
Our pleasant home when spring began,
A long, long year before.

A day it was when I could bear
Some fond regrets to entertain;
With so much happiness to spare,

---

* This was suggested in front of Alfoxden. The Boy was a son of my friend, Basil Montagu, who had been two or three years under our care. The name of Kilve is from a village on the Bristol Channel, about a mile from Alfoxden; and the name of Liswyn Farm was taken from a beautiful spot on the Wye. When Mr. Coleridge, my Sister, and I, had been visiting the famous John Thelwall, who had taken refuge from politics, after a trial for high treason, with a view to bring up his family by the profits of agriculture, which proved as unfortunate a speculation as that he had fled from, Coleridge and he had both been public lecturers; Coleridge mingling, with his politics, Theology, from which the other elocutionist abstained, unless it were for the sake of a sneer. This quondam community of public employment induced Thelwall to visit Coleridge at Nether Stowey, where he fell in my way. He really was a man of extraordinary talent, an affectionate husband, and a good father. Though brought up in the City, he was truly sensible of the beauty of natural objects. I remember once, when Coleridge, he, and I were seated together upon the turf on the brink of a stream in the most beautiful part of the most beautiful glen of Alfoxden, Coleridge exclaimed, "This is a place to reconcile one to all the jarrings and conflicts of the wide world."-"Nay," said Thelwall, "to make one forget them altogether." The visit of this man to Coleridge was, as I believe Coleridge has related, the occasion of a spy being sent by Government to watch our proceedings, which were, I can say with truth, such as the world at large would have thought ludicrously harmless.

1) *Kilve*: West Somerset에 있는 마을

I could not feel a pain.

The green earth echoed to the feet
Of lambs that bounded through the glade,
From shade to sunshine, and as fleet
From sunshine back to shade.

Birds warbled round me-and each trace
Of inward sadness had its charm;
Kilve, thought I, was a favoured place,
And so is Liswyn[1] farm.

My boy beside me tripped, so slim
And graceful in his rustic[2] dress!
And, as we talked, I questioned him,
In very idleness.

"Now tell me, had you rather be,"
I said, and took him by the arm,
"On Kilve's smooth shore, by the green sea,
Or here at Liswyn farm?"

In careless mood he looked at me,
While still I held him by the arm,
And said, "At Kilve I'd rather be
Than here at Liswyn farm."

"Now, little Edward, say why so:
My little Edward, tell me why."—
"I cannot tell, I do not know."—
"Why, this is strange," said I;

---

1) *Liswyn*: Wye 강변에 있는 농촌 마을
2) *rustic*: roughly made

"For, here are woods, hills smooth and warm:
There surely must some reason be
Why you would change[1] sweet Liswyn farm
For Kilve by the green sea."

At this, my boy hung down his head,
He blushed with shame, nor made reply;
And three times to the child I said,
"Why, Edward, tell me why?"[2]

His head he raised—there was in sight,
It caught his eye, he saw it plain—
Upon the house-top, glittering bright,
A broad and gilded vane[3].

Then did the boy his tongue unlock[4],
And eased his mind[5] with this reply:
"At Kilve there was no weather-cock;
And that's the reason why."

O dearest, dearest boy! my heart
For better lore would seldom yearn,
Could I but teach the hundredth part
Of what from thee I learn.

---

1) *change*: exchange
2) 세 번씩이나 Kilve를 선호하는 이유를 다그쳐 묻는다. 그러나 어린아이는 인과율에 근거한 논리적 사고를 하지 못한다. 계속해서 대답을 강요하면 어린아이는 사실을 왜곡시키거나 거짓말을 하게 된다.
3) *vane*: weather-vane; weather-cock: 바람개비, 풍향계
4) *his tongue unlock*: unlock his tongue (말문을 열다)
5) *ease his mind*: 긴장을 풀다, 마음을 편히 가지다 (feel less worried or nervous)

We Are Seven

A Simple Child, dear brother Jim,
That lightly draws its breath,
And feels its life in every limb,
What should it know of death?

I met a little cottage Girl:
She was eight years old, she said;
Her hair was thick with many a curl
That clustered round her head.

She had a rustic, woodland air,
And she was wildly clad:
Her eyes were fair, and very fair;
—Her beauty made me glad.

"Sisters and brothers, little Maid,
How many may you be?"
"How many? Seven in all," she said
And wondering looked at me.

"And where are they? I pray you tell."
She answered, "Seven are we;
And two of us at Conway dwell,
And two are gone to sea.

"Two of us in the church-yard lie,
My sister and my brother;
And, in the church-yard cottage, I
Dwell near them with my mother."

"You say that two at Conway dwell,
And two are gone to sea,
Yet ye are seven!—I pray you tell,

Sweet Maid, how this may be."

Then did the little Maid reply,
"Seven boys and girls are we;
Two of us in the church-yard lie,
Beneath the church-yard tree."

"You run above, my little Maid,
Your limbs they are alive;
If two are in the church-yard laid,
Then ye are only five."

"Their graves are green, they may be seen,"
The little Maid replied,
"Twelve steps or more from my mother's door,
And they are side by side.

"My stockings there I often knit,
My kerchief there I hem[1];
And there upon the ground I sit,
And sing a song to them.

"And often after sun-set, Sir,
When it is light and fair,
I take my little porringer[2],
And eat my supper there.

"The first that died was sister Jane;
In bed she moaning lay,
Till God released her of her pain;
And then she went away.

---

1) *hem*: 가장자리를 꿰매다, 옷단을 감치다;

2) *porringer*: 죽 그릇 (a small bowl for soup, broth, porridge etc.); porridge: 오트밀에 우유 또는 물을 넣어 만든 죽

"So in the church-yard she was laid;
And, when the grass was dry,
Together round her grave we played,
My brother John and I.

"And when the ground was white with snow,
And I could run and slide,
My brother John was forced to go,
And he lies by her side."

"How many are you, then," said I,
"If they two are in heaven?"
Quick was the little Maid's reply,
"O Master! we are seven."

"But they are dead; those two are dead!
Their spirits are in heaven!"
'Twas throwing words away; for still
The little Maid would have her will[1],
And said, "Nay, we are seven!"

---

1) *have her will*: 고집대로 하다

To My Sister

It is the first mild day of March:
Each minute sweeter than before
The redbreast sings from the tall larch[1)]
That stands beside our door.

There is a blessing in the air,
Which seems a sense of joy to yield
To the bare trees, and mountains bare,
And grass in the green field.

My sister! ('tis a wish of mine)
Now that our morning meal is done,
Make haste, your morning task resign[2)];
Come forth and feel the sun.

Edward will come with you;—and, pray,
Put on with speed your woodland dress;
And bring no book: for this one day
We'll give to idleness[3)].

No joyless forms shall regulate
Our living calendar:
We from to-day, my Friend, will date
The opening of the year.

Love, now a universal birth,
From heart to heart is stealing,

---

* "Observed in the holly-grove at Alfoxden, where these verses were written in the spring of 1799. I had the pleasure of again seeing, with dear friends, this grove in unimpaired beauty forty-one years after." (Wordsworth)

1) *larch*: 낙엽송

2) *your morning task resign*: 아침 설거지를 그만두라.

3) 오늘 하루 한가롭게 지내자; "this one day"는 give의 목적어.

From earth to man, from man to earth:
—It is the hour of feeling.

One moment now may give us more
Than years of toiling reason:
Our minds shall drink at every pore
The spirit of the season.

Some silent laws our hearts will make,
Which they shall long obey:
We for the year to come may take
Our temper[1] from to-day.

And from the blessed power that rolls
About, below, above,
We'll frame the measure[2] of our souls:
They shall be tuned to love.

Then come, my Sister! come, I pray,
With speed put on your woodland dress;
And bring no book: for this one day
We'll give to idleness.

1798

1) *temper*: actual state or attitude of the mind or feelings; 오늘부터 새로운 정신적 태도를 갖자는 의미.

2) *measure*: 가락, 선율, 노래 (an air, a tune, a melody)

Lines Written in Early Spring

I heard a thousand blended notes,
While in a grove I sate reclined,
In that sweet mood when pleasant thoughts
Bring sad thoughts to the mind.

To her fair works did Nature link
The human soul that through me ran;
And much it grieved my heart to think
What man has made of man.

Through primrose tufts[1], in that green bower,
The periwinkle[2] trailed its wreaths[3];
And 'tis my faith that every flower
Enjoys the air it breathes.

The birds around me hopped and played,
Their thoughts I cannot measure—
But the least motion which they made
It seemed a thrill of pleasure.

The budding twigs spread out their fan,
To catch the breezy air;
And I must think, do all I can,
That there was pleasure there.

If this belief from heaven be sent,
If such be Nature's holy plan,
Have I not reason to lament
What man has made of man?

1798

---

* "Actually composed while I was sitting by the side of the brook that runs down from the Comb, in which stands the village of Alford, through the grounds of Alfoxden. It was a chosen resort of mine...." (Wordsworth)

1) *primrose tufts*: 앵초 덤불

2) *periwinkle*: 일일초, 협죽도

3) *wreath*: 화관

Expostulation and Reply

"Why, William, on that old grey stone,
Thus for the length of half a day,
Why, William, sit you thus alone,
And dream your time away?

"Where are your books?—that light bequeathed
To Beings else forlorn and blind!
Up! up! and drink the spirit breathed
From dead men to their kind.

"You look round on your Mother Earth,
As if she for no purpose bore you;
As if you were her first-born birth,
And none had lived before you!"[1)]

One morning thus, by Esthwaite lake,
When life was sweet, I knew not why,
To me my good friend Matthew spake,
And thus I made reply:

"The eye it cannot choose but see;
We cannot bid the ear be still;
Our bodies feel, where'er they be,
Against, or with our will.

"Nor less I deem that there are powers
Which of themselves our minds impress;
That we can feed this mind of ours

---

* "This poem is a favourite among the Quakers, as I have learnt on many occasions. It was composed in front of the house at Alfoxden, in the spring of 1798." (Wordsworth) *expostulation*: 충고, 훈계 (a spoken remonstrance, protest or reproof).

1) "최초의 인간(Adam)인 것처럼"이라는 표현은 새로운 시대(또는 정신)의 시작을 암시하는 말임.

In a wise passiveness[1].

"Think you, 'mid all this mighty sum
Of things for ever speaking,
That nothing of itself will come,
But we must still be seeking?

"—Then ask not wherefore, here, alone,
Conversing as I may,
I sit upon this old grey stone,
And dream my time away."

1798

1) *a wise passiveness*: 현명한 수용적 태도; 잔잔한 수면에 주위의 사물이 비치듯, 지적 판단을 중지하고 감각인상을 받아들이는 태도를 말함.

The Tables[1] Turned

Up! up! my Friend, and quit your books;
Or surely you'll grow double[2]:
Up! up! my Friend, and clear your looks;
Why all this toil and trouble?

The sun above the mountain's head,
A freshening lustre mellow
Through all the long green fields has spread,
His first sweet evening yellow.

Books! 'tis a dull and endless strife:
Come, hear the woodland linnet,
How sweet his music! on my life,
There's more of wisdom in it.

And hark! how blithe the throstle[3] sings!
He, too, is no mean preacher:
Come forth into the light of things,
Let Nature be your teacher.

She has a world of ready wealth,
Our minds and hearts to bless—
Spontaneous wisdom breathed by health,
Truth breathed by cheerfulness.

One impulse from a vernal wood
May teach you more of man,

---

1) *tables*: 법전; (고대에 법률을 새겨 넣은) 판; *the two tables of the law*: 모세의 십계명을 새겨 넣은 두 개의 석판; the Ten Commandments; *the Twelve Tables of Rome*: (로마의 가장 오래된 법전인) 12 동판법; *turn the tables*: 형세를 역전시키다 (reverse relations, esp. pass from inferior to superior position)
2) *grow double*: 허리가 꼬부라지다. Cf. *double*=bent; folded; stooping forward
3) *throstle*: 개똥지빠귀

Of moral evil and of good,
Than all the sages can.
Sweet is the lore[1] which Nature brings;
Our meddling intellect[2]
Mis-shapes the beauteous forms of things:—
We murder to dissect[3].

Enough of Science and of Art;
Close up those barren leaves;
Come forth, and bring with you a heart
That watches and receives.

1798

1) *lore*: 지식, 학문 (body of traditions and knowledge)
2) *meddling intellect*: 간섭하는 지성
3) *murder to dissect*: 해부하기 위해 죽인다; 분석적 지성을 비판하는 표현.

Lines

Composed a Few Miles above Tintern Abbey,
on revisiting the banks of the Wye during a tour
July 13, 1798

Five years have past; five summers, with the length
Of five long winters![1] and again I hear
These waters, rolling from their mountain-springs
With a soft inland murmur.—Once again
Do I behold these steep and lofty cliffs,
Which on a wild secluded scene impress
Thoughts of more deep seclusion; and connect
The landscape with the quiet of the sky.
The day is come when I again repose
Here, under this dark sycamore, and view
These plots of cottage-ground, these orchard-tufts,
Which, at this season, with their unripe fruits,
Are clad in one green hue, and lose themselves
'Mid groves and copses. Once again I see
These hedge-rows, hardly hedge-rows[2], little lines
Of sportive wood run wild[3]; these pastoral farms,
Green to the very door; and wreathes of smoke[4]
Sent up, in silence, from among the trees,
With some uncertain notice[5], as might seem,
Of vagrant[6] dwellers in the houseless woods,
Or of some Hermit's[7] cave, where by his fire

---

* "No poem of mine was composed under circumstances more pleasant for me to remember than this. I began it upon leaving Tintern, after crossing the Wye, and concluded it just as I was entering Bristol in the evening, after a ramble of four or five days, with my Sister. Not a line of it was altered, and not any part of it written down till I reached Bristol."-I. F. Note.

1) Wordsworth는 1793년 Salisbury Plain으로부터 Wales로 도보여행을 하는 길에 틴턴 사원과 Wye강 계곡을 방문했었다.

2) *hedge-rows*: a row of small bushes or trees growing close together, usually dividing one field or garden from another

3) *sportive wood run wild*: 멋대로 자란 관목숲; (*run wild*: grow unchecked; *sportive*: playful)

4) *wreaths of smoke*: 피어오르는 몇 가닥의 연기(curving or spiral masses of smoke)

5) *with some uncertain notice*: 얼핏 보면

6) *vagrant*: wandering; "vagrant dweller"(떠도는 거주자)는 모순어법임.

The Hermit sits alone.

These beauteous forms,
Through a long absence, have not been to me,
As is a landscape to a blind man's eye[1]:
But oft, in lonely rooms, and 'mid the din
Of towns and cities, I have owed to them,
In hours of weariness, sensations[2] sweet,
Felt in the blood, and felt along the heart,
And passing even into my purer mind
With tranquil restoration[3]:—feelings too
Of unremembered pleasure; such, perhaps,
As have had no slight or trivial influence
On that best portion of a good man's life;
His little, nameless[4], unremembered, acts
Of kindness and of love. Nor less, I trust,
To them I may have owed another gift,
Of aspect more sublime[5]; that blessed mood[6],
In which the burthen of the mystery[7],
In which the heavy and the weary weight
Of all this unintelligible world,
Is lighten'd:—that serene and blessed mood,
In which the affections[8] gently lead us on,—
Until, the breath of this corporeal frame[9],
And even the motion of our human blood
Almost suspended, we are laid asleep

---

7) *hermit*: 종교적 은둔자(a person who from religious motives has retired into solitary life: early Christian recluse)

1) 장님 눈에 비친 풍경 같지는 않았다.

2) *sensation*: a feeling that you get from one of the five senses; sense impressions; sense experience

3) *with tranquil restoration*: 조용하게 (지난날의 경험을) 회복시켜주는

4) *nameless*: unknown; obscure

5) *sublime*: producing an overwhelming sense of awe, reverence, or high emotion, by reason of great beauty, vastness, or grandeur

6) *blessed mood*: blissful state of mind or feeling

7) *mystery*: religious truth divinely revealed, esp. one beyond human reason

8) *affections*: mental states; feelings

9) *corporeal frame*: body

In body, and become a living soul:
While with an eye made quiet by the power
Of harmony[1], and the deep power of joy,
We see into the life[2] of things.

If this
Be but a vain belief, yet, oh! how oft,
In darkness, and amid the many shapes
Of joyless daylight; when the fretful stir
Unprofitable[3], and the fever of the world,
Have hung upon the beatings of my heart—
How oft, in spirit, have I turned to thee,
O sylvan Wye! thou wanderer through the wood,
How often has my spirit turned to thee!

And now, with gleams of half-extinguish'd thought,
With many recognitions[4] dim and faint,
And somewhat of a sad perplexity[5],
The picture of the mind revives[6] again:
While here I stand, not only with the sense
Of present pleasure, but with pleasing thoughts
That in this moment there is life and food
For future years. And so I dare to hope
Though changed, no doubt, from what I was when first
I came among these hills; when like a roe
I bounded o'er the mountains, by the sides
Of the deep rivers, and the lonely streams,
Wherever nature led: more like a man
Flying from something that he dreads, than one

---

1) *harmony*: the state being harmonious (harmonious=forming a consistent or orderly or pleasing whole)
2) *life*: vitality; energy; spirit
3) *unprofitable*: not useful or fruitful
4) *recognition*: the act of knowing something; cf. *recognize*=know who someone is or what something is, because you have seen, heard, experienced or learned about them in the past
5) *perplexity*: 당혹감(=the feeling of being confused or worried by something you cannot understand)
6) *revive*: come back to consciousness

Who sought the thing he loved. For nature then
(The coarser[1]) pleasures of my boyish days,
And their glad animal movements all gone by)
To me was all in all.—I cannot paint
What then I was. The sounding cataract
Haunted me like a passion: the tall rock,
The mountain, and the deep and gloomy wood,
Their colours and their forms, were then to me
An appetite[2]): a feeling and a love,
That had no need of a remoter charm,
By thought supplied, nor any interest
Unborrowed from the eye.—That time is past,
And all its aching joys are now no more,
And all its dizzy raptures[3]). Not for this
Faint I, nor mourn nor murmur; other gifts
Have followed, for such loss, I would believe,
Abundant recompence[4]). For I have learned
To look on nature, not as in the hour
Of thoughtless youth, but hearing oftentimes
The still, sad music of humanity[5]),
Nor harsh nor grating[6]), though of ample power
To chasten[7]) and subdue[8]). And I have felt
A presence that disturbs me with the joy
Of elevated thoughts; a sense sublime
Of something far more deeply interfused[9]),
Whose dwelling is the light of setting suns,
And the round ocean, and the living air,
And the blue sky, and in the mind of man:

---

1) *coarse*: unrefined; vulgar
2) *appetite*: desire to satisfy natural needs
3) *rapture*: great excitement and happiness; ecstatic delight
4) *recompense*: reward
5) *humanity*: human attributes
6) *grating*: hard and unpleasant
7) *chasten*: render pure in character
8) *subdue*: check or repress (an emotion)
9) *interfuse*: permeate, blend

A motion and a spirit, that impels[1]
All thinking things, all objects of all thought,
And rolls through all things. Therefore am I still
A lover of the meadows and the woods,
And mountains; and of all that we behold
From this green earth; of all the mighty world
Of eye and ear,—both what they half-create,
And what perceive[2]; well pleased to recognize
In nature and the language of the sense,
The anchor of my purest thoughts, the nurse,
The guide, the guardian of my heart, and soul
Of all my moral being.

                                        Nor, perchance,
If I were not thus taught, should I the more
Suffer my genial spirits[3] to decay[4]:
For thou art with me, here upon the banks
Of this fair river; thou my dearest Friend,
My dear, dear Friend, and in thy voice I catch
The language of my former heart, and read
My former pleasures in the shooting lights
Of thy wild eyes. Oh! yet a little while
May I behold in thee what I was once,
My dear, dear Sister! And this prayer I make,
Knowing that Nature never did betray[5]
The heart that loved her; 'tis her privilege,
Through all the years of this our life, to lead
From joy to joy: for she can so inform[6]
The mind that is within us, so impress
With quietness and beauty, and so feed[7]
With lofty thoughts, that neither evil tongues,

---

1) *impel*: drive, force
2) *what perceive*: what (they half) perceive
3) *genial spirits*: cheerful feelings; 生氣(=natural vivacity)
4) *decay*: decline (in power)
5) *betray*: be disloyal to; disappoint the expectations of
6) *inform*: inspire
7) impress와 feed 다음에 목적어 the mind가 생략되었음

Rash judgments, nor the sneers of selfish men,
Nor greetings where no kindness is, nor all
The dreary intercourse of daily life,
Shall e'er prevail[1] against us, or disturb[2]
Our cheerful faith, that all which we behold
Is full of blessings. Therefore let the moon
Shine on thee in thy solitary walk;
And let the misty mountain-winds be free
To blow against thee: and in after years,
When these wild ecstasies shall be matured
Into a sober pleasure; when thy mind
Shall be a mansion for all lovely forms,
Thy memory be as a dwelling-place
For all sweet sounds and harmonies; oh! then,
If solitude, or fear, or pain, or grief,
Should be thy portion, with what healing thoughts
Of tender joy wilt thou remember me,
And these my exhortations! Nor, perchance—
If I should be where I no more can hear
Thy voice, nor catch from thy wild eyes these gleams
Of past existence—wilt thou then forget
That on the banks of this delightful stream
We stood together; and that I, so long
A worshipper of Nature, hither came,
Unwearied in that service: rather say
With warmer love, oh! with far deeper zeal
Of holier love. Nor wilt thou then forget
That after many wanderings, many years
Of absence, these steep woods and lofty cliffs,
And this green pastoral landscape, were to me
More dear, both for themselves and for thy sake!

1798

---

1) *prevail*: be victorious
2) *disturb*: agitate and destroy

Strange Fits of Passion Have I Known

Strange fits of passion[1] have I known:
And I will dare to tell,
But in the Lover's ear alone,
What once to me befell.

When she I loved looked every day
Fresh as a rose in June,
I to her cottage bent my way,
Beneath an evening-moon.

Upon the moon I fixed my eye,
All over the wide lea[2];
With quickening pace my horse drew nigh
Those paths so dear to me.

And now we reached the orchard-plot;
And, as we climbed the hill,
The sinking moon to Lucy's cot
Came near, and nearer still.

In one of those sweet dreams I slept,
Kind Nature's gentlest boon![3]
And all the while my eyes I kept
On the descending moon.

My horse moved on; hoof after hoof
He raised, and never stopped:
When down behind the cottage roof,
At once, the bright moon dropped.

---

* "The next three poems were written in Germany." (Wordsworth)

1) *Strange fits of passion*: 문득 떠오르는 불길한 예감

2) *lea*: a tract of open ground, esp. grassland

3) *boon*: a gift, a gratuity

What fond[1] and wayward[2] thoughts will slide
Into a lover's head!
"O mercy!"[3] to myself I cried,
"If Lucy should be dead!"

1799 (1800)

She Dwelt among the Untrodden Ways

She dwelt among the untrodden[4] ways
  Beside the springs[5] of Dove,
A Maid whom there were none to praise[6]
  And very few to love:

A violet by a mossy stone
  Half hidden from the eye!
– Fair as a star, when only one
  Is shining in the sky.

She lived unknown, and few could know
  When Lucy ceased to be;
But she is in her grave, and, oh,
  The difference to me![7]

1799 (1800)

---

1) *fond*: foolish; foolishly optimistic
2) *wayward*: childishly self-willed; capricious
3) O mercy!: O mercy on us!; 저런! 어쩌나! (놀람, 난처함 등을 나타냄)
4) *untrodden*: 인적 없는(not trodden or stepped on)
5) spring: 원류(原流: a place where water wells up from earth)
6) *praise*: laud; extol; express warm approval or admiration of
7) Lucy가 없음으로 인하여 세상이 달라졌다는 의미임.

Three Years She Grew in Sun and Shower

Three years she grew in sun and shower,
Then Nature said, "A lovelier flower
On earth was never sown;
This Child I to myself will take;
She shall be mine, and I will make
A Lady of my own.

"Myself will to my darling be
Both law and impulse[1]: and with me
The Girl, in rock and plain,
In earth and heaven, in glade and bower,
Shall feel an overseeing[2] power
To kindle[3] or restrain[4].

"She shall be sportive as the fawn
That wild with glee across the lawn,
Or up the mountain springs;
And hers shall be the breathing balm[5],
And hers the silence and the calm
Of mute insensate things.

"The floating clouds their state shall lend
To her; for her the willow bend;
Nor shall she fail to see
Even in the motions of the Storm
Grace[6] that shall mould the Maiden's form
By silent sympathy.

---

1) *impulse*: 충동(a sudden strong desire to do something)
2) *oversee*: 감독하다(superintend; officially supervise), 보살피다(keep watch over)
3) kindle: (감정을) 불러일으키다(inflame, arouse, inspire)
4) restrain: 억제하다(keep in check or under control; repress, keep down)
5) *balm*: fragrance; healing or soothing influence
6) *grace*: an attractive or pleasing quality; something that imparts beauty

"The stars of midnight shall be dear
To her; and she shall lean her ear
In many a secret place
Where rivulets dance their wayward round,
And beauty born of murmuring sound
Shall pass into her face.

"And vital[1] feelings of delight
Shall rear her form to stately height,
Her virgin bosom swell;
Such thoughts to Lucy I will give
While she and I together live
Here in this happy dell."

Thus Nature spake—The work was done—
How soon my Lucy's race[2] was run!
She died, and left to me
This heath[3], this calm, and quiet scene;
The memory of what has been,
And never more will be.

1799 (1800)

---

1) *vital*: full of life or energy; lively
2) *race*: course of life
3) *heath*: open uncultivated ground covered by heather or related plants

A Slumber Did My Spirit Seal

A slumber did my spirit seal;
I had no human fears:
She seemed a thing that could not feel
The touch of earthly years.

No motion has she now, no force;
She neither hears nor sees;
Rolled round in earth's diurnal course,
With rocks, and stones, and trees.

1799 (1800)

I Travelled Among Unknown Men

I travelled among unknown men
In lands beyond the sea;
Nor, England! did I know till then
What love I bore to thee.

'Tis past, that melancholy dream!
Nor will I quit thy shore
A second time; for still I seem
To love thee more and more.

Among thy mountains did I feel
The joy of my desire;
And she I cherished turned her wheel[1]
Beside an English fire.

Thy mornings showed, thy nights concealed,
The bowers where Lucy played;
And thine too is the last green field
That Lucy's eyes surveyed.

1801 (1807)

---

1) *wheel*: spinning wheel

The Two April Mornings

We walk'd along, while bright and red
Uprose the morning sun,
And Matthew stopp'd, he look'd, and said,
"The will of God be done!"

A village schoolmaster was he,
With hair of glittering grey;
As blithe a man as you could see
On a spring holiday.

And on that morning, through the grass,
And by the steaming rills,
We travell'd merrily to pass
A day among the hills.

"Our work," said I, "was well begun;
Then, from thy breast what thought,
Beneath so beautiful a sun,
So sad a sigh has brought?"

A second time did Matthew stop,
And fixing still his eye
Upon the eastern mountain-top
To me he made reply.

Yon cloud with that long purple cleft[1)]
Brings fresh into my mind
A day like this, which I have left
Full thirty years behind.

---

1) *cleft*: a natural crack (in the surface of rocks or the Earth)

And on that slope of springing corn
The self-same crimson hue
Fell from the sky that April morn,
The same which I now view!

With rod and line my silent sport
I plied[1] by Derwent's wave,
And, coming to the churchyard, stopp'd short
Beside my daughter's grave.

Nine summers had she scarcely seen
The pride[2] of all the vale;
And then she sang:—she would have been
A very nightingale.

Six feet in earth my Emma lay;
And yet I lov'd her more,
For so it seem'd, than till that day
I e'er had loved before.

And, turning from her grave, I met
Beside the churchyard Yew
A blooming[3] Girl, whose hair was wet
With points of morning dew.

A basket on her head she bare,
Her brow was smooth and white,
To see a child so very fair,

---

1) *ply*: work at; devote one's energy to
2) *the pride of*: 자랑거리 (the thing or person that the people in a particular place are most proud of)
3) *blooming*: 꽃다운, 한창인 (in full beauty or vigour)

It was a pure delight!

No fountain from its rocky cave
E'er tripp'd with foot so free,
She seemed as happy as a wave
That dances on the sea.

There came from me a sigh of pain
Which I could ill confine;
I look'd at her and look'd again:
—And did not wish her mine.

1800

The Fountain,

A Conversation

We talked with open heart, and tongue
Affectionate and true,
A pair of friends, though I was young,
And Matthew seventy-two.

We lay beneath a spreading oak,
Beside a mossy seat;
And from the turf a fountain broke
And gurgled[1] at our feet.

Now, Matthew! said I, let us match
This water's pleasant tune
With some old border-song[2], or catch[3]
That suits a summer's noon.

Or of the church-clock and the chimes[4]
Sing here beneath the shade,
That half-mad thing of witty rhymes
Which you last April made!

In silence Matthew lay, and eyed[5]
The spring beneath the tree;
And thus the dear old man replied,
The grey-haired man of glee.

"Down to the vale this water steers[6],

---

1) *gurgle*: 콸콸 소리 내다 (make bubbling sound)
2) *border song*: 변방의 노래
3) catch: 윤창(輪唱) (round for three or more equal voices, so devised as to produce punning or other humorous verbal combinations)
4) *chimes*: 종소리, 종악 (set of attuned bells; series of sounds given by this).
5) *eye*: observe, watch
6) *steer*: direct one's course

How merrily it goes!
'Twill murmur on a thousand years,
And flow as now it flows.

And here, on this delightful day,
I cannot choose but think
How oft, a vigorous man, I lay
Beside this fountain's brink.

My eyes are dim with childish tears,
My heart is idly stirr'd,
For the same sound is in my ears,
Which in those days I heard.

Thus fares it still in our decay:
And yet the wiser mind
Mourns less for what Age takes away
Than what it leaves behind.

The blackbird in the summer trees,
The lark upon the hill,
Let loose[1)] their carols[2)] when they please,
Are quiet when they will.

With Nature never do they wage
A foolish strife; they see
A happy youth, and their old age
Is beautiful and free:

But we are pressed by heavy laws,
And often, glad no more,
We wear a face of joy, because
We have been glad of yore.

---

1) *let loose*: sing
2) *carol*: joyous song, esp. Christmas hymn (hymn=song of praise to God)

If there be one who need bemoan[1])
His kindred laid in earth,
The household hearts that were his own,
It is the man of mirth.

My days, my friend, are almost gone,
My life has been approv'd[2]),
And many love me, but by none
Am I enough beloved."

"Now both himself and me he wrongs,
The man who thus complains!
I live and sing my idle songs
Upon these happy plains,

And, Matthew, for thy children dead
I'll be a son to thee!"
At this he grasp'd my hand and said
"Alas! that cannot be."

We rose up from the fountain-side,
And down the smooth descent
Of the green sheep-track did we glide,
And through the wood we went,

And, ere we came to Leonard's Rock,
He sang those witty rhymes
About the crazy old church-clock
And the bewildered chimes.

1800

1) *bemoan*: express sorrow for
2) *approved*: considered good or satisfactory

My Heart Leaps Up

My heart leaps up when I behold
  A rainbow[1)] in the sky:
So was it when my life began;
So is it now I am a man;
So be it when I shall grow old,
  Or let me die!
The Child is father of the Man[2)];
And I could wish my days to be
Bound each to each by natural piety.[3)]

1802 (1807)

---

* Wordsworth의 시 중에서 가장 짧은 작품이다. 얼핏 보기에 단순하고 평이한 작품처럼 보이지만, 이 작품 속에는 워즈워스가 반복해서 다루는 중요한 주제들이 모두 포함되어 있다.

1) *A rainbow*: 자연의 아름다운 형상들 중 하나이다. 성경에서 무지개는 인간에 대한 하나님의 약속, 즉 지상의 생명이 영원히 번성하게 하겠다는 하나님의 약속을 상징한다. "I do set my bow in the cloud, and it shall be for a token of a covenant between me and the earth. And it shall come to pass, when I bring a cloud over the earth, that the bow shall be seen in the cloud. And I will remember my covenant, which is between me and you and every living creature of all flesh; and the waters shall no more become a flood to destroy all flesh."(Genesis 9:13-15) 무지개는 또한 시인의 상상력을 상징한다. 워즈워스는 *Lyrical Ballads* (1800) 서문에서 그의 목표가 평범한 일상생활에서 "incidents and situations"를 선택하여 거기에 상상의 색채("a certain colouring of imagination")를 첨가함으로써 평범한 것이 특이하게 보이도록 만드는 것이라 말했다. 무색투명한 빛이 프리즘을 통과하면 일곱 가지 찬란한 빛으로 이루어진 무지개가 되는 것은 시인의 상상력에 의한 제재의 시적 변용을 보여주는 좋은 예이다.

2) *The Child is father of the Man*: 흔히 "어린이는 어른의 아버지이다"라고 번역된다. 여기서 "The Child"와 "the Father"는 "어린이"와 "어른"이라는 보통명사가 아니라 "어린이의 속성"과 "어른의 속성"이라는 추상적 의미를 갖는다. 그리고 "father"는 "아버지"를 의미하는 보통명사가 아니라 "원천"이라는 추상적 의미를 갖는다. 사전에는 "tendencies in childhood foreshadow adult development"라고 풀이되어 있다. 이 역설적인 표현 속에는 "it(poetry) takes its origin from emotion recollected in tranquility"라는 그의 시론이 함축되어 있다. 이 말은 어릴 적에 자연으로부터 받아들인 감각경험들이 후일 어른이 되어 시를 쓸 때 회상되어 시의 제재가 된다는 것을 의미한다. *The Prelude*에는 회상된 어릴 적의 경험이 "spots of time"(1850; XII, 208-225)으로 묘사되어 있다.

3) *natural piety*: 자연에 대한 경건한 마음; "piety"는 신과 종교에 대한 존경과 복종을 의미한다. 따라서 "natural piety"라는 표현에는 자연을 신성시하는 워즈워스의 태도가 함축되어 있다. 이 작품에서 "natural piety"는 구체적으로 하늘의 무지개를 볼 때 가슴이 뛰는 정서반응을 의미한다. "이 piety는 성경에 기초를 둔 경건감과는 다르다; 일상적 사물의 신비로움에 대한 지속적 반응은 어른이 된 워즈워스와 그의 어린 시절을 연결시키는 종교적 감정이다."

Written in March

While Resting on the Bridge at the Foot of Brother's Water[1)]

The cock is crowing,
The stream is flowing,
The small birds twitter,
The lake doth glitter,
The green field sleeps in the sun;

The oldest and youngest
Are at work with the strongest;
The cattle are grazing,
Their heads never raising;
There are forty feeding like one!

Like an army defeated
The snow hath retreated,
And now doth fare ill
On the top of the bare hill;
The ploughboy is whooping—anon—anon:

There's joy in the mountains;
There's life in the fountains;
Small clouds are sailing,
Blue sky prevailing;
The rain is over and gone!

1802 (1807)

---

* Dorothy Wordsworth's Journal (April 16, 1802): "When we came to the Brother's Water I left William sitting on the bridge... When I returned I found William writing a poem descriptive of the sights and sounds we saw and heard. There was the gentle flowing of the stream, the glittering, lively lake... behind us, a flat pasture with forty-two cattle feeding.... William finished the poem before we got to the foot of Kirkstone."

Composed upon Westminster Bridge

SEPT. 3, 1802

Earth has not anything to show more fair:
Dull would he be of soul who could pass by
A sight so touching in its majesty:
This City[1] now doth, like a garment, wear
The beauty of the morning; silent, bare,
Ships, towers, domes, theatres, and temples lie
Open unto the fields, and to the sky;
All bright and glittering in the smokeless air.
Never did sun more beautifully steep[2]
In his first splendour, valley, rock, or hill;
Ne'er saw I, never felt, a calm so deep!
The river[3] glideth at his own sweet will[4]:
Dear God! the very houses seem asleep;
And all that mighty heart[5] is lying still!

1807

---

* "Composed on the roof of a coach, on my way to France" (Wordsworth). 그러나 실제 여행한 날자는 1802년 7월 31일이었다. 워즈워스는 한 때 열렬한 혁명 지지자였고, Annette Vallon을 사랑하여 사생아를 낳은 그 나라로 잠시 돌아갔을 때 느낀 심리적 갈등을 소재로 여러 편의 소네트를 남겼다.

1) *This city*: London

2) *steep*: 적시다 (soak or bathe in water or other liquid)

3) *the river*: the Thames

4) *at will*: 마음대로 (whenever one wants and in whatever way one wants); *at his own sweet will*: 마음대로 아름답게

5) *that mighty heart*: the heart of London; 런던을 인간의 심장에 비유한 표현임.

It Is a Beauteous Evening

It is a beauteous evening, calm and free,
The holy time[1] is quiet as a nun
Breathless with adoration; the broad sun
Is sinking down in its[2] tranquility;
The gentleness of heaven broods o'er the sea:[3]
Listen! the mighty Being[4] is awake,
And doth with his eternal motion make
A sound like thunder[5]—everlastingly.
Dear Child![6] dear Girl! that walkest with me here,
If thou appear untouched by solemn thought[7],
Thy nature is not therefore less divine:
Thou liest in Abraham's bosom[8] all the year,
And worship'st at the Temple's inner shrine,
God being with thee when we know it not.

1807

---

* "This was composed on the beach near Calais in the autumn of 1802" (Wordsworth).

1) *the holy time*: 성스러운 시간: 저녁을 의인화하여 숨죽이고 기도하는 수녀에 비유하고 있다.

2) *its*: "it"는 "성스러운 시간" 즉 "저녁"을 가리킨다.

3) "부드러운 하늘이 바다를 품고 있다"; 하늘을 의인화한 표현임.

4) *the mighty Being*: 거대한 존재; "Tintern Abbey"의 "A presence"처럼 우주에 충만한 존재.

5) "거대한 존재"는 "영원한 운동으로 우레 같은 소리를 내고 있다." 여기서 "motion"은 "Tintern Abbey"의 "A motion"과 같은 의미를 갖는다. 이 존재가 내는 소리는 육신의 귀에 들리지는 않지만 상상의 귀에는 "우레 같은 소리"로 들린다.

6) *Dear Child*: 시인과 Annette Vallon 사이에 태어난 딸 Caroline

7) solemn thought: 엄숙한 사상: 즉 우주 속에 만유의 신성인 "거대한 존재"가 살아 움직이고 있다는 생각을 의미한다. 이것은 "우리가 의식하지 못하는 순간에도 하나님이 우리와 함께 계신다"는 생각으로 이어진다.

8) *Abraham's bosom*: 의로운 자의 영혼이 죽은 후에 쉬는 곳: 천국; "And it came to pass, that the beggar died, and was carried by the angels into Abraham's bosom" (Luke 16:22).

London, 1802

Milton! thou shouldst be living at this hour:
England hath need of thee: she is a fen
Of stagnant waters[1]): altar, sword, and pen[2]),
Fireside, the heroic wealth of hall and bower[3]),
Have forfeited[4]) their ancient English dower[5])
Of inward happiness. We are selfish men;
Oh! raise us up, return to us again;
And give us manners, virtue, freedom, power[6]).
Thy soul was like a Star, and dwelt apart:
Thou hadst a voice whose sound was like the sea:
Pure as the naked heavens[7]), majestic, free,
So didst thou travel on life's common way[8]),
In cheerful godliness[9]); and yet thy heart
The lowliest duties on herself did lay[10]).

1802 (1807)

---

* One of the series "written immediately after my return from France to London, when I could not but be struck, as here described, with the vanity and parade of our own country...as contrasted with the quiet, and I may say the desolation, that the revolution had produced in France." (Wordsworth)

1) *a fen / Of stagnant waters*: 물이 고여 있는 늪; 고인 물은 썩기 마련이다. 워즈워스는 당시의 영국 사회적 타락과 정체성을 물이 고여 썩어가는 늪에 비유하여 묘사하고 있다.

2) altar, sword, and pen: 제단과 칼과 펜, 즉 교회와 군대와 문단을 의미하는 환유(metonymy)이다.

3) Fireside, the heroic wealth of hall and bower: 난롯가(가정), 홀과 규방의 장엄한 부, 즉 소박한 평민의 가정과 화려한 상류사회를 의미한다; *hall*=대저택(mansion, large residence); *bower*=내실, 규방(inner room; bedroom for ladies)

4) *forfeit*: lose (something valuable)

5) dower: 과부산, 유산 (widow's share for life of husband's estate); 타고난 자질 (endowment, gift of nature); 시인은 고래로 영국이 가지고 있던 내면적 행복이라는 유산을 잃어버렸다고 탄식한다.

6) 시인은 영국이 상실한 것이 "예의, 덕행, 자유, 힘"이라고 말한다.

7) *naked heavens*: 구름 한 점 없는 맑은 하늘

8) 인생의 평범한 길을 여행했다: 즉 평범한 삶을 살았다는 의미.

9) *in cheerful godliness*: 흔쾌히 신의 뜻에 순종하며; *godly*=obeying God and leading a good life

10) 그대의 마음은 가장 천한 의무도 자신에게 부과했다.

The World Is Too Much with Us

The world is too much with us[1]; late and soon[2],
Getting and spending, we lay waste our powers:
Little we see in Nature that is ours;
We have given our hearts away, a sordid boon![3]
The Sea that bares her bosom to the moon;
The winds that will be howling at all hours,
And are up-gathered now like sleeping flowers;
For this, for everything, we are out of tune[4];
It moves us not.—Great God! I'd rather be
A Pagan suckled in a creed outworn;[5]
So might I, standing on this pleasant lea,
Have glimpses that would make me less forlorn[6];
Have sight of Proteus[7] rising from the sea;
Or hear old Triton[8] blow his wreathed horn.[9]

1807

1) *The world is too much with us*: 우리는 너무나 세속에 물들어 있다. *the world*: 세속적인 관심과 일들 (secular interests and occupations)
2) *late and soon*: 늦게 자고 일찍 일어나고; *(go to bed) late and (get up) soon.*
3) *boon*: gift; "더러운 선물"이란 우리의 마음을 내버리는 행위를 의미한다.
4) *be out of tune (with)*: be unable to realize, understand, or agree with
5) 낡은 신앙을 빨아 먹는 이교도
6) *forlorn*: lonely and unhappy
7) *Proteus*: 해신 (海神); 모습을 자유자재로 바꿀 수 있는 능력과 예언 능력을 가졌다는 바다의 노인.
8) *Triton*: 해신 (海神); 상반신은 사람의 모습, 하반신은 물고기의 모습한 한 바다의 신; 소라고둥을 불어 파도를 다스리는 힘을 가졌다고 전해진다.
9) *wreathed horn*: 해초가 얽힌 소라 나팔

Resolution and Independence

I

There was a roaring in the wind all night;
The rain came heavily and fell in floods;
But now the sun is rising calm and bright;
The birds are singing in the distant woods;
Over his own sweet voice the Stock-dove broods;[1)]
The Jay makes answer as the Magpie chatters;[2)]
And all the air is filled with pleasant noise of waters.

II

All things that love the sun are out of doors;
The sky rejoices in the morning's birth;
The grass is bright with rain-drops;—on the moors
The hare is running races in her mirth[3)];
And with her feet she from the plashy[4)] earth
Raises a mist, that, glittering in the sun,
Runs with her all the way, wherever she doth run.

---

* "This old man I met a few hundred yards from my cottage at Town End, Grasmere [October 3, 1800]; and the account of him is taken from his own mouth. I was in the state of feeling described in the beginning of the poem, while crossing over Barton Fell from Mr. Clarkson's, at the foot of Ullswater, towards Askam. The image of the hare I then observed on the ridge of the Fell" (Wordsworth). Dorothy는 1800년 10월 3일자 일기에서 이 작품의 기초가 된 경험을 이렇게 설명했다: "We met an old man almost double. He had had a wife, and she was a good woman, and 'it pleased God to bless us with ten children.' All of them were dead but one, of whom he had not heard for many years. He had been hurt in driving a cart, his leg broken, his body driven over, his skull fractured. His trade was to gather leeches, but now leeches were scarce, and he had not the strength for it." 그로부터 2년 후 이 사소한 사건은 "평정 속에서 회상되어" 이 작품의 제재가 되었다. 시인은 이 작품에서 신비로운 비전처럼 찾아온 거머리 잡이 노인의 묘사를 통하여 인간정신의 위대함과 견인불굴의 정신을 표현하고 있다.

1) 들비둘기는 제 목소리를 (알을 품듯이) 품는다.
2) 까치가 재잘대면 어치가 화답한다. *Jay*: 어치; *magpie*: 까치
3) *mirth*: 환희, 흥겨움 (happiness and laughter)
4) *plashy*: splashy; 질척질척한, 웅덩이가 많은

III

I was a Traveller then upon the moor,
I saw the hare that raced about with joy;
I heard the woods and distant waters roar;
Or heard them not, as happy as a boy:
The pleasant season did my heart employ[1]:
My old remembrances went from me wholly;
And all the ways of men, so vain and melancholy.

IV

But, as it sometimes chanceth, from the might
Of joy in minds that can no further go,
As high as we have mounted in delight
In our dejection do we sink as low;[2]
To me that morning did it happen so;
And fears and fancies[3] thick upon me came;
Dim sadness—and blind thoughts, I knew not, nor could name.

V

I heard the sky-lark warbling in the sky;
And I bethought me of[4] the playful hare:
Even such a happy Child of earth am I;
Even as these blissful creatures do I fare[5];
Far from the world I walk, and from all care;
But there may come another day[6] to me—
Solitude, pain of heart, distress, and poverty.

---

1) *employ*: 사로잡다 (keep occupied)
2) 기쁠 때는 마음이 한없이 들뜨다가도 낙담하면 한없이 우울해진다는 의미.
3) *fears and fancies*: 공포와 환상들; 시인은 기쁨의 절정에서 갑자기 기분의 변화를 일으켜 최악의 실의에 빠지게 된다.
4) *bethink me (myself) of*: 생각나다 (remind myself of; stop to think)
5) *fare*: go travel
6) *another day*: 또 다른 날; 시인은 "고독, 가슴앓이, 고통, 그리고 가난"을 겪을 날이 올 것이라는 불안한 생각에 젖어든다. 이러한 불안한 생각은 다음 연에서 인생살이가 뜻대로 되지만은 않을 것이라는 생각으로 이어진다.

VI

My whole life I have lived in pleasant thought,
As if life's business were a summer mood;
As if all needful things would come unsought
To genial[1] faith, still rich in genial good;
But how can he expect that others should
Build for him, sow for him, and at his call
Love him, who for himself will take no heed at all?

VII

I thought of Chatterton[2], the marvellous Boy,
The sleepless Soul that perished in his pride;
Of Him[3] who walked in glory and in joy
Following his plough, along the mountain-side:
By our own spirits are we deified[4]:
We Poets in our youth begin in gladness;
But thereof come in the end despondency and madness.[5]

VIII

Now, whether it were by peculiar grace,
A leading from above[6], a something given[7],

---

1) genial: 정다운, 유쾌한 (kindly, jovial)

2) *Chatterton*: Thomas Chatterton (1752-70); 극심한 가난과 고독 때문에 17세의 나이에 독약을 마시고 자살한 천재 시인; 낭만파 시인들이 사회로부터 버림받고 요절한 천재 시인의 상징으로 생각했다.

3) *Him*: Robert Burns (1759-96). 37세에 죽은 스코틀랜드의 농부 시인; 그 또한 사회로부터 인정받지 못하고 젊은 나이에 가난하게 죽은 시인으로 여겨졌다.

4) *deify*: render godlike in character, spirit, or quality; 우리는 기분이 좋을 때는 신이 된다.

5) "우리 시인들은 젊을 때는 기쁨으로 시작하지만, 마지막엔 실의와 광기가 찾아온다." 낭만주의 시인들은 상상력으로 무한과 영원을 추구할 수 있다고 믿고 시를 쓰기 시작하지만, 결국은 육신을 가진 인간으로서의 한계를 극복하지 못하고 절망하게 된다는 것을 의미한다. 실의 또는 낙담이 낭만주의 시의 주제로 등장한 것은 이 때문이다. 워즈워스는 여기서 요절한 천재 시인들의 운명을 생각하고 있다. 이 무렵 그는 자신의 건강을 걱정하고 있었다. 그는 두통과 불면증에 시달렸고, 자신의 창작능력이 소진되지 않을까 걱정하고 있었다(Noyes 132). 그는 요절한 젊은 시인들의 운명이 자신에게도 일어날 수 있다는 불안감에 젖어 있다.

6) *A leading from above*: 위로부터의 인도, 즉 신(하늘)의 인도; *leading*=a directing influence or guidance. 시인은 "위로부터의 인도" 즉 신의 섭리의 개입으로 거머리 잡이 노인을 만나고 우울증에서 벗어난다. 이 노인은 마치 그가 불길한 예감에서 벗어나라고 신이 보낸 선물처럼 보인다.

7) *a something given*: 주어진 어떤 것 즉 선물

Yet it befell, that, in this lonely place,
When I with these untoward[1] thoughts had striven,
Beside a pool bare to the eye of heaven[2]
I saw a Man before me unawares:
The oldest man he seemed that ever wore grey hairs.

IX

As a huge stone is sometimes seen to lie
Couched on the bald top of an eminence[3];
Wonder to all who do the same espy,
By what means it could thither come, and whence;[4]
So that it seems a thing endued[5] with sense:
Like a sea-beast crawled forth, that on a shelf
Of rock or sand reposeth, there to sun itself;

X

Such seemed this Man[6], not all alive nor dead,
Nor all asleep—in his extreme old age:
His body was bent double, feet and head
Coming together in life's pilgrimage[7];
As if some dire constraint[8] of pain, or rage[9]

---

1) *untoward*: 비뚤어진 (perverse); 어울리지 않는 (unseemly)
2) *the eye of heaven*: the sun
3) eminence: 고지, 언덕 (an elevated or lofty position
4) "그 바위를 본 사람들은 모두 / 그것이 어떻게 거기에 왔고 어디서 왔는지 궁금하게 여긴다." *Wonder*: 이상한 것(일), 놀라운 일 (strange or remarkable thing or performance or event).
5) *endue*: endow, furnish (a person) with (power, qualities, etc.)
6) 시인은 노인을 바위와 해수에 비유하여 "자연의 과정을 초월한 영적 존재"(Noyes 132)로 변형시켜 놓았다. 그는 1807년 시집 *Poems*의 서문에서 상상력의 작용을 설명하면서 이 부분을 자세히 분석하였다. 그는 상상력이 사물에 없는 속성을 부여하고(conferring), 사물이 가진 속성을 소거하여(abstracting), 상호 수정하는(modifying) 능력을 가지고 있다고 설명했다. 이 작품에서는 바위에 없는 생명력을 부여하고, 바다짐승이 가진 생명의 속성을 제거하여, 바위와 해수를 동화시키며, 노인에게서 생명력과 운동을 제거하여 바위 또는 해수와 결합시킴으로써 시적 심상을 창조하였다고 설명했다. 이러한 과정을 통하여 노인은 자연 풍경과 하나가 되어 자연 속의 장엄하고 영원한 속성과 연결된다.
7) *life's pilgrimage*: 인생여정; *pilgrimage*=moral life viewed as a journey
8) *constraint*: 압박 (oppression)
9) rage: 격심함, 강렬함, 맹위 (violent operation of some natural force or some sentiment); *rage / Of sickness*: 격심한 질병

Of sickness felt by him in times long past,
A more than human weight upon his frame had cast.[1)]

XI

Himself he propped, limbs, body, and pale face,
Upon a long grey staff of shaven wood[2)]:
And, still as I drew near with gentle pace,
Upon the margin of that moorish flood
Motionless as a cloud the old Man stood,
That heareth not the loud winds when they call
And moveth all together, if it move at all.

XII

At length, himself unsettling[3)], he the pond
Stirred with his staff, and fixedly did look
Upon the muddy water, which he conned[4)],
As if he had been reading in a book:
And now a stranger's privilege I took;
And, drawing to his side, to him did say,
"This morning gives us promise of a glorious day."[5)]

XIII

A gentle answer did the old Man make,
In courteous speech which forth he slowly drew:[6)]
And him with further words I thus bespake[7)],
"What occupation do you there pursue?
This is a lonesome place for one like you."
Ere he replied, a flash of mild surprise

---

1) As if some...had cast: 마치 오래 전에 그가 느꼈던 끔찍한 고통의 압박 혹은 격심한 질병이 그의 육신에 인간이 견딜 수 없는 무거운 짐을 짊어지게 한 듯.
2) shaven wood: 깎은 나무; *shave*=pare surface of (wood).
3) *himself unsettling*: 몸을 움직이면서; *unsettle*=disturb settled state of
4) *con*: 자세히 살피다 (study)
5) 오늘은 날씨가 좋을 것 같다는 의미; promise: 전망, 가망 (signs that something will be good)
6) 천천히 꺼내는 정중한 말로
7) *bespeak*: 말을 걸다 (speak to)

Broke from the sable orbs[1] of his yet-vivid eyes,

XIV

His words came feebly, from a feeble chest,
But each in solemn order followed each,
With something of a lofty utterance drest[2]—
Choice word and measured phrase[3], above the reach
Of ordinary men; a stately speech;
Such as grave livers do in Scotland use,[4]
Religious men, who give to God and man their dues[5].

XV

He told, that to these waters he had come
To gather leeches, being old and poor:
Employment hazardous and wearisome![6]
And he had many hardships to endure:
From pond to pond he roamed, from moor to moor;
Housing, with God's good help, by choice or chance[7],
And in this way he gained an honest maintenance[8].

XVI

The old Man still stood talking by my side;
But now his voice to me was like a stream
Scarce heard; nor word from word could I divide;

---

1) *the sable orbs*: 검은 눈동자 (black eyeball)
2) 고상한 말투로 다듬어진; *dress*=꾸미다, 장식하다 (ornament, adorn); 고상한 말씨로 다듬어진 한마디 한마디의 말이 엄숙하게 이어졌다는 의미.
3) *choice word and measured phrase*: 엄선된 단어와 정연한 구절; *choice*=carefully chosen; *measured*=accurately regulated, correctly proportioned
4) 근엄하게 살아가는 스코틀랜드 사람들이 사용하는; *grave*=dignified, serious, solemn
5) *Religious men, who give to God and man their dues*: 하나님을 공경하고 인간을 사랑하는 신자(信者)들; 앞줄의 "grave livers"와 동격임; *give a person his/her due*=공평하게 다루다 (treat a person fairly or with justice); 하나님과 인간을 공평하게 대한다는 말은 곧 신을 공경하고 인간을 사랑한다는 뜻임.
6) (거머리를 잡는 일은) 위험하고 지루한 일이었다.
7) *Housing...by choice or chance*: 고르거나 운에 맡겨 잠자리를 구하며
8) *maintenance*: 생계 (livelihood; means of subsistence); *gained an honest subsistence*: 정직하게 생계를 꾸려 나갔다.

And the whole body of the Man did seem
Like one whom I had met with in a dream;
Or like a man from some far region sent,
To give me human strength, by apt admonishment[1].

XVII

My former thoughts[2] returned: the fear that kills;
And hope that is unwilling to be fed[3];
Cold, pain, and labour, and all fleshly ills;
And mighty Poets in their misery dead.
—Perplexed, and longing to be comforted,
My question eagerly did I renew,
"How is it that you live, and what is it you do?"

XVIII

He with a smile did then his words repeat;
And said, that, gathering leeches, far and wide
He travelled; stirring thus about his feet
The waters of the pools where they abide.
"Once I could meet with them on every side;
But they have dwindled[4] long by slow decay[5];
Yet still I persevere[6], and find them where I may."

XIX

While he was talking thus, the lonely place,
The old Man's shape, and speech—all troubled[7] me:
In my mind's eye I seemed to see him pace
About the weary moors continually,

---

1) *admonishment*: admonition: 훈계, 충고; *admonish*=give advice to; reprove, warn
2) *My former thoughts*: 지난날의 생각들: 즉 "생명을 위협하는 공포, / 만족을 원치 않는 희망, / 추위, 고통, 노동, 그리고 온갖 육체적 질병,/ 그리고 비참하게 죽은 시인들"
3) *hope that is unwilling to be fed*: 만족을 원치 않는 희망
4) *dwindle*: become gradually smaller
5) *by slow decay*: 서서히 줄어들어; *decay*=decrease in quantity.
6) *persevere*: continue steadfastly, persist
7) *trouble*: agitate, disturb

Wandering about alone and silently.
While I these thoughts within myself pursued,
He, having made a pause, the same discourse renewed.

XX

And soon with this he other matter blended,
Cheerfully uttered, with demeanour kind,
But stately in the main; and when he ended,
I could have laughed myself to scorn to find
In that decrepit[1] Man so firm a mind.[2]
"God," said I, "be my help and stay[3] secure;
I'll think of the Leech-gatherer on the lonely moor!"

May 3~July 4, 1802 (1807)

---

1) *decrepit*: 노쇠한 (enfeebled with age and infirmities)
2) 시인은 "저 노쇠한 인간에게서 확고한 정신"을 발견하고 자신을 비웃는다. 즉 그는 이 노인에게서 자연인의 삶에 활력을 주고 인내하게 하며 승리하게 하는 영적인 삶의 가치를 깨닫는다. 이 노인에게는 육신의 쇠퇴에 상응하는 내적 생명의 쇠퇴가 없으며, 따라서 영혼의 낙심은 육체적 노쇠의 필연적 결과가 아니라는 진리를 웅변적으로 보여주고 있다.
3) *stay*: (정신적) 지주 (support); 의지, 믿고 의지하는 대상

The Sparrow's Nest

Behold, within the leafy shade,
Those bright blue eggs together laid!
On me the chance-discovered sight
Gleamed like a vision of delight.
I started—seeming to espy
The home and sheltered bed,
The Sparrow's dwelling, which, hard by
My Father's house, in wet and dry
My sister Emmeline[1)] and I
Together visited.

She looked at it and seemed to fear it;
Dreading, tho' wishing, to be near it:
Such heart was in her, being then
A little Prattler among men.
The Blessing of my later years
Was with me when a boy:
She gave me eyes, she gave me ears;
And humble cares, and delicate fears;
A heart, the fountain of sweet tears;
And love, and thought, and joy.

1801 (1807)

---

* "Written in the Orchard, Town-end, Grasmere. At the end of the garden of my father's house at Cockermouth was a high terrace that commanded a fine view of the river Derwent and Cockermouth Castle. This was our favourite play-ground. The terrace-wall, a low one, was covered with closely-clipt privet and roses, which gave an almost impervious shelter to birds that built their nests there. The latter of these stanzas alludes to one of those nests." (Wordsworth) 이 시는 Dove Cottage 시편들 중의 하나이다. 워즈워스 남매는 1799년 12월에 이 집으로 이사하여 1808년 5월까지 살면서 많은 훌륭한 작품들을 창작했다. 이 시는 시인이 부친의 집에서 누이와 함께 보낸 어린 시절을 생각하며 쓴 작품이다. 그는 우연히 Dove Cottage 정원의 수풀 속에서 참새 둥지를 발견하고 어릴 때 부친의 집 울타리에서 본 새둥지를 생각해낸다.

1) *Emmeline*: 시인의 누이 Dorothy Wordsworth에 대한 애칭이다. 그녀는 뛰어난 감수성과 관찰력으로 시인에게 눈과 귀가 되어 주었다.

To A Butterfly

Stay near me—do not take thy flight!
A little longer stay in sight!
Much converse[1] do I find in thee,
Historian of my infancy!
Float near me; do not yet depart!
Dead times revive in thee:[2]
Thou bring'st, gay creature as thou art!
A solemn image to my heart,
My father's family!

Oh! pleasant, pleasant were the days,
The time, when, in our childish plays,
My sister Emmeline and I
Together chased the butterfly!
A very hunter did I rush
Upon[3] the prey—with leaps and springs[4]
I followed on from brake to bush;
But she, God love her, feared to brush
The dust[5] from off its wings

1801 (1807)

---

* "Written in the orchard, Town-end, Grasmere. My sister and I were parted immediately after the death of our mother, who died in 1778, both being very young." (Wordsworth) 부친의 집에서 Dorothy와 함께 보낸 어린 시절을 생각하며 지은 시이다. 시인은 나비를 보고 어린 시절을 생각해낸다. 그는 나비를 쫓아다녔으나, 누이는 나비 날개에서 꽃가루를 털기조차 두려워하는 섬세함을 보였다.

1) *converse*: 이야기, 대화 (conversation)
2) 너를 보면 지난 시절이 되 살아난다. *dead*=past
3) *rush upon*: 덮치다, (별안간에) 덤벼들다 (capture by sudden vehement assault)
4) *with leaps and springs*: by leaps and bounds; 빠른 속도로 (with startlingly rapid progress)
5) dust: 꽃가루 (pollen), 가루 (fine powder of any material)

To the Cuckoo

O blithe New-comer! I have heard,
I hear thee and rejoice.
O Cuckoo! shall I call thee Bird,
Or but a wandering Voice?

While I am lying on the grass
Thy twofold shout[1] I hear;
From hill to hill it seems to pass,
At once far off, and near.

Though babbling only to the Vale
Of sunshine and of flowers,
Thou bringest unto me a tale
Of visionary hours.

Thrice welcome, darling of the Spring!
Even yet thou art to me
No bird, but an invisible thing,
A voice, a mystery;

The same whom in my school-boy days
I listened to; that Cry
Which made me look a thousand ways
In bush, and tree, and sky.

To seek thee did I often rove
Through woods and on the green;
And thou wert still a hope, a love;
Still longed for, never seen.

---

* Composed in the orchard, Town-end, Grasmere. (Wordsworth)
1) twofold shout: 이중(二重)의 외침

And I can listen to thee yet;
Can lie upon the plain
And listen, till I do beget
That golden time again.

O blessèd Bird! the earth we pace
Again appears to be
An unsubstantial, faery place;
That is fit home for Thee!

1804 (1807)

I Wandered Lonely as a Cloud

I wandered lonely as a cloud
That floats on high o'er vales and hills,
When all at once I saw a crowd,
A host of[1] golden[2] daffodils;
Beside the lake, beneath the trees,
Fluttering and dancing in the breeze.

Continuous as the stars that shine
And twinkle on the Milky Way[3],
They stretched in never-ending line
Along the margin of a bay:
Ten thousand saw I at a glance,
Tossing their heads in sprightly[4] dance.

The waves beside them danced; but they
Out-did[5] the sparkling waves in glee[6]:
A poet could not but be gay,

---

* "Written at Town-end, Grasmere. The Daffodils grew and still grow on the margin of Ullswater and probably may be seen to this day as beautiful in the month of March, nodding their golden heads beside the dancing and foaming waves."(Wordsworth) Cf. Dorothy Wordsworth's *Journals* (April 15, 1802): "I never saw daffodils so beautiful. They grew among the mossy stones about and about them; some rested their heads upon these stones, as on a pillow, for weariness; and the rest tossed and reeled and danced, and seemed as if they verily laughed with the wind, that blew upon them over the lake; they looked so gay, ever glancing, ever changing."

1) *a host of*: 한 무리의 (a large number of); host: an armed company or multitude of men, an army; Cf. "무질서한 군중"(a number of people gathered together so as to press upon or impede each other)을 의미하는 "a crowd"와는 다른 의미를 함축하고 있다.

2) *golden*: ① 황금색의 (of the colour of gold), 황금처럼 반짝이는 (shining like gold) ② 황금처럼 귀중한 (resembling gold in value, precious) ③ 황금기의 (characterized by great prosperity and happiness) ④ 황금시대의 (of the golden age); 특히 ②의 의미는 제3연의 "wealth"와 연결된다.

3) *the Milky Way*: 은하수 (galaxy); 수선화를 은하수의 별들에 비유한 것은 "golden"과 더불어 수선화의 가치를 강화한다. 또한 수선화의 춤은 우주적 질서의 일부분임을 암시한다.

4) *sprightly*: 활발한, 기운찬, 경쾌한 (full of animation and cheerful vitality; vigorous, lively)

5) *out-do*: 능가하다 (surpass, excel); 시인은 수선화의 춤과 물결의 춤을 비교하면서, 수선화의 춤이 더 아름답다고 말한다.

6) *glee*: 환희(歡喜) (triumphant or exuberantly displayed delight); Wordsworth는 특히 창조적 기쁨을 표현할 때 이 단어를 사용한다.

In such a jocund company[1];
I gazed—and gazed—but little thought[2]
What wealth the show to me had brought:

For oft, when on my couch I lie
In vacant or in pensive mood,
They flash upon that inward eye
Which is the bliss of solitude[3];
And then my heart with pleasure fills,
And dances with the daffodils.

1804 (1807)

---

1) *company*: 친구, 동석한 사람들; 함께 있음 (the state of being companion or fellow)

2) *I gazed—and gazed—but little thought*: 응시하고 또 응시하였으나 생각하지는 않았다; 이 말은 "간섭하는 지성(meddling intellect)"의 방해를 받지 않는 "현명한 수용의 태도(a wise passiveness)"를 견지하였음을 의미한다. 제3연에서 "시인"을 언급한 것은 이 작품이 창작의 과정을 묘사한 것임을 암시한다. 마치 잔잔한 수면에 외부의 사물이 잘 비치듯이, 창조적 지각의 순간에 일체의 지적 판단이 중지되어야 한다.

3) *the bliss of solitude*: 고독의 축복; 시인은 홀로 고요하게 명상에 잠겨 있을 때 "마음의 눈(inward eye)이 열린다."고 한다. 여기서 "solitude"는 자연으로부터 소외된 상태를 의미하는 "lonely"와 달리 "홀로 있음"을 의미한다. 마지막 연은 워즈워스가 "서문"에서 설명한 정서의 회상 과정을 예시한 것이다. 그는 "시는 평정 상태에서 회상된 정서에서 유래한다.(it takes its origin from emotion recollected in tranquility)"고 말했다.

The Solitary Reaper

Behold her, single in the field,
Yon solitary Highland[1)] Lass!
Reaping and singing by herself;
Stop here, or gently pass!
Alone she cuts and binds the grain,
And sings a melancholy strain;
O listen! for the Vale profound
Is overflowing with the sound.

No Nightingale did ever chaunt
More welcome notes to weary bands
Of travellers in some shady haunt[2)],
Among Arabian sands:
A voice so thrilling ne'er was heard
In spring-time from the Cuckoo-bird,
Breaking the silence of the seas
Among the farthest Hebrides[3)].
Will no one tell me what she sings?[4)]—

---

* 1803년 8월에 누이 Dorothy와 함께 Scotland를 여행했다. 이 여행 기간에 남매는 여자들이 추수하는 모습을 보았다. Dorothy는 이 여행에서 얻은 경험을 *Recollections of a Tour Made in Scotland* 에 기록했고 Wordsworth는 여러 편의 시로 묘사했다. 그는 집에 돌아와서 Thomas Wilkins의 *Tour in Scotland* 에 나오는 한 구절을 읽고 이 시를 지었다: "Passed by a female who was reaping alone, she sung in Erse [the Gaelic language of Scotland] as she bended over the sickle, the sweetest human voice I ever heard. Her strains were tenderly melancholy, and felt delicious long after they were heard no more." Cf. Dorothy는 다음과 같이 적었다: "As we descended, the scene became more fertile....It was harvest time, and the fields were quietly—might I be allowed to say pensively—enlivened by small companies of reapers. It is not uncommon in the more lonely parts of the Highlands to see a single person so employed."

1) *Highland*: 스코틀랜드의 고원지대

2) *shady haunt*: 그늘진 곳 즉 오아시스; *haunt*=a place where someone likes to go to often.

3) *the Hebrides*: 헤브리디즈 군도 (스코틀랜드 서쪽에 있는 군도); 시인은 제2연에서 아라비아 사막에서 헤브리디즈 군도까지 공간을 확대하고, 제3연에서 먼 옛날에서부터 오늘에 이르기까지 시간을 확대하여, 제1연에 제시된 외로운 추수꾼의 노래를 모든 인간의 보편적 감정(기쁨, 슬픔, 또는 고통)을 표현하는 노래로 승화시킨다.

4) 처녀는 게일어(캘트어에 속하는 고대 아일랜드 또는 스코틀랜드 방언)로 노래하기 때문에 화자가(또는 시인이) 알아듣지 못한다.

Perhaps the plaintive numbers[1] flow
For old, unhappy, far-off things,
And battles long ago:
Or is it some more humble lay[2],
Familiar matter of to-day?
Some natural[3] sorrow, loss, or pain,
That has been, and may be again?

Whate'er the theme, the Maiden sang
As if her song could have no ending;
I saw her singing at her work,
And o'er the sickle bending;—
I listened, motionless and still;
And, as I mounted up the hill
The music in my heart I bore,
Long after it was heard no more.

November 5, 1805 (1807)

---

1) *plaintive numbers*: 슬픈 노래 (mournful verses)
2) *lay*: 노래 (song)
3) *natura*l: 타고난 (innate, existing in nature)

Stepping Westward

"What, you are stepping westward?"—"Yea."

—'T would be a wildish destiny,
If we, who thus together roam
In a strange land, and far from home,
Were in this place the guests of Chance[1]):
Yet who would stop, or fear to advance,
Though home or shelter he had none,
With such a sky to lead him on?

The dewy ground was dark and cold;
Behind, all gloomy to behold;
And stepping westward seemed to be
A kind of heavenly destiny:
I liked the greeting; 't was a sound
Of something without place or bound;
And seemed to give me spiritual right
To travel through that region bright.

The voice was soft, and she who spake
Was walking by her native lake:
The salutation had to me
The very sound of courtesy:
Its power was felt; and while my eye
Was fixed upon the glowing sky,
The echo of the voice enwrought
A human sweetness with the thought
Of traveling through the world that lay
Before me in my endless way.

1807

---

* "While my Fellow-traveller and I were walking by the side of Loch Ketterine, one fine evening after sunset, in our road to a Hut where in the course of our Tour we had been hospitably entertained some weeks before, we met, in one of the loneliest parts of that solitary region, two well dressed Women, one of whom said to us, by way of greeting, What, you are stepping westward?" (Wordsworth)

1) *guests of Chance*: 우연히 만난 손님

Ode:

Intimations of Immortality
from Recollections of Early Childhood

"This was composed during my residence at Town-end, Grasmere. Two years at least passed between the writing of the four first stanzas and the remaining part. To the attentive and competent reader the whole sufficiently explains itself; but there may be no harm in adverting here to particular feelings or 'experiences' of my own mind on which the structure of the poem partly rests. Nothing was more difficult for me in childhood than to admit the notion of death as a state applicable to my own being. I have said elsewhere—

"A simple child,
That lightly draws its breath,
And feels its life in every limb,
What should it know of death!"—

But it was not so much from feelings of animal vivacity that 'my' difficulty came as from a sense of the indomitableness of the Spirit within me. I used to brood over the stories of Enoch and Elijah, and almost to persuade myself that, whatever might become of others, I should be translated, in something of the same way, to heaven. With a feeling congenial to this, I was often unable to think of external things as having external existence, and I communed with all that I saw as something not apart from, but inherent in, my own immaterial nature. Many times while going to school have I grasped at a wall or tree to recall myself from this abyss of idealism to the reality. At that time I was afraid of such processes. In later periods of life I have deplored, as we have all reason to do, a subjugation of an opposite character, and have rejoiced over the remembrances, as is expressed in the lines—

"Obstinate questionings
Of sense and outward things,
Fallings from us, vanishings;" etc.

To that dream-like vividness and splendour which invest objects of sight in childhood, every one, I believe, if he would look back, could bear testimony, and I need not dwell upon it here: but having in the poem regarded it as presumptive evidence of a prior state of existence, I think it right to protest against a conclusion, which has given pain to some good and pious persons, that I meant to inculcate such a belief. It is far too shadowy a notion to be recommended to faith, as more than an element in our instincts of immortality. But let us bear in mind that, though the idea is not advanced in revelation, there is nothing there to contradicear , and the fall of Man presents an analogy in me gfavour. Accordingly, a pre-existent state has entered into the popular creeds of many nations; and, among all persons acqpointed with classic literature, is n ton as an mngredient in Platonic philosophy. Archimedes said that he could move the wor notf he had a point whereon to rest his machine. sho has not felt is n ton aspirations as regards the wor noof his own mind? Having to wield s amonf its elements when I was impelled to write this poem on the "Immortality of the Soul," I took hold of the notion of pre- existence as having sufficient foundation in humanity for authorising me to make for my purpose the best use of it I could as a poet." (Wordsworth)

Ode

Intimations of Immortality
from Recollections of Early Childhood

The Child is father of the Man;
And I could wish my days to be
Bound each to each by natural piety.

I

There was a time when meadow, grove, and stream,
The earth, and every common sight,
To me did seem
Apparelled in celestial light[1],
The glory and the freshness of a dream[2].
It is not now as it hath been of yore;—
Turn wheresoe'er I may,
By night or day,
The things which I have seen I now can see no more.

II

The Rainbow comes and goes,
And lovely is the Rose;
The Moon doth with delight
Look round her when the heavens are bare;
Waters on a starry night
Are beautiful and fair;
The sunshine is a glorious birth;
But yet I know, where'er I go,
That there hath past away a glory from the earth.[3]

---

1) *celestial light*: 천국의 빛; *celestial*=heavenly, divine; 이 작품의 제1부(제1연~제4연)는 빛을 상실을 묘사한 부분이다.

2) 꿈의 영광과 생생함; celestial light와 동격으로 사용되었다. 워즈워스는 "천국의 빛"이라는 생소한 개념을 설명하기 위해 "꿈"의 이미지를 사용하고 있다. 또한 glory 자체도 "heavenly light"의 뜻을 함축하고 있다; *glory*=splendour; effulgence of heavenly light; bliss and splendour of heaven; circle of light round head or figure of deity.

3) 제2연에 제시된 "무지개," "장미," "달," "태양," "별" 등은 모두 빛과 관계가 있는 이미지들이다. 시인은 이것들이 있음에도 불구하고 빛이 사라졌다고 역설적으로 표현한다. (이 작품에 나타난 "빛의 역설"에 관해서는 Cleanth Brooks의 *The Well-Wrought Urn, pp.* 170-187을 참조할 것.)

III

Now, while the birds thus sing a joyous song,
And while the young lambs bound
As to the tabor's sound,
To me alone there came a thought of grief:
A timely utterance[1] gave that thought relief,
And I again am strong:
The cataracts blow their trumpets from the steep;
No more shall grief of mine the season wrong;
I hear the echoes through the mountains throng[2],
The winds come to me from the fields of sleep[3],
And all the earth is gay;
Land and sea
Give themselves up to jollity[4],
And with the heart of May
Doth every beast keep holiday;—
Thou Child of Joy,
Shout round me, let me hear thy shouts, thou happy
Shepherd-boy!

IV

Ye blessèd Creatures, I have heard the call
Ye to each other make; I see
The heavens laugh with you in your jubilee[5];
My heart is at your festival,
My head hath its coronal[6],
The fullness of your bliss, I feel—I feel it all.
O evil day! if I were sullen

---

1) *A timely utterance*: 적시의 표현; Garrod는 이것이 워즈워스가 이 작품을 시각하기 하루 전에 쓴 무지개에 관한 시를 가리키는 것이라 설명했다 (113).

2) *throng*: 모여들다 (come/go in multitudes)

3) *the fields of sleep*: 바람이 잠 든 들판 (the fields where the winds sleep)

4) *jollity*: merry-making; festivity; *Give themselves up to jollity*: 홍겨움(즐거움)에 몸을 맡기다, 마음껏 즐기다.

5) *jubilee*: 축제 (a season or occasion of joyful celebration); 기념제(anniversary). Cf. silver jubilee (25년제), golden jubilee (50년제), diamond jubilee (60년제)

6) *coronal*: 화관 (garland); 오월제(May Day)에 목동들이 모자를 장식하는 화관.

While Earth herself is adorning,
This sweet May-morning,
And the Children are culling
On every side,
In a thousand valleys far and wide,
Fresh flowers[1]; while the sun shines warm,
And the babe leaps up on his Mother's arm:—
I hear, I hear, with joy I hear!
—But there's a tree, of many, one[2],
A single Field which I have looked upon,
Both of them speak of something that is gone:
The pansy at my feet
Doth the same tale[3] repeat:
Whither is fled the visionary gleam[4]?
Where is it now, the glory and the dream?

V

Our birth is but a sleep and a forgetting:[5]
The Soul that rises with us, our life's Star[6],
Hath had elsewhere its setting,
And cometh from afar:
Not in entire forgetfulness,
And not in utter nakedness,
But trailing clouds of glory[7] do we come
From God, who is our home:

---

1) *Fresh flowers*: culling의 목적어.
2) *of many, one;* 각운을 맞추기 위해 one of many의 어순을 도치시킨 것.
3) *the same tale*: 사라진 것이 있다는 말
4) *visionary gleam*: 상상의 빛 (imaginary light); 제1연의 "celestial light"와 같은 표현임. Cf. *gleam*=transient light
5) 우리의 출생은 잠이요 망각에 지나지 않는다. 시인은 빛의 상실을 설명하기 위해 전생신화(myth of pre-existence)를 도입하고 있다. 우리의 영혼은 태어나면서부터 잠들기 시작하고 전생의 기억을 망각하기 시작한다는 의미이다. 제2부(제5연~제8연)에서 시인은 "전생신화"를 도입하여 빛의 상실과정을 설명하고 있다.
6) *our life's Star*: 우리의 생명의 별; 시인은 이 작품에서 일관되게 영혼을 태양에 비유하고 있다.
7) *trailing clouds of glory*: 영광의 구름을 이끌면서; 여기서 "영광"은 "천국의 빛"과 같은 것이며 한때 지상의 만물이 천국의 빛으로 옷 입고 있는 듯이 보였던 것은 바로 이것 때문이다.

Heaven lies about us in our infancy!
Shades of the prison-house[1] begin to close
Upon the growing Boy,
But He
Beholds the light, and whence it flows,
He sees it in his joy;
The Youth, who daily farther from the east
Must travel, still is Nature's priest[2],
And by the vision splendid
Is on his way attended;
At length the Man perceives it die away,
And fade into the light of common day.[3]

VI

Earth fills her lap with pleasures of her own;
Yearnings she hath in her own natural kind,[4]
And, even with something of a Mother's mind,
And no unworthy aim,
The homely Nurse[5] doth all she can
To make her foster-child, her Inmate Man[6],
Forget the glories he hath known,
And that imperial palace[7] whence he came.

---

1) *prison-house*: 시인은 현세를 영혼을 가두는 "감옥"에 비유하고 있다.

2) *Nature's priest*: 자연의 사제, 즉 자연의 숭배자; "청년은 아직도 자연의 사제"라는 말은 감옥과 같은 현실세계를 숭배한다는 의미가 아니라, 아직도 자연에서 천국의 빛을 본다는 것을 의미한다. 이 시에서 "Nature"와 "Earth"는 전혀 다른 의미로 사용되어 있음에 유의해야 한다.

3) 시인은 "영광" 즉 "천국의 빛"이 "일상의 빛(the light of common day)" 속으로 사라진다고 묘사한다. 이 부분은 제9연에 묘사된 빛의 회복의 가능성을 암시하고 있다. 일상의 빛 속에 숨은 "영광"은, 마치 무색투명한 빛이 프리즘을 통과하면 찬란한 무기개가 되듯이, 시인의 상상력을 통해 재생될 수 있다는 것을 암시한다.

4) 대지는 그 나름의 타고난 모정을 가지고 있다; *yearning*: 갈망, 동경, 그리움 (a deep longing)

5) *the homely Nurse*: 소박한 유모; 대지는 영혼의 어머니가 아니라 "유모"에 비유되어 있다.

6) *her Inmate Man*: 대지의 동거인인 인간; 대지는 유모이므로 그 유모가 기르는 영혼은 "양자"이며, 대지는 영혼을 가두는 감옥이므로 영혼은 "죄수"라 할 수 있다.

7) *imperial*: 장엄한 (majestic, magnificent); "장엄한 궁전"은 영혼의 본향(本鄕)인 영원의 세계를 의미한다.

VII

Behold the Child among his new-born blisses,
A six years' Darling[1] of a pigmy size!
See, where 'mid work of his own hand he lies,
Fretted[2] by sallies of his mother's kisses[3],
With light upon him from his father's eyes!
See, at his feet, some little plan or chart,
Some fragment from his dream of human life,
Shaped by himself with newly-learnèd art;
A wedding or a festival,
A mourning or a funeral;
And this hath now his heart,
And unto this he frames his song:
Then will he fit his tongue
To dialogues of business, love, or strife;
But it will not be long
Ere this be thrown aside,
And with new joy and pride
The little actor cons[4] another part;
Filling from time to time his "humorous stage"[5]
With all the Persons, down to palsied Age,
That Life brings with her in her equipage[6];
As if his whole vocation
Were endless imitation.

VIII

Thou, whose exterior semblance[7] doth belie[8]

---

1) *Darling*: 총아, 귀염둥이 (favoured person or thing)
2) *fret*: 괴롭히다, 짜증나게 하다 (annoy, irritate, distress)
3) *sallies of his mother's kisses*: 갑자기 퍼부어 대는 엄마의 입맞춤; *sally*: 반격, 갑작스런 행동 (sudden start into activity).
4) *con*: 배우다 (study, learn by heart)
5) "*humorous stage*": "변덕스런 무대"; 이것은 엘리자베스 조 시인 Samuel Daniel의 소네트에 대한 인유이다. 여기서 "humorous"는 "capricious"라는 고어적인 의미로 사용되어 있다.
6) *equipage*: (시종이 딸린) 마차 (a carriage and horses with attendants); 행장(行裝) (equipment for a journey)
7) *exterior semblance*: 외형, 외모 (outward appearance)
8) *belie*: 속이다 (give a false idea of); *whose exterior semblance doth belie / Thy Soul's immensity*:

Thy soul's immensity;
Thou best philosopher, who yet dost keep
Thy heritage[1], thou eye among the blind,
That, deaf and silent, read'st the eternal deep[2],
Haunted[3] for ever by the eternal mind,—
Mighty Prophet! Seer blest!
On whom those truths do rest,
Which we are toiling all our lives to find,
In darkness lost, the darkness of the grave;
Thou, over whom thy Immortality
Broods like the Day[4], a Master o'er a Slave,
A Presence which is not to be put by[5];
Thou little Child, yet glorious in the might
Of Heaven-born freedom on thy being's height,
Why with such earnest pains dost thou provoke
The years to bring the inevitable yoke[6],
Thus blindly with thy blessedness at strife?
Full soon thy Soul shall have her earthly freight,
And custom lie upon thee with a weight,
Heavy as frost, and deep almost as life!

IX

O joy! that in our embers[7]
Is something that doth live,
That nature[8] yet remembers

외모로 보아서는 거대한 영혼이 들어 있을 것 같지 않은

1) *heritage*: 유산 (what is inherited); 여기서는 전생의 기억, 또는 "천국의 빛"을 의미한다.

2) *eternal deep*: 영원의 바다

3) *haunt*: 자주 가다 (frequent, visit frequently)

4) *Broods like the Day*: 태양처럼 굽어보고 있다; *brood*=hang close over

5) *put by*: 거부하다, 피하다 (reject, evade); 여기서 "거부할 수 없는 존재(A Presence which is not to be put by)"는 "thy Immortality"와 동격이다.

6) *provoke / The years...yoke*: 피할 수 없는 멍에를 씌우도록 세월을 재촉하는가?; *provoke*=incite or urge

7) *ember*: 등걸불, 여신(餘燼) (a hot fragment left in a dying fire); 타다 남은 잿더미 속의 불씨의 이미지는 제4연에서 일상의 빛 속으로 사라진 "천국의 빛"을 회복할 수 있는 가능성을 암시한다. 제3부(제9연~제11연)는 빛의 회복을 다룬 부분이다.

8) *nature*: 외부의 자연과 내부의 인간본성(human nature)을 의미한다. 외부의 잿더미와 내부의

What was so fugitive[1)]!
The thought of our past years in me doth breed
Perpetual benediction: not indeed
For that which is most worthy to be blest;[2)]
Delight and liberty, the simple creed
Of Childhood, whether busy or at rest,
With new-fledged hope[3)] still fluttering in his breast—
Not for these[4)] I raise
The song of thanks and praise;
But for those obstinate questionings[5)]
Of sense and outward things,
Fallings from us, vanishings[6)];
Blank misgivings[7)] of a Creature
Moving about in worlds not realized[8)],
High instincts[9)] before which our mortal Nature
Did tremble like a guilty Thing surprised[10)]:

기억 속에는 잃어버린 빛의 회복을 가능케 하는 "불씨"가 살아 있다.

1) *fugitive*: 덧없는, 무상한 (transient)
2) 가장 축복 받을 가치가 있는 것; 그 다음에 이어지는 "기쁨과 자유, 가슴 속에 새로 깃털이 난 희망이 파닥이는, 어린 시절의 소박한 신조"를 의미한다. creed=system of religious belief
3) *new-fledged hope*: 깃털이 새로 난 희망; 그 다음의 "fluttering"과 함께 희망을 새에 비유한 은유이다. 그리고 "With new-fledged...in his breast"는 Childhood를 수식한다.
4) *these*: "Delight and liberty, the simple creed / Of Childhood"를 가리킨다.
5) *obstinate*: 집요한 (stubborn), 떨쳐버릴 수 없는 (difficult to get rid of); "감각과 외부의 사물에 대한 집요한 의문"이란 어릴 적엔 만물을 덮고 있던 천국의 빛이 어디로 갔는가 하는 의문을 의미한다.
6) *Fallings from us, vanishings*: 우리로부터 떨어져 나가는 것들, 사라지는 것들; 워즈워스는 이 작품에 붙인 주석에서 외부 세계의 사물들이 사라져 존재하지 않는 것처럼 느껴질 때가 있었다고 말했다. 그래서 벽이나 나무를 만져보고 그 실재를 확인했다고 다음과 같이 말했다: "I was often unable to think of external things as having external existence, and I communed with all that I saw as something not apart from, but inherent in, my own immaterial nature. Many times while going to school have I grasped at a wall or tree to recall myself from this abyss of idealism to the reality." (*PW*, IV, 463)
7) *blank misgiving*: 망연한 의혹; *blank*=멍한, 망연한(puzzled); *misgiving*=a feeling of doubt
8) *worlds not realized*: 실현되지 않은 세계; 비현실적인 세계. 즉 이해할 수 없는 외부세계를 의미한다. 그에게는 오직 정신세계만이 실재하며 외부의 물질세계는 존재하지 않는 것처럼 느껴졌다.
9) *High instinct*: 고매한 본능, 즉 영적 본성을 의미하며, 뒤에 나오는 "숙명적 본성(mortal Nature)"과 대조를 이룬다.
10) *a guilty Thing surprised*: 기습당한 죄인; *surprise*=capture by surprise.

But for those first affections[1],
Those shadowy recollections,
Which, be they what they may,
Are yet the fountain-light of all our day,
Are yet a master-light of all our seeing;
Uphold us, cherish[2], and have power to make
Our noisy years seem moments in the being
Of the eternal Silence: truths that wake,
To perish never:
Which neither listlessness, nor mad endeavour,
Nor Man nor Boy,
Nor all that is at enmity with joy,
Can utterly abolish or destroy!
Hence in a season of calm weather
Though inland far we be,
Our souls have sight of that immortal sea[3]
Which brought us hither,
Can in a moment travel thither,
And see the Children sport upon the shore,
And hear the mighty waters rolling evermore.

X

Then sing, ye birds, sing, sing a joyous song!
And let the young lambs bound
As to the tabor's sound!
We in thought will join your throng,
Ye that pipe and ye that play,
Ye that through your hearts to-day

---

1) *first affections*: 최초의 애정: 즉 갓 태어난 어린아이와 세계를 이어주는 애정을 의미한다. *The Prelude* (1805)에 나오는 "젖먹이의 혈관 속에는 인간과 세계를 연결하는 자연의 중력과 애정(모자의 유대)이 녹아 흐른다.(Along his infant veins are interfused / The gravitation and filial bond / Of Nature that connect him with the world.)"라는 표현을 참고할 것 (*The Prelude* 1805; IV, 262-4). 워즈워스는 인간과 자연을 최초로 연결해주는 "중력"과도 같은 힘을 마치 탯줄과도 같은 모자간의 "애정(filial bond)"으로 이해한다, 또한 그는 이것을 "최초의 시 정신(the first / Poetic spirit of our human life-IV, 275-6)"이라고 표현했다.

2) *cherish*: 소중히 하다 (protect lovingly)

3) *immortal sea*: 불멸의 바다, 즉 출생 이전의 영혼의 세계.

Feel the gladness of the May!
What though the radiance which was once so bright
Be now for ever taken from my sight,
Though nothing can bring back the hour
Of splendour in the grass, of glory in the flower;
We will grieve not, rather find
Strength in what remains behind;
In the primal sympathy[1])
Which having been must ever be;
In the soothing thoughts that spring
Out of human suffering;
In the faith that looks through death,
In years that bring the philosophic mind.

XI

And O ye Fountains, Meadows, Hills, and Groves,
Forebode not any severing of our loves!
Yet in my heart of hearts I feel your might;
I only have relinquish'd one delight
To live beneath your more habitual sway.[2])
I love the brooks which down their channels fret,
Even more than when I tripp'd lightly as they;
The innocent brightness of a new-born Day
Is lovely yet;
The clouds that gather round the setting sun
Do take a sober colouring from an eye
That hath kept watch o'er man's mortality;
Another race hath been, and other palms are won.
Thanks to the human heart by which we live,
Thanks to its tenderness, its joys, and fears,
To me the meanest flower that blows can give
Thoughts that do often lie too deep for tears.

1802-4 (1807)

---

1) *primal sympathy*: 원초적 공감; Cf. *The Prelude* (1805) I, 582-3: "those first-born affinities that fit / Our new existence to existing things." 이것은 제9연의 "최초의 애정"과 같은 의미를 갖는다.
2) 보다 습관적인 영향 하에 살기 위해 하나의 기쁨을 포기했다

Ode to Duty

Stern Daughter of the Voice of God![1)]
O Duty! if that name thou love,
Who art a light to guide, a rod
To check the erring and reprove;
Thou, who art victory and law
When empty terrors overawe[2)];
From vain temptations dost set free[3)];
And calm'st the weary strife of frail humanity!

There are who ask not if thine eye
Be on them; who, in love and truth,
Where no misgiving is, rely
Upon the genial sense[4)] of youth:
Glad hearts! without reproach or blot[5)];
Who do thy work, and know it not:
O, if through confidence misplaced

---

* "This ode is on the model of Gray's *Ode to Adversity*, which is copied from Horace's *Ode to Fortune*. Many and many a time have I been twitted by my wife and sister for having forgotten this dedication of myself to the stern lawgiver...." (Wordsworth) 이 시는 이전의 명상적 구조를 버리고 추상개념을 의인화한 18세기 송시(ode)의 형식을 따르고 있다. 또한 이 시에 표현된 윤리적 사상은 워즈워스가 젊은 시절 본능적 충동에 의존하던 것에서 정통 윤리의 전통으로 복귀한 것을 보여준다. 이 시에서 "의무(Duty)"는 밀턴의 "올바른 이성(right reason)"의 개념과 일치한다. 밀턴은 이성을 인간의 내부에 있는 신성(神性)으로 보았다. 이것은 기독교적 인본주의자들이 스토아학파의 엄격한 윤리와 기독교에서 말하는 내면적인 "양심"의 목소리의 개념을 결합하여 발전시킨 것이다. 이 시에서 워즈워스의 목표는 개인의 의지를 신의 의지에 완전히 종속시킴으로써 얻어지는 마음의 평화이다. 워즈워스는 1837년에 Seneca, *Moral Epistles*에 나오는 한 구절(CXX. 10)을 따서 이 시의 제사(epigraph)로 삼았다: "Jam non consilio bonus, sed more eo perductus, ut non tantum recte facere possim, sed nisi recte facere non possim." (Now I am not good by taking thought, but have been brought by habit to such a point that it is not so much that I am able to act rightly, but that I am unable to act except rightly.)

1) 밀턴의 『실낙원』에 나오는 다음 구절에 대한 인유이다: "God so commanded, and left that Command / Sole Daughter of his voice; the rest we live / Law to ourselves, our Reason is our Law"(IX. 652-4).

2) *overawe*: 겁주다, 위압하다 (fill with awe)

3) *set free*: 주어는 Thou이다.

4) *the genial sense*: 타고난 선한 본성 (innate good nature); *genial*=natural, of natural disposition

5) *blot*: 오점 (a moral stain)

They fail, thy saving arms, dread Power! around them cast.

Serene will be our days and bright,
And happy will our nature be,
When love is an unerring light,
And joy its own security.
And they[1] a blissful course may hold
Even now, who, not unwisely bold,
Live in the spirit of this creed;
Yet seek thy firm support, according to their need.

I, loving freedom, and untried[2],
No sport[3] of every random gust,
Yet being to myself a guide,
Too blindly have reposed my trust[4]:
And oft, when in my heart was heard
Thy timely mandate, I deferr'd
The task, in smoother walks to stray[5];
But thee I now would serve more strictly, if I may.

Through no disturbance of my soul,
Or strong compunction[6] in me wrought,
I supplicate for[7] thy control;
But in the quietness of thought.
Me this unchartered[8] freedom tires;
I feel the weight of chance-desires[9];

---

1) *they*: 다음 줄에 나오는 who의 선행사이다. 이러한 신념으로 살아가는 사람들은 행복한 삶을 살게 될 것이라는 의미이다.
2) *untried*: 경험이 없는 (inexperienced);
3) *sport*: 노리개 (plaything, laughing-stock)
4) 너무나 맹목적으로 자신을 믿었다는 의미이다. *repose*=put or place
5) *in smoother walks to stray*: 평탄한 옆길로 빗나가느라고
6) *compunction*: 양심의 가책 (sting of conscience, remorse); 그 다음의 *in me wrought*는 형용사구이다. 즉 내 안에서 일어나는 양심의 가책을 의미한다.
7) *supplicate for*: 애원하다, 간청하다 (beg humbly for, make humble petition for)
8) *unchartered*: 허가받지 못한 (not authorized), 불법의 (lawless)
9) *chance-desires*: 무심결의 욕망 (casual desires)

My hopes no more must change their name[1],
I long for a repose that ever is the same.

Stern Lawgiver![2] yet thou dost wear
The Godhead's most benignant grace;
Nor know we anything so fair
As is the smile upon thy face:
Flowers laugh before thee on their beds,
And fragrance in thy footing[3] treads
Thou dost preserve the stars from wrong;
And the most ancient heavens, through Thee, are fresh and strong.

To humbler functions, awful Power!
I call thee: I myself commend[4]
Unto thy guidance from this hour;
O, let my weakness have an end!
Give unto me, made lowly wise,
The spirit of self-sacrifice;
The confidence of reason give;
And in the light of truth thy Bondman[5] let me live!

1804 (1807)

---

1) 내 희망은 더 이상 변하지 않을 것이다 (My hopes will be constant).
2) *Stern Lawgiver*: 엄한 입법자 즉 "의무"를 의미한다.
3) *footing*: 발걸음 (footsteps)
4) *commend*: 맡기다, 의탁하다 (entrust)
5) *Bondman*: 노예 (slave); "thy Bondman"은 me와 동격이다.

Elegiac Stanzas

Suggested by a Picture of Peele Castle, in a Storm,
Painted by Sir George Beaumont

I was thy neighbour once, thou rugged Pile[1])!
Four summer weeks I dwelt in sight of thee:
I saw thee every day; and all the while
Thy Form was sleeping on a glassy[2]) sea.

So pure the sky, so quiet was the air!
So like, so very like, was day to day!
Whene'er I looked, thy Image still was there;
It trembled, but it never passed away.

How perfect was the calm! it seemed no sleep;
No mood, which season takes away, or brings:
I could have fancied that the mighty Deep
Was even the gentlest of all gentle Things.

Ah! then, if mine had been the Painter's hand,
To express what then I saw; and add the gleam,
The light that never was, on sea or land,
The consecration[3]), and the Poet's dream;

---

* "Sir George Beaumont painted two pictures of this subject, one of which he gave to Mrs. Wordsworth, saying she ought to have it; but Lady Beaumont interfered, and after Sir George's death she gave it to Sir Uvedale Price, in whose house at Foxley I have seen it" (Wordsworth). Sir George Beaumont(1753-1827)는 워즈워스의 절친한 친구이자 후원자였던 아마추어 풍경화가 이다. Peele Castle은 Lancashire 주의 Rampside 건너편 곳에 있는 성인데, 워즈워스가 Beaumont의 그림을 보기 11년 전인 1794년에 한 달을 그곳에서 보낸 적이 있었다.

1) *rugged Pile*: 견고한 성채; *rugged*=strong, sturdy, strongly constructed; *pile*=a large imposing building; a large group of tall buildings

2) *glassy*: (거울 같이) 잔잔한 (having a smooth unruffled surface like glass)

3) *consecration*: 신성하게 함, 정화; 빵과 포도주를 그리스도의 몸으로 성변화(聖變化)시키는 것. 여기서 "바다에도 육지에도 없는 빛, 정화와 시인의 꿈"은 *Lyrical Ballads* 서문의 시론에서 말한 "모종의 상상의 색채(a certain colouring of imagination)"와 일치한다. 시인은 평범한 일상생활에서 "사건과 상황"을 선택하여 거기에 "모종의 상상의 색채"를 첨가하여 평범한 것을 특이하게 보이게 만드는 것이 자신의 목표라고 했다. 이것은 제재의 시적 변용을 의미한다.

I would have planted thee, thou hoary Pile
Amid a world how different from this![1]
Beside a sea that could not cease to smile;
On tranquil land, beneath a sky of bliss.

Thou shouldst have seemed a treasure-house divine[2]
Of peaceful years; a chronicle of heaven;—
Of all the sunbeams that did ever shine
The very sweetest had to thee been given[3].

A Picture had it been of lasting ease,
Elysian quiet[4], without toil or strife;
No motion but the moving tide, a breeze,
Or merely silent Nature's breathing life.

Such, in the fond illusion of my heart[5],
Such Picture would I at that time have made:
And seen[6] the soul of truth in every part,
A stedfast peace that might not be betrayed[7].

So once it would have been,—'tis so no more;
I have submitted to a new control[8]:
A power is gone, which nothing can restore;
A deep distress hath humanised[9] my Soul[10].

---

1) 나는 이와는 매우 다른 세계 속에 너를 놓았을 것이다; 시인은 자신이 그렸을 가상적 그림과 보몬트 경의 그림을 대조하고 있다; 인생의 쓴 경험(즉 "a deep distress")을 하기 전에 이 성을 그렸다면, 폭풍 속의 피일 성을 그린 보몬트 경의 그림과는 전혀 다르게 그렸을 것이다.

2) *a treasure-house divine*: 신성한 보고(寶庫)

3) *had been given*: would have been given.

4) *Elysian quiet*: 낙원의 고요; *Elysium*: 선량한 사람들이 죽은 후 사는 곳 (abode of the blessed after death), 극락, 낙원, 이상향 (place or state of ideal happiness)

5) *the fond illusion of my heart*: 내 마음의 어리석은 환상; 시인은 순진했던 과거의 예술적 환상이 삶의 비극적 현실을 반영하지 못했음을 반성하고 있다.

6) *seen*: I would have seen

7) *betray*: (적에게) 팔아넘기다 (give up treacherously)

8) *a new control*: 새로운 통제; 즉 삶의 비극적 성격을 실감한 이가 얻은 극기(克己)와 인종(忍從)의 정신을 의미한다(이영걸, 『영미시 개관』, p. 13).

9) *humanize*: 교화하다 (make humane, refine, civilize)

10) 깊은 슬픔이 내 영혼을 교화했다; 여기서 "깊은 슬픔"이란 아우의 죽음에 대한 슬픔을 의

Not for a moment could I now behold
A smiling sea, and be what I have been:
The feeling of my loss will ne'er be old;
This, which I know, I speak with mind serene.

Then, Beaumont, Friend! who would have been the Friend,
If he had lived, of Him whom I deplore[1],
This work of thine I blame not, but commend[2];
This sea in anger, and that dismal shore.

O 'tis a passionate Work!—yet wise and well[3],
Well chosen is the spirit that is here;
That Hulk which labours in the deadly swell,[4]
This rueful[5] sky, this pageantry[6] of fear!

And this huge Castle, standing here sublime[7],
I love to see the look with which it braves[8],
Cased in the unfeeling armour of old time[9],
The lightning, the fierce wind, and trampling waves.

Farewell, farewell the heart that lives alone,
Housed in a dream, at distance from the Kind[10]!
Such happiness, wherever it be known,

미한다. 상선 선장이었던 John Wordsworth는 1805년 2월 5일에 배가 난파하여 익사했다. 이 비극적 사건을 통해 시인은 인생이 항상 평화롭고 행복하기만 한 것이 아니며 참고 견디어야 할 일이 많다는 것을 깨닫는다.

1) *Him whom I deplore*: John Wordsworth. *deplore*=show grief for a person's death, lament, mourn
2) *commend*: praise
3) *wise and well*: 슬기롭고 훌륭하다.
4) 사나운 파도에 흔들리는 저 선체. *labour*: 흔들리다 (roll or pitch heavily)
5) *rueful*: 슬픈 (expressing sorrow, doleful)
6) *pageantry*: 장관, 화려한 구경거리 (an elaborate display or spectacle)
7) *sublime*: 높이 솟은 (situated or rising high up, towering)
8) brave: 용감하게 맞서다 (meet with courage)
9) 해묵은 시간의 무감각한 갑옷을 입고
10) *the Kind*: the humankind; 인간세상으로부터 멀리 떨어져, 인간세상을 등지고.

Is to be pitied; for 'tis surely blind.
But welcome fortitude[1], and patient cheer[2],
And frequent sights of what is to be borne![3]
Such sights, or worse, as are before me here.—
Not without hope we suffer and we mourn.

1805 (1807)

1) *fortitude*: 불굴의 정신, 견인불발(堅忍不拔) (moral strength or courage, esp. in the endurance of pain or adversity); 역경 속에서도 꿋꿋이 참고 견디는 용기를 의미함.

2) *cheer*: 기분, 생기 (a frame of mind, disposition, mood)

3) 견뎌야 할 것들의 잦은 광경들

The Prelude
Or, Growth of a Poet's Mind

From BOOK FIRST

INTRODUCTION—CHILDHOOD AND SCHOOL-TIME

OH there is blessing in this gentle breeze,
A visitant[1] that while it[2] fans my cheek
Doth seem half-conscious of the joy it brings
From the green fields, and from yon azure sky.
Whate'er its mission, the soft breeze can come
To none more grateful than to me; escaped
From the vast city[3], where I long had pined
A discontented sojourner[4]: now free,
Free as a bird to settle where I will.
What dwelling shall receive me? in what vale
Shall be my harbour? underneath what grove
Shall I take up my home? and what clear stream
Shall with its murmur lull me into rest?
The earth is all before me. With a heart
Joyous, nor scared at its own liberty,
I look about; and should the chosen guide
Be nothing better than a wandering cloud,
I cannot miss my way. I breathe again!
Trances of thought and mountings of the mind

---

1) *visitant*: a visitor, esp. a supernatural one

2) it: "breeze"를 지시하는 대명사이다. 초고에는 he로 되어 있었으나, 후일에 Christopher Wordsworth가 정통적인 기독교에 반하는 animism의 요소를 제거하기 위해 it로 고친 것 같다. (Jonathan Wordsworth [ed.], *The Prelude* 각주 참조.)

3) Exodus 13:3의 인유: "And Moses said unto the people, Remember this day, in which ye came out from Egypt, out of the house of bondage." 이 부분을 쓸 당시 워즈워스는 호수지방에 있었다. 여기 언급된 도시는 London 또는 Goslar이다. 시인은 도시에서 답답한 정신 상태를 경험했고, 이제 그 도시를 벗어나 자유를 느낀다.

4) *sojourner*: a visitor, a guest

Come fast upon me[1]: it is shaken off,
That burthen of my own unnatural self,
The heavy weight of many a weary day
Not mine, and such as were not made for me.
Long months of peace (if such bold word accord
With any promises of human life),
Long months of ease and undisturbed delight
Are mine in prospect; whither shall I turn,
By road or pathway, or through trackless field,
Up hill or down, or shall some floating thing
Upon the river point me out my course?

Dear Liberty! Yet what would it avail
But for a gift that consecrates the joy?
For I, methought, while the sweet breath of heaven
Was blowing on my body, felt within
A correspondent[2] breeze, that gently moved
With quickening[3] virtue, but is now become
A tempest, a redundant[4] energy,
Vexing its own creation. Thanks to both,
And their congenial[5] powers, that, while they join
In breaking up a long-continued frost,
Bring with them vernal promises, the hope
Of active days urged on by flying hours,—
Days of sweet leisure, taxed with patient thought
Abstruse[6], nor wanting punctual service high,
Matins and vespers[7], of harmonious verse!

---

1) *The earth is all before me*: *Paradise Lost* 마지막 부분에 대한 인유이다. 이 작품은 *Paradise Lost*가 끝나는 부분에서 시작되는 것처럼 되어 있다. 즉 이 작품은 워즈워스의 『복낙원』(*Paradise Regained*)이라 할 수 있다. Cf. "The world was all before them, where to choose / Their place of rest, and providence their guide: / They hand in hand with wandering steps and slow, / Through Eden took their solitary war."(*PL*)
2) *correspondent*: 상응하는 (corresponding), 유사한 (similar)
3) *quickening*: 활력을 주는 (animating, giving life to)
4) *redundant*: 넘쳐흐르는 (overflowing; superfluous)
5) *congenial*: 동질의 (kindred)
6) *abstruse*: 난해한 (hard to understand), 심오한 (profound)
7) *Matins and vespers*: 아침 기도와 저녁 기도

Thus far, O Friend![1] did I, not used to make
A present joy the matter of a song[2],
Pour forth that day my soul in measured strains[3]
That would not be forgotten, and are here
Recorded: to the open fields I told
A prophecy: poetic numbers[4] came
Spontaneously[5] to clothe in priestly robe
A renovated spirit singled out[6],
Such hope was mine, for holy services.
My own voice cheered me, and, far more, the mind's
Internal echo of the imperfect sound[7];
To both I listened, drawing from them both
A cheerful confidence in things to come.

* * *

[River-bathing]

Was it for this[8]
That one, the fairest of all rivers, loved
To blend his murmurs with my nurse's song,
And, from his alder shades and rocky falls,
And from his fords and shallows, sent a voice
That flowed along my dreams? For this, didst thou,
O Derwent![9] winding among grassy holms[10]

---

1) *Friend*: S. T. Coleridge; 이 시는 Coleridge에게 보낸 운문 서간의 형식으로 되어 있다.
2) 시인은 현재의 감정을 시의 제재로 삼지 않는다. 워즈워스는 "회상된 정서"를 시의 제재로 삼는다고 했다.
3) *measured strains*: 율동적인 노래; *measured*=rhythmical; *strains*=a passage of a song or poem
4) *poetic numbers*: 시 (verses); *numbers*=rhythm, verses
5) *spontaneously*: 저절로, 자연발생적으로 (done of one's own accord); 무의식적으로
6) *singled out*: 선택받은 (chosen); 시인은 자신이 "성스러운 일(holy service)"을 하도록 선택받은 사람이라 생각한다.
7) *the imperfect voice*: 내면의 목소리가 더 완전하다는 의미를 함축하고 있다.
8) *Was it for this*: 이것 때문이었던가?; 이 작품의 초고인 "The Two part Prelude" (1799)는 여기서부터 시작된다. 반복해서 나오는 대명사 "this"가 무엇을 가리키는 가는 작품 속에 나타나 있지 않다. Jonathan Wordsworth는 이것이 그가 구상했던 철학시 *The Recluse*를 쓰지 못하게 된 것을 가리킨다고 설명한다(1). 그러나 문맥으로 유추해 볼 때 "this"는 이 작품을 의미한다고 봄이 타당하다.
9) *Derwent*: 더윈트 강; 이 강은 워즈워스 생가의 담을 끼고 흐른다. 강은 의식의 흐름을 상징한다. 이 강물 소리를 회상하면서부터 그의 마음속에 자리 잡고 있던 어린 시절의 경험들이 되살아나기 시작한다. 그는 이러한 경험들을 "spots of time"이라 불렀다.
10) *holms*: islands

Where I was looking on, a babe in arms,
Make ceaseless music that composed my thoughts
To more than infant softness, giving me
Amid the fretful dwellings of mankind
A foretaste[1], a dim earnest, of the calm
That Nature breathes among the hills and groves.
When he had left the mountains and received
On his smooth breast the shadow of those towers
That yet survive, a shattered monument
Of feudal sway[2], the bright blue river passed
Along the margin of our terrace walk[3];
A tempting playmate whom we dearly loved.
Oh, many a time have I, a five years' child,
In a small mill-race[4] severed from his stream,
Made one long bathing of a summer's day;
Basked in the sun, and plunged and basked again
Alternate, all a summer's day, or scoured[5]
The sandy fields, leaping through flowery groves
Of yellow ragwort[6]; or, when rock and hill,
The woods, and distant Skiddaw's[7] lofty height,
Were bronzed with deepest radiance, stood alone
Beneath the sky, as if I had been born
On Indian plains, and from my mother's hut
Had run abroad in wantonness[8], to sport
A naked savage, in the thunder shower[9].

[Trap-robbing]

Fair seed-time[10] had my soul, and I grew up

---

1) *foretaste*: 예감 (anticipation); *earnest*=foretaste, presage
2) a shattered monument / Of feudal sway: 봉건 제도의 부서진 기념비; Cockermouth Castle
3) *terrace walk*: 정원 산책로
4) *mill-race*: 물레방아용 도랑
5) *scour*: 바쁘게 돌아다니다 (hasten along or over)
6) *ragwort*: ragweed: 개쑥갓
7) *Skiddaw*: Cockermouth 동쪽에 있는 산; 호수지방에서 네 번째로 높은 산.
8) *in wantonness*: 장난치며
9) *thunder shower*: 뇌우(雷雨) (shower accompanied by thunder)
10) *seed-time*: 파종기 (sowing season); 시인은 "내 영혼에 파종기가 있었다"고 말한다. 파종기

Fostered alike by beauty and by fear:
Much favoured in my birth-place, and no less
In that beloved Vale[1] to which erelong
We were transplanted;—there were we let loose
For sports of wider range. Ere I had told
Ten birth-days, when among the mountain slopes
Frost, and the breath of frosty wind, had snapped
The last autumnal crocus[2], 'twas my joy
With store of springes[3] o'er my shoulder hung
To range[4] the open heights where woodcocks run
Along the smooth green turf. Through half the night,
Scudding away[5] from snare to snare, I plied[6]
That anxious visitation;—moon and stars
Were shining o'er my head. I was alone,
And seemed to be a trouble to the peace
That dwelt among them. Sometimes it befell
In these night wanderings, that a strong desire
O'erpowered my better reason, and the bird
Which was the captive of another's toil[7]
Became my prey; and when the deed was done
I heard among the solitary hills
Low breathings coming after me, and sounds
Of undistinguishable[8] motion, steps
Almost as silent as the turf they trod.

에 영혼의 토양에 뿌려진 씨앗(이미지)은 자라서 후일에 시의 원료가 된다. 이 작품 제1권과 제2권은 주로 파종기의 일화들로 이루어져 있다.

1) *beloved Vale*: Hawkshead; 워즈워스는 1779년에 고향집에서 35마일 떨어진 곳에 위치한 Hawkshead Grammar School에 입학했다. 다음에 이어지는 일화들은 그 시절의 경험을 기록한 것들이다.

2) *autumnal crocus*: 사프란(saffron); Cf. *crocus*: 크로커스 꽃 (영국에서 봄에 맨 먼저 피는 꽃)

3) *springe*: 올가미, 덫 (noose or snare for catching small game); *store of springes*: 여러 개의 덫

4) *range*: 찾아 헤매다 (traverse in all directions; roam over or through)

5) *scud away*: 질주하다 (run fast with easy motion)

6) *ply*: 열중하다 (devote one's energy to; work at)

7) *the bird...toil*: 남의 덫에 잡힌 새; 여기서 "toil"은 "snare" 또는 "labour"의 의미를 갖는다.

8) *undistinguishable*: 분간할 수 없는

[Raven's Nest]

Nor less, when spring had warmed the cultured Vale,
Moved we as plunderers[1] where the mother-bird
Had in high places built her lodge; though mean
Our object and inglorious, yet the end
Was not ignoble[2]. Oh! when I have hung
Above the raven's nest, by knots of grass
And half-inch fissures in the slippery rock
But ill sustained[3], and almost (so it seemed)
Suspended by the blast that blew amain[4],
Shouldering the naked crag, oh, at that time
While on the perilous ridge I hung alone,
With what strange utterance did the loud dry wind
Blow through my ear! the sky seemed not a sky
Of earth-and with what motion moved the clouds!

Dust as we are, the immortal spirit grows
Like harmony in music[5]; there is a dark
Inscrutable workmanship[6] that reconciles
Discordant elements, makes them cling together
In one society[7]. How strange, that all
The terrors, pains, and early miseries,
Regrets, vexations[8], lassitudes[9] interfused
Within my mind, should e'er have borne a part,
And that a needful part, in making up
The calm existence that is mine when I

---

1) *plunderer*: 약탈자, 도둑
2) 목표는 비열하고 수치스러웠지만, 결과는 부끄럽지 않았다.
3) 엉킨 풀과 미끄러운 바위틈을 잡고 간신히 몸을 지탱하고 매달려 있을 때
4) *amain*: vehemently
5) 우리의 육신은 비록 흙이지만, 우리의 불멸의 영혼은 마치 음악의 화음처럼 자란다.
6) *inscrutable workmanship*: 신비로운 솜씨 (mysterious craftsmanship); 모든 공포, 고통, 불행, 후회, 초조, 권태 등과 같은 부조화의 요소를 조화시켜 하나의 유기적 전체로 만드는 "신비로운 솜씨"는 곧 상상력의 작용을 의미한다.
7) *one society*: an intimate relationship
8) vexation: 초조 (irritation)
9) *lassitude*: 권태 (weariness of body or mind; langour)

Am worthy of myself![1] Praise to the end!
Thanks to the means which Nature deigned[2] to employ;
Whether her fearless visitings, or those
That came with soft alarm, like hurtless[3] light
Opening the peaceful clouds; or she would use
Severer interventions[4], ministry
More palpable[5], as best might suit her aim.

[Boat-stealing]

One summer evening (led by her[6]) I found
A little boat tied to a willow tree
Within a rocky cave, its usual home.
Straight I unloosed her chain, and stepping in
Pushed from the shore. It was an act of stealth
And troubled pleasure[7], nor without the voice
Of mountain-echoes did my boat move on;
Leaving behind her still, on either side,
Small circles glittering idly in the moon,
Until they melted all into one track
Of sparkling light. But now, like one who rows,
Proud of his skill, to reach a chosen point
With an unswerving line[8], I fixed my view
Upon the summit of a craggy ridge,
The horizon's utmost boundary; far above
Was nothing but the stars and the grey sky.
She was an elfin pinnace[9]; lustily[10]

---

1) *when I / Am worthy of myself*: 내가 가장 나다울 때
2) deign: 황송하게도...하여 주시다 (condescend to grant)
3) *hurtless*: harmless
4) *severer interventions*: 더 엄한 간섭; 자연은 인간에게 폭풍, 지진, 우레 등으로 공포감을 준다. Cf. "I grew up / Fostered alike by beauty and by fear."(I. 301-2)
5) *ministry / More palpable*: 더욱 명백한 작용; *ministry*: 역할 (a function, an office), 작용 (agency); *palpable*: 지각할 수 있는, 명백한 (able to be touched; perceptible, obvious)
6) *her*: Nature
7) *troubled pleasure*: 혼란된 쾌감; 남의 배를 훔친 데 대한 불안감이 뒤섞인 쾌감이라는 의미이다.
8) *With an unswerving line*: 곧장 일직선으로; Cf. *swerve*=turn aside, deviate from a direct course
9) *an elfin pinnace*: (요정의) 작은 배; *elfin*=diminutive; *pinnace*=small boat
10) *lustily*: 힘차게; Cf. *lusty*=healthy and strong, vigorous

I dipped my oars into the silent lake,
And, as I rose upon the stroke, my boat
Went heaving through the water like a swan;
When, from behind that craggy steep till then
The horizon's bound, a huge peak, black and huge,
As if with voluntary power instinct[1],
Upreared its head. I struck and struck again,
And growing still in stature the grim shape
Towered up between me and the stars, and still,
For so it seemed, with purpose of its own
And measured motion like a living thing,
Strode[2] after me. With trembling oars I turned,
And through the silent water stole my way
Back to the covert[3] of the willow tree;
There in her mooring-place[4] I left my bark,—
And through the meadows homeward went, in grave
And serious mood; but after I had seen
That spectacle, for many days, my brain
Worked with a dim and undetermined sense
Of unknown modes of being[5]; o'er my thoughts
There hung a darkness, call it solitude
Or blank desertion[6]. No familiar shapes
Remained, no pleasant images of trees,
Of sea or sky, no colours of green fields;
But huge and mighty forms, that do not live
Like living men, moved slowly through the mind
By day, and were a trouble to my dreams[7].
   Wisdom and Spirit of the universe![8]

---

1) *As if with voluntary power instinct*: 마치 자발적인 의지력을 가진 듯이; *instinct (with)*: 가득 찬 (charged, imbued)
2) *stride*: 성큼성큼 따라오다 (walk with long steps)
3) *covert*: 은닉처 (shelter); 배를 매어 두었던 바위동굴을 의미한다.
4) *mooring place*: 계선장, 정박지 (the place where the boat was moored)
5) 알 수 없는 존재 양식에 대한 희미하고 막연한 느낌
6) blank desertion: 텅 빈 폐허(황폐);
7) *were a trouble to my dreams*: 내 꿈자리를 사납게 했다
8) *Wisdom and Spirit of the universe*: 우주의 지혜와 정신; 자연의 신성(神性)을 의미한다. 워즈

Thou Soul that art the eternity of thought
That givest to forms and images a breath
And everlasting motion, not in vain
By day or star-light thus from my first dawn
Of childhood didst thou intertwine for me
The passions that build up our human soul;
Not with the mean and vulgar works of man,
But with high objects[1], with enduring things—
With life and nature—purifying thus
The elements of feeling and of thought,
And sanctifying[2], by such discipline[3],
Both pain and fear, until we recognise
A grandeur in the beatings of the heart.
Nor was this fellowship[4] vouchsafed to me
With stinted kindness. In November days,
When vapours rolling down the valley made
A lonely scene more lonesome, among woods,
At noon and 'mid the calm of summer nights,
When, by the margin of the trembling lake,
Beneath the gloomy hills homeward I went
In solitude, such intercourse was mine;
Mine was it in the fields both day and night,
And by the waters, all the summer long.

[Skating]

And in the frosty season, when the sun

워스의 범신론적 사상이 가장 두드러진 "Tintern Abbey"에서 우주에 충만한 신성을 "A motion and a spirit, that impels / All thinking things, all objects of all thought, / And rolls through all things"라고 묘사했다. 이 정신은 인간의 마음속에도 존재한다. 그 다음에 이어지는 "우리의 생각 속에 영원히 존재하는 영혼"(Soul that art the eternity of thought)는 인간의 마음속에 존재하는 신성을 의미한다.

1) *didst thou intertwined.../ The passions... with high objects*: 그대는...감정을 숭고한 사물과 연결시켰다; 이것은 인간 정신 안에서 이루어진다. 영혼의 토양에 심어진 사물의 이미지는 인간 정서와 결합하여 성장하게 된다.

2) *sanctify*: 정화시키다 (purify, free from sin); 목적어는 "Both pain and fear"이다.

3) *discipline*: 수련, 가르침, 훈련 (education, teaching, training)

4) *fellowship*: 자연과의 친교 (intercourse with Nature)

Was set, and visible for many a mile
The cottage windows blazed through twilight gloom,
I heeded not their summons[1]: happy time
It was indeed for all of us—for me
It was a time of rapture! Clear and loud
The village clock tolled six,—I wheeled about,
Proud and exulting like an untired horse
That cares not for his home. All shod with steel[2],
We hissed along the polished ice in games
Confederate[3], imitative of the chase
And woodland pleasures[4],—the resounding horn,
The pack[5] loud chiming, and the hunted hare.
So through the darkness and the cold we flew,
And not a voice was idle; with the din
Smitten, the precipices rang aloud;
The leafless trees and every icy crag
Tinkled[6] like iron; while far distant hills
Into the tumult sent an alien sound
Of melancholy not unnoticed, while the stars
Eastward were sparkling clear, and in the west
The orange sky of evening died away.
Not seldom from the uproar[7] I retired
Into a silent bay, or sportively
Glanced sideway, leaving the tumultuous throng,
To cut across the reflex[8] of a star

---

1) *I heeded not their summons*: 나는 그들의 부름에 개의치 않았다; 즉 땅거미가 내리고 집집마다 창문에 불이 켜졌음에도 불구하고 집으로 돌아가지 않았음을 의미한다.

2) *All shod with steel*: 쇠신(스케이트)을 신고서; *shod*=shoed (shoe: 신을 신기다, 말에 편자를 박다). 바로 앞의 "집 걱정을 하지 않는 지칠 줄 모르는 말처럼"이라는 표현과 연결된다.

3) *games / Confederate*: 여럿이 함께 하는 놀이; *confederate*=allied

4) *imitative of the chase / And woodland pleasures*: 사냥과 숲속의 재미있는 놀이를 흉내 내며; *chase*=hunting; 그 다음에 사냥에 관한 묘사가 이어진다: 뿔 나팔 소리가 울려 퍼지고, 사냥개들이 종을 울리며 토끼를 추격한다. 스케이팅을 사냥놀이에 비유하여 묘사하고 있다.

5) *pack*: 한 무리의 사냥개 (a group of dogs trained for hunting)

6) *tinkle*: 금속음을 내다 (make light ringing sounds)

7) *uproar*: 소란 (noisy confusion; noise of shouting or tumult)

8) *reflex*: image or reflection; 스케이트를 타면서 빙판 위에 비친 별의 영상을 볼 때 마치 별이 빠르게 움직이는 것처럼 보인다.

That fled, and, flying still before me, gleamed
Upon the glassy plain; and oftentimes,
When we had given our bodies to the wind,
And all the shadowy banks on either side
Came sweeping through the darkness, spinning[1] still
The rapid line of motion, then at once
Have I, reclining back upon my heels,
Stopped short; yet still the solitary cliffs
Wheeled by me—even as if the earth had rolled
With visible motion her diurnal round![2]
Behind me did they stretch in solemn train,
Feebler and feebler, and I stood and watched
Till all was tranquil as a dreamless sleep.

Ye Presences of Nature[3] in the sky
And on the earth! Ye Visions of the hills!
And Souls of lonely places! can I think
A vulgar hope was yours when ye employed
Such ministry, when ye, through many a year
Haunting me thus among my boyish sports,
On caves and trees, upon the woods and hills,
Impressed, upon all forms, the characters[4]
Of danger or desire; and thus did make
The surface of the universal earth,
With triumph and delight, with hope and fear,
Work like a sea?

*　　*　　*

Thus oft amid those fits of vulgar joy[5]

---

1) *spin*: 돌리다, 회전시키다 (cause to whirl round)

2) *diurnal round*: 지구의 자전; 빙글 빙글 돌다가 갑자기 멈추어 설 때, 주위의 사물이 도는 것처럼 보인다.

3) *Presences of Nature*: 자연의 존재; 그 다음에 나오는 Visions 및 Souls와 더불어 자연 속에 내재한 신성을 가리킨다. 이것은 소년 시절의 놀이에 항상 신비로운 영향을 미친다.

4) *character*: 글자, 문자 (inscribed letters); 동굴과 나무, 숲과 산에 위험과 욕망의 글자를 새겼다는 말은 위험을 알려주고 욕망을 느끼게 했다는 것을 의미한다.

5) *fits of vulgar joy*: 일상적인 것이 주는 충동적인 쾌감; *fit*=capricious impulse; *vulgar joy*=ordinary pleasures

Which, through all seasons, on a child's pursuits[1]
Are prompt attendants, 'mid that giddy bliss[2]
Which, like a tempest, works along the blood
And is forgotten; even then I felt
Gleams like the flashing of a shield[3];—the earth
And common face of Nature spake to me
Rememberable things; sometimes, 'tis true,
By chance collisions and quaint accidents[4]
(Like those ill-sorted unions, work supposed
Of evil-minded fairies), yet not vain
Nor profitless, if haply they impressed
Collateral[5] objects and appearances,
Albeit[6] lifeless then, and doomed to sleep
Until maturer seasons called them forth

To impregnate[7] and to elevate[8] the mind.
—And if the vulgar joy by its own weight
Wearied itself out of the memory,
The scenes which were a witness of that joy
Remained in their substantial lineaments[9]
Depicted on the brain, and to the eye
Were visible, a daily sight; and thus
By the impressive discipline of fear,
By pleasure and repeated happiness,
So frequently repeated, and by force

1) *child's pursuit*: 어린아이의 놀이(활동)

2) *giddy bliss*: 어지러운 행복감; "fits of vulgar joy"와 "giddy bliss"는 Tintern Abbey에 묘사된 "짜릿한 쾌감과 어지러운 황홀감(aching joys and dizzy raptures)"과 같은 것이다.

3) *Gleams like the flashing of a shield*: 방패에 순간적으로 번쩍이는 빛과 같은 섬광

4) chance collisions and quaint accidents: 우연한 충돌이나 이상한 사고; 괄호 속에 들어있는 "심술궂은 요정의 작용으로 맺어진 것 같은 잘못된 결합"과 같은 우연한 만남을 의미한다. 이러한 만남의 부수적인 결과로 자연의 사물과 형상이 정신에 각인되고, 그 당시에는 생명이 없이 잠들어 있으나 세월이 흐른 후 "성숙한 계절"이 오면 회상되어 마음의 양식이 된다.

5) *collateral*: 부수적인 (subordinate, attendant, concomitant)

6) *albeit*: even though

7) *impregnate*: 충만하게 하다, 가득 채우다 (fill, saturate)

8) *elevate*: 고양시키다 (raise the moral, intellectual, or cultural level of)

9) *in their substantial lineaments*: 실체적 외형(윤곽) 그대로

Of obscure feelings representative
Of things forgotten, these same scenes so bright,
So beautiful, so majestic in themselves,
Though yet the day was distant, did become
Habitually dear, and all their forms
And changeful colours by invisible links
Were fastened to the affections[1].

From BOOK SECOND SCHOOL-TIME (continued)

Blest the infant Babe,
(For with my best conjecture I would trace
Our Being's earthly progress,) blest the Babe,
Nursed[2] in his Mother's arms, who sinks to sleep[3]
Rocked[4] on his Mother's breast; who with his soul
Drinks in the feelings of his Mother's eye!
For him, in one dear Presence, there exists
A virtue[5] which irradiates[6] and exalts
Objects through widest intercourse of sense[7].
No outcast he[8], bewildered and depressed:
Along his infant veins are interfused[9]
The gravitation and the filial bond[10]
Of nature that connect him with the world.

---

1) *affections*: feelings
2) nurse: 젖을 먹이다 (suckle), 기르다 (foster)
3) *sink to sleep*: fall asleep
4) *rock*: 흔들어 재우다 (move gently to and fro as in cradle)
5) *virtue*: 힘 (inherent power; the power inherent in a divine being)
6) *irradiate*: 밝히다, 비추다 (throw light on, shine upon)
7) *intercourse of sense*: 감각을 통한 교류 (교감)
8) *No outcast he*: He is no outcast; 그는 버림받지 않았다.
9) *interfuse*: 혼합하다 (fuse and blend with eath other)
10) *filial bond*: 모자(母子)의 인연; 젖먹이의 핏줄 속에는 그와 세상을 이어주는 중력과 모자의 인연이 녹아 흐른다. 즉 유에게는 중력 또는 탯줄처럼 그와 세상을 이어주는 힘이 내재하고 있다는 의미이다. *filial*=자식으로서의 (of a child, due from a child); *bond*=유대(a tie), 인연(a uniting force). 모자의 인연은 인간과 자연 간의 더 큰 인연을 맺어준다.

Is there a flower, to which he points with hand
Too weak to gather it, already love
Drawn from love's purest earthly fount for him
Hath beautified that flower; already shades
Of pity cast from inward tenderness
Do fall around him upon aught that bears
Unsightly marks of violence or harm.
Emphatically[1] such a Being lives,
Frail creature as he is, helpless as frail,
An inmate of this active universe.
For, feeling has to him imparted power
That through the growing faculties of sense
Doth like an agent of the one great Mind[2]
Create, creator and receiver both[3],
Working but in alliance with the works
Which it beholds.—Such, verily, is the first
Poetic spirit of our human life,
By uniform control[4] of after years,
In most, abated or suppressed; in some,
Through every change of growth and of decay,
Pre-eminent[5] till death.

* * *

'Twere long to tell
What spring and autumn, what the winter snows,
And what the summer shade, what day and night,

---

1) *emphatically*: 외견상으로는 (in appearance)

2) *an agent of the one great Mind*: 한 위대한 정신의 대리인; *the one great Mind*=God

3) *creator and receiver both*: 창조자요 수용자로서; 지각능력에 관한 언급이다. 워즈워스는 지각이 단순히 수동적으로 외부의 감각인상을 받아들이는 수동적 기능이 아니라 능동적으로 창조하는 기능이라고 생각했다. 콜리지는 창조적 지각능력을 "제1상상력(primary imagination)"이라 불렀다. 워즈워스는 이것을 "최초의 시 정신(the first / Poetic spirit)," "유아기의 감수성(infant sensibility-II. 270)," 또는 "내 최초의 창조적 감수성(My first creative sensibility-II. 360)"이라 부르고 있다. Cf. "Tintern Abbey" ll. 106-8: "both what they[eye and ear] half create, / And what perceive."

4) *uniform control*: 획일적인 통제; 이 "최초의 시 정신"은 획일적인 교육이나 사회적 관습의 영향으로 대부분의 경우 쇠퇴하거나 억제되지만, 일부(즉 시인들)의 경우 죽을 때까지 다른 사람들보다 뛰어나게 유지된다고 한다.

5) *pre-eminent*: 탁월한, 남보다 뛰어난 (excelling others)

Evening and morning, sleep and waking, thought
From sources inexhaustible, poured forth
To feed the spirit of religious love
In which I walked with Nature. But let this
Be not forgotten, that I still retained
My first creative sensibility;
That by the regular action of the world
My soul was unsubdued. A plastic power[1]
Abode with me; a forming hand, at times
Rebellious, acting in a devious mood;
A local spirit of his own, at war
With general tendency, but, for the most,
Subservient[2] strictly to external things
With which it communed. An auxiliar[3] light
Came from my mind, which on the setting sun
Bestowed new splendour; the melodious birds,
The fluttering breezes, fountains that run on
Murmuring so sweetly in themselves, obeyed
A like dominion[4], and the midnight storm
Grew darker in the presence of my eye:
Hence my obeisance[5], my devotion hence,
And hence my transport.

                                        Nor should this, perchance,
Pass unrecorded, that I still[6] had loved
The exercise and produce of a toil,
Than analytic industry to me
More pleasing, and whose character I deem

---

1) *A plastic power*: 성형적(成形的)인 힘, 즉 상상력을 의미한다; *plastic*=formative, creative. Cf. Coleridge는 "esemplastic power"라 불렀다. 이것은 이질적인 요소를 통합하여 하나의 유기적 전체를 만들어 내는 힘을 의미한다(esemplastic=forming into one, unifying).

2) *subservient*: 보조적인(serving as means, subordinate)

3) *auxiliar*: auxiliary: 보조적인 (subsidiary), 부가적인 (additional); 마음에서 나와 석양에 새로운 광채를 부여하는 "부가적인 빛"은 상상력을 의미한다. 이것은 일상적 제재에 부여하는 "a certain colouring of imagination"과 같은 것이다.

4) *dominion*: 영향 (influence), 지배 (control)

5) *obeisance*: 존경 (respect), 복종 (submission)

6) *still*: always

Is more poetic as resembling more
Creative agency. The song would speak
Of that interminable building reared
By observation of affinities
In objects where no brotherhood exists
To passive minds. My seventeenth year was come
And, whether from this habit rooted now
So deeply in my mind, or from excess
In the great social principle of life
Coercing[1]) all things into sympathy,
To unorganic natures were transferred
My own enjoyments; or the power of truth
Coming in revelation, did converse
With things that really are; I, at this time,
Saw blessings spread around me like a sea.
Thus while the days flew by, and years passed on,
From Nature and her overflowing soul,
I had received so much, that all my thoughts
Were steeped in feeling; I was only then
Contented, when with bliss ineffable
I felt the sentiment of Being[2]) spread
O'er all that moves and all that seemeth still;
O'er all that, lost beyond the reach of thought
And human knowledge, to the human eye
Invisible, yet liveth to the heart;
O'er all that leaps and runs, and shouts and sings,
Or beats the gladsome air; o'er all that glides
Beneath the wave, yea, in the wave itself,
And mighty depth of waters. Wonder not
If high the transport, great the joy I felt,
Communing in this sort through earth and heaven

---

1) *coerce*: 강제하다 (forcibly constrain or impel)
2) 만물 속에 충만한 존재의 느낌은 "Tintern Abbey"(ll. 93-012)에 묘사된 것과 일치한다. "I have felt / A presence... / Whose dwelling is the light of setting suns, / And the round ocean and the living air, / And the blue sky, and in the mind of man..."

With every form of creature, as it looked
Towards the Uncreated[1] with a countenance
Of adoration, with an eye of love.
One song they sang, and it was audible,
Most audible, then, when the fleshly ear,
O'ercome by humblest prelude of that strain
Forgot her functions, and slept undisturbed.

From BOOK THIRD : RESIDENCE AT CAMBRIDGE[2]

IT was a dreary[3] morning when the wheels
Rolled over a wide plain o'erhung with clouds,
And nothing cheered our way till first we saw
The long-roofed chapel of King's College[4] lift
Turrets[5] and pinnacles in answering files,
Extended high above a dusky grove.

Advancing, we espied[6] upon the road
A student clothed in gown and tasselled cap[7],
Striding along as if o'ertasked by Time,
Or covetous of exercise and air[8];
He passed—nor was I master of my eyes
Till he was left an arrow's flight behind.

---

1) *the Uncreated*: 신의 창조행위에 의해 창조되지 않은 존재(not created by the divine act of creation), 스스로 존재하는 영원한(self-existent and eternal) 존재, 즉 신(God)을 의미한다.

2) Wordsworth는 1787년 10월 30일에 Cambridge에 도착했고, 1791년 1월 21일에 학위(BA)를 받았다.

3) *dreary*: 쓸쓸한, 우울한, 지루한 (dismal, gloomy, dull); Cambridge 대학생활의 전반적인 분위기를 암시하는 형용사이다.

4) Wordsworth는 1787년 10월 30일에 Cambridge에 도착하였고, 1791년 1월 21일에 학위(BA)를 받았다.

5) turret: 작은 탑 (small tower connected with main building)

6) *espy*: catch sight of

7) *tasselled cap*: 술 달린 모자

8) *as if o'ertasked by Time, / Or covetous of exercise and air*: 시간 쫓기거나 옥외 운동을 하려는 듯; *covetous*=eagerly desirous

As near and nearer to the spot we drew,
It seemed to suck us in with an eddy's force[1].
Onward we drove beneath the Castle; caught,
While crossing Magdalene Bridge, a glimpse of Cam;
And at the "Hoop" alighted, famous Inn.

*　　　*　　　*

Of College labours, of the Lecturer's room
All studded[2] round, as thick as chairs could stand,
With loyal students, faithful to their books,
Half-and-half idlers, hardy recusants,
And honest dunces—of important days,
Examinations, when the man was weighed
As in a balance! of[3] excessive hopes,
Tremblings withal[4] and commendable[5] fears,
Small jealousies, and triumphs[6] good or bad—
Let others that know more speak as they know.
Such glory[7] was but little sought by me,
And little won. Yet from the first crude[8] days
Of settling time in this untried[9] abode,
I was disturbed at times by prudent thoughts,
Wishing to hope without a hope[10], some fears
About my future worldly maintenance[11],
And, more than all, a strangeness in the mind,

---

1) 워즈워스의 인생을 강물에 비유한다면, 대학생활은 소용돌이(small whirlpool)에 해당한다.
2) *studded*: 산재해 있는 (scattered about)
3) 64, 68, 70 행의 전치사 "of"는 모두 73행의 "Let others...speak"에 연결된다.
4) *withal*: 그와 동시에 (at the same time), 게다가 (in addition, moreover); as well
5) *commendable*: 칭찬할만한 (praiseworthy),
6) *triumph*: 성공, 업적 (great success or achievement), 성공의 기쁨 (joy at success)
7) *glory*: 영예 (honorable fame)
8) *crude*: 미숙한 (unrefined)
9) *untried*: 경험해보지 못한, 생소한 (inexperienced)
10) "절망적인 희망을 품는 신중한 생각": 당시 그는 가족들이 그가 St. John's College의 연구원 (fellow)의 직을 얻기를 희망하고 있어서 부담을 느끼고 있었다.
11) *worldly maintenance*: 세속적인 생계수단(means of subsustence; livelihood), (장래의) 직업

A feeling that I was not for that hour,
Nor for that place. But wherefore be cast down?
For (not to speak of Reason and her pure
Reflective acts to fix the moral law
Deep in the conscience, nor of Christian Hope,
Bowing her head before her sister Faith
As one far mightier), hither I had come,
Bear witness Truth[1]), endowed with holy powers
And faculties, whether to work or feel.
Oft when the dazzling show no longer new
Had ceased to dazzle, ofttimes did I quit
My comrades, leave the crowd, buildings and groves,
And as I paced alone the level fields
Far from those lovely sights and sounds sublime
With which I had been conversant[2]), the mind
Drooped not[3]); but there into herself returning,
With prompt rebound seemed[4]) fresh as heretofore.
At least I more distinctly recognised
Her native instincts[5]): let me dare to speak
A higher language, say that now I felt
What independent solaces were mine,
To mitigate the injurious sway of place
Or circumstance, how far soever changed
In youth, or to be changed in manhood's prime;
Or for the few who shall be called to look
On the long shadows in our evening years,
Ordained precursors to the night of death.

---

1) *bear witness Truth*: 진리여 증언하라, 진실로, 사실은 (in truth, surely); 명령형으로서 삽입절로 보아야 한다. *bear witness*=증언하다 (state one's belief in)

2) *as I paced...sounds sublime*: 내가 아름다운 풍경과 숭고한 소리로부터 멀리 떨어진 평원을 거닐 때; 여기서 "those lovely sights and sounds sublime"은 "Tintern Abbey"의 "These beauteous forms" 즉 그가 떠나온 고향의 아름다운 자연을 의미한다. 그는 "오랜 부재의 기간 동안에도 이 아름다운 형상들은 맹인의 눈에 비친 풍경 같지는 않았다"고 말했다.

3) *Drooped not*: 우울하지 않았다; droop=풀이 죽다 (lose heart; flag in spirit or courage)

4) *seemed*: 주어는 "the mind"이다; 정신이 "즉각적인 반동으로 내부세계로 되돌아갈 때" 전처럼 생기를 되찾게 되었다는 뜻이다. *heretofore*=before this time, formerly

5) *Her native instincts*: 정신의 타고난 본능

As if awakened, summoned, roused, constrained,
I looked for universal things; perused
The common countenance of earth and sky[1]:
Earth, nowhere unembellished by some trace
Of that first Paradise whence man was driven[2];
And sky, whose beauty and bounty are expressed
By the proud name she bears—the name of Heaven.[3]
I called on both to teach me what they might;
Or, turning the mind in upon herself,
Pored, watched, expected, listened, spread my thoughts
And spread them with a wider creeping; felt
Incumbencies more awful[4], visitings
Of the Upholder[5], of the tranquil soul,
That tolerates the indignities of Time,
And, from the centre of Eternity
All finite motions overruling, lives
In glory immutable. But peace! enough
Here to record that I was mounting now
To such community with highest truth.

A track pursuing, not untrod before[6],
From strict analogies by thought supplied
Or consciousnesses not to be subdued[7],
To every natural form, rock, fruits, or flower,
Even the loose stones that cover the highway,
I gave a moral life[8]: I saw them feel,

---

1) 대지와 하늘의 평범한 얼굴: 이것은 눈앞에 펼쳐진 풍경이 아니라 마음속의 풍경이다.
2) *nowhere unembellished...was driven*: 인간이 쫓겨난 최초의 낙원의 흔적이 여전히 남아 있는 (대지); *embellish*=아름답게 하다, 장식하다 (beautify, adorn)
3) *And sky... the name of Heaven*: 자랑스러운 이름, 즉 천국이라는 이름으로 아름다움과 베푸는 마음을 표현하고 있는 하늘; *bounty*=베푸는 마음 (goodness shown in giving; munificence)
4) *Incumbencies more awful*: 더욱 경외감을 자아내는 영적인 그림자 (spiritual overshadowing); *encumbency*=brooding, the condition of pressing on something
5) *visitings / Of the Upholder*: 지탱해주는 존재의 방문; "Upholder"는 "Presence"와 마찬가지로 신성(Divinity) 또는 신(God)을 의미한다.
6) 전에 다녔던 길을 되짚어 걸으며: 시인은 내면 성찰(introspection)을 계속하고 있다.
7) 억누를 수 없는 생각이나 의식이 제공하는 엄격한 추론의 과정을 통해

Or linked them to some feeling: the great mass
Lay bedded in a quickening soul, and all
That I beheld respired with inward meaning.
Add that whate'er of Terror or of Love
Or Beauty, Nature's daily face put on
From transitory passion, unto this
I was as sensitive as waters are
To the sky's influence in a kindred mood
Of passion; was obedient as a lute
That waits upon the touches of the wind.
Unknown, unthought of, yet I was most rich—
I had a world about me[1]—'twas my own;
I made it, for it only lived to me,
And to the God who sees into the heart.
Such sympathies[2], though rarely, were betrayed
By outward gestures and by visible looks:
Some called it madness—so indeed it was,
If child-like fruitfulness in passing joy,
If steady moods of thoughtfulness matured
To inspiration, sort with such a name[3];
If prophecy be madness; if things viewed
By poets in old time, and higher up
By the first men, earth's first inhabitants,
May in these tutored days no more be seen
With undisordered sight[4]. But leaving this,

---

8) 시인은 마음의 풍경을 이루고 있는 모든 사물에 윤리적 생명을 부여했다고 말한다. 여기서 "moral life"란 정서적 에너지를 의미한다. 그는 사물의 이미지와 감정을 결합시킨 복합체 즉 "the great mass"를 다시 영혼의 토양에 심는다.

1) *I had a world about me*: 나의 내부는 하나의 세계가 있었다. 여기서 "about"는 "주위에"라는 의미이지만, 그 다음에 나와 하나님만이 알고 있는 세계라고 말한 것을 보면, 자신의 내부에 있는 세계임이 분명하다.

2) *Such sympathies*: 이러한 공감; 이것은 자신의 내부 세계와의 교감, 즉 내성(introspection)을 의미한다. 이것은 때로는 몸짓이나 표정으로 드러나 남들이 보면 미쳤다고 오해하기도 한다고 말한다. *betray*=reveal involuntarily

3) 끊임없이 사색에 몰입한 정신상태(mood)가 무르익어 얻어진 영감이 광기라는 이름에 어울린다면. *sort with*=어울리다 (agree with)

4) *if things viewed / By poets...undisordered sight*: 옛날 시인들이나 그보다 오래 전에 최초의 인간들, 즉 대지의 첫 주민들이 본 것이 교육받은 시대인 오늘날 혼란스러운 광경으로 보인다면.

It was no madness, for the bodily eye
Amid my strongest workings evermore
Was searching out the lines of difference
As they lie hid in all external forms,
Near or remote, minute or vast; an eye
Which, from a tree, a stone, a withered leaf,
To the broad ocean and the azure heavens
Spangled with kindred multitudes of stars,
Could find no surface where its power might sleep;
Which spake perpetual logic to my soul,
And by an unrelenting agency
Did bind my feelings even as in a chain.

* * *

From BOOK FOURTH : SUMMER VACATION[1]

* * *

Among the favourites whom it pleased me well
To see again[2], was one by ancient right
Our inmate, a rough terrier of the hills;
By birth and call of nature pre-ordained[3]
To hunt the badger[4] and unearth the fox
Among the impervious[5] crags, but having been
From youth our own adopted[6], he had passed
Into a gentler service[7]. And when first

---

1) Wordsworth는 대학에 입학한 이듬해인 1788년에 첫 여름방학을 Hawkshead에서 보냈다. 그는 고향으로 돌아가 산 위에서 Windermere 후수를 내려다본다. 마을 사람들이 반갑게 인사하고, 하숙집 아주머니 Ann Tyson이 반갑게 그를 맞는다. 고향의 낯익은 사물들을 보고 지난날을 회상한다. 외로운 산책길에 사냥개의 이미지를 떠 올린다. 어느 날 환락의 밤을 지새우고 새벽녘에 집으로 돌아가는 길에 시에 헌신할 것을 결심한다. 제대군인 일화로 제4권을 끝맺는다.

2) 이 절(93-130)은 Wordsworth가 1786-7년에 쓴 "The Dog: An Idillium"을 고쳐 쓴 것이다.

3) *pre-ordain*: 운명을 미리 정하다 (predestine; predetermine)

4) *badger*: 오소리

5) *impervious*: 뚫기 어려운 (impenetrable)

6) *having been / From youth our own adopted*: 어릴 때부터 우리가 길렀기 때문에

7) *had passed / Into a gentler service*: 순한 일을 하도록 길들여졌다.

The boyish spirit flagged, and day by day
Along my veins I kindled with the stir,
The fermentation[1], and the vernal heat
Of poesy, affecting private shades
Like a sick Lover[2], then this dog was used
To[3] watch me, an attendant and a friend,
Obsequious to[4] my steps early and late,
Though often of such dilatory[5] walk
Tired, and uneasy at the halts I made.
A hundred times when, roving high and low,
I have been harassed with the toil of verse[6],
Much pains and little progress, and at once
Some lovely Image in the song rose up
Full-formed, like Venus rising from the sea;
Then have I darted forwards to let loose
My hand upon his back with stormy joy,
Caressing him again and yet again.
And when at evening on the public way
I sauntered, like a river murmuring
And talking to itself when all things else
Are still, the creature trotted on before;
Such was his custom; but whene'er he met
A passenger approaching, he would turn
To give me timely notice[7], and straightway,
Grateful for that admonishment, I hushed
My voice, composed my gait[8], and, with the air
And mien of one whose thoughts are free, advanced

---

1) *fermentation*: 흥분 (excitement), 동요 (agination)
2) *affecting private shades / Like a sick Lover*: 사랑의 열병을 앓는 사람처럼 혼자 우울해하며; *affect*=pretend to feel; *shade*=a cloud on a person's face
3) *was used to (watch)*: used to (watch)
4) *obsequious to*: following
5) *dilatory*: 느린 (slow)
6) *I have been harnessed with the toil of verse*: 시 창작에 열중했다.
7) *notice*: warning
8) *composed my gait*: 걸음걸이를 단정하게 했다; compose=가다듬다 (arrange one's face etc. so as to conceal one's feelings)

To give and take a greeting that might save
My name from piteous rumours, such as wait
On men suspected to be crazed in brain.

*　　*　　*

[Dedication]

Yes, that heartless[1] chase
Of trivial pleasures was a poor exchange
For books and nature at that early age.
'Tis true, some casual knowledge might be gained
Of character or life; but at that time,
Of manners put to school[2] I took small note,
And all my deeper passions lay elsewhere.
Far better had it been to exalt the mind
By solitary study, to uphold
Intense desire through meditative peace;
And yet, for chastisement of these regrets,
The memory of one particular hour
Doth here rise up against me. 'Mid a throng
Of maids and youths, old men, and matrons staid[3],
A medley of all tempers, I had passed
The night in dancing, gaiety, and mirth,
With din of instruments and shuffling feet,
And glancing forms, and tapers glittering,
And unaimed prattle flying up and down;
Spirits upon the stretch[4], and here and there
Slight shocks of young love-liking interspersed,
Whose transient pleasure mounted to the head,
And tingled through the veins. Ere we retired,
The cock had crowed, and now the eastern sky

---

1) *heartless*: 어리석은 (stupid, foolish), 우울한 (depressing)
2) *put to school*: 교육받은
3) *matrons staid*: 점잖은 부인들; *matron*=married woman; *staid*=dignified and serious
4) *Spirits on the stretch*: 긴장된 마음; *on the stretch*=긴장된

Was kindling, not unseen, from humble copse
And open field, through which the pathway wound,
And homeward led my steps. Magnificent
The morning rose, in memorable pomp,
Glorious as e'er I had beheld—in front,
The sea lay laughing at a distance; near,
The solid mountains shone, bright as the clouds,
Grain-tinctured, drenched in empyrean[1] light;
And in the meadows and the lower grounds
Was all the sweetness of a common dawn—
Dews, vapours, and the melody of birds,
And labourers going forth to till the fields.
Ah! need I say, dear Friend! that to the brim
My heart was full; I made no vows, but vows
Were then made for me; bond unknown to me
Was given, that I should be, else sinning greatly,
A dedicated Spirit. On I walked
In thankful blessedness, which yet survives.

*　　　*　　　*

[Discharged Soldier]

Once, when those summer months
Were flown, and autumn brought its annual show
Of oars with oars contending, sails with sails,
Upon Winander's[2] spacious breast, it chanced
That—after I had left a flower-decked room
(Whose in-door pastime, lighted up, survived
To a late hour), and spirits overwrought
Were making night do penance for a day
Spent in a round of strenuous idleness—
My homeward course led up a long ascent,
Where the road's watery surface, to the top
Of that sharp rising, glittered to the moon

1) empyrean: 천상의; n. the highest heaven, the sphere of the pure element of fire
2) *Winander*: Windermere

And bore the semblance of another stream
Stealing with silent lapse to join the brook
That murmured in the vale. All else was still;
No living thing appeared in earth or air,
And, save the flowing water's peaceful voice,
Sound there was none—but, lo! an uncouth[1] shape,
Shown by a sudden turning of the road,
So near that, slipping back into the shade
Of a thick hawthorn, I could mark him well,
Myself unseen. He was of stature tall,
A span above man's common measure, tall,
Stiff, lank, and upright; a more meagre[2] man
Was never seen before by night or day.
Long were his arms, pallid his hands; his mouth
Looked ghastly in the moonlight: from behind,
A mile-stone propped him; I could also ken[3]
That he was clothed in military garb,
Though faded, yet entire. Companionless,
No dog attending, by no staff sustained,
He stood, and in his very dress appeared
A desolation, a simplicity,
To which the trappings[4] of a gaudy world
Make a strange back-ground. From his lips, ere long,
Issued low muttered sounds, as if of pain
Or some uneasy thought; yet still his form
Kept the same awful steadiness—at his feet
His shadow lay, and moved not. From self-blame
Not wholly free, I watched him thus; at length
Subduing my heart's specious cowardice[5],
I left the shady nook where I had stood
And hailed him. Slowly from his resting-place

1) *uncouth*: strange, unusual
2) *meagre*: lean, thin
3) *ken*: know
4) *trappings*: 장식 (ornamental accessories)
5) *my heart's specious cowardice*: the cowardice of my specious heart; 겉으로만 선량한 척하는 내 마음의 비겁함. *specious*=superficially genuine but in reality false

He rose, and with a lean and wasted arm
In measured[1] gesture lifted to his head
Returned my salutation; then resumed
His station as before; and when I asked
His history, the veteran, in reply,
Was neither slow nor eager; but, unmoved,
And with a quiet uncomplaining voice,
A stately air of mild indifference,
He told in few plain words a soldier's tale—
That in the Tropic Islands he had served,
Whence he had landed scarcely three weeks past;
That on his landing he had been dismissed,
And now was travelling towards his native home.
This heard, I said, in pity, "Come with me."
He stooped, and straightway from the ground took up
An oaken staff by me yet unobserved—
A staff which must have dropped from his slack hand
And lay till now neglected in the grass.
Though weak his step and cautious, he appeared
To travel without pain, and I beheld,
With an astonishment but ill suppressed,
His ghostly figure moving at my side;
Nor could I, while we journeyed thus, forbear[2]
To turn from present hardships to the past,
And speak of war, battle, and pestilence,
Sprinkling this talk with questions, better spared[3],
On what he might himself have seen or felt.
He all the while was in demeanour calm,
Concise in answer; solemn and sublime
He might have seemed, but that in all he said
There was a strange half-absence, as of one
Knowing too well the importance of his theme,
But feeling it no longer. Our discourse
Soon ended, and together on we passed

1) *measured*: rhythmical, regular in movement
2) *forbear*: 참다, 삼가다 (refrain from)
3) *better spared*: 하지 않았으면 좋았을

In silence through a wood gloomy and still.
Up-turning, then, along an open field,
We reached a cottage. At the door I knocked,
And earnestly to charitable care
Commended him as a poor friendless man,
Belated and by sickness overcome.
Assured that now the traveller would repose
In comfort, I entreated that henceforth
He would not linger in the public ways,
But ask for timely furtherance and help
Such as his state required. At this reproof,
With the same ghastly mildness in his look,
He said, "My trust is in the God of Heaven,
And in the eye of him who passes me!"
  The cottage door was speedily unbarred,
And now the soldier touched his hat once more
With his lean hand, and in a faltering voice,
Whose tone bespake[1] reviving interests
Till then unfelt, he thanked me; I returned
The farewell blessing of the patient man,
And so we parted. Back I cast a look,
And lingered near the door a little space,
Then sought with quiet heart my distant home.

From BOOK FIFTH: BOOKS[2]

[Dream of the Arab]

                    Oh! why hath not the Mind

---

1) *bespeak*: 나타내다 (suggest, be evidence of)

2) 제5권에서 Wordsworth는 어린 시절의 독서의 영향에 관해 이야기한다. 책은 보존되어야 할 가치를 지니고 있으나 결국은 사라지고 만다는 탄식을 한다. 그는 아랍인에 관한 꿈을 이야기한다. Don Quixote를 읽다가 잠이 들었는데, 꿈에 한 손에 책(기하학)과 다른 손에 조가비(시)를 들고 단봉낙타를 타고 오는 아랍인을 만난다. 조가비에서 홍수에 의해 대지가 파괴될 것이라는 예언의 말을 듣고 책을 보존하려고 노력하지만 파도가 밀려와 아랍인을 삼킨다. 시인은 아랍인의 열망에 공감한다. 그 다음 "There Was a Boy"와 "The Drowned Man"을 소개한다. 책은 자연보다 열등하나 위대한 힘이다. 학창시절에 학교공부보다 책을 마음대로 읽을 수 있었던 것에 감사한다. 그는 어른의 축소판을 만드는 그릇된 학교교육을 비판한다. 자연 속에서 자유롭게 뛰노는 것이 진짜 아이들을 만드는 데 도움이 된다고 생각한다.

Some element to stamp her image on
In nature somewhat nearer to her own?
Why, gifted with such powers to send abroad
Her spirit, must it lodge in shrines so frail?[1)]
  One day, when from my lips a like complaint
Had fallen in presence of a studious[2)] friend,
He with a smile made answer, that in truth
'Twas going far to seek disquietude[3)];
But on the front of his reproof[4)] confessed
That he himself had oftentimes given way
To kindred hauntings[5)]. Whereupon I told,
That once in the stillness of a summer's noon,
While I was seated in a rocky cave
By the sea-side, perusing, so it chanced,
The famous history of the errant knight
Recorded by Cervantes[6)], these same thoughts
Beset[7)] me, and to height unusual rose[8)],
While listlessly[9)] I sate, and, having closed
The book, had turned my eyes toward the wide sea.
On poetry and geometric truth,
And their high privilege of lasting life,
From all internal injury exempt[10)],
I mused; upon these chiefly: and at length,
My senses yielding to the sultry air,
Sleep seized me, and I passed into a dream.

---

1) Wordsworth는 대격변이 일어나 인간의 지혜와 시를 담고 있는 모든 책이 소실될 것을 염려하고 있다.
2) *studious*: 학구적인 (assiduous in study); *when from my lips...friend*: 학구적인 친구의 면전에서 내가 이와 같은 불평을 했을 때
3) *to seek disquietude*: 불안해하는 것; *disquietude*=불안, 걱정 (state of uneasiness, anxiety)
4) *on the front of his reproach*: 책망하기에 앞서
5) *give way / To kindred hauntings*: 유사한 고민에 빠지다; *give way to*=be overcome by an emotion, break down; *haunting*=worry
6) i. e. *Don Quixote*; *errant knight*: 편력기사 (a knight in former times who was travelled looking for adventure)
7) *beset*: 포위하다(surround, besiege), 몰려들다, 괴롭히다
8) *to unusual height rose*: rose to unusual height; (생각이) 몹시 고조되었다
9) listlessly: 나른하게 (languidly), 맥이 풀려
10) *From all internal injury exempt*: 마음 아파하지 않고; *exempt from*=free from

I saw before me stretched a boundless plain
Of sandy wilderness[1], all black and void,
And as I looked around, distress and fear
Came creeping over me, when at my side,
Close at my side, an uncouth shape appeared
Upon a dromedary[2], mounted high.
He seemed an Arab of the Bedouin tribes[3]:
A lance he bore, and underneath one arm
A stone, and in the opposite hand a shell
Of a surpassing brightness. At the sight
Much I rejoiced, not doubting but a guide
Was present, one who with unerring skill
Would through the desert lead me; and while yet
I looked and looked, self-questioned what this freight[4]
Which the new-comer carried through the waste
Could mean, the Arab told me that the stone
(To give it in the language of the dream)
Was "Euclid's Elements[5]," and "This," said he,
"Is something of more worth;" and at the word
Stretched forth the shell, so beautiful in shape,
In colour so resplendent[6], with command
That I should hold it to my ear. I did so,
And heard that instant in an unknown tongue,
Which yet I understood, articulate sounds,
A loud prophetic blast of harmony[7];
An Ode, in passion uttered, which foretold
Destruction to the children of the earth
By deluge, now at hand. No sooner ceased
The song, than the Arab with calm look declared

---

1) sandy wilderness: 모래벌판; 사막
2) *dromedary*: 단봉낙타 (a one-humped camel bred for riding)
3) *Bedouin tribe*: 베두인족, 아랍계 유목민 (nomadic Arabs)
4) *freight*: 손에 들고 있는 물건, 즉 돌과 조가비
5) *Euclid's Elements*: 유클리드 기하학 (Euclid's Elements of Geometry); *Euclid*: 기원전 300년경에 Alexandria에 살았던 그리스의 기하학자
6) *resplendent*: brilliant, dazzlingly bright
7) *A loud prophetic blast of harmony*: 크고 조화로운 예언의 소리; *blast*=sound of wind-instrument

That all would come to pass[1] of which the voice
Had given forewarning, and that he himself
Was going then to bury those two books:
The one that held acquaintance with the stars,
And wedded soul to soul in purest bond
Of reason, undisturbed by space or time;
The other that was a god, yea many gods,
Had voices more than all the winds, with power
To exhilarate[2] the spirit, and to soothe,
Through every clime, the heart of human kind.
While this was uttering, strange as it may seem,
I wondered not, although I plainly saw
The one to be a stone, the other a shell;
Nor doubted once but that they both were books,
Having a perfect faith in all that passed.
Far stronger, now, grew the desire I felt
To cleave unto[3] this man; but when I prayed
To share his enterprise, he hurried on
Reckless of me: I followed, not unseen,
For oftentimes he cast a backward look,
Grasping his twofold treasure.—Lance in rest,
He rode, I keeping pace with him; and now
He, to my fancy, had become the knight
Whose tale Cervantes tells; yet not the knight,
But was an Arab of the desert too;
Of these was neither, and was both at once.
His countenance, meanwhile, grew more disturbed;
And, looking backwards when he looked, mine eyes
Saw, over half the wilderness diffused[4],
A bed of glittering light[5]: I asked the cause:
"It is," said he, "the waters of the deep
Gathering upon us;" quickening then the pace

---

1) *come to pass*: 일어나다 (happen)
2) *exhilarate*: 기쁘게 하다 (gladden, enliven)
3) *cleave unto*: 매달리다 (cling to)
4) *diffuse*: disperse, spread widely
5) *A bed of glittering light*: 한 바닥의 반짝이는 빛; *bed*=a level surface

Of the unwieldy[1] creature he bestrode[2],
He left me: I called after him aloud;
He heeded not; but, with his twofold charge[3]
Still in his grasp, before me, full in view,
Went hurrying o'er the illimitable waste[4],
With the fleet[5] waters of a drowning world
In chase of him; whereat I waked in terror,
And saw the sea before me, and the book,
In which I had been reading, at my side.[6]

* * *

[There Was a Boy]

There was a Boy: ye knew him well, ye cliffs
And islands of Winander!—many a time
At evening, when the earliest stars began
To move along the edges of the hills,
Rising or setting, would he stand alone
Beneath the trees or by the glimmering lake,
And there, with fingers interwoven[7], both hands
Pressed closely palm to palm, and to his mouth
Uplifted, he, as through an instrument,
Blew mimic hootings[8] to the silent owls,
That they might answer him; and they would shout
Across the watery vale, and shout again,
Responsive to his call, with quivering peals[9],

---

1) *unwieldy*: 육중한 (difficult to manage owing to size or weight), 느린 (slow of movement)
2) *bestride*: 걸터앉다 (get on with legs astride)
3) *charge*:짐 (load); *with his twofold charge / Still in his grasp*: 두 개의 짐(즉 돌과 조가비)을 여전히 손에 들고
4) *the illimitable waste*: 끝없는 사막
5) *fleet*: 빠른 (swift)
6) 아랍인에 관한 꿈 이야기는 1619년에 철학자 Descartes가 꾼 꿈 이야기를 변형시킨 것이라 한다. Jane Worthington Smyser는 콜리지가 Descartes의 꿈 이야기를 워즈워스에게 들려주었을 것이라 주장한다("Wordsworth's Dream of Poetry and Science," *PMLA*, LXXI [1956], pp. 269-75 참조).
7) *with fingers interwoven*: 손가락을 깍지 끼고
8) *blow mimic hootings*: 올빼미 소리를 흉내 내다
9) *peal*: 울림, 종소리 (loud ringing of bells)

And long halloos[1] and screams, and echoes loud,
Redoubled and redoubled[2], concourse wild
Of jocund din[3]; and, when a lengthened pause
Of silence came and baffled his best skill,
Then sometimes, in that silence while he hung
Listening, a gentle shock of mild surprise
Has carried far into his heart the voice
Of mountain torrents; or the visible scene
Would enter unawares into his mind,
With all its solemn imagery, its rocks,
Its woods, and that uncertain heaven, received
Into the bosom of the steady lake.

[The Drowned Man]

  Well do I call to mind the very week
When I was first intrusted[4] to the care
Of that sweet Valley; when its paths, its shores,
And brooks were like a dream of novelty
To my half-infant thoughts; that very week,
While I was roving up and down alone,
Seeking I knew not what, I chanced to cross
One of those open fields, which, shaped like ears,
Make green peninsulas on Esthwaite's Lake:
Twilight was coming on, yet through the gloom
Appeared distinctly on the opposite shore
A heap of garments, as if left by one
Who might have there been bathing. Long I watched,
But no one owned them[5]; meanwhile the calm lake
Grew dark with all the shadows on its breast,
And, now and then, a fish up-leaping snapped[6]

---

1) *halloo*: 어이하고 외치는 소리 (calling attention at a distance; the shout of 'halloo')
2) *redouble*: repeat, echo
3) concourse wild / Of jocund din: 즐거운 소란의 열광적인 합주; *concourse*=합류 (a flowing together, confluence)
4) *intrust*: entrust: 맡기다, 위탁하다
5) *no one owned them*: 그 옷의 주인은 나타나지 않았다
6) *snap*: break with a sudden sharp moise; *a fish...stillness*: 물고기 뛰는 소리가 숨죽인 적막을 깼다.

The breathless stillness. The succeeding day,
Those unclaimed garments[1] telling a plain tale
Drew to the spot an anxious crowd; some looked
In passive expectation from the shore,
While from a boat others hung o'er the deep,
Sounding with grappling irons[2] and long poles.
At last, the dead man[3], 'mid that beauteous scene
Of trees and hills and water, bolt upright[4]
Rose, with his ghastly face, a spectre shape
Of terror; yet no soul-debasing fear[5],
Young as I was, a child not nine years old,
Possessed me, for my inner eye had seen
Such sights before, among the shining streams
Of faery land, the forest of romance.
Their spirit hallowed[6] the sad spectacle
With decoration of ideal grace;
A dignity, a smoothness[7], like the works
Of Grecian art, and purest poesy.

* * *

From BOOK SIXTH : CAMBRIDGE AND THE ALPS[8]

* * *

[Imagination]

Imagination—here the Power so called

---

1) *unclaimed garments*: 주인 없는 옷
2) *grappling irons*: 쇠갈고리 (an iron tool with several hooks)
3) 이웃마을 교사인 James Jackson이 1779년 6월 18일에 Esthwaite 후수에서 멱 감다가 익사했다.
4) *bolt upright*: 꼿꼿하게 (rigidly erect)
5) *soul-debasing fear*: 영혼을 타락시키는 공포; 오싹한 공포
6) *hallow*: 신성하게 하다 (make holy), 정화하다 (purify)
7) *smoothness*: 평온함 (calmness)
8) 제6권에서는 대학 2학년과 3학년 때의 경험을 이야기한다. Wordsworth는 대학 재학기간 동안 자신에 충실한 삶을 살았고, 공부에는 무관심했다. 그는 1790년 대학에 입학한 후 세 번째 여름방학을 맞아 친구 Robert Jones와 함께 프랑스, 스위스, 알프스 산, 그리고 이탈리아를 도보로 여행했다. 이 여행은 기억에 남은 모험여행이었고, 그가 시인이 되는 데에 크게 기여했다.

Through sad incompetence of human speech[1]),
That awful Power rose from the mind's abyss
Like an unfathered vapour[2]) that enwraps[3]),
At once, some lonely traveller. I was lost;
Halted without an effort to break through;
But to my conscious soul I now can say—
"I recognise thy glory:" in such strength
Of usurpation[4]), when the light of sense
Goes out, but with a flash that has revealed
The invisible world, doth greatness make abode,
There harbours; whether we be young or old,
Our destiny, our being's heart and home,
Is with infinitude[5]), and only there;
With hope it is, hope that can never die,
Effort, and expectation, and desire,
And something evermore about to be.
Under such banners militant[6]), the soul
Seeks for no trophies, struggles for no spoils
That may attest her prowess, blest[7]) in thoughts
That are their own perfection and reward,
Strong in herself and in beatitude

---

1) *Through sad...speech*: 슬프게도 인간의 언어가 너무나 무력하여

2) *unfathered vapour*: 근원을 알 수 없는 안개; *unfathered*=of unknown origin; 상상력을 "근원 모를 안개"에 비유한 것은 상상력이 무의식의 심연에서 나오는 것임을 의미한다.

3) *enwrap*: 싸다, 에워싸다 (enfold, surround)

4) *usurpation*: 강탈 (seizure by force), 침범 (encroachment); *in such strength...invisible world*: 감각의 빛을 빼앗고 섬광과 더불어 불가시의 세계를 드러내 보여주는 강탈의 힘 속에, (위대함이 거처를 마련한다). Wordsworth는 감각이 지배하는 동안에는 상상력이 작용할 수 없다고 생각했다. 그는 "spots of time"이 "정신이 주인이 되고—외적 감각이 정신의 의지의 하인이 되는" 순간에 형성된다고 말했다(XII, 222-3). 이 말은 현재의 감정을 시의 제재로 삼지 않는다는 말과 맥을 같이한다(I, 46-47).

5) *Our destiny... infinitude*: 우리의 운명, 우리 존재의 중심과 고향은 무한에 있다. 이 말은 우리 존재(영혼)가 궁극적으로 도달하는 곳은 영원의 세계 또는 무한의 세계임을 의미한다. 여기서 "destiny"는 "destination"의 의미로 사용되고 있다.

6) *banners militant*: 전쟁의 깃발; 영혼이 영원의 세계를 추구하는 노력을 전투에 비유하여 묘사하고 있다. 이 전투에서 영혼은 승리의 포상 (즉 "trophies")이나 "무용(prowess)"을 입증해 줄 "전리품(spoils)"을 추구하지 않는다고 한다.

7) *blest*: as it is blest; *blest in...reward*: 그 자체의 완성이요 보상인 사상으로 축복을 받기 때문에

That hides her, like the mighty flood of Nile
Poured from his fount of Abyssinian[1] clouds
To fertilise the whole Egyptian plain.[2]

[The Simplon Pass[3]]

The melancholy slackening that ensued
Upon those tidings by the peasant given
Was soon dislodged[4]. Downwards we hurried fast,
And, with the half-shaped road which we had missed,
Entered a narrow chasm[5]. The brook and road
Were fellow-travellers in this gloomy strait[6],
And with them did we journey several hours
At a slow pace. The immeasurable height
Of woods decaying, never to be decayed[7],
The stationary blasts of waterfalls[8],
And in the narrow rent[9] at every turn
Winds thwarting winds, bewildered and forlorn,
The torrents shooting from the clear blue sky,
The rocks that muttered close upon our ears,
Black drizzling crags that spake by the way-side
As if a voice were in them, the sick sight
And giddy prospect of the raving[10] stream,
The unfettered clouds[11] and region of the Heavens,

---

1) *Abyssinian*: 아비시니아(Ethiopia)의
2) 영혼의 전투에서 승리하여 얻는 행복감(beatitude)을 아비시니아의 구름에서 내린 비로 내려 나일 강이 범람하여 이집트 평원을 비옥하게 하는 것에 비유하고 있다.
3) *The Simplon Pass*: 심플론 고개 (Alps 산맥에 있는 스위스 남부의 산길)
4) *The melancholy...dislodged*; 이미 알프스 산을 넘어왔다("we had crossed the Alps")는 농부의 말(VI, 591)을 듣고 실망하여 걸음이 느려졌으나, 다시 걸음이 빨라졌다는 의미이다. *tidings*: news, information; *dislodge*: 제거하다 (remove from fixed position)
5) *chasm*: 좁은 골짜기 (an opening up of the earth in an earthquake)
6) strait: 협곡 (a narrow passage or gorge between mountains)
7) *decaying, never to be decayed*: 썩어가고 있으나 결코 썩지 않는, 즉 한편으로는 썩어가지만 다른 한편으로는 성장하고 있는
8) *The stationary blasts of waterfalls*: 정지해 있는 것 같은 폭포 소리 (아득히 높은 곳에서 떨어지는 폭포의 모양과 소리를 공감각심상으로 표현한 것임)
9) *rent*: 좁은 길, 협곡 (gorge)
10) raving stream: 소리(아우성)치는 강물; *rave*=rush or roar furiously
11) *unfettered clouds*: 흩어지는 구름

Tumult and peace, the darkness and the light—
Were all like workings of one mind, the features
Of the same face, blossoms upon one tree;
Characters of the great Apocalypse[1],
The types and symbols of Eternity,
Of first, and last, and midst, and without end[2].

*   *   *

From BOOK SEVEHTH : RESIDENCE IN LONDON[3]

*   *   *

[Blind London Beggar]

As the black storm upon the mountain top
Sets off[4] the sunbeam in the valley, so
That huge fermenting mass[5] of human-kind
Serves as a solemn back-ground, or relief,
To single forms and objects, whence they draw,
For feeling and contemplative regard,
More than inherent liveliness and power.
How oft, amid those overflowing streets,
Have I gone forward with the crowd, and said

---

1) *Characters of the great Apocalypse*: 위대한 묵시의 글자들

2) *first, last, and midst, and without end*: 처음이자 끝이고 중간이며 끝이 없는 존재, 즉 신(God)을 의미한다. Cf. Revelation, 1:8: "I am Alpha and Omega, the beginning and the ending, saith the Lord, which is, and which was, and which is to come, the Almighty." 워즈워스는 나무, 폭포, 바람, 바위, 강물, 구름, 등 모든 자연 현상에서 신성을 느끼는 범신론적 경향을 드러내고 있다.

3) 제7권에서 Wordsworth는 두 번의 London 체류에 관해 서술한다. 그는 1791년 대학을 졸업한 후에, 그리고 1792년 12월 프랑스에서 귀국한 후에 런던에 머물렀었다. 런던에 가보기 전에 그는 멋진 런던의 모습을 꿈꾸었다. 그러나 실제로 분주한 도시에서 시간을 보내면서 실망하게 되었다. 거리를 배회하면서 거리 연주를 보고, 군중들 사이에서 인간의 표본을 찾았다. 실내에서, 미술관에서, 무언극이나 Sadler's Wells에서 공연한 멜로드라마를 즐겼다. 그는 비열한 인간들에 둘러싸인 순진한 어린아이를 보고 괴로워했다. 눈먼 거지(A blind Beggar)는 우리 자신과 우주에 대해 알 수 있는 극단의 상징이었다. 소란한 낮의 모습과는 대조적으로 밤의 런던은 고요하고 아름답고 평화로웠다.

4) *set off*: 돋보이게 하다 (make more striking)

5) *fermenting mass*: 소란한 군중

Unto myself, "The face of every one
That passes by me is a mystery!"
Thus have I looked, nor ceased to look, oppressed
By thoughts of what and whither, when and how,
Until the shapes before my eyes became
A second-sight procession[1], such as glides
Over still mountains, or appears in dreams;
And once, far-travelled in such mood, beyond
The reach of common indication, lost
Amid the moving pageant, I was smitten[2]
Abruptly, with the view (a sight not rare)
Of a blind Beggar, who, with upright face,
Stood, propped against a wall, upon his chest
Wearing a written paper, to explain
His story, whence he came, and who he was.
Caught by the spectacle my mind turned round
As with the might of waters; and apt type
This label seemed of the utmost[3] we can know,
Both of ourselves and of the universe;
And, on the shape of that unmoving man,
His steadfast face and sightless eyes, I gazed,
As if admonished from another world.

*　　*　　*

From BOOK TWELFTH : IMAGINATION AND TASTE, HOW IMPAIRED AND RESTORED

*　　*　　*

[Spots of Time]

There are in our existence spots of time[4],

---

1) *a second-sight procession*: 미래를 예견케 하는 행렬
2) *was smitten*: 감명을 받았다; *smite*=impress strongly
3) *the utmost*: 궁극적 진리
4) *spots of time*: 시간의 반점; 상상력을 회복시켜주는 특수한 기억의 한 형태

That with distinct pre-eminence retain
A renovating virtue[1]), whence—depressed
By false opinion and contentious thought[2]),
Or aught of heavier or more deadly weight,
In trivial occupations, and the round
Of ordinary intercourse—our minds
Are nourished and invisibly repaired;
A virtue, by which pleasure is enhanced,
That penetrates, enables us to mount,
When high, more high, and lifts us up when fallen.
This efficacious spirit[3]) chiefly lurks
Among those passages of life that give
Profoundest knowledge to what point, and how,
The mind is lord and master—outward sense
The obedient servant of her will. Such moments
Are scattered everywhere, taking their date
From our first childhood.

[Gibbet-Scene]

I remember well,
That once, while yet my inexperienced hand
Could scarcely hold a bridle, with proud hopes
I mounted, and we journeyed towards the hills:
An ancient servant of my father's house
Was with me, my encourager and guide:
We had not travelled long, ere some mischance
Disjoined me from my comrade; and, through fear
Dismounting, down the rough and stony moor
I led my horse, and, stumbling on, at length
Came to a bottom, where in former times
A murderer had been hung in iron chains[4]).

---

1) *a renovating virtue*: 원기를 회복시켜주는 힘; *renovate*=restore to good condition or vigor
2) *contentious thought*: 논쟁적 사상 (합리적 사고에 의해 논리를 따지는 것을 의미한다); *contentious*=quarrelsome (contention=dispute)
3) *efficacious spirit*: 치유의 힘; efficacious=효험이 있는 (producing desired effect)
4) 1767년에 Penrith 지방에서 Thomas Nicholson이라는 사람이 어느 푸주한을 살해한 사건과, 그로

The gibbet-mast[1]) had mouldered down, the bones
And iron case were gone; but on the turf,
Hard by, soon after that fell deed[2]) was wrought,
Some unknown hand had carved the murderer's name.
The monumental letters were inscribed
In times long past; but still, from year to year
By superstition of the neighbourhood,
The grass is cleared away, and to this hour
The characters are fresh and visible:
A casual glance had shown them, and I fled,
Faltering and faint, and ignorant of the road:
Then, reascending the bare common, saw
A naked pool that lay beneath the hills,
The beacon on the summit[3]), and, more near,
A girl, who bore a pitcher on her head,
And seemed with difficult steps to force her way
Against the blowing wind.[4]) It was, in truth,
An ordinary sight; but I should need
Colours and words that are unknown to man,
To paint the visionary dreariness[5])
Which, while I looked all round for my lost guide,
Invested moorland waste and naked pool,
The beacon crowning the lone eminence,
The female and her garments vexed and tossed
By the strong wind. When, in the blessed hours

부터 백 년 전에 Thomas Lancaster라는 사람이 아내를 독살한 사건이 있었다. 워즈워스는 이 두 사건을 중첩시키고 있다. 1799년 편에는 "아내의 살인자"로 되어 있었다(Jonathan Wordsworth, 9n).

1) *gibbet-mast*: 교수대 기둥

2) *fell deed*: 잔인한 행위, 즉 살인자 처형; fell=ruthless, terrible

3) 산 정사의 봉화대; 이 봉화대는 1719년에 Penrith 산 정상에 세워졌고, Nicholson은 그곳에서 동쪽으로 1마일 떨어진 곳에서 처형되었다.

4) 워즈워스는 "연못," "봉화대," "물동이 이고 가는 처녀"의 심상을 세 번 반복하여 묘사하고 있다. 이것은 동일한 심상이 정서의 굴절을 통하여 변용되는 과정을 보여주기 위함이다.

5) 평범한 광경에 "상상의 색채"를 더한 것이 시다. 워즈워스는 *Lyrical Ballads*(1800) 서문에서 평범한 일상생활에서 "사건과 상황"을 제재로 선택하여 거기에 "모종의 상상의 색채"를 더하여 평범한 것이 신비롭게 보이도록 만드는 것이 자신의 시작 목표라고 말했다. 여기서 "인간이 모르는 색채와 언어"란 다름 아닌 "상상의 색채"를 의미한다.

Of early love, the loved one at my side[1],
I roamed, in daily presence of this scene,
Upon the naked pool and dreary crags,
And on the melancholy beacon, fell
A spirit of pleasure[2] and youth's golden gleam;
And think ye not with radiance more sublime
For these remembrances, and for the power
They had left behind? So feeling comes in aid
Of feeling, and diversity of strength
Attends us, if but once we have been strong.
Oh! mystery of man, from what a depth
Proceed thy honours. I am lost, but see
In simple childhood something of the base
On which thy greatness stands[3]; but this I feel,
That from thyself it comes, that thou must give,
Else never canst receive. The days gone by
Return upon me almost from the dawn
Of life: the hiding-places of man's power
Open; I would approach them, but they close.
I see by glimpses now; when age comes on,
May scarcely see at all;[4] and I would give,
While yet we may, as far as words can give,
Substance and life to what I feel, enshrining,
Such is my hope, the spirit of the Past
For future restoration.[5]—Yet another
Of these memorials:—

---

1) "사랑하는 사람"은 후일 아내가 된 Mary Hutchinson이다. 워즈워스는 1787년 여름에 Mary와 누이 Dorothy와 함께 그곳에 갔었다. 사랑과 관련된 "쾌감의 힘"과 "청춘의 황금 빛"은 세 가지 심상에 새로운 의미를 부여한다.

2) *A spirit of pleasure*: 쾌감의 힘; *spirit*=the active power of an emotion, attitude, etc. 이 작품 제6권에도 동일한 장면이 다음과 같이 묘사되어 있다: "And o'er the Border Beacon, and the waste / Of naked pools, and common crags that lay / Exposed on the bare fell, were scattered love, / The spirit of pleasure, and youth's golden gleam" (VI. 233-6)

3) 소박한 어린 시절에 인간의 위대함의 토대가 마련된다고 한다. Cf. "The Child is father of the Man." ("My Heart Leaps Up")

4) 나이가 들면 "최초의 시 정신"이 쇠퇴함을 의미한다.

5) 워즈워스의 시론에서, 미래의 회복을 위해 언어로써 "과거의 정신"에 "실체와 생명"을 부여한 것이 시다.

[Waiting for Horses]

One Christmas-time,
On the glad eve of its dear holidays,
Feverish, and tired, and restless, I went forth
Into the fields, impatient for the sight
Of those led palfreys that should bear us home;
My brothers and myself.[1] There rose a crag,
That, from the meeting-point of two highways
Ascending, overlooked them both, far stretched[2];
Thither, uncertain on which road to fix
My expectation, thither I repaired,
Scout-like[3], and gained the summit; 'twas a day
Tempestuous, dark, and wild, and on the grass
I sate half-sheltered by a naked wall;
Upon my right hand couched a single sheep,
Upon my left a blasted hawthorn stood;
With those companions at my side, I watched
Straining my eyes intensely, as the mist
Gave intermitting prospect of the copse
And plain beneath. Ere we to school returned,—
That dreary time,—ere we had been ten days
Sojourners in my father's house, he died;
And I and my three brothers, orphans then,
Followed his body to the grave.[4] The event,
With all the sorrow that it brought, appeared
A chastisement; and when I called to mind
That day so lately past, when from the crag
I looked in such anxiety of hope;
With trite reflections of morality,

---

1) 정확한 날자는 1783년 12월 19일이다. 그때 워즈워스의 나이는 13세였고, 그 당시 두 동생들, 즉 Richard와 John도 Hawkshead Grammar School에 다니고 있었다. 1805년 판에는 "those two horses"로 되어 있었으나 여기서는 "those led palfreys"로 수정되어 있다. *palfrey*=승용마(saddle-horse for ordinary riding); *led palfreys*=끌려가는 말, 즉 (바꿔타기 위한) 예비 말.

2) 그는 학교에서 1.5마일 떨어진 Borwick Lodge의 언덕 위에서 말을 기다렸다.

3) *scout-like*: 정찰병(수색병)처럼

4) 그의 부친 John Wordsworth(Senior)는 1783년 12월 30일에 별세했다. 그의 모친은 그로부터 5년 전에 작고했다. 따라서 그는 고아가 된 셈이다. 부친의 장례식에 참석한 형제들은 Richard와 John이었다. 1805년 판에는 "two brothers"로 되어 있다.

Yet in the deepest passion, I bowed low
To God, Who thus corrected my desires;
And, afterwards, the wind and sleety rain,
And all the business of the elements[1],
The single sheep, and the one blasted tree,
And the bleak music from that old stone wall,
The noise of wood and water, and the mist
That on the line of each of those two roads
Advanced in such indisputable shapes;
All these were kindred spectacles and sounds
To which I oft repaired, and thence would drink,
As at a fountain; and on winter nights,
Down to this very time, when storm and rain
Beat on my roof, or, haply, at noon-day,
While in a grove I walk, whose lofty trees,
Laden with summer's thickest foliage, rock
In a strong wind, some working of the spirit,
Some inward agitations thence are brought,
Whate'er their office, whether to beguile
Thoughts over busy in the course they took,
Or animate an hour of vacant ease.

From BOOK FOURTEENTH: CONCLUSION[2]

*　　*　　*

[The Ascent of Snowdon]

---

1) all the business of the elements: 모든 자연현상의 작용; *elements*=4 원소(air, earth, water, fire); *business*=busy-ness, activity

2) 어느 안개 짙은 여름날 일출을 보려고 안내자를 데리고 친구 Jones와 함께 Snowdon 산을 등반한 경험을 묘사한다. 산을 오르는 동안 하늘은 낮게 드리우고 구름이 끼어 비가 올 것만 같았다. 안개 때문에 앞이 보이지 않았다. 정상에 다가가자 땅이 밝아오기 시작했다. 고개를 들었을 때, 하늘에는 밝은 달이 떠있었다. 발아래 거대한 안개 바다가 펼쳐져 있고, 저만치 안개 속에 균열이 보인다. 그 깊고 어두운 숨구멍에서 수많은 물소리가 들려왔다. 이 장엄한 풍경은 시인에게 완벽한 창조적 정신의 이미지로 보였다. 이 창조적 능력, 즉 상상력은 인간이 알고 있는 최고의 능력이다. 시인은 이와 같은 자신의 정신을 형성하는 데에 Dorothy와 Coleridge가 진지하고 애정 어린 도움을 주었음에 찬사를 보낸다. 시인은 단 몇 년 만이라도 인간에게 사랑을 가르쳐 줄 위대한 작품을 쓸 수 있게 해달라는 기원으로 작품을 끝맺는다.

It was a close, warm, breezeless summer night,
Wan, dull, and glaring, with a dripping fog
Low-hung and thick that covered all the sky;
But, undiscouraged, we began to climb
The mountain-side. The mist soon girt us round,
And, after ordinary travellers' talk
With our conductor, pensively we sank
Each into commerce with his private thoughts:
Thus did we breast the ascent, and by myself
Was nothing either seen or heard that checked
Those musings or diverted, save that once
The shepherd's lurcher[1]), who, among the crags,
Had to his joy unearthed a hedgehog[2]), teased
His coiled-up prey with barkings turbulent.
This small adventure, for even such it seemed
In that wild place and at the dead of night,
Being over and forgotten, on we wound
In silence as before. With forehead bent
Earthward, as if in opposition set
Against an enemy, I panted up
With eager pace, and no less eager thoughts.
Thus might we wear a midnight hour away,
Ascending at loose distance each from each,
And I, as chanced, the foremost of the band;
When at my feet the ground appeared to brighten,
And with a step or two seemed brighter still;
Nor was time given to ask or learn the cause,
For instantly a light upon the turf
Fell like a flash, and lo! as I looked up,
The Moon hung naked in a firmament
Of azure without cloud, and at my feet
Rested a silent sea of hoary mist.
A hundred hills their dusky backs upheaved
All over this still ocean; and beyond,

---

1) *lurcher*: (잡종)개 (mongrel)
2) *hedgehog*: 고스도치

Far, far beyond, the solid vapours stretched,
In headlands, tongues, and promontory shapes,
Into the main Atlantic, that appeared
To dwindle, and give up his majesty,
Usurped upon far as the sight could reach.
Not so the ethereal vault; encroachment none
Was there, nor loss; only the inferior stars
Had disappeared, or shed a fainter light
In the clear presence of the full-orbed Moon,
Who, from her sovereign elevation, gazed
Upon the billowy ocean, as it lay
All meek and silent, save that through a rift—
Not distant from the shore whereon we stood,
A fixed, abysmal, gloomy, breathing-place—
Mounted the roar of waters, torrents, streams
Innumerable, roaring with one voice![1]
Heard over earth and sea, and, in that hour,
For so it seemed, felt by the starry heavens.[2]
  When into air had partially dissolved
That vision, given to spirits of the night
And three chance human wanderers, in calm thought
Reflected, it appeared to me the type
Of a majestic intellect, its acts
And its possessions, what it has and craves,
What in itself it is, and would become.
There I beheld the emblem of a mind
That feeds upon infinity[3], that broods
Over the dark abyss, intent to hear
Its voices issuing forth to silent light
In one continuous stream; a mind sustained

---

1) 최초의 Snowdon 풍경 묘사는 워즈워스가 Wales 도보여행을 한지 1년이 지난 1792년 여름에 지은 *Descriptive Sketches*, 492-505행에 나타나 있다.

2) 마지막 두 줄은 Wordsworth가 영국국교의 정통성(orthodoxy)에 맞추기 위해 작품을 수정한 것들 중에서 최악의 수정이라는 평을 듣는 부분이다. 1805년 판은 다음과 같이 되어 있었다: "The universal spectacle throughout / Was shaped for admiration and delight, / Grand in itself alone, but in that breach / Through which the homeless voice of waters rose, / That dark deep thoroughfare, had Nature lodged / The soul, the imagination of the whole"(XIII. 60-65).

3) *the emblem...infinity*: 무한을 먹고 사는 정신의 상징

By recognitions of transcendent power,
In sense conducting to ideal form,
In soul of more than mortal privilege.
One function, above all, of such a mind
Had Nature shadowed there, by putting forth,
'Mid circumstances awful and sublime,
That mutual domination which she loves
To exert upon the face of outward things,
So moulded, joined, abstracted, so endowed
With interchangeable supremacy,
That men, least sensitive, see, hear, perceive,
And cannot choose but feel. The power, which all
Acknowledge when thus moved, which Nature thus
To bodily sense exhibits, is the express
Resemblance of that glorious faculty
That higher minds bear with them as their own.[1]
This is the very spirit in which they deal
With the whole compass of the universe:
They from their native selves can send abroad
Kindred mutations; for themselves create
A like existence; and, whene'er it dawns
Created for them, catch it, or are caught
By its inevitable mastery,
Like angels stopped upon the wing by sound
Of harmony from Heaven's remotest spheres.

---

1) 자연은 "외부 사물의 외형에 작용하는 지배력"으로써 사물의 형태를 만들고(moulded), 사물에 내재하지 않은 속성을 "첨가하며(endowed)", 사물이 가진 속성을 "제거하며(abstracted)", 모든 이질적인 요소를 "종합하여(joined)" 전체 풍경에 통일성을 부여하는 힘을 가지고 있다. 이처럼 자연이 보여주는 힘은 숭고한 정신을 가진 사람들("higher minds"), 즉 시인들이 가진 "영광스러운 능력(that glorious faculty)"을 꼭 닮았다고 한다. 이와 같은 설명은 1815년 시집 서문에 서술된 시적 상상력의 작용과정과 일치한다(*PW*. II. 438-9). Snowdon 풍경 묘사에는 이와 같은 상상력의 작용이 예시되어 있다. 상상력의 상관물인 안개는 바다를 뒤덮음으로써 바다의 물리적 속성을 제거하여 "근원 모를 물소리" (homeless voice of waters-1805)로 변형시키고, 산에 운동을 부여하여 동물처럼 꿈틀거리게 만든다. 또한 안개는 풍경을 하나의 "거대한 안개 바다"로 만들어 전체 풍경에 통일성을 부여한다. 워즈워스는 자연도 시인의 상상력과 같은, 아니 오히려 훨씬 더 위대한, "거룩한 정신기능"을 가지고 있으며, 그 기능이 자연물이나 풍경의 외양에 작용하여 시적 변용을 일으키는 것으로 묘사하고 있다. 다시 말해서 Snowdon 풍경은 자연이 쓴 위대한 한 편의 시이다. (졸저 『회상의 시』, pp. 302-321 참조)

Them the enduring and the transient both
Serve to exalt; they build up greatest things
From least suggestions[1]; ever on the watch,
Willing to work and to be wrought upon,
They need not extraordinary calls
To rouse them; in a world of life they live,
By sensible impressions not enthralled,
But by their quickening impulse made more prompt
To hold fit converse with the spiritual world,
And with the generations of mankind
Spread over time, past, present, and to come,
Age after age, till Time shall be no more.
Such minds are truly from the Deity,
For they are Powers; and hence the highest bliss
That flesh can know is theirs—the consciousness
Of Whom they are, habitually infused
Through every image and through every thought,
And all affections by communion raised
From earth to heaven, from human to divine;
Hence endless occupation for the Soul,
Whether discursive or intuitive[2];
Hence cheerfulness for acts of daily life,
Emotions which best foresight need not fear,
Most worthy then of trust when most intense.
Hence, amid ills that vex and wrongs that crush
Our hearts—if here the words of Holy Writ
May with fit reverence be applied—that peace
Which passeth understanding, that repose
In moral judgments which from this pure source
Must come, or will by man be sought in vain.

*　　*　　*

1) *they build up greatest things / From least suggestions*: 그들(higher minds)은 최소한의 암시로부터 가장 위대한 것을 창조한다. "The Thorn"에 붙인 주석에도 유사한 표현이 나온다: "Imagination, by which word I mean the faculty which produces impressive effects out of simple elements"(*PW*. Ⅱ. 512).

2) *Whether discursive or intuitive*: 논증적이든 직관적이든 간에

Selected Bibliography

1. Primary Sources:

Wordsworth, William. *The Poetical Works of William Wordsworth*, 5 Vols. Ed. by Ernest de Selincourt and Helen Darbishire. Oxford: Clarendon Press, 1952-63.

__________. *The Prelude 1799, 1805, 1850*. A Norton Critical Edition. Eds. by Jonathan Wordsworth, M. H. Abrams, and Stephen Gill. New York: Norton, 1979.

2. Secondary Sources:

Bateson, F. W. *Wordsworth: A Re-interpretation*. London & Colchester: Spottiswoode, Ballantyne and Co. Ltd., 1954.

Bloom, Harold (ed.). *William Wordsworth's The Prelude*. New York: Chelsea House Publishers, 1986.

Clarke, C. C. *Romantic Paradox: An Essay on the Poetry of Wordsworth*. London: Routledge & Kegan Paul, 1962

Durrant, Geoffrey. *William Wordsworth*. Cambridge UP, 1969.

_____. *Wordsworth and the Great System: A Study of Wordsworth's Poetic World*. Cambridge: Cambridge UP, 1970.

Ferry, David. *The Limits of Mortality: An Essay on Wordsworth's Major Poems*. Middletown, Conn.: Wesleyan UP, 1959.

Hartman, Geoffrey H. *Wordsworth's Poetry 1787-1814*. New Haven and London: Yale UP, 1964.

Jones, John. *The Egotistical Sublime: A History of Wordsworth's Imagination*. Westpost, Conn.: 1954.

Noyes, Russell. *William Wordsworth*. Boston: Twayne Publishers, 1971.

Rader, Melvin M. *Presiding Ideas in Wordswort's Poetry*. New York: Gordian Press, 1968.

Read, Herbert. *Wordsworth*. London: Faber and Faber, 1930.

Wordsworth, Jonathan. *William Wordsworth: The Borders of Vision*. Oxford: Clarendon Press, 1982.

朴, 柄熙. 『회상의 시: 워즈워스의 시론』. 울산: 울산대학교 출판부, 2005.

Samuel Taylor Coleridge
(1772~1834)

Coleridge in 1795, aged 23.

A statue of the Ancient Mariner at Watchet Harbour, Somerset, England, unveiled in September 2003 as a tribute to Samuel Taylor Coleridge.

콜리지의 생애와 작품

1772년 10월 21일 영국 데본셔(Devonshire)의 Ottery St. Mary라는 작은 마을에서 목사의 9남1녀 중 막내로 태어났다. 1781년 부친이 별세하고 이듬해에 런던에 있는 Christ's Hospital Preparatory School에 다녔다. 그는 몽상적이고 다혈질적이며 남달리 조숙한 학생이었다. 1791년에 Cambridge 대학의 Jesus College에 입학했다. 진학 당시 그는 모범학생이었으나, 대학에서 지적 자극을 찾지 못하여 나태와 방종을 일삼게 되어 절망적으로 런던으로 도망하게 된다. 거기서 그는 Silas Tomkyn Comberbache라는 가명으로 용기병에 입대했다. 형제들이 그를 구출하여 다시 대학에 복학했으나, 1794년에 끝내 학위를 받지 못하고 대학을 떠나고 말았다.

1794년 6월 그는 Oxford 대학에 다니고 있던 Robert Southey를 만났고, 이들은 전망 없는 영국을 떠나 미국의 써스퀴해너 강 유역에 이상적인 공동체인 Pantisocracy의 건설 계획을 함께 추진했다. 이것은 열렬한 프랑스혁명 지지자였던 그에게 혁명 실패에 대한 보상적 대안이었고, 이를 위해 Southey의 처제인 Sara Fricker와 사랑이 없는 결혼을 할 정도로 적극적이었다. 그러나 두 사람은 웨일즈에서 공동체를 시범운영하는 문제로 싸웠고, 콜리지는 1795년에 Bristol에서 정치와 종교에 관한 일련의 대중간연을 했다. 그가 워즈워스를 만난 것은 이 무렵이었다.

콜리지는 1795년에 Wordsworth를 만나 친교를 맺었고, 그와 함께 『서정담시집』을 출판하였는데, 이것은 영국 낭만주의의 시작을 알리는 중요한 문학사적 사건이었다. 이 시집의 첫 부분에 수록된 "The Rime of the Ancient Mariner", 아편을 피우고 환상 속에서 창작했다고 하는 "Kubla Khan", 미완성의 서사시 "Christabel" 등은 환상적이고 상징적인 상황묘사를 통해 인간의식의 심연을 탐구한 걸작들이다. 그 밖에도 1797년에서 1798년 사이에 소위 대화시(conversation poems)라 불리는 작품들을 썼다.

콜리지는 시집을 출판하고 나서 워즈워스 남매와 함께 독일로 갔다. 그곳에서 그는 괴팅겐 대학에 다니면서 후기 칸트파 독일철학자 및 비평가들에 관한 평생에 걸친 연구를 시작하였다. 이것은 철학과 종교와 미학에 관한 그의 사상을 심화시키는데 결정적인 역할을 하였다. 1800년 귀국한 그는 호수지방의 케지크(Keswick)에 있는 그레타 홀(Greta Hall)에 정착하였다. 그는 아내에 대해 불만을 품어오다가 워즈워스의 아내가 된 메리의 언니인 사라 허치슨(Sara Hutchinson)과 절망적인 사랑에 빠지게 되었다.

콜리지는 일생동안 갖가지 질병에 시달렸고, 때때로 갑작스런 발작을 일으키기도 했다. 그래서 그는 의사의 처방에 따라 장기간 아편을 복용하고 있었다. 1800년부터 1801년 사이에 류머티즘을 치료하기 위해 아편을 과다복용한 나머지 아편 중독자가 되었다. 그와 동시에 그의 창작능력은 급속히 감퇴되었고, 1802년에 발표한 "Dejection: An Ode"는 그의 건강과 행복 및 시 창작에 대한 절망적인 고별사였다.

1804년 그는 아내와 헤어지기로 결심하고 지중해의 Malta 섬에 가서 2년간 요양을 하였으나 건강은 더욱 악화되었다. 1806년 여름에 영국에 돌아왔을 때는 거의 폐인이 되다시피 했다. 이러한 상황에서 콜리지가 보인 문학에 대한 열정은 실로 영웅적인 것이었다. 그는 1808년 1월부터 6월 사이에 런던에서 "시의 원리"에 관한 일련의 공개강연을 했다. 그리고 1809년에는 신문에 기고하는 한편 The Friend라는 문예지를 혼자 힘으로 집필하고 제작하여 배포하였다. 이 일은 그 후 약 14개월간 지속되었다. 그러다가 1810년에는 잡지 편집을 그만두었고, 심한 언쟁 끝에 워즈워스와 결별하고 런던으로 떠났다. 1813년에는 그의 희곡 Remorse가 드루리 레인(Drury Lane) 극장에서 20회나 공연되는 성공을 거두기도 했다.

콜리지는 1816년 런던 북쪽 교외의 Highgate에 거처를 마련하고 훌륭한 의사 길먼(James Gillman)의 치료를 받기 시작하였다. 그의 치료는 콜리지의 아편 복용을 근절시키지는 못했으나 다행히 복용량을 줄여주었다. 길먼 부부와 함께 보낸 그의 여생은 그 어느 때보다 평온하고 행복했다. 아내와의 관계도 원만해지고 워즈워스와도 화해하여 1828년에는 라인 지방을 함께 여행했다. 그는 1834년 7월 25일 길먼 박사의 집에서 세상을 떠났다.

하이게이트에 있던 그의 방은 친구들과 런던의 문인들 그리고 순례자들이 모이는 장소가 되었다. 왜냐하면 콜리지의 입담은 쇠퇴기에 접어들어서도 여전히 마력을 지니고 있었기 때문이었다.

그는 시와 더불어 평론으로 대성하였으며, 대표적 평론집인『문학평전』(Biographia Literaria) (1817)을 출판했다. 이 평론집은 영국 낭만주의 시대의 가장 중요한 비평서이며, 이 책에서 18세기말과 19세기 초 독일 관념철학을 영국 독자들에게 소개했다.

콜리지가 18세기 경험주의를 비판하여, 인간 최고의 능력으로서 상상력의 우위를 강조한 이론은 후대에 영향을 끼쳤다. 그의 사상은 종교와 정치 영역에까지 미쳤으며, 19세기 중엽의 그리스도교 사상에도 영향을 주었다. 오늘날에야 비로소 발간되고 있는 그의 방대한 <수첩>은 프로이드를 예언하는 심리적 통찰로 가득 찬 기록이기도 하다.

The Æolian Harp

My pensive[1)] Sara! thy soft cheek reclined
Thus on mine arm, most soothing sweet it is
To sit beside our Cot, our Cot o'ergrown
With white-flower'd Jasmin, and the broad-leav'd Myrtle,
(Meet[2)] emblems they of Innocence and Love!)
And watch the clouds, that late were rich with light,
Slow saddenning round[3)], and mark the star of eve[4)]
Serenely brilliant (such should Wisdom be)
Shine opposite! How exquisite the scents
Snatch'd from yon bean-field! and the world so hush'd!
The stilly murmur of the distant Sea
Tells us of silence.

---

* Composed August 20th 1795 at Clevedon, Somersetshire. 원숙기의 대화시(conversation poems)와 초자연적인 주제를 다룬 작품의 경향을 미리 엿볼 수 있는 초기 시이다. 이 작품에서 시인은 자연의 풍경과 그 속에 살고 있는 자비로운 신성을 아름답게 묘사하고 있다. "*The Eolian Harp* (1975) is a honeymoon poem in which we encounter a dialectic between two Coleridges, the imaginative and intellectually daring poet, and the timidly orthodox young husband...." (Bloom 195).

* 대화시(conversation poems): "시인이 사사로운 계기에 친밀한 대화체의 어조와 리듬을 통해 그의 생각에 공감할 수 있는 가까운 주변 인물들에게 말을 건네는 형식의 시"(윤준 20). "Coleridge wanted to mimic the patterns and cadences of everyday speech in his poetry. Many of his poems openly address a single figure—the speaker's wife, son, friend, and so on—who listens silently to the simple, straightforward language of the speaker. Unlike the descriptive, long, digressive poems of Coleridge's classicist predecessors, Coleridge's so-called conversation poems are short, self-contained, and often without a discernable poetic form. Colloquial, spontaneous, and friendly, Coleridge's conversation poetry is also highly personal, frequently incorporating events and details of his domestic life in an effort to widen the scope of possible poetic content. Although he sometimes wrote in blank verse, unrhymed iambic pentameter, he adapted this metrical form to suit a more colloquial rhythm. Both Wordsworth and Coleridge believed that everyday language and speech rhythms would help broaden poetry's audience to include the middle and lower classes, who might have felt excluded or put off by the form and content of neoclassicists, such as Alexander Pope, Lady Mary Wortley Montagu, and John Dryden." (Spark Notes)

1) *pensive Sara*: 명상에 잠긴 사라(Sara Fricker); pensive=plunged in thought, sorrowfully thoughtful; Coleridge는 Robert Southey와 함께 만민평등사회(Pantisocracy) 건설을 계획하고 그 사회의 일원이 되기 위해 1794년 8-9월에 Sara Fricker와 약혼하였고 1795년 10월에 그녀와 결혼했다.
2) *meet*: suitable, proper
3) *Slow saddening round*: 주변이 서서히 슬픔에 물드는; 앞줄의 cloud를 수식한다.
4) *the star of eve*: 저녁별 (개밥바라기)

And that simplest Lute[1),]
Plac'd length-ways in the clasping casement[2)], hark!
How by the desultory[3)] breeze caress'd,
Like some coy maid half-yielding to her lover,
It pours such sweet upbraiding[4)], as must needs
Tempt to repeat the wrong[5)]! And now, its strings
Boldlier swept, the long sequacious[6)] notes
Over delicious surges sink and rise,
Such a soft floating witchery of sound[7)]
As twilight Elfins make, when they at eve
Voyage on gentle gales from Faery-Land,
Where Melodies round honey-dropping flowers,
Footless and wild, like birds of Paradise,
Nor pause, nor perch, hovering on untam'd wing!
O! the one Life within us and abroad[8)],
Which meets all motion and becomes its soul,
A light in sound, a sound-like power in light,[9)]
Rhythm in all thought, and joyance every where—
Methinks, it should have been impossible
Not to love all things in a world so fill'd;
Where the breeze warbles, and the mute still air

---

1) *lute*: 류트 (기타 비슷한 14-17세기 현악기); 이 작품의 제목으로 사용된 "에올리언 하프"를 의미한다. 바람이 불면 저절로 소리를 낸다는 이 악기는 흔히 낭만적 감수성의 상징으로 사용된다. Cf. 워즈워스도 *The Prelude* (1850)에서 유사한 이미지를 사용했다: "[I] was obedient as the lute / That waits upon the touches of the wind" (III. 141-2).
2) *clasping casement*: 애무하는 창틀; 창들이 마치 류트를 껴안고 애무하고 있는 것처럼 묘사되어 있다. 이것은 또한 "애인에게 반쯤 몸을 맡긴 수줍은 처녀"와 연결된다.
3) *desultory*: 변덕스런, 산만한 (going constantly from one subject to another)
4) upbraiding: 비난, 책망; *upbraid*=chide or reproach
5) *the wrong*: 비행 (wrong action, what is morally wrong); 즉 애무를 의미한다; 류트는 바람에게 좀 더 적극적인 애무를 하라고 유혹한다.
6) *sequacious*: 유연한 (pliable), 일관된 (following one another with consistent and ordered regularity)
7) *a soft floating witchery of sound*: 부드럽게 떠다니는 소리의 마법; 앞에 나온 the long sequacious notes와 동격이다.
8) *the one Life within us and abroad*: 우리의 내부와 외부에 존재하는 하나의 생명; 이것은 워즈워스가 "Tintern Abbey"와 *The Prelude* 에서 우주에 충만한 신성이라는 범신론적 의미로 사용한 "Being" 또는 "Presence"의 개념과 유사하다.
9) 소리 속의 빛, 빛 속의 소리 같은 힘; 공감각 심상의 하나이다. 빛은 일종의 소리 같은 힘을 가지며, 소리는 빛처럼 마음에 영향을 준다: 소리와 빛은 바람과 하프처럼, 콜리지와 사라처럼 창조적 조화 속에 "하나의 생명" 안에 통합된다.

Is Music slumbering on her instrument.[1)]

And thus, my Love! as on the midway slope
Of yonder hill I stretch my limbs at noon,
Whilst thro' my half-clos'd eye-lids I behold
The sunbeams dance, like diamonds, on the main,
And tranquil[2)] muse upon tranquility;
Full many a thought uncall'd and undetain'd[3)],
And many idle flitting phantasies,
Traverse[4)] my indolent[5)] and passive brain,
As wild and various, as the random gales[6)]
That swell and flutter on this subject Lute![7)]

And what if all of animated nature
Be but organic Harps[8)] diversly fram'd,
That tremble into thought, as o'er them sweeps
Plastic and vast[9)], one intellectual breeze[10)],
At once the Soul of each, and God of all?

But thy more serious eye a mild reproof[11)]
Darts, O belovéd Woman! nor such thoughts

---

1) "침묵하는 바람"은 하프 위에 잠든 (잠재적) 음악이다.
2) *tranquil*: 고요하게 (tranquilly, calmly)
3) *undetain'd*: 붙잡지 않은; *detain*: 붙잡다 (keep in a place, delay, hold)
4) *traverse*: move through
5) *indolent*=lazy, averse to exertion
6) *random gales*: 멋대로 부는 광풍; *random*=not sent in a special direction; *gale*=very strong wind, storm
7) *subject Lute*: 순응하는 류트; *subject*=obedient, submissive. 이 paragraph에서 시인은 자신을 에올리언 하프에 비유하고 있다. 산기슭에 누워 명상에 잠겨 있으면, "부르지도 붙잡지도 않은(uncall'd and undetain'd)" 온갖 생각과 환상들이 "수동적인 뇌"를 스쳐지나간다.
8) *what if ... organic Harps*: 만약 생동하는 자연의 만물이 살아있는 하프라면 어떨까. 시인은 자기 자신 뿐만 아니라 모든 생명체를 "하나의 생명"이라는 바람이 사상을 연주하는 에올리언 하프에 비유하고 있다.
9) *palstic and vast*: 유연하고 거대하게
10) *one intellectual breeze*: 하나의 영적인 바람; *intellectual*=spiritual; 자연 속에 충만한 "하나의 생명"을 영적인 바람에 비유하고 있다.
11) *a mild reproof*: 부드러운 책망; Sara는 콜리지의 범신론적 상상이 정통 기독교 사상과 맞지 않는다고 나무란다. 그러나 그녀는 그의 생각을 부정하지 않고 단지 "하나님과 겸허하게 걸어가라고 명한다."

Dim and unhallow'd dost thou not reject,[1]
And biddest me walk humbly with my God.
Meek Daughter in the Family of Christ![2]
Well hast thou said and holily disprais'd[3]
These shapings of the unregenerate mind[4];
Bubbles that glitter as they rise and break
On vain Philosophy's aye-babbling spring.[5]
For never guiltless may I speak of him,
The Incomprehensible![6] save when with awe
I praise him, and with Faith that inly feels[7];
Who with his saving mercies[8] healéd me,
A sinful and most miserable man,
Wilder'd[9] and dark[10], and gave[11] me to possess
Peace, and this Cot, and thee, heart-honour'd[12] Maid!

August 20, 1975 (1976)

---

1) *nor such thoughts / Dim and unhallow'd dost thou not reject*: 그대는 이러한 생각이 불분명하고 부정하다고 거부하지 않는다; *reject*=refuse to accept; *unhallowed*=unholy, profane
2) *Meek daughter of the Family of Christ*: 그리스도 가족의 유순한 딸; Sara가 독실한 기독교인(orthodox Christian)임을 의미한다.
3) *dispraise*: 나무라다, 책망하다 (censure)
4) *shapings of the unregenerate mind:* 사악한(갱생하지 못한) 정신이 만들어낸 생각; *unregenerate*=not regenerate(=spiritually reborn), 사악한, 죄 많은 (sinful, inveterately wrong)
5) 시인은 자신의 생각을 "한가로이 떠다니는 환상" 또는 "끝없이 재잘대는 공허한 철학의 샘물위에 / 일어나 부서지며 반짝이는 거품"에 비유하고 있다. 그는 진지한(신앙심 깊은) Sara 앞에서 자신의 자유로운 상상을 농담처럼 가볍게 취급한다. 이러한 태도는 자신의 사색이 범신론적 경향에 빠질 위험성을 깨달은 데서 나온 것이다. "The Imagination wishes to be indulged, and Coleridge feared the moral consequences of such indulgence"(Bloom 196).
6) *The Incomprehensible*: 이해할 수 없는 존재; 즉 신(God)을 의미한다. 정통 기독교에서 신은 초자연적이고 인간의 이성이나 상상력으로 파악할 수 없는 신비로운 존재로 여겨진다. 이러한 신의 개념은 4연까지의 시인의 사색과 배치된다.
7) *inly feel*: be consciously perceived in the heart
8) *saving mercies*: 구원의 자비, 나약한 인간을 죄악에서 구원해주는 신의 자비를 의미한다; *save*=preserve from damnation; *mercy*=God's forbearance and forgiveness of sins
9) *wilder'd*: 당황한 (bewildered), 어쩔 줄을 모르는 (confused, led astray)
10) *dark*: 어둠에 싸인, 사악한 (evil, devoid of moral or spiritual light), 우울한 (gloomy, 무지몽매한 (totally blind, ignorant)
11) *gave*: allowed
12) *heart-honour'd*: 마음으로부터 존경 받는. 고결한 (noble-minded)

This Lime-Tree Bower My Prison

Well, they[1] are gone, and here must I remain,
This lime-tree bower my prison![2] I have lost
Beauties and feelings, such as would have been
Most sweet to my remembrance even when age
Had dimm'd mine eyes to blindness! They, meanwhile,
Friends, whom I never more may meet again,
On springy heath[3], along the hill-top edge,
Wander in gladness, and wind down, perchance,
To that still roaring dell, of which I told;
The roaring dell, o'erwooded[4], narrow, deep,
And only speckled by the mid-day sun;
Where its slim trunk the ash from rock to rock
Flings arching like a bridge[5];—that branchless ash,
Unsunn'd and damp, whose few poor yellow leaves
Ne'er tremble in the gale, yet tremble still,
Fann'd by the water-fall! and there my friends
Behold the dark green file of long lank weeds[6],
That all at once (a most fantastic sight!)
Still nod and drip beneath the dripping edge
Of the blue clay-stone.[7]

---

* "In the June of 1797 some long-expected friends paid a visit to the author's cottage; and on the morning of their arrival, he met with an accident, which disabled him from walking during the whole of their stay. One evening, when they had left him for a few hours, he composed the following lines in the garden-bower."(Coleridge's Note) 이 시는 자연과 인간의 조화로운 관계, 행복한 우정, 자연의 아름다움을 함께 나누는 기쁨을 노래한 시이다. 우리 인간은 "the one Life within us and abroad" ("The Aeolian Harp")로 인하여 직접 눈으로 보든 보지 못하든 간에 자연에서 기쁨을 얻는다.

1) *they*: 벗들 (즉 Lamb과 Wordsworth)

2) 혼자 남겨진 처지를 한탄하며 보리수 그늘을 감옥으로 생각한다.

3) *springy heath*: 탄력 있는 히스; *springy*=탄력 있는, 용수철 같은 (elastic, resilient)

4) *o'erwooded*: over-wooded; 숲이 우거진

5) *Where its slim...like a bridge*: 물푸레나무가 가느다란 줄기로 바위들 사이에 다리 모양의 아치를 만들어 놓은 곳; where의 선행사는 the roaring dell이며, 이 절의 주어는 the ash이다.

6) *the dark green file of long lank weeds*: 짙은 초록으로 줄 지어 늘어선 길고 가느다란 잡초들

7) 이 paragraph에서 시인은 자연과 접촉할 기회를 상실한 채 고립된 상태에서 친구들이 가고 있을 산책 경로를 상상하고 있다. *clay-stone*: 점토암

Now, my friends emerge
Beneath the wide wide Heaven—and view again
The many-steepled tract magnificent[1])
Of hilly fields and meadows, and the sea,
With some fair bark, perhaps, whose sails light up
The slip of smooth clear blue[2]) betwixt two Isles
Of purple shadow! Yes! they wander on
In gladness all; but thou, methinks[3]), most glad,
My gentle-hearted Charles[4])! for thou hast pined
And hunger'd after Nature, many a year,
In the great City pent[5]), winning thy way
With sad yet patient soul, through[6]) evil and pain
And strange calamity[7])! Ah! slowly sink
Behind the western ridge, thou glorious Sun!
Shine in the slant beams of the sinking orb[8]),
Ye purple heath-flowers! richlier burn, ye clouds!
Live in the yellow light, ye distant groves!
And kindle, thou blue Ocean! So my friend
Struck with deep joy may stand, as I have stood,
Silent with swimming sense[9]); yea, gazing round
On the wide landscape, gaze[10]) till all doth seem
Less gross than bodily; and of such hues
As veil the Almighty Spirit[11]), when yet he makes

---

1) 첨탑이 많은 웅장한 지대; *tract*: 넓은 지대 (a large stretch of land)
2) *the slip of smooth clear blue*: 한 조각 잔잔하고 맑은 바다; *slip*=a long, relatively thin and narrow piece or strip
3) *methinks*: it seems to me
4) *Charles*: i. e., Charles Lamb
5) *pent*: pen의 과거분사; *pen*=가두다 (enclose, shut in, confine)
6) *win one way through*: 헤쳐 나가다
7) *calamity*: 역경, 불행 (adversity, a grievous disaster)
8) *the slant beams of the sinking orb*: 비스듬히 비치는 석양; *orb*=구체 (sphere), 천체 (heavenly body)
9) swimming sense: 어지러운 감각; *swim*=have dizzy effect, appear to reel or whirl
10) *gaze*: my friend...may gaze; 시인은 친구 Charles가 석양에 물든 히스 꽃, 구름, 수풀, 바다, 등으로 이루어진 아름다운 자연 풍경을 보고 감명을 받고 있을 것이라 상상한다.
11) till all doth...*the Almighty Spirit*: 만물이 물질적인 것보다 덜 비천해 보이고, 전능한 영혼을 감싸고 있는 그런 빛깔을 띠고 있는 것처럼 보일 때까지; *the Almighty Spirit*=전능한 영혼,

Spirits perceive his presence.[1)]

A delight
Comes sudden on my heart, and I am glad
As I myself were there![2)] Nor in this bower,
This little lime-tree bower, have I not mark'd
Much that has sooth'd me.[3)] Pale beneath the blaze
Hung the transparent foliage; and I watch'd
Some broad and sunny leaf, and lov'd to see
The shadow of the leaf and stem above
Dappling its sunshine! And that walnut-tree
Was richly ting'd, and a deep radiance lay
Full on the ancient ivy, which usurps[4)]
Those fronting[5)] elms, and now, with blackest mass
Makes their dark branches gleam a lighter hu
Through the late twilight: and though now the bat
Wheels silent by, and not a swallow twitters,
Yet still the solitary humble-bee[6)]
Sings in the bean-flower! Henceforth I shall know
That Nature ne'er deserts the wise and pure[7)];
No plot so narrow, be but Nature there,[8)]

즉 신(God); seem...of such hues로 연결된다. "물질저긴 것보다 덜 비천해 보인다."는 말은 만물이 영적인 것으로 보인다는 의미이다. 그리고 신(God)을 감싸고 있는 빛은 "천국의 빛"과 같은 것이다.

1) 영혼이 그의 존재를 느끼게 만든다는 말은 그도 영적인 존재가 된다는 것을 의미한다.
2) 그러한 상상을 하고 있을 때, 시인도 마치 친구들과 함께 걷고 있는 것처럼 기쁨을 느낀다. 그는 더 이상 보리수 그늘을 감옥으로 생각하지 않는다. 보리수 그늘에서도 자연은 매우 아름답기에, 그도 사랑과 미를 느낀다. 그 장소에 가 있든 그렇지 않든 간에 자연은 현명하고 순수한 사람들에게 풍부한 기쁨의 원천이 된다.
3) *Nor in this bower...sooth'd me*: 나는 이 그늘에서, 이 작은 보리수 그늘에서 내게 위안을 준 많은 것을 보아왔다. 그 다음 이어지는 47-59행에서 넓은 보리수 잎, 후두나무, 담쟁이, 느릅나무, 박쥐, 땅벌 등 보리수 그늘에서 볼 수 있는 아름다운 자연 풍경을 묘사한다.
4) *usurp*: 침범하다 (encroach)
5) *fronting*: 마주 보는 (facing, confronting)
6) *humble-bee*: 땅벌 (bumble-bee)
7) *I shall know / That Nature ne'er deserts the wise and pure*: 나는 자연이 현명하고 순수한 사람들을 버리지 않는다는 것을 알게 되리라. Cf. "And this prayer I make, / Knowing that Nature never did betray / The heart that loved her."(Wordsworth, "Tintern Abbey," ll. 121-3)
8) 자연이 그곳에 있기만 하면, 어떤 장소도 좁은 곳이 아니다; *be but Nature* there=if but there be Nature there

No waste so vacant, but may well employ
Each faculty of sense, and keep the heart
Awake to Love and Beauty![1] and sometimes
'Tis well to be bereft of promis'd good[2],
That we may lift the soul, and contemplate
With lively joy the joys we cannot share.
My gentle-hearted Charles! when the last rook
Beat its straight path across the dusky air
Homewards, I blest it! deeming its black wing
(Now a dim speck, now vanishing in light)
Had cross'd the mighty Orb's dilated glory[3],
While thou stood'st gazing; or, when all was still,
Flew creaking o'er thy head[4], and had a charm
For thee, my gentle-hearted Charles, to whom
No sound is dissonant which tells of Life[5].

June 1797

---

1) *No waste...Love and Beauty*: 황무지도 모든 감각을 사로잡아 가슴이 사랑과 미에 깨어있게 만들지 못할 정도도 텅 비어 있지는 않다. 즉 "황무지도 텅 빈 것 같지만, 우리의 감각을 사로잡아 사랑과 미를 느끼게 만든다."는 뜻이다. No waste is so vacant...but may....의 구문이다. 여기서 but는 "that...not"의 뜻을 가진 관계대명사이다. Cf. There is no one but knows it. (그것을 모르는 사람은 아무도 없다.)

2) *'Tis well to be bereft of promis'd good*: 약속된 이득을 빼앗겨도 좋다; 즉 친구들과 함께 아름다운 자연 속을 몸소 산책하지 못해도 상상 속에서 생생한 기쁨을 공감할 수 있다는 뜻이다.

3) *the mighty Orb's dilated glory*: 거대한 천구(태양)의 팽창된 빛; *dilate*=make larger, enlarge, expand

4) *flew creaking over thy head*: 그대 머리 위로 까옥까옥 울음 울며 날아갔다; *creak*=(of a crow, rook, goose) 까옥까옥 울다 (utter a harsh cry)

5) 그대에게는 생명을 알리는 어떤 소리도 불협화음이 아니다.

Frost at Midnight

The Frost performs its secret ministry[1],
Unhelped by any wind. The owlet's cry
Came loud—and hark, again! loud as before.
The inmates of my cottage, all at rest,
Have left me to that solitude, which suits
Abstruser musings: save that at my side
My cradled infant[2] slumbers peacefully.
'Tis calm indeed! so calm, that it disturbs
And vexes[3] meditation with its strange
And extreme silentness. Sea, hill, and wood,
This populous village[4]! Sea, and hill, and wood,
With all the numberless goings-on of life[5],
Inaudible as dreams! the thin blue flame
Lies on my low-burnt fire, and quivers not;
Only that film[6], which fluttered on the grate,
Still flutters there, the sole unquiet thing.
Methinks, its motion in this hush of nature
Gives it dim sympathies with me who live,[7]
Making it a companionable form[8],
Whose puny flaps and freaks[9] the idling Spirit
By its own moods interprets, every where
Echo or mirror seeking of itself[10],

---

1) *performs its secret ministry*: 은밀하게 임무를 수행한다; *ministry*=function, office
2) *My cradled infant*: 요람에 잠든 내 아기, 즉 아들 Hartley
3) *vex*: agitate, disturb
4) *populous village*: 사람들로 붐비는 마을; *populous*=thickly inhabited
5) *goings-on of life*: 인생사; *goings-on*=proceedings, frolics
6) *film*: 피막(被膜), 검댕; 벽난로 받침쇠 위에서 파닥이는 검댕을 의미한다. 이것은 당대에 예기치 않은 방문객의 도착을 알리는 징조라는 속설이 있었다. 이 작품 26행의 "a fluttering stranger"는 여기서 유래한 표현이다. "In all parts of the kingdom these films are called strangers and supposed to portend the arrival of some absent friend(Coleridge's Note)".
7) its motion...who live: 자연의 정적 속에서 그 움직임은 살아있는 나와 어렴풋이 공감한다.
8) *a companionable form*: 어울리는 형태, 벗할 수 있는 형태; *companionable*=fitted to match
9) *puny flaps and freaks*: 미약한 펄럭임과 변덕; *freak*=caprice, whim
10) 그 자체의 메아리 혹은 닮은꼴을 찾으며; 어순은 "seeking echo or mirror of itself"이다.

And makes a toy of Thought.

But O! how oft,
How oft, at school, with most believing mind,
Presageful[1], have I gazed upon the bars,
To watch that fluttering stranger[2]! and as oft
With unclosed lids, already had I dreamt
Of my sweet birth-place[3], and the old church-tower,
Whose bells, the poor man's only music, rang
From morn to evening, all the hot Fair-day[4],
So sweetly, that they stirred and haunted me
With a wild pleasure, falling on mine ear
Most like articulate sounds[5] of things to come!
So gazed I, till the soothing things, I dreamt,
Lulled me to sleep, and sleep prolonged my dreams!
And so I brooded all the following morn,
Awed by the stern preceptor's face[6], mine eye
Fixed with mock study[7] on my swimming book[8]:
Save if the door half opened, and I snatched
A hasty glance, and still my heart leaped up,
For still I hoped to see the stranger's face,
Townsman, or aunt, or sister more beloved,
My play-mate when we both were clothed alike!

Dear Babe, that sleepest cradled by my side,
Whose gentle breathings, heard in this deep calm,

---

mirror=본보기, 귀감 (pattern, exemplar)

1) *presageful*: 예감하는 (having a presentiment)

2) *that fluttering stranger*: 저 나풀거리는 '손님': 15행의 "that film"을 의미한다.

3) Coleridge의 출생지는 Devonshire의 Ottery St. Mary이다.

4) *Fair-day*: 장날

5) *articulate sounds*: 분명한 소리; *articulate*=뜻이 분명한 (with clearly distinguishable parts, each having meaning)

6) *Awed by the stern preceptor's face*: 엄한 선생의 얼굴이 두려워; "엄한 선생"은 콜리지가 다니던 학교(Christ's Hospital)의 Rev. James Boyer이다 (*Biographia Literaria*, Chapter I 참조)

7) *with mock study*: 공부하는 척하며

8) *swimming book*: (글자가) 어른거리는 책

Fill up the interspersed vacancies[1)]
And momentary pauses of the thought!
My babe so beautiful! it thrills my heart
With tender gladness, thus to look at thee,
And think that thou shall learn far other lore,
And in far other scenes! For I was reared
In the great city, pent 'mid cloisters dim[2)],
And saw nought lovely but the sky and stars.
But thou, my babe! shalt wander like a breeze
By lakes and sandy shores, beneath the crags
Of ancient mountain, and beneath the clouds,
Which image[3)] in their bulk both lakes and shores
And mountain crags: so shalt thou see and hear
The lovely shapes and sounds intelligible
Of that eternal language, which thy God
Utters, who from eternity doth teach
Himself in all, and all things in himself.
Great universal Teacher! he shall mould
Thy spirit, and by giving make it ask.
  Therefore all seasons shall be sweet to thee,
Whether the summer clothe the general earth
With greenness, or the redbreast sit and sing
Betwixt the tufts of snow on the bare branch
Of mossy apple-tree, while the nigh thatch
Smokes in the sun-thaw; whether the eave-drops fall
Heard only in the trances of the blast,
Or if the secret ministry of frost
Shall hang them up in silent icicles,
Quietly shining to the quiet Moon.

February, 1798 (1798)

---

1) *interspersed vacancies*: 간헐적인 공백
2) *dim cloisters*: 어둠침침한 수도원
3) *image*: 닮다 (copy, resemble)

The Nightingale

A Conversation Poem, April, 1798

No cloud, no relique[1] of the sunken day
Distinguishes[2] the West, no long thin slip
Of sullen light, no obscure[3] trembling hues.
Come, we will rest on this old mossy bridge!
You see the glimmer of the stream beneath,
But hear no murmuring: it flows silently.
O'er its soft bed[4] of verdure. All is still.
A balmy[5] night! and though the stars be dim,
Yet let us think upon the vernal showers
That gladden the green earth, and we shall find
A pleasure in the dimness of the stars.
And hark! the Nightingale begins its song,
'Most musical, most melancholy'[6] bird!
A melancholy bird? Oh! idle[7] thought!
In Nature there is nothing melancholy.
But some night-wandering man whose heart was pierced
With the remembrance of a grievous[8] wrong,
Or slow distemper[9], or neglected love,
(And so, poor wretch! filled all things with himself,
And made all gentle sounds tell back the tale
Of his own sorrow) he, and such as he,
First named these notes a melancholy strain.
And many a poet echoes the conceit[10];

---

1) *relique*: what is left behind
2) *distinguish*: make noteworthy or outstanding
3) *obscure*: dark, gloomy
4) *bed*: bottom of a river
5) *balmy*: fragrant, soft and mild, soothing
6) *'Most musical, most melancholy'*: '가장 음악적이고, 가장 우울한'; John Milton, "Il Penseroso", 62행. 나이팅게일은 전통적으로 슬픈 노래를 부르는 새로 묘사되어왔다.
7) *idle*: vain, groundless, useless
8) *grievous*: causing grief, severe, flagrant, heinous
9) *distemper*: ailment of body or mind, illness, disease
10) *echoed the conceit*: 그 같은 생각을 모방했다; *conceit*: an idea, a fanciful notion; *echo*= repeat, imitate

Poet who hath been building up the rhyme
When he had better far have stretched his limbs
Beside a brook in mossy forest-dell,
By sun or moon-light, to the influxes[1)]
Of shapes and sounds and shifting elements[2)]
Surrendering his whole spirit, of his song
And of his fame forgetful! so his fame
Should share in Nature's immortality,
A venerable thing! and so his song
Should make all Nature lovelier, and itself
Be loved like Nature! But 'twill not be so;
And youths and maidens most poetical[3)],
Who lose the deepening twilights of the spring
In ball-rooms and hot theatres, they still
Full of meek sympathy must heave their sighs
O'er Philomela's[4)] pity-pleading strains.

My Friend, and thou, our Sister! we have learnt
A different lore[5)]: we may not thus profane
Nature's sweet voices, always full of love
And joyance! 'Tis the merry Nightingale
That crowds and hurries, and precipitates[6)]
With fast thick warble his delicious notes,
As he were fearful that an April night
Would be too short for him to utter forth
His love-chant, and disburthen[7)] his full soul
Of all its music!

And I know a grove

---

1) *influx*: flowing in
2) *elements*: atmospheric agencies, esp. wind and storm
3) *poetical*: fond of poetry, able to appreciate poetry
4) *Philomela*: Procne's sister in Greek mythology, who was transformed into a nightingale.
5) *different lore*: 다른 가르침, 즉 나이팅게일의 노래가 우울한 노래가 아니라고 배웠다는 의미이다. lore=가르침 (the act of teaching, instruction, education), 지식 (that which is taught, learning)
6) *precipitate*: 내던지다 (throw down headlong, hurl or fling down)
7) *disburthen*: 짐을 내리다 (unload, remove a burden from), 쏟아내다 (discharge)

Of large extent, hard by a castle huge,
Which the great lord inhabits not; and so
This grove is wild[1] with tangling underwood[2],
And the trim[3] walks are broken up, and grass,
Thin grass and king-cups grow within the paths.
But never elsewhere in one place I knew
So many nightingales; and far and near,
In wood and thicket, over the wide grove,
They answer and provoke each other's song,
With skirmish[4] and capricious passagings[5],
And murmurs musical[6] and swift jug jug,
And one low piping[7] sound more sweet than all
Stirring the air with such a harmony,
That should you close your eyes, you might almost
Forget it was not day![8] On moonlight bushes,
Whose dewy leaflets are but half-disclosed,
You may perchance behold them on the twigs,
Their bright, bright eyes, their eyes both bright and full,
Glistening, while many a glow-worm in the shade
Lights up her love-torch.
                    A most gentle Maid,
Who dwelleth in her hospitable home
Hard by the castle, and at latest eve
(Even like a Lady vowed and dedicate
To something more than Nature in the grove)

---

1) *wild*: disorderly, uncultivated
2) *underwood*: 덤불 (underbrush; small trees, shrubs, etc. growing beneath higher timber trees)
3) *trim*: well arranged, neat
4) *skirmish*: 사소한 싸움 (a bout of irregular fighting), 작은 충돌 (slight engagement)
5) *passaging*: 치고받기(an exchange of blows), 말다툼 (an amorous exchange of words); *passage*=fence with words, argue
6) *murmurs musical*: 아름다운 속삭임; musical=harmonious, melodious
7) *piping*: high-pitched and clear, whistling
8) 58-64행: 영주의 숲에서 일어난 나이팅게일의 합주를 묘사한 이 부분은 Wordsworth의 "There Was a Boy"에 묘사된 소년과 올빼미들의 합주와 흡사하다. "they would shout / Across the watery vale, and shout again, / Responsive to his call, with quivering peals, / And long halloos and screams, and echoes loud, / Redoubled and redoubled, concourse wild / Of jocund dim." (*The Prelude*; 1850, V, 374-9)

Glides through the pathways; she knows all their notes,
That gentle Maid! and oft, a moment's space,
What time the moon was lost behind a cloud,
Hath heard a pause of silence; till the moon
Emerging, hath awakened earth and sky
With one sensation[1], and those wakeful birds
Have all burst forth in choral minstrelsy[2],
As if some sudden gale had swept at once
A hundred airy harps![3] And she hath watched
Many a nightingale perch giddily
On blossomy twig still swinging from the breeze,
And to that motion tune his wanton[4] song
Like tipsy[5] Joy that reels with tossing head.

Farewell! O Warbler! till tomorrow eve,
And you, my friends! farewell, a short farewell!
We have been loitering long and pleasantly,
And now for our dear homes. That strain again!
Full fain it would delay me! My dear babe,
Who, capable of no articulate sound,
Mars all things with his imitative lisp,
How he would place his hand beside his ear,
His little hand, the small forefinger up,
And bid us listen! And I deem it wise
To make him Nature's play-mate. He knows well
The evening-star; and once, when he awoke
In most distressful mood (some inward pain
Had made up that strange thing, an infant's dream)
I hurried with him to our orchard-plot,

---

1) *sensation*: 강한 자극 (strong stimulation)

2) *minstrelsy*: 음유시인의 노래 (minstrel poetry)

3) 75-82행: 빛과 소리, 달빛과 나이팅게일의 노래의 조화(공명)는 "The Aeolian Harp"에 나오는 "A light in sound, a sound-like power in light"라는 표현을 연상시킨다. 이것은 우주에 충만한 신성인 "the one Life within and abroad"를 느끼는 순간을 의미한다. *airy harps*: Aeolian harps

4) *wanton*: 흥겨운, 경쾌한 (gay, lively)

5) *tipsy*: slightly intoxicated

And he beheld the moon, and, hushed at once,
Suspends his sobs, and laughs most silently,
While his fair eyes, that swam with undropped tears,
Did glitter in the yellow moon-beam! Well!
It is a father's tale: But if that Heaven
Should give me life, his childhood shall grow up
Familiar with these songs, that with the night
He may associate joy. Once more, farewell,
Sweet Nightingale! once more, my friends! farewell.

April 1798 (1798)

The Rime of the Ancient Mariner

IN SEVEN PARTS

Facile credo, plures esse Naturas invisibiles quam visibiles in rerum universitate. Sed horum omnium familiam quis nobis enarrabit? et gradus et cognationes et discrimina et singulorum munera? Quid agunt? quae loca habitant? Harum rerum notitiam semper ambivit ingenium humanum, nunquam attigit. Juvat, interea, non diffiteor, quandoque in animo, tanquam in tabulâ, majoris et melioris mundi imaginem contemplari: ne mens assuefacta hodiernae vitae minutiis se contrahat nimis, et tota subsidat in pusillas cogitationes. Sed veritati interea invigilandum est, modusque servandus, ut certa ab incertis, diem a nocte, distinguamus.[1)]

T. Burnet, Archaeol. Phil., p. 68

Argument[2)]

How a Ship having passed the Line was driven by storms to the cold Country towards the South Pole; and how from thence she made her course to the tropical Latitude of the Great Pacific Ocean; and of the strange things that befell; and in what manner the Ancyent Marinere came back to his own Country.

PART I[3)]

An ancient Mariner meeteth three Gallants[4)] *bidden to a wedding-feast, and*

---

1) Latin epigraph: "I readily believe that there are more invisible than visible Natures in the universe. But who will explain for us the family of all these beings, and the ranks and relations and distinguishing features and functions of each? What do they do? What places do they inhabit? The human mind has always sought the knowledge of these things, but never attained it. Meanwhile I do not deny that it is helpful sometimes to contemplate in the mind, as on a tablet, the image of a greater and better world, lest the intellect, habituated to the petty things of daily life, narrow itself and sink wholly into trivial thoughts. But at the same time we must be watchful for the truth and keep a sense of proportion, so that we may distinguish the certain from the uncertain, day from night."—Adapted by Coleridge from Thomas Burnet, *Archaeologiae philosophicae* (1692)

2) *Argument*: summary; Cf. "How a Ship, *having first sailed to the Equator*, was driven by Storms to the cold Country towards the South Pole; how *the Ancient Mariner cruelly and in contempt of the laws of hospitality killed a Seabird and how he was followed by many and strange Judgements*: and in what manner he came back to his own Country."(1800)

3) 제1부: 노수부가 결혼하객 한 사람을 멈춰 세우고 이야기를 시작한다. 배는 폭풍으로 남극까지 밀려간다. 노수부가 Christ의 상징인 신천옹(Albatross)을 죽인다.

4) *gallant*: 멋쟁이(man of fashion), 신사 (fine gentleman)

detaineth one.

It is an ancient Mariner,
And he stoppeth one of three.
"By thy long beard and glittering eye,
Now wherefore stopp'st thou me?

The Bridegroom's doors are opened wide,
And I am next of kin;
The guests are met, the feast is set:
May'st hear the merry din."

He holds him with his skinny hand,
"There was a ship," quoth[1] he.
"Hold off! unhand me, grey-beard loon[2]!"
Eftsoons[3] his hand dropt he.

The Wedding-Guest is spell-bound by the eye of the old seafaring man, and constrained to hear his tale.

He holds him with his glittering eye—
The Wedding-Guest stood still,
And listens like a three years' child:
The Mariner hath his will[4].

The Wedding-Guest sat on a stone :
He cannot choose but hear;
And thus spake[5] on that ancient man,
The bright-eyed Mariner.
"The ship was cheered, the harbour cleared[6],

---

1) *quoth*: said
2) *loon*: 건달, 불량배 (rogue, idler, a worthless person)
3) *eftsoons*: at once
4) *hath his will*: 뜻을 이루다 (gets what he desires)
5) *spake*: spoke
6) *cleared*: was cleared: *clear*: (항구를) 벗어나다 (pass through or away from)

Merrily did we drop[1)]
Below the kirk[2)], below the hill,
Below the lighthouse top.

The Mariner tells how the ship sailed southward with a good wind and fair weather, till it reached the Line.

The Sun came up upon the left,
Out of the sea came he!
And he shone bright, and on the right
Went down into the sea.

Higher and higher every day,
Till over the mast at noon[3)]—"
The Wedding-Guest here beat his breast,
For he heard the loud bassoon.

The Wedding-Guest heareth the bridal music ; but the Mariner continueth his tale.

The bride hath paced into the hall,
Red as a rose is she;
Nodding their heads before her goes
The merry minstrelsy[4)].

The Wedding-Guest he beat his breast,
Yet he cannot choose but hear;
And thus spake on that ancient man,
The bright-eyed Mariner.

The ship driven by a storm toward the south pole.

"And now the STORM-BLAST came, and he

---

1) *drop*: be carried gently downstream by the wind or current
2) *kirk*: church
3) 배가 적도(equator)에 도착했음을 의미한다.
4) *minstrelsy*: 음유시인들 (body of minstrels)

Was tyrannous and strong:
He struck with his o'ertaking wings[1)],
And chased us south along.

With sloping masts and dipping prow,
As who[2)] pursued with yell and blow
Still treads the shadow of his foe,
And forward bends his head,
The ship drove fast, loud roared the blast,
The southward aye[3)] we fled.

And now there came both mist and snow,
And it grew wondrous[4)] cold:
And ice, mast-high, came floating by,
As green as emerald.

The land of ice, and of fearful sounds where no living thing was to be seen.

And through the drifts the snowy clifts[5)]
Did send a dismal sheen[6)]:
Nor shapes of men nor beasts we ken[7)]—
The ice was all between.

The ice was here, the ice was there,
The ice was all around:
It cracked and growled, and roared and howled[8)],

---

1) *overtaking wings*: 덮치는 날개
2) *as who*: as one who
3) *aye*: ever, always
4) *wondrous*: 놀랄 만큼, 굉장히 (wonderfully)
5) *clifts*: cliffs
6) *sheen*: brightness, splendour; *dismal sheen*: 어두운 광채 (gloomy brightness)
7) *ken*: 보다 (see), 알다 (know)
8) *cracked and growled, and roared and howled*; 얼음은 깨어지고, 으르렁거리고, 고함치고, 울부짖었소, *growl*: (개가 성이 나서) 으르렁거리다, (천둥이) 울리다 (rumble); *roar*: (사자가) 노호하다, 울부짖다; *howl*: (늑대가) 소리를 길게 뽑으며 짖다 (emit a long loud doleful cry); 시인은 남극에서 얼음이 갈라지는 신비로운 소리를 이 모든 소리가 한꺼번에 울리는 것에 비유하여

Like noises in a swound[1]!

Till a great sea-bird, called the Albatross, came through the snow-fog, and was received with great joy and hospitality.

At length did cross an Albatross,
Thorough[2] the fog it came;
As if it had been a Christian soul,
We hailed it in God's name.

It ate the food it ne'er had eat[3],
And round and round it flew.
The ice did split with a thunder-fit;
The helmsman steered us through!

And lo! the Albatross proveth a bird of good omen, and followeth the ship as it returned northward through fog and floating ice.

And a good south wind sprung[4] up behind;
The Albatross did follow,
And every day, for food or play,
Came to the mariner's hollo!

In mist or cloud, on mast or shroud[5],
It perched for vespers nine;
Whiles all the night, through fog-smoke white,
Glimmered the white Moon-shine."

The ancient Mariner inhospitably killeth the pious bird of good omen.

묘사하고 있다.

1) *swound*: swoon, 기절, 졸도 (fainting-fit); 얼음이 갈라지는 소리를 다시 졸도할 때 들리는 소리에 비유하고 있다.

2) *thorough*: through

3) *had eat*: had eaten

4) *sprung*: sprang

5) *shroud*: 돛대 밧줄 (rope supporting the mast)

"God save thee, ancient Mariner!
From the fiends, that plague thee thus!—
Why look'st thou so?"—With my cross-bow[1]
I shot the Albatross.[2]

PART II[3]

The Sun now rose upon the right:[4]
Out of the sea came he,
Still hid in mist, and on the left
Went down into the sea.

And the good south wind still blew behind,
But no sweet bird did follow,
Nor any day for food or play
Came to the mariners' hollo!

His shipmates cry out against the ancient Mariner, for killing the bird of good luck.

And I had done an hellish thing,
And it would work 'em woe[5]:
For all averred, I had killed the bird
That made the breeze to blow.
Ah wretch[6]! said they, the bird to slay,
That made the breeze to blow!

---

1) *cross-bow*: 십자궁, 석궁

2) 노수부가 신천옹을 죽이는 행위는 "하나의 생명"(the one Life)에 대한 범죄이다. "The Eolian Harp"에 묘사된 대로 "하나의 생명"은 우리의 내부와 외부에 존재한다. 따라서 노수부의 죄는 창조된 세계에 대한 죄인 동시에 그 자신에 대한 죄이다. (Watson 163)

3) 제2부: 배는 북쪽으로 태평양을 향해 항해한다. 적도에 다다르자 무풍상태에 직면한다. 무풍상태는 상상력의 고갈, 또는 죽음의 상태를 상징한다. 선원들이 모든 죄를 노수부에게 덮어씌운다.

4) 배는 Cape Horn을 돌아서 북쪽에 있는 태평양으로 향한다.

5) *work 'em woe*: 선원들에게 화가 미치다

6) *wretch*: 비열한 놈 (a despicable person, a person without conscience or shame)

But when the fog cleared off, they justify the same, and thus make themselves accomplices in the crime.

Nor dim nor red, like God's own head,
The glorious Sun uprist[1]):
Then all averred, I had killed the bird
That brought the fog and mist.
'Twas right, said they, such birds to slay,
That bring the fog and mist.[2])

The fair breeze continues; the ship enters the Pacific Ocean, and sails northward, even till it reaches the Line.

The fair breeze blew, the white foam flew,
The furrow followed free;
We were the first that ever burst
Into that silent sea.

The ship hath been suddenly becalmed.

Down dropt the breeze, the sails dropt down,
'Twas sad as sad could be;
And we did speak only to break
The silence of the sea!

All in a hot and copper sky,
The bloody Sun, at noon,
Right up above the mast did stand,
No bigger than the Moon.

Day after day, day after day,
We stuck, nor breath nor motion[3]);

---

1) *uprist:* uprose
2) 노수부의 범죄에 대한 세평이 엇갈린다.
3) *nor breath nor motion*: neither wind nor tide

As idle[1] as a painted ship
Upon a painted ocean.

And the Albatross begins to be avenged.

Water, water, every where,
And all the boards did shrink;
Water, water, every where,
Nor any drop to drink.

The very deep did rot: O Christ![2]
That ever this should be!
Yea, slimy things did crawl with legs
Upon the slimy sea.

About, about, in reel and rout[3]
The death-fires[4] danced at night;
The water, like a witch's oils,
Burnt green, and blue and white.

A Spirit had followed them; one of the invisible inhabitants of this planet, neither departed souls nor angels; concerning whom the learned Jew, Josephus[5], and the Platonic Constantinopolitan[6], Michael Psellus[7], may be consulted. They are very numerous, and there is no climate or element without one or more.

And some in dreams assuréd were
Of the Spirit that plagued us so;
Nine fathom deep[8] he had followed us

---

1) *idle*: motionless
2) *O Christ!*: 맙소사! (놀람을 나타내는 감탄사)
3) *in reel or rout*: 요란하게 선회하며; *reel*=선회 (a whirl), (스코틀랜드의) 경쾌한 민속춤(a lively folk dance): *rout*=riot, tumult, uproar
4) *death-fires*: 도깨비불, 성엘모의 불 (St. Elmo's fire, corposant); 폭풍우의 밤에 돛대나 비행기 날개 등에 나타나는 방전 현상으로 죽음의 징조로 여겨짐.
5) *Josephus*: Flavius Josephus (37?-100), 요세푸스, 유태의 역사가
6) *Constantinopolitan*: 콘스탄티노플(이스탄불) 사람
7) Michael Psellus: 미카엘 프셀루스(1018-1078), 비잔틴의 정치가, 학자, 작가
8) *nine fathom deep*: 아홉 길 물속에서

From the land of mist and snow.

And every tongue, through utter drought[1],
Was withered at the root;
We could not speak, no more than if
We had been choked with soot.

The shipmates, in their sore distress, would fain throw the whole guilt on the ancient Mariner: in sign whereof they hang the dead sea-bird round his neck.

Ah! well a-day![2] what evil looks
Had I from old and young!
Instead of the cross, the Albatross
About my neck was hung.

PART III[3]

There passed a weary time. Each throat
Was parched, and glazed[4] each eye.
A weary time! a weary time!
How glazed each weary eye,
When looking westward, I beheld
A something in the sky.

The ancient Mariner beholdeth a sign in the element afar off.

At first it seemed a little speck,
And then it seemed a mist;
It moved and moved, and took at last
A certain shape, I wist[5].

---

1) *through utter drought*: 심한 갈증으로, 너무나 목이 말라; *drought*=thirst
2) *well a-day*: welladay, 슬프도다
3) 제3부: 유령선 나타나, 그 배의 두 유령, 즉 Death와 Life-in-Death가 싸워 후자가 Mariner의 영혼을 차지한다. 다른 선원들은 모두 죽는다. 노수부는 죄의식에 고립되어 고행을 한다.
4) *glaze*: 흐려지다 (become glassy)
5) *wist*: knew; wit의 과거, 과거분사 형

A speck, a mist, a shape, I wist!
And still it neared and neared :
As if it dodged a water-sprite[1],
It plunged and tacked and veered.[2]

At its nearer approach, it seemeth him to be a ship ; and at a dear ransom he freeth his speech from the bonds of thirst.

With throats unslaked[3], with black lips baked,
We could nor laugh nor wail;
Through utter drought all dumb we stood!
I bit my arm, I sucked the blood,
And cried, A sail! a sail!

A flash of joy[4];

With throats unslaked, with black lips baked,
Agape[5] they heard me call :
Gramercy![6] they for joy did grin,
And all at once their breath drew in,
As they were drinking all.

And horror follows. For can it be a ship that comes onward without wind or tide?

See! see! (I cried) she tacks no more!
Hither[7] to work us weal[8];
Without a breeze, without a tide,

---

1) water-sprite: 물의 요정; *sprite*=elf, fairy
2) 물에 잠기고 이리 저리 방향을 바꾸었다; tack=갈지자로 나아가다, 방향을 바꾸다 (change ship's course by turning head to wind)
3) with throats unslaked: 목이 마르고; *slake*=갈증을 해소하다 (quench one's thirst)
4) A flash of joy: 한 순간의 기쁨; *flash*=instant
5) *agape*: 입을 벌린 채 (open-mouthed with wonder or expectation)
6) *Gramercy!*: Great thanks! (프랑스어 'grand-merci'에서 유래)
7) *Hither*: She comes hither
8) *weal*: benefit, good fortune

She steadies[1] with upright keel!

The western wave was all a-flame.
The day was well nigh done!
Almost upon the western wave
Rested the broad bright Sun;
When that strange shape drove suddenly
Betwixt us and the Sun.

It seemeth him[2] but the skeleton of a ship.

And straight the Sun was flecked with bars[3],
(Heaven's Mother send us grace!)
As if through a dungeon-grate[4] he peered[5]
With broad and burning face.

And its ribs are seen as bars on the face of the setting Sun.

Alas! (thought I, and my heart beat loud)
How fast she nears and nears!
Are those her sails that glance in the Sun,
Like restless gossameres[6]?

The Spectre-Woman and her Death-mate, and no other on board the skeleton ship.

And those her ribs through which the Sun
Did peer, as through a grate?
And is that Woman all her crew?
Is that a DEATH? and are there two?
Is DEATH that woman's mate?

---

1) *steady*: move steadily
2) *seemed him*: seemed to him
3) the Sun was flecked with bars: 태양이 막대 무늬로 얼룩져 있었다; *fleck*=얼룩지게 하다 (mark with flecks, dapple)
4) *dungeon-grate*: 지하 감옥의 쇠창살
5) *peer*: 들여다보다 (peep)
6) *restless gossameres*: 바람에 떠있는 거미줄

Like vessel, like crew![1]

Her lips were red, her looks were free,
Her locks were yellow as gold:
Her skin was as white as leprosy,
The Night-mare[2] LIFE-IN-DEATH[3] was she,
Who thicks man's blood with cold.

Death and Life-in-Death have diced for the ship's crew, and she (the latter) winneth the ancient Mariner.

The naked hulk alongside came,
And the twain were casting dice;
'The game is done! I've won! I've won!'
Quoth she, and whistles thrice.

No twilight within the courts of the Sun[4]. ·

The Sun's rim dips; the stars rush out :
At one stride comes the dark;
With far-heard whisper, o'er the sea,
Off shot the spectre-bark[5].

At the rising of the Moon,

We listened and looked sideways up!
Fear at my heart, as at a cup,
My life-blood seemed to sip![6]
The stars were dim, and thick the night,
The steerman's face by his lamp gleamed white;
From the sails the dew did drip—

1) *Like vessel, like crew!*: 그 배에 그 승무원이라!
2) *nightmare*: 몽마 (female monster supposedly sitting on and seeming to suffocate sleeper)
3) LIFE-IN-DEATH: 사중생(死中生)
4) *courts of the Sun*: 태양의 궁정
5) 유령선이 손살 같이 사라졌다; *Off shot*: shot off; 손살 같이 사라졌다
6) "My life's blood"는 동사 "sip"의 목적어

Till clomb[1] above the eastern bar[2]
The hornéd Moon, with one bright star
Within the nether tip.

One after another,

One after one, by[3] the star-dogged Moon[4],
Too quick for groan or sigh,
Each turned his face with a ghastly pang,
And cursed me with his eye.

His shipmates drop down dead.

Four times fifty living men,
(And I heard nor sigh nor groan)
With heavy thump, a lifeless lump,
They dropped down one by one.

But Life-in-Death begins her work on the ancient Mariner.

The souls did from their bodies fly,—
They fled to bliss or woe!
And every soul, it passed me by,
Like the whizz of my cross-bow!

PART IV[5]

The Wedding-Guest feareth that a Spirit is talking to him;
"I fear thee, ancient Mariner!

---

1) *clomb*: climbed
2) *eastern bar*: 동쪽 수평선; *bar*=horizon
3) *by*: by the light of
4) *star-dogged Moon*: 별에게 좇기는 달; Cf. "It is a common superstition among sailors that something evil is about to happen whenever a star dogs the moon." (MS. note by Coleridge)
5) 제4부에서는 노수부의 참담한 고행이 묘사된다, 노두부는 물뱀의 모습에서 아름다움과 사랑을 느끼고 그들을 축복한다. 그때 기도의 말문이 열린다.

I fear thy skinny hand!
And thou art long, and lank, and brown,
As is the ribbed sea-sand.

I fear thee and thy glittering eye,
And thy skinny hand, so brown"—
Fear not, fear not, thou Wedding-Guest!
This body dropt not down.

But the ancient Mariner assureth him of his bodily life, and proceedeth to relate his horrible penance[1].

Alone, alone, all, all alone,
Alone on a wide wide sea!
And never a saint took pity on
My soul in agony.

He despiseth the creatures of the calm,

The many men, so beautiful!
And they all dead did lie:
And a thousand thousand slimy things
Lived on; and so did I.

And envieth that they should live, and so many lie dead.

I looked upon the rotting sea,
And drew my eyes away;
I looked upon the rotting deck,
And there the dead men lay.

I looked to heaven, and tried to pray;
But or ever a prayer had gusht,

---

1) *penance*: 고행(苦行); (가톨릭) 고해(告解), 통회(痛悔), 사죄(赦罪) 성사 (the sacrament of confession, contrition and absolution)

A wicked whisper came, and made
My heart as dry as dust.

I closed my lids, and kept them close,
And the balls like pulses beat;
For the sky and the sea, and the sea and the sky
Lay like a load on my weary eye,
And the dead were at my feet.

But the curse liveth for him in the eye of the dead men.

The cold sweat melted from their limbs,
Nor rot nor reek[1] did they:
The look with which they looked on me
Had never passed away.

An orphan's curse would drag to hell
A spirit from on high;
But oh! more horrible than that
Is the curse in a dead man's eye!
Seven days, seven nights, I saw that curse,
And yet I could not die.

In his loneliness and fixedness he yearneth towards the journeying Moon, and the stars that still sojourn, yet still move onward ; and every where the blue sky belongs to them, and is their appointed rest, and their native country and their own natural homes, which they enter unannounced, as lords that are certainly expected and yet there is a silent joy at their arrival.

The moving Moon went up the sky,
And no where did abide:
Softly she was going up,
And a star or two beside—

Her beams bemocked[2] the sultry main,

---

1) *reek*: 악취가 나다 (smell unpleasantly, of corruption)
2) *bemock*: 비웃다 (mock, flout)

Like April hoar-frost spread;
But where the ship's huge shadow lay,
The charméd water burnt alway[1]
A still and awful red.

By the light of the Moon he beholdeth God's creatures of the great calm.

Beyond the shadow of the ship,
I watched the water-snakes :
They moved in tracks of shining white,
And when they reared, the elfish light
Fell off in hoary flakes.

Within the shadow of the ship
I watched their rich attire:
Blue, glossy green, and velvet black,
They coiled and swam; and every track
Was a flash of golden fire.

Their beauty and their happiness. He blesseth them in his heart.

O happy living things! no tongue
Their beauty might declare:
A spring of love gushed from my heart,
And I blessed them unaware[2]:
Sure my kind saint took pity on me,
And I blessed them unaware.

The spell begins to break.

The self-same moment I could pray;
And from my neck so free
The Albatross fell off, and sank

---

1) *alway*: always (운을 맞추기 위해 s를 생략하였음)
2) *unaware*: unawares

Like lead into the sea.

PART V[1]

Oh sleep! it is a gentle thing,
Beloved from pole to pole!
To Mary Queen the praise be given!
She sent the gentle sleep from Heaven,
That slid into my soul.

By grace of the holy Mother, the ancient Mariner is refreshed with rain.

The silly[2] buckets on the deck,
That had so[3] long remained,
I dreamt that they were filled with dew;
And when I awoke, it rained.

My lips were wet, my throat was cold,
My garments all were dank;
Sure I had drunken in my dreams,
And still my body drank.

I moved, and could not feel my limbs:
I was so light—almost
I thought that I had died in sleep,
And was a blesséd ghost.

He heareth sounds and seeth strange sights and commotions in the sky and the element.

And soon I heard a roaring wind:
It did not come anear[4];

---

1) 제5부에서는 비가 내리고 바람이 불기 시작한다. 배가 다시 움직인다. 정령으로 채워진 죽은 수부들이 일어나 노를 젓는다. 다음날 다시 배가 멈춘다. Polar Spirit의 복수가 시작된다.
2) silly: simple, futile
3) so: silly; "so"는 "long"을 수식하는 것이 아니라 remained와 연결된다.
4) *anear*: near

But with its sound it shook the sails,
That were so thin and sere.

The upper air burst into life!
And a hundred fire-flags sheen[1],
To and fro they were hurried about!
And to and fro, and in and out,
The wan stars danced between.

And the coming wind did roar more loud,
And the sails did sigh like sedge;
And the rain poured down from one black cloud;
The Moon was at its edge.

The thick black cloud was cleft, and still
The Moon was at its side:
Like waters shot from some high crag,
The lightning fell with never a jag,
A river steep and wide.

The bodies of the ship's crew are inspired, and the ship moves on;

The loud wind never reached the ship,
Yet now the ship moved on!
Beneath the lightning and the Moon
The dead men gave a groan.

They groaned, they stirred, they all uprose,
Nor spake, nor moved their eyes;
It had been strange, even in a dream,
To have seen those dead men rise.

The helmsman steered, the ship moved on;
Yet never a breeze up-blew;

---

1) *fire-flags sheen*: 밝은 불 깃발 (bright meteoric flames)

The mariners all 'gan[1] work the ropes,
Where they were wont to do;
They raised their limbs like lifeless tools—
We were a ghastly crew.

The body of my brother's son
Stood by me, knee to knee:
The body and I pulled at one rope,
But he said nought to me.

But not by the souls of the men, nor by dæmons of earth or middle air, but by a blessed troop of angelic spirits, sent down by the invocation of the guardian saint.

"I fear thee, ancient Mariner!"
Be calm, thou Wedding-Guest!
'Twas not those souls that fled in pain,
Which to their corses[2] came again,
But a troop of spirits blest:

For when it dawned—they dropped their arms,
And clustered round the mast;
Sweet sounds rose slowly through their mouths,
And from their bodies passed.

Around, around, flew each sweet sound,
Then darted to the Sun;
Slowly the sounds came back again,
Now mixed, now one by one.

Sometimes a-dropping from the sky
I heard the sky-lark sing;
Sometimes all little birds that are,

1) '*gan*: began
2) *corses*: corpses

How they seemed to fill the sea and air
With their sweet jargoning[1])!

And now 'twas like all instruments,
Now like a lonely flute;
And now it is an angel's song,
That makes the heavens be mute.

It ceased; yet still the sails made on
A pleasant noise till noon,
A noise like of a hidden brook
In the leafy month of June,
That to the sleeping woods all night
Singeth a quiet tune.

Till noon we quietly sailed on,
Yet never a breeze did breathe:
Slowly and smoothly went the ship,
Moved onward from beneath.

The lonesome Spirit from the south-pole carries on the ship as far as the Line, in obedience to the angelic troop, but still requireth vengeance.

Under the keel nine fathom deep,
From the land of mist and snow,
The spirit slid: and it was he
That made the ship to go.
The sails at noon left off their tune,
And the ship stood still also.

The Sun, right up above the mast,
Had fixed her to the ocean:
But in a minute she 'gan stir,
With a short uneasy motion—

---

1) *jargoning*: warbling

Backwards and forwards half her length
With a short uneasy motion.

Then like a pawing horse let go,
She made a sudden bound:
It flung the blood into my head,
And I fell down in a swound.

The Polar Spirit's fellow-dæmons, the invisible inhabitants of the element, take part in his wrong; and two of them relate, one to the other, that penance long and heavy for the ancient Mariner hath been accorded to the Polar Spirit, who returneth southward.

How long in that same fit I lay,
I have not to declare;
But ere my living life returned,
I heard and in my soul discerned
Two voices in the air.

"Is it he?" quoth one, "Is this the man?
By him who died on cross,
With his cruel bow he laid full low
The harmless Albatross.

The spirit who bideth by himself
In the land of mist and snow,
He loved the bird that loved the man
Who shot him with his bow."

The other was a softer voice,
As soft as honey-dew:
Quoth he, "The man hath penance done,
And penance more will do."

PART VI[1)]

FIRST VOICE

"But tell me, tell me! speak again,
Thy soft response renewing—
What makes that ship drive on so fast?
What is the ocean doing?"

SECOND VOICE

"Still as a slave before his lord,
The ocean hath no blast;
His great bright eye most silently
Up to the Moon is cast—

If he may know which way to go;
For she guides him smooth or grim.
See, brother, see! how graciously
She looketh down on him."

The Mariner hath been cast into a trance ; for the angelic power causeth the vessel to drive northward faster than human life could endure.

FIRST VOICE

"But why drives on that ship so fast,
Without or wave or wind?"

SECOND VOICE

"The air is cut away before,
And closes from behind.

---

1) 제6부: 노수부가 혼수상태에서 깨어나고 고행이 다시 시작된다. 선원들의 시체가 노수부에게 저주의 눈길을 보낸다. 다시 순풍이 불고 배가 움직이고, 노수부는 고향에 도착한다. 천사의 무리가 선원들의 시체를 떠난다. 곧 노 젓는 소리가 들리고 수로안내인(Pilot)의 함성이 들리고 보트가 나타난다. 수로안내인과 그의 아들이 다가오고 선량한 은자(Hermit)의 음성이 들려온다. 은자가 노수부의 고해를 듣고 죄를 용서하고 천신홍의 피를 씻어줄 것이라 생각한다.

Fly, brother, fly! more high, more high!
Or we shall be belated:
For slow and slow that ship will go,
When the Mariner's trance is abated."

The supernatural motion is retarded ; the Mariner awakes, and his penance begins anew.

I woke, and we were sailing on
As in a gentle weather:
'Twas night, calm night, the moon was high;
The dead men stood together.

All stood together on the deck,
For a charnel-dungeon fitter:
All fixed on me their stony eyes,
That in the Moon did glitter.

The pang, the curse, with which they died,
Had never passed away:
I could not draw my eyes from theirs,
Nor turn them up to pray.

The curse is finally expiated[1].

And now this spell was snapt: once more
I viewed the ocean green,
And looked far forth, yet little saw
Of what had else been seen—

Like one, that on a lonesome road
Doth walk in fear and dread,
And having once turned round walks on,
And turns no more his head;

---

1) *expiate*: put an end to

Because he knows, a frightful fiend
Doth close behind him tread.

But soon there breathed a wind on me,
Nor sound nor motion made:
Its path was not upon the sea,
In ripple or in shade.

It raised my hair, it fanned my cheek
Like a meadow-gale of spring—
It mingled strangely with my fears,
Yet it felt like a welcoming.

Swiftly, swiftly flew the ship,
Yet she sailed softly too:
Sweetly, sweetly blew the breeze—
On me alone it blew.

And the ancient Mariner beholdeth his native country.

Oh! dream of joy! is this indeed
The light-house top I see?
Is this the hill? is this the kirk?
Is this mine own countree?

We drifted o'er the harbour-bar[1],
And I with sobs did pray—
O let me be awake, my God!
Or let me sleep alway.

The harbour-bay was clear as glass,
So smoothly it was strewn!
And on the bay the moonlight lay,
And the shadow of the Moon.

---

1) *harbour-bar*: 항구의 모래톱; bar=a bank of sand across the mouth of a harbour)

The rock shone bright, the kirk no less,
That stands above the rock:
The moonlight steeped in silentness[1]
The steady weathercock.

The angelic spirits leave the dead bodies,

And the bay was white with silent light,
Till rising from the same[2],
Full many shapes, that shadows were,
In crimson colours came.

And appear in their own forms of light.

A little distance from the prow
Those crimson shadows were:
I turned my eyes upon the deck—
Oh, Christ! what saw I there!

Each corse lay flat, lifeless and flat,
And, by the holy rood[3]!
A man all light, a seraph-man,
On every corse there stood.

This seraph-band, each waved his hand:
It was a heavenly sight!
They stood as signals to the land,
Each one a lovely light;

This seraph-band, each waved his hand:
No voice did they impart—

---

1) *silentness*: silence
2) *the same*: i. e., the bay
3) *rood*: cross

No voice; but oh! the silence sank
Like music on my heart.

But soon I heard the dash of oars,
I heard the Pilot's cheer;
My head was turned perforce[1] away
And I saw a boat appear.

The Pilot and the Pilot's boy,
I heard them coming fast:
Dear Lord in Heaven! it was a joy
The dead men could not blast.

I saw a third—I heard his voice :
It is the Hermit good!
He singeth loud his godly hymns
That he makes in the wood.
He'll shrieve[2] my soul, he'll wash away
The Albatross's blood.

PART VII[3]

The Hermit of the Wood,

This Hermit good lives in that wood
Which slopes down to the sea.
How loudly his sweet voice he rears!

---

1) *perforce*: by force

2) *shrieve*: shrive, 고해를 듣다 (hear the confessions), 고해를 듣고 죄를 용서하다

3) 제7부: 보트가 배에 다가오자 배가 요란한 굉음을 내며 침몰한다. 노수부의 몸이 물위에 떠오르고, 수로 안내인이 비명을 지르며 기절한다. 은자는 앉은 자리에서 기도를 한다. 노수부가 노를 젓자 소년이 놀란다. 노수부는 뭍에 오른다. 은자가 성호를 그리며 "당신 어떤 사람이요?"하고 묻는다. 그러자 노수부의 몸이 비틀리며 고통을 받는다. 이야기를 하고 나면 다시 자유로워진다. 때때로 고통이 찾아오면 가슴이 뜨거워지고 이야기를 들어줄 사람을 찾아 자신이 겪은 이야기를 들려준다. 노인은 이야기를 마치고 결혼하객과 작별을 한다. 그는 결혼하객에게 교훈적인 말을 남긴다. 결혼하객은 잔칫집에 들어가지도 않고 돌아간다. 다음날 일어났을 때, 그는 더 슬프고 더 현명한 사람이 되어 있었다.

He loves to talk with marineres
That come from a far countree.

He kneels at morn, and noon, and eve—
He hath a cushion plump[1]:
It is the moss that wholly hides
The rotted old oak-stump.

The skiff-boat[2] neared: I heard them talk,
"Why, this is strange, I trow[3]!
Where are those lights so many and fair,
That signal made but now?"

Approacheth the ship with wonder.

"Strange, by my faith!" the Hermit said—
"And they answered not our cheer!
The planks looked warped! and see those sails,
How thin they are and sere!
I never saw aught like to them,
Unless perchance it were

Brown skeletons of leaves that lag
My forest-brook along;
When the ivy-tod[4] is heavy with snow,
And the owlet whoops to the wolf below,
That eats the she-wolf's young."

"Dear Lord! it hath a fiendish look—
(The Pilot made reply)
I am a-feared[5]"—"Push on, push on!"

---

1) plump: 폭신폭신한 (having a full rounded shape, filled out)
2) *skiff-boat*: 작은 보트 (a light rowing boat)
3) *trow*: believe
4) *ivy-tod*: 담쟁이덩굴 (clump of ivy)
5) *a-feared*: afraid

Said the Hermit cheerily.

The boat came closer to the ship,
But I nor spake nor stirred;
The boat came close beneath the ship,
And straight a sound was heard.

The ship suddenly sinketh.

Under the water it rumbled on,
Still louder and more dread:
It reached the ship, it split the bay;
The ship went down like lead.

The ancient Mariner is saved in the Pilot's boat.

Stunned[1] by that loud and dreadful sound,
Which sky and ocean smote,
Like one that hath been seven days drowned
My body lay afloat;
But swift as dreams, myself I found
Within the Pilot's boat.

Upon the whirl, where sank the ship,
The boat spun round and round;
And all was still, save that the hill
Was telling of[2] the sound.

I moved my lips—the Pilot shrieked
And fell down in a fit;
The holy Hermit raised his eyes,
And prayed where he did sit.

---

1) *Stunned*: 귀가 멍멍해져서; *stun*=deafen temporarily
2) *telling of*: echoing

I took the oars: the Pilot's boy,
Who now doth crazy go,
Laughed loud and long, and all the while
His eyes went to and fro.
"Ha! ha!" quoth he, "full plain I see,
The Devil knows how to row."

And now, all in my own countree,
I stood on the firm land!
The Hermit stepped forth from the boat,
And scarcely he could stand.

The ancient Mariner earnestly entreateth the Hermit to shrieve him ; and the penance of life falls on him.

"O shrieve me, shrieve me, holy man!"
The Hermit crossed his brow.
"Say quick," quoth he, "I bid thee say—
What manner[1] of man art thou?"

Forthwith[2] this frame of mine was wrenched[3]
With a woful[4] agony,
Which forced me to begin my tale;
And then it left me free.

And ever and anon through out his future life an agony constraineth him to travel from land to land;

Since then, at an uncertain hour,
That agony returns:
And till my ghastly tale is told,
This heart within me burns.

---

1) *manner*: kind, sort
2) *forthwith*: 즉시 (immediately, without delay)
3) *wrench*: twist
4) *woful*: woeful, wretched

I pass, like night, from land to land;
I have strange power of speech;
That moment that his face I see,
I know the man that must hear me:
To him my tale I teach.

What loud uproar bursts from that door!
The wedding-guests are there:
But in the garden-bower the bride
And bride-maids singing are:
And hark the little vesper bell,
Which biddeth me to prayer!

O Wedding-Guest! this soul hath been
Alone on a wide wide sea:
So lonely 'twas, that God himself
Scarce seemed there to be.

O sweeter than the marriage-feast,
'Tis sweeter far to me,
To walk together to the kirk
With a goodly company!—

To walk together to the kirk,
And all together pray,
While each to his great Father bends,
Old men, and babes, and loving friends
And youths and maidens gay!

And to teach, by his own example, love and reverence to all things that God made and loveth.

Farewell, farewell! but this I tell
To thee, thou Wedding-Guest!

He prayeth well, who loveth well
Both man and bird and beast.

He prayeth best, who loveth best
All things both great and small;
For the dear God who loveth us,
He made and loveth all.

The Mariner, whose eye is bright,
Whose beard with age is hoar[1],
Is gone: and now the Wedding-Guest
Turned from the bridegroom's door.

He went like one that hath been stunned,
And is of sense forlorn[2]:
A sadder and a wiser man,
He rose the morrow morn.

1797–98 (1798)

---

1) *hoar*: greyish white
2) *forlorn*: deprived

Kubla Khan

OR A VISION IN A DREAM, A FRAGMENT

In Xanadu[1]) did Kubla Khan[2])
A stately pleasure-dome decree:[3])
Where Alph[4]), the sacred river, ran
Through caverns measureless to man[5])
  Down to a sunless sea.
So twice five miles of fertile ground
With walls and towers were girdled round[6]):
And there were gardens bright with sinuous rills,
Where blossomed many an incense-bearing tree[7]);
And here were forests ancient as the hills,
Enfolding sunny spots of greenery[8]).

---

* "1797년 여름에 시인은 건강이 좋지 않아서 Somerset와 Devonshire의 경계에 위치한 Porlock과 Linton 사이의 외로운 농가에 은거하고 있었다. 경미한 병으로 진통제(아편)를 복용하고 의자에 앉아서 *Purchas's Pilgrimage*의 다음 구절을 읽다가 잠이 들었다. 'Here the Khan Kubla commanded a palace to be built, and a stately garden thereunto. And thus ten miles of fertile ground were enclosed with a wall.' 두세 시간 동안 곤히 잠들었는데, 그 동안 그는 200 또는 300 행은 족히 쓸 수 있을 것 같은 확신이 들었다. 아무 감각이나 의식적 노력이 없이 눈앞에 이미지들과 그에 상응하는 표현이 "사물로서" 생생하게 떠오른 상태를 창작이라 할 수 있다면 말이다. 잠에서 깨었을 때 그는 모든 내용을 분명히 기억할 수 있을 것 같아, 팬과 잉크와 종이를 들고 곧장 써 내려갔다. 지금 남아 있는 부분까지 썼을 때, Porlock에서 어떤 사람이 볼 일이 있어서 그를 방문했고, 한 시간 이상을 그와 함께 보냈다. 그가 방에 돌아왔을 때, 창피하고 놀랍게도 그가 본 것의 전체적 의미는 희미하게 기억이 되었으나, 대략 8 내지 10 줄 또는 이미지를 제외하고는 마치 개울물 속에 돌을 던질 때 표면의 영상이 사라지듯이 사라져 버리고 더 이상 회복할 수 없게 되었다." (Coleridge's Note: 1816년 5월에 출판된 시집 *Christabel; Kubla Khan, a Vision; The Pains of Sleep*의 서문으로 발표된 것.)

1) *Xanadu*: 상도(上都) (만주 열하성의 고도; Kublai Khan이 1256년에 이궁을 세운 땅), 도원경

2) *Kubla Khan*: Kublai Khan 또는 Kubilai Khan: 쿠빌라이 칸 (忽必熱汗) (1216-94), 몽고제국 제5대 황제; 징기스칸(Genghis Khan)의 손자로 원(元)나라의 시조가 됨.

3) *pleasure-dome*: 환락궁(歡樂宮); 쿠빌라이는 자신의 말로써 환락궁(지상낙원)을 창조한다. 그는 비옥한 땅을 성벽과 탑으로 둘러싸고, 실개천이 반짝이며 흐르고 향기로운 나무들이 꽃을 피우며 태고의 숲이 양지바른 녹지를 에워싸고 있는 정원을 만든다. 이것은 환경에 대한 인간의 지배력을 보여주는 동시에 인간은 스스로 낙원을 만든다는 사실을 말해준다.

4) *Alph*: 알프강; 그리스 신화에 나오는 강의 신 Alpheus 또는 그리스 자모의 첫 글자 Alpha에서 유래한 이름이며 "기원"의 의미를 함축하고 있다 (윤준 197).

5) *measureless to man*: 인간이 측량할 수 없는; *measureless*=immeasurable, unlimited

6) *girdled round*: surrounded

7) *incense-bearing tree*: 향이 열리는 나무; 향나무

8) *sunny spots of greenery*: 양지바른 녹지; *greenery*=green foliage or vegetation

But oh! that deep romantic chasm[1] which slanted
Down the green hill athwart a cedarn cover[2]!
A savage[3] place! as holy and enchanted
As e'er beneath a waning moon was haunted
By woman wailing for her demon-lover!
And from this chasm, with ceaseless turmoil seething[4],
As if this earth in fast thick pants were breathing[5],
A mighty fountain momently was forced:
Amid whose swift half-intermitted burst[6]
Huge fragments vaulted[7] like rebounding hail,
Or chaffy grain[8] beneath the thresher's flail[9]:
And 'mid these dancing rocks at once and ever
It flung up[10] momently the sacred river.
Five miles meandering with a mazy motion
Through wood and dale the sacred river ran,
Then reached the caverns measureless to man,
And sank in tumult to a lifeless ocean:
And 'mid this tumult Kubla heard from far
Ancestral voices prophesying war![11]

---

1) *deep romantic chasm*: 깊은 낭만적 균열; 성하(聖河) 알프의 발원지이다. 콜리지는 제2연 12-24행에서 성적 이미지를 사용하여 성하가 발원하는 순간을 인상적으로 묘사하고 있다. 이 "균열"은 제1연에 묘사된 인공적인 "환락궁"과는 대조적으로 "야생의 장소"이며 원시적 에너지가 충만한 곳이다. *chasm*=a deep fissure, a wide crack. Cf. Wordsworth의 *The Prelude*(1805)에도 유사한 묘사가 나온다: "from the shore / At distance.../ Was a blue chasm, a fracture in the vapour, / A deep and gloomy breathing-place, through which / Mounted the roar of waters...." (XIII, 54-58)
2) *athwart a cedarn cover*: 삼(杉)나무 숲을 가로질러; *athwart*=across from side to side; *cover*=woods or undergrowth sheltering game
3) *savage*: 야생의, 황량한 (wild, uncultivated)
4) *seethe*: 끓어오르다, 들끓다 (boil, bubble up; be in a state of agitation); *with ceaseless turmoil seething*: 끊임없는 소란으로 들끓는
5) *As if...breathing*: 마치 대지가 가쁜 숨을 몰아쉬듯; *pant*=헐떡거림 (gasp)
6) *Amid whose...burst:* 그 샘의 단속적인 분출에 섞여; *intermitted*=intermittent; *burst*=sudden issuing forth
7) *vault*: 뛰다, 도약하다 (spring, leap)
8) *chaffy grain*: 왕겨에 싸인 곡식 낟알
9) *thresher's flail*: 도리깨; *thresher*=탈곡자, 도리깨질하는 사람
10) *fling up*: 던져 올리다, 밀어 올리다 (throw up); 주어 "It"는 "the deep chasm"을 가리킨다.
11) 바다로 쏟아지는 강물의 소란 속에서 쿠빌라이는 "전쟁을 예언하는 선조들의 목소리"를 듣는다. 쿠빌라이의 낙원은 "성벽과 탑"에 둘러싸여 있지만, 미래의 격변과 파괴의 가능성을 내포하고 있다. 즉 시인은 쿠빌라이가 만든 인공적인 낙원이 진정한 낙원과는 거리가

The shadow of the dome of pleasure
Floated midway on the waves[1];
Where was heard the mingled measure[2]
From the fountain and the caves.
It was a miracle of rare device[3],
A sunny pleasure-dome with caves of ice!

A damsel with a dulcimer[4]
In a vision once I saw:
It was an Abyssinian maid,
And on her dulcimer she played,
Singing of Mount Abora[5].
Could I revive within me
Her symphony and song,
To such a deep delight 'twould win me,
That with music loud and long,
I would build that dome in air,[6]
That sunny dome! those caves of ice!
And all who heard should see them there,[7]

먼 곳임을 암시한다.

1) *The shadow... the waves*: 환락궁의 그림자가 / 파도의 중간에 어른거렸다. 이 말은 쿠빌라이의 환락궁이 실체가 아니라 그림자임을 암시한다. 이것은 또한 제1연의 "환락궁"과 제3연에 묘사된 (시인이 상상력으로 지은) 공중의 궁전("that dome in air")을 중간에서 연결하는 역할을 한다.

2) *mingled measure*: 혼합된 가락; *measure*=melody, tune

3) *a miracle of rare device*: 절묘하게 만들어진 기적 (뜨거운 햇빛과 차가운 얼음이 공존하기 때문에 기적이라 부른다); *device*=the action of devising, ingenuity

4) *A damsel with a dulcimer*: 덜시머를 들고 있는 처녀; 이 처녀는 시신(詩神)과 같은 존재이며, "원형적 시인(Fogle 49)"이라 할 수 있다. 제3연에서 시인은 이 처녀가 연주하는 노래에 영감을 받아 공중에 궁전, 즉 "that dome"을 짓고 싶어 한다. 시인이 언어로 지은 궁전 즉 상상적 창조물은 쿠빌라이의 환락궁보다 영속적이다.

5) *Mount Abora*: 아보라 산; 이 산은 Milton의 *Paradise Lost* 제4권에 나오는 Mount Amara를 고친 것이다 (윤준 205). 밀턴의 작품에서 이 산은 아비시니아(Ethiopia) 왕들이 그들의 자손을 지키던 곳으로 진정한 낙원보다는 열등한 곳으로 묘사되어 있다. 처녀가 부르는 노래의 주제인 이 산은 이상향 또는 진정한 낙원을 의미한다.

6) *with that music... in air*: 높고 긴 음악으로 / 나는 공중에 저 궁전을 지으리라; 음악으로 궁전을 짓겠다는 말은 그리스 신화의 Amphion에 대한 인유이다. 암피온은 Zeus와 Antiope 사이에 태어난 쌍둥이 형제 중의 하나이다. 그는 하프의 명수로 쌍둥이 Zethus와 함께 테베(Thebes)의 성벽을 쌓았는데, 그가 타는 하프 소리에 돌이 저절로 움직여 성벽이 완성되었다고 한다.

7) 제3연의 마지막 부분(48행-끝)은 시인의 상상적 창조물에 대한 독자의 반응을 다룬 부분이다.

And all should cry, Beware! Beware!
His flashing eyes, his floating hair!
Weave a circle round him thrice,
And close your eyes with holy dread,[1]
For he on honey-dew hath fed,
And drunk the milk of Paradise[2].

1797-98(1816)

여기서 "all who heard"는 시인의 음악을 들은 사람, 즉 독자들을 의미한다.

1) 콜리지는 시인을 초월적인 존재, 즉 신들린 사람으로 묘사하고 있다. 노수부처럼 "번쩍이는 눈"과 "나부끼는 머리카락"을 가진 시인은 "성스러운 두려움"의 대상이다. 시인을 본 사람들은 "주의하라! 주의하라!"고 외치면서 마치 종교의식을 행하듯 시인의 주위에 "세 겹의 울타리를 치고" 가까이 하기를 두려워하며, 감히 바로 쳐다보지 못하고 눈을 감아버린다. 시인은 초월적인 예언의 능력을 가진 신성한 존재로 경원시해야 할 인물이다. 시인은 감로와 낙원의 우유를 먹고 사는 신성한 존재다.

2) 이 작품을 "Paradise"라는 말로 끝맺는 것도 중요한 의미를 지닌다. 시인은 낙원에 사는 존재이며, 시인들이 궁극적으로 추구하는 세계 또한 낙원이다. "무한한 가능성이 열리는 것처럼 보이는 순수한 순간에 느끼는 창조적 기분"(Bowra 11)이야말로 낙원의 경지라 할 수 있을 것이다.

Dejection: An Ode

Late, late yestreen I saw the new Moon,
With the old Moon in her arms;
And I fear, I fear, my Master dear!
We shall have a deadly storm.
Ballad of Sir Patrick Spence[1].

I

Well! if the Bard was weather-wise[2], who made
The grand old ballad of Sir Patrick Spence,
This night, so tranquil now, will not go hence[3]
Unroused by winds, that ply a busier trade[4]
Than those which mould yon cloud in lazy flakes[5],
Or the dull sobbing draft, that moans and rakes
Upon the strings of this Aeolian lute[6],

---

* 이 시의 초고는 콜리지가 Wordsworth의 "Ode: Intimations of Immortality" 첫 4연(3월 27일에 중단)을 읽고 나서 1802년 4월 4일 밤에 지은 340행에 달하는 서한시 "A Letter to _____"이다. 이 서한시는 워즈워스의 아내가 된 Mary Hutchinson의 동생 Sara에게 바친 시이다. 이 서한시에는 워즈워스가 다룬 상실의 주제와 아울러 콜리지 자신의 불행한 결혼생활과 Sara에 대한 절망적 사랑이 장황하게 취급되어 있었다. 콜리지는 반년에 걸쳐 초고의 절반을 삭제하고 나머지 행들을 재구성하여 워즈워스의 결혼식 날인 그해 10월 4일에 "Dejection: An Ode"라는 제목으로 발표하였다. 이 시는 워즈워스가 "Ode"에서 제시한 상실의 주제를 다루고 있기 때문에 워즈워스가 4연의 끝부분에서 던진 물음("Whither is fled the visionary gleam? / Where is it now, the glory and the dream?")에 대한 대답의 성격을 갖고 있다. 콜리지의 경우 자아와 자연의 상호작용은 단지 실패의 얼굴을 비출 뿐이었다. 콜리지는 이 시에서 에너지가 소진된 한 인간의 자화상을 그리고 있다. (이 두 작품의 관계에 관해서는 Stephen Prickett의 *Coleridge and Wordsworth*를 참조할 것.)

1) *Sir Patrick Spence*: 옛 스코틀랜드의 민요. 공주를 모시고 노르웨이로 간 Sir Patrick Spence가 스코틀랜드로 돌아오는 도중에 난파한 사건을 소재로 한 작품이다. 콜리지가 이 시를 인용한 것은 시인이 "날씨를 알아맞히는" 예언자라는 의미를 함축하는 동시에, 날씨에 관한 미신적인 민간속설을 이용하여 자연의 날씨를 묘사하면서 시인 자신의 내면의 날씨를 암시하기 위함이다.

2) *weather-wise*: 날씨를 잘 알아맞히는 (able to forecast the weather)

3) *go hence*: 지나가다 (pass), 죽다 (die); *hence*=away, from here; *This night... will not go hence / Unroused by winds*: 오늘 밤은 바람 때문에 잠을 잘 못잘 것이라는 의미이다. *rouse*=잠을 깨우다 (startle out of sleep)

4) *that ply a busier trade*: 더 거세게(시끄럽게) 부는; *ply*=부지런히 일하다 (work steadily at); *trade*=야단법석, 소란 (fuss, commotion)

5) *lazy flake*: 느리게 움직이는 조각(구름); *lazy*=slow-moving; flake=thin broad piecepeeled off, chiplike piece

6) *Aeolian lute*: 에올리언 하프(류트); 풍명금(風鳴琴) (wind harp); *Aeolian*=of Aeolus (바람의 신); 바람에 의해 연주되는 이 악기는 낭만파 시인들이 즐겨 사용하는 이미지의 하나다. 콜리지는 자신을 에올리언 하프에 비유하고 있으며, 그는 이 하프가 거친 음악을 연주하기

Which better far were mute.
For lo! the New-moon winter-bright[1])!
And overspread with phantom[2]) light,
(With swimming phantom light o'erspread
But rimmed and circled by a silver thread)
I see the old Moon in her lap[3]), foretelling
The coming-on of rain and squally blast.
And oh! that even now the gust[4]) were swelling,
And the slant[5]) night-shower driving loud and fast!
Those sounds which oft have raised me, whilst they awed,
And sent my soul abroad[6]),
Might now perhaps their wonted impulse[7]) give,
Might startle this dull pain[8]), and make it move and live!

II

A grief without a pang, void, dark, and drear,
A stifled, drowsy, unimpassioned grief,
Which finds no natural outlet, no relief,
In word, or sigh, or tear—[9])
O Lady! in this wan and heartless mood[10]),
To other thoughts by yonder throstle woo'd[11]),

때문에 "침묵하는 것이 나았을" 것이라 말한다. (Geoffrey Grigson, *The Harp of Aeolus and Other Essays* [1947] 참조)

1) *winter-bright*: 차갑게 빛나는
2) *phantom:* 환영(幻影)의, 유령 같은 (merely apparent, illusive)
3) *the old Moon in her lap*: 새 달 무릎에 안긴 옛 달; "새 달"은 초승달이며, 달은 "유령 같은 빛"으로 덮여 있고 가장자리에는 은 빛 실로 띠를 두르고 있다. 즉 달무리가 서 있다. 달무리는 궂은 날씨, 즉 "비와 돌풍(squally blast)"을 예고한다.
4) *gust*: 돌풍, 일진광풍 (sudden violent rush of wind), 감정의 폭발 (an outburst of feeling)
5) *slant*: 비스듬한 (sloping)
6) *abroad*: astray
7) *wonted impulse*: 익숙한 충격, 예전의 충격; *wonted*=익숙한(accustomed), 평소의(usual); *impulse* 충격(impetus), 자극(mental incitement)
8) *dull pain*: 둔한 통증; 이것은 제2연의 "A grief without a pang"과 연결된다.
9) 22-24행: 말이나 한숨이나 눈물로도 / 어떤 자연스런 배출구나 위안을 찾지 못하는 / 답답하고, 졸리고, 차분한 슬픔: *unimpassioned*=calm, free from passion; *outlet* =means of expressing emotion; *relief*=deliverance from pain;
10) *wan and heartless mood*: 나른하고 풀이 죽은 기분; wan=지친, 나른한 (looking worn and exhausted); heartless=기운 없는, 풀이 죽은 (lacking spirit)
11) 26행: 저 너머 지빠귀 소리에 딴 생각에 잠겨; 어순은 *Woo'd to other thoughts by yonder*

All this long eve, so balmy and serene,
Have I been gazing on the western sky,
And its peculiar tint of yellow green:
And still I gaze—and with how blank an eye!
And those thin clouds above, in flakes and bars,
That give away their motion to the stars;
Those stars, that glide behind them or between,
Now sparkling, now bedimmed, but always seen:
Yon crescent Moon, as fixed as if it grew
In its own cloudless, starless lake of blue;
I see them all so excellently fair,
I see, not feel, how beautiful they are![1]

III

My genial spirits fail[2];
And what can these avail
To lift[3] the smothering weight from off my breast?
It were a vain endeavour,
Though I should gaze for ever
On that green light that lingers in the west:
I may not hope from outward forms to win
The passion and the life, whose fountains are within.

---

*throstle*이다. 이것은 능동태로 고치면 yonder throstle woo'd me to other thoughts가 된다. *woo* =win, induce

1) 38행: "나는 보지만, 그들이 얼마나 아름다운지 느끼지는 못한다." 이것은 "이지(理智)와 감성(感性)의 분리"(이영걸 17)를 의미한다. 여기서 자연은 너무나 아름답게 묘사되어 있다: 저녁하늘은 황록색을 띠고 있고, 하늘에는 조각구름과 막대구름이 떠있으며, 구름 사이로 별이 반짝이고, 호수 같은 하늘에 초승달이 떠 있다. 그러나 시인은 그 아름다움을 느끼지 못한다. 이처럼 외부세계와 시인의 정신은 단절되어 있다. 시인이 느끼는 슬픔 또는 "둔한 통증"의 본질은 자연의 아름다움을 보면서도 느끼지 못하는 데 있다. 이 부분은 Wordsworth의 "Ode: Intimations of Immortality"에서 빛의 상실을 탄식한 부분(Ⅰ-Ⅳ)과 상응한다.

2) 제3연에서 시인은 낙담 상태에서 "원기"가 쇠퇴하는 것을 느낀다. 그는 그 원인을 내부에서 찾는다. 콜리지는 서쪽 하늘에 머물고 있는 "저 녹색 빛"의 원천이 "외적인 형태"가 아니라 자신의 내부에 있다고 말한다. 그는 여기서 "초원의 빛"이 외부의 빛이 아니라 내부에서 나오는 빛이라고 워즈워스의 질문에 대답하고 있다.
genial spirits: 타고난 원기 (innate powers; creative powers); *genial*=natural, native, inborn; *spirits*=liveliness, vivacity; Cf. *spirit* =animating or life-giving principle

3) *lift*: take up and remove, take away

IV

O Lady! we receive but what we give[1],
And in our life alone does Nature live:
Ours is her wedding garment, ours her shroud![2]
And would we aught behold, of higher worth,
Than that inanimate cold world allowed
To the poor loveless ever-anxious crowd[3],
Ah! from the soul itself must issue forth
A light, a glory, a fair luminous cloud
Enveloping the Earth—[4]
And from the soul itself must there be sent
A sweet and potent voice, of its own birth,
Of all sweet sounds the life and element!

V

O pure of heart! thou need'st not ask of me
What this strong music in the soul may be!
What, and wherein it doth exist,
This light, this glory, this fair luminous mist,
This beautiful and beauty-making power.
Joy[5], virtuous Lady! Joy that ne'er was given,
Save to the pure, and in their purest hour,
Life, and Life's effluence[6], cloud at once and shower,

---

1) *we receive but what we give*: 우리는 우리가 준 것만 받는다.

2) 49행: "자연의 혼례복은 우리의 혼례복, 자연의 수의는 우리의 수의"라는 말은 우리의 마음이 기쁘면 자연도 아름답게 보이고, 우리의 마음이 슬프면 자연도 슬퍼 보인다는 것을 의미한다. 즉 "우리의 생명 속에 자연이 살고 있다." 이 "wedding garment"는 워즈워스의 "Trailing clouds of glory"를 연상시킨다. *ours*: our wedding garment; our shroud

3) *that inanimate...crowd*: 사랑 없이 늘 초조해하는 가엾은 무리들에게 허용된 저 차갑고 생명 없는 세계; 사랑이 없는 가엾은 무리들에게 자연은 단지 죽음의 세계로만 보일 뿐이다.

4) 54-55행: "대지를 감싸고 있는 빛, 영광, 아름답게 빛나는 구름"은 Wordsworth의 "celestial light" 또는 "the glory"와 일치한다. 콜리지는 이 빛이 우리의 영혼에서 나오는 빛이라 설명한다.

5) *Joy*: 환희 (a pleasurable, happy, felicitous state); 콜리지는 "a state of abounding vitality and a sense of harmony between one's inner life and the life of nature"의 의미로 사용한다(Norton 219n).

6) *effluence*: 흘러나오는 것(a flowing out), 발산물 (that which flows out, emanation); "Life, and Life's effluence"는 그 다음의 "cloud at once and shower"와 함께 "Joy"와 동격이다. 환희는 생명 그 자체이면서 생명에서 나오는 것이다. "구름인 동시에 소나기"는 생명과 생명의 발

Joy, Lady! is the spirit and the power,
Which wedding Nature to us gives in dower
  A new Earth and new Heaven,[1]
Undreamt of by the sensual and the proud—
Joy is the sweet voice, Joy the luminous cloud—
    We in ourselves rejoice![2]
And thence[3] flows all that charms or ear or sight,
  All melodies the echoes of that voice,
All colours a suffusion from that light.[4]

VI

There was a time[5] when, though my path was rough,
  This joy within me dallied with distress,
And all misfortunes were but as the stuff
  Whence Fancy made me dreams of happiness:
For hope grew round me, like the twining vine,
And fruits, and foliage, not my own, seemed mine.
But now afflictions bow me down to earth:
Nor care I that they rob me of my mirth;
    But oh! each visitation[6]

산물의 관계를 시각적으로 보여주는 심상으로 사용되어 있다. 즉 소나기는 구름에서 쏟아져 나오는 발산물이다. 다시 말해서, 환희는 인간과 자연을 결혼시키는 원동력이다.

1) *the spirit and power / Which wedding Nature to us gives in dower / A new Earth and new Heaven*: 자연과 우리를 결혼시키면서 / 새로운 대지와 새로운 하늘을 지참금으로 우리에게 주는 / 정신이요 힘이다. 즉 "환희"는 생명에서 발산되는 힘이며, 이것이 있으면 인간 정신은 자연과의 소외를 극복하고 자연과 조화로운 관계를 유지하게 되고, 그 결과로 외부 세계에 대한 새로운 경험을 얻게 된다는 의미이다. "wedding Nature to us"는 분사구문

2) *We rejoice in ourselves!*: 우리는 우리 자신을 기뻐한다. 이 말은 우리 자신의 내부에 있는 환희의 힘(또는 창조적 상상력)을 기뻐한다는 것을 의미한다. 환희는 상상력이 창조적 활동을 하는 순간에 느껴지는 감정이다.

3) *Thence*: 그것으로부터 (From that), 즉 환희로부터 (From joy);

4) 73-75행: 우리의 내면에 환희가 있으면, 모든 자연의 형상, 선율, 색채가 아름답게 느껴진다는 뜻이다. 모든 선율은 환희의 음성에 메아리이며, 모든 색깔은 환희의 빛이 넘쳐 나와 표면을 뒤덮은 것이다. Coleridge는 Wordsworth가 "Ode"에서 말한 "초원의 빛"이 우리 내부의 "환희"에서 유래함을 역설하고 있다. *suffusion*=a colouring spread over a surface; Cf. *suffuse*=내부에서 넘쳐 나와 표면을 뒤덮다 (spread over from within)

5) 76-79행: 비록 내 길이 험했어도, 내 안의 환희가 / 고통을 희롱하고, 환상은 모든 불행을/ 재료로 사용하여 내게 행복한 꿈을 / 만들어주었던 시절이 있었다. *There was a time*: Cf. "There was a time when meadow, grove, and stream, / The earth and every common sight, / To me did seem / Apparelled in celestial light...." (Wordsworth, "Ode: Intimations of Immortality," 1-4); *dally with*=flirt or trifle with

6) *visitation*: 고통, 시련 (a grave affliction, blow, or trial)

Suspends what nature gave me at my birth,
  My shaping spirit of Imagination[1].
For not to think of what I needs must feel,
  But to be still and patient, all I can;[2]
And haply by abstruse research to steal
  From my own nature all the natural man[3]—
  This was my sole resource, my only plan:
Till that which suits a part infects the whole,
And now is almost grown the habit of my soul.[4]

VII

Hence, viper thoughts, that coil around my mind,
    Reality's dark dream![5]
I turn from you, and listen to the wind,
  Which long has raved unnoticed. What a scream
Of agony by torture lengthened out
That lute sent forth! Thou Wind, that rav'st without,
  Bare crag, or mountain-tairn[6], or blasted tree[7],
Or pine-grove whither woodman never clomb,

---

1) *My shaping spirit of Imagination*: 내 상상력의 성형(成形) 능력; "내가 태어날 때 자연이 내게 준 것(what nature gave me at my birth)"과 동격; 콜리지는 *Biographia Literaria*에서 상상력을 "plastic power"(X) 또는 "esemplastic power"(VIII)라 불렀다. 이 중에서 후자는 콜리지가 그리스어에서 만든 "to shape into one"의 뜻을 가진 신조어이다. 이것은 모든 이질적인 요소를 통합하여 하나의 유기적 전체를 창조하는 능력을 의미한다. Cf. "A plastic power / Abode with me, a forming hand..."(*The Prelude*[1850], II, 362-3).

2) *For not to think of what I needs must feel, / But to be still and patient, all I can*; 왜냐하면 나는 고작해야 내가 느껴야 하는 것을 생각하지 않고, 조용히 인내할 따름이니까. 어순은 For all I can [is] not to think....이다.

3) 89-90행: 그리고 아마도 심오한 연구로 나 자신의 본성으로부터 모든 자연스러운 인간을 훔쳐내기만 할 뿐이니까. 이 말은 자신의 내부에서("from my own nature") 모든 타고난 인간의 능력("all the natural man")을 연구하는 일만 하게 되었다는 것, 즉 창작보다는 비평에 몰두하게 되었다는 것을 의미한다. (실제로 Coleridge는 이 작품을 쓴 이후 상상력이 감퇴하여 시 창작보다는 비평에 몰두하게 되었다는 주장도 있다.) *steal*=develop by insensible degrees (from); 어순은 [all I can is] haply to steal all the natural man from my own nature by abstruse research이다.

4) 92-3행: 마침내 부분에 적합한 것이 전체를 오염시키고, / 이제는 [그것이] 거의 내 영혼의 습관이 되어버렸다. 이것은 분석적 이성의 폐해에 관해 언급한 말이다.

5) 94-95행: 분석적 사고 습관을 "내 마음을 휘감는 살모사 같은 생각, / 현실의 악몽"이라 묘사한다.

6) *mountain-tairn*: 산정호수

7) *blasted tree*: 말라죽은 나무; *blast*=blight, destroy (plants) with disease

Or lonely house, long held the witches' home,
  Methinks were fitter instruments for thee,
Mad Lutanist[1]! who in this month of showers,
Of dark-brown gardens, and of peeping flowers,
Mak'st Devils' yule[2], with worse than wintry song,
The blossoms, buds, and timorous leaves[3] among.
  Thou Actor, perfect in all tragic sounds![4]
Thou mighty Poet, e'en to frenzy bold[5]!
    What tell'st thou now about?
    'Tis of the rushing of an host in rout[6],
  With groans, of trampled men, with smarting wounds—
At once they groan with pain, and shudder with the cold!
But hush! there is a pause of deepest silence![7]
  And all that noise, as of a rushing crowd,
With groans, and tremulous shudderings[8]—all is over—
  It tells another tale, with sounds less deep and loud!
    A tale of less affright[9],
    And tempered with delight[10],
As Otway's[11] self had framed the tender lay,—

---

1) *lutanist*: 류트(lute) 연주자
2) *devils' yule*: 악마들의 축제; *yule*=Christmas and the festivities connected with it
3) *timorous leaves*: 소심한 나뭇잎들; *timorous*=timid, easily alarmed
4) 시인은 자조적으로 자신을 "온갖 비극적인 소리에 완벽한 배우" 즉 비극배우에 비유하고 있다.
5) *to frenzy bold*: 미칠 정도로 대담한; *frenzy*=발광, 광란 (temporary insanity, wild folly)
6) *the rushing of an host in rout*: 패주하는 군대의 돌진; *host*=army; *rout*=disorderly retreat of defeated army
7) *But hush! there is a pause of deepest silence!* 그러나 쉿! 잠시 아주 깊은 정적이 깃드는구나! 이 정적은 폭풍이 멎었음을 의미할 수도 있고, 시인 자신의 내면에 고요가 찾아왔음을 의미할 수도 있다. 여기서부터 시인의 상상력은 "낙심" 상태를 서서히 벗어나 창조적인 힘을 회복한다. 그 다음에 "덜 무섭고, 기쁨으로 누그러진 이야기"를 한다. 이 이야기의 주인공인 어린아이는 길을 잃었으나 어머니가 그의 부름을 듣기를 바라는 희망을 가지고 있다.
8) *With groans, and tremulous shudderings*; 신음하며 몸서리치며 떠는; *tremulous* =trembling; *shuddering*=sudden shivering due to fear or horror
9) *affright*: 공포 (fright)
10) *tempered with delight*: 기쁨으로 누그러진; *temper*=완화시키다 (modify, mitigate)
11) *Otway*: Thomas Otway (1652-85); 영국의 극작가; Otway는 Chatterton처럼 조직화된 사회에서 버림받은 굶주린 시인이다. 초고에서는 "As Wordsworth's self made the tender lay"로 되어 있었다고 한다(Bloom 219). 워즈워스가 지은 "정겨운 노래"는 "Lucy Gray"이다. Lucy Gray는 밤새 눈보라 속에서 길을 잃고 헤매다가 실종된 비극의 주인공으로 묘사되어 있다 (Wordsworth의 "Lucy Gray" 참조). 콜리지가 다른 작가의 이야기를 인유한 목적은 실제로 슬픈 이야기도

'Tis of a little child
Upon a lonesome wild,
Not far from home, but she hath lost her way:
And now moans low in bitter grief and fear,
And now screams loud, and hopes to make her mother hear.

VIII

'Tis midnight, but small thoughts have I of sleep[1]:
Full seldom may my friend such vigils keep![2]
Visit her, gentle Sleep! with wings of healing,
And may this storm be but a mountain-birth[3]
May all the stars hang bright above her dwelling,
Silent as though they watched the sleeping Earth!
With light heart may she rise,
Gay fancy[4], cheerful eyes,
Joy lift her spirit, joy attune her voice[5];
To her may all things live, from pole to pole,
Their life the eddying of her living soul[6]!
O simple spirit, guided from above[7],
Dear Lady! friend devoutest of my choice[8],
Thus mayest thou ever, evermore rejoice.

April 4, 1802 (1802, 1817)

예술적 승화(또는 정화)를 통해 심미적 기쁨을 줄 수 있다는 것을 암시하기 위함이다.

1) small thoughts have I of sleep: 별로 잠이 올 것 같지 않다. 마지막 연에서 시인은 여인에 대한 기원으로 끝맺는다. 콜리지가 Sara에 대한 기원으로 끝맺는 것은 워즈워스가 "Tintern Abbey"를 Dorothy에 대한 기원으로 끝맺은 것과 유사하다. Dorothy는 워즈워스의 alter ego 이다. 이 작품의 전체적인 구조는 Grief-Joy-Grief-Joy로 되어 있으며(Watson 178), 마지막 연에서 콜리지는 Sara를 통해 낙심 상태를 벗어나 자신의 창조적 능력의 회복을 기원한다.

2) *Full seldom may my friend such vigils keep!*: 내 친구(Sara)에겐 이런 불면의 밤이 없기를!; *vigil*=밤샘 (keeping awake during the time usually given to sleep)

3) *mountain-birth*: 산에서 태어난 것; 시인은 폭풍이 단지 산에서만 부는 바람이기를 기원한다.

4) *gay fancy*: 즐거운 공상; *gay*=full of mirth, carefree; *fancy*=delusory imagination

5) *joy attune her voice*: 기쁨으로 아름다운 노래를 부르기를; *attune*=make tuneful melodious

6) *Their life the eddying of her living soul!*: 만물의 생명이 그녀의 살아 있는 영혼에 소용돌이치기를!

7) *guided from above*: 하늘에서 인도된, 즉 하늘에서 내려온; *above*=heaven, a higher place

8) *friend devoutest of my choice*: 내가 선택한 가장 헌신적인 친구; *devout*=pious, earnestly religious

Selected Bibliography

1. Primary Sources:

Coleridge, Samuel Taylor. *Poetical Works*, ed. Ernest Hartley Coleridge. Oxford: Oxford UP, 1969, 1983.

Coleridge, Samuel Taylor. *Biographia Literaria or Biographical Sketches of My Literary Life and Opinions*, 2 vols., ed. by James Engell and W. Jackson Bate. Princeton, N. J.: Princeton UP, 1983.

2. Secondary Sources:

Bloom, Harold (ed.). *Samuel Taylor Coleridge (Modern Critical Views 61)*, New York and Philadelphia: Chelsea House, 1986.

Beer, J. B. (ed.). *Coleridge's Poems*, Everyman edition (Rev.). London, 1974.

Bloom, Herold (ed.). *Samuel Taylor Coleridge (Modern Critical Views 61)*, New York and Philadelphia: Chelsea House, 1986.

______. (ed.). *Samuel Taylor Coleridge's The Rime of the Ancient Mariner*. New York: Chelsea House, 1986.

Brett, R. L (ed.). S. T. *Coleridge*. London: Bell and Sons, 1971.

House, Humphry. *Coleridge*: *The Clark Lectures 1951-52*. London: Rupert Hart-Davis, 1953.

Brett, R. L. (ed.). *S. T. Coleridge*. Athens: Ohio UP, 1972.

Prickett, Stephen. *Coleridge and Wordsworth, The Poetry of Growth*. Cambridge, 1970.

Wheeler, Kathleen M. *The Creative Mind in Coleridge's Poetry*. Cambridge, Mass.: Harvard UP, 1981.

윤 준. 『코울리지의 시 연구』. 서울: 동인, 2001.

George Gordon, Lord Byron
(1788~1824)

Lord Byron
Born 22 January 1788

Newstead Abbey in 1880

Byron's Stone in Tepelene, Albania

바이런의 생애와 작품

바리런(George Gordon, Lord Byron)은 셸리(Shelley) 및 키츠(Keats)와 더불어 제2세대 낭만주의 시인 혹은 후기 낭만주의 시인으로 분류된다. 그는 남작의 지위를 물려받은 귀족신분으로 태어났고, 정치 사상적으로 급진적인 혁명가였다. 그는 다른 낭만주의 시인들과는 달리 드라이든(Dryden)과 포우프(Pope)와 같은 신고전주의 시인들을 본받아 풍자시를 썼으며, 낭만주의 시인이면서도 가장 반낭만주의적인 시인이었다. 그는 낙관적인 낭만주의 비전에 대해 회의하며, 인간영혼이 유한하고 암울하여 죽음에서 벗어날 수 없다는 어둠의 비전을 토로했다. 그는 빛과 생명은 잠정적인 상태이고 어둠과 죽음이 궁극적이고 영원하다고 생각했다.

바이런은 생존 시에 가장 훌륭한 영국 시인으로 알려져 있었고, 작고한 후에도 오래 동안 널리 모방의 대상이 되었다. 그가 당대에 대중적 인기를 누린 것은 그의 독특하고 복잡한 성격 탓도 있겠으나 무엇보다도 그가 "Byronic hero"라는 인물을 창조했기 때문이다. 이 인물은 바이런의 작품 속에 여러 가지 모습으로 등장하는데, "바이런적 영웅"을 그린 가장 대표적인 작품은 「해롤드 공자」(Childe Harold's Pilgrimage)와 극시「맨프레드」(Manfred)이다. "바이런적 영웅"은 우울하면서도 열정적이며, 보통사람보다 우수한 정서적 지적 능력을 가지고 있어서 오만하고 자신감에 차 있고 극도로 민감한 감수성을 갖고 있다. 게다가 강한 성적 매력으로 가지고 남을 매료시킨다. 그는 신분과 특권을 무시하며 인습과 사회제도 및 규범에 반항하여 사회로부터 고립된 방랑자이다. 그는 알 수 없는 죄악에 대한 기억에 시달리며 스스로를 피할 수 없는 파멸로 몰아넣기도 한다. 그는 혼자 고립된 채 자기의존적인 태도를 취하며, 어떠한 반대도 무릅쓰고 스스로 부과한 도덕률에 따라 확고부동하게 자신의 목적을 추구한다. 이와 같은 "바이런적 영웅"은 『폭풍의 언덕』(Wuthering Heights)의 히스클리프, 『모비 딕』(Moby Dick)의 에이허브 선장, 푸쉬킨의 『예브게니 오네긴』(Eugene Onegin)의 주인공, 등의 인물 창조에 영향을 주었다.

바이런은 귀족의 후예다. 부친은 방탕아였고, 어머니는 병적으로 성미가 급한 지주의 후예였다. 그는 런던에서 태어나 세 살 때 아버지를 여읜 후 스코틀랜드의 Aberdeen에서 과히 유복하지 못한 환경에서 어머니의 손에 자랐다. 열 살 때인 1798년에 제6대 남작(男爵)(Baron Byron)이 되었고, 종가인 Newstead Abbey로 이사했다. Harrow School을 거쳐 1805년에 케임브리지 대학의 Trinity College에 입학하였다. 바이런은 타고난 기형족이 잘못받은 수술로 악화되어 그것이 평생을 통한 신체적 고통과 이상성격과 무절제한 생활의 원인이 되었다. 절름발이이기 때문에 더욱 용맹심에 불타 전문가 이상으로 권투, 검도, 승마, 수영에 열중했다. 그는 성적으로 조숙하여 일곱 살 때 사촌 Mary Duff와 열렬한 연애를 할 정도였다. 케임브리지 대학 시절에 그는 화려하게 꾸민 방과 종자를 거느린 마차와 애완용 곰과 정부를 거느리고서 사치와 낭비를 일삼았다. 이런 생활을 통하여 경제적 파탄을 가져왔지만 많은 친구를 사귀었고, 시를 썼다.

그는 1807년 3월에 상원의원이 되었고, 다음 해 7월에 문학 석사 학위를 받았다. 그해 후반에 시집 *Hours of Idleness*를 출판하였으나, 『에딘버러 리뷰』로부터 혹평을 받았다. 이에 화가 난 그는 당대의 주요 시인들을 조롱한 풍자시 「영국 시인과 스코틀랜드 비평가」(*English Bards and Scottish Reviewers*) (1809)를 발표했다.

1809년에는 대학 친구 호브하우스(John Cam Hobhouse)와 함께 포르투갈, 스페인, 몰타 섬(Malta), 그리스, 소아시아 등지를 여행했다. 이 2년간의 모험여행에서 얻은 소재로 「해롤드 공자」(*Childe Harold's Pilgrimage*) 1, 2권(1812)

을 완성했고, 후일에 「돈 주안」(*Don Juan*) (1819-24)을 썼다. 귀국 후 출판한 「해롤드 공자」는 그가 말한 대로 "하루아침에 깨어보니 유명해져" 있을 정도로 돌연한 명성을 가져다줌으로써 일약 런던 사교계의 명사가 되었다. 상원의원 자리를 차지하고, 막대한 인세 수입으로 귀족의 지위를 호화롭게 장식하면서 많은 연문을 퍼뜨렸다. 선천적으로 미모였던 바이런은 사교계 여인들과 일련의 추문을 남겼다. 특히 세속적인 레이디 캐롤라인 램(Lady Caroline Lamb)의 광적인 구애를 피하기 위해 애너벨러 밀뱅크(Annabella Milbanke)와 결혼하게 되었다. 1812년에 처음 만나 1815년 1월에 정식으로 결혼한 밀뱅크는 바이런이 이복누이 Augusta Leigh와 근친상간 관계에 있는 것을 알게 되어 딸 Augusta Ada를 낳고 겨우 1년 만에 이혼했다. 이복누이에 대한 바이런의 애정은 진실했으며 일생동안 계속되었다. 이 사건으로 인하여 바이런은 몇몇 친구들을 제외한 모든 사람들로부터 배척을 당하여, 1816년 4월에 그는 어쩔 수 없이 영국을 영원히 떠나게 되었다.

바이런은 제네바에서 셸리(Percy Bysshe Shelley)와 친교를 맺었다. 셸리는 그 무렵 아내 및 아내의 이복여동생 클레어 클레어먼트(Claire Clairmont)와 제네바에 머물고 있었다. 그리고 1817년 1월에 바이런과 클레어 사이에 딸 Allegra가 태어났고, 그해 가을 로마 여행에서 돌아와 베니스에 머물면서 그의 난봉행각의 절정을 이루는 사건들을 벌이기 시작했다. 추정에 의하면 그는 2백 명 이상의 여자들과 난잡한 관계를 맺었는데, 대게는 하층계급의 여자들이었다. 그럼에도 불구하고 이 기간은 그의 생에서 가장 위대한 창조의 시기였다. 그는 극 「맨프레드」(*Manfred*)를 탈고했고, 「해롤드 공자」 제4편을 완성하였으며, 「돈 주안」을 쓰기 시작했다.

문란한 생활에 싫증을 느낀 바이런은 1819년 노 백작 알레산드로 깃치올리(Allesandro Guiccioli)의 젊은 아내 테레사(Teresa)와 조용한 관계를 맺음으로써 안정을 찾았다. 당시 상류사회의 관습에 따라 정략결혼을 한 테레사는 바이런을 공공연한 애인으로 곁에 둘 수 있었다. 테레사의 집안인 감바 가(the Gambas)는 오스트리아 통치에 반대하는 이탈리아 혁명 음모에 연루되어 1821년에 피사로 강제 추방되었고, 바이런도 그들을 따라 피사로 가서 그곳에서 셸리와 합류하였다.

부도덕한 그의 생활과 작품에 대한 사회적 비난 속에서 그는 문학을 버리고 행동의 세계를 택하여 희랍독립전쟁에 가담했다. 결국 그 전쟁 중에 열병에 걸려 36세의 젊은 나이에 세상을 떠났다. 그가 보인 영웅주의와 자유 애호 정신은 희랍인들에게 큰 힘이 되었고, 그 때문에 아직도 그들은 바이런을 국민적 영웅으로 추앙하고 있다.

Written After Swimming From Sestos To Abydos

If, in the month of dark December,
  Leander, who was nightly wont[1])
(What maid will not the tale remember?)
  To cross thy stream, broad Hellespont[2])!

If, when the wintry tempest roared,
  He sped to Hero, nothing loath[3]),
And thus of old thy current poured,
  Fair Venus! how I pity both!

For me, degenerate modern wretch,
  Though in the genial month of May,
My dripping limbs I faintly stretch,
  And think I've done a feat today.

But since he crossed the rapid tide,
  According to the doubtful story,
To woo—and—Lord knows what beside[4]),
  And swam for Love, as I for Glory;

'Twere hard to say who fared the best:
  Sad mortals! thus the gods still plague you!
He lost his labour, I my jest;
  For he was drowned, and I've the ague.

May 9, 1810 (1812)

---

* 헬레스폰트는 유럽과 아시아 사이에 있는 좁은 해협이다. 아시아 쪽에 있는 아비도스(Abydos)의 청년 레안드로스(Leander)는 밤마다 이 해협을 헤엄쳐 건너가서 (비너스의 여 신관) 헤로(Hero)를 만나곤 했다. 그러다가 폭풍이 휘몰아치던 어느 날 레안드로스가 익사하자 헤로도 그를 따라 물에 빠져 죽었다고 한다. 바이런은 1810년 5월 3일 유럽 쪽에서 헬레스폰트를 헤엄쳐 건넜다.

1) *wont*: accustomed

2) *Hellespont*: 헬레스폰트 (지금의 Dardanelles 해협; 유럽과 아시아 터키의 경계를 이룸)

3) *nothing loath*: 기꺼이 (quite willingly); *loath*: unwilling

4) *Lord knows what beside*: (사랑 이외에) 무슨 다른 목적이 있었는지 모르지만

She Walks in Beauty

She walks in beauty, like the night
Of cloudless climes and starry skies;
And all that's best of dark and bright[1)]
Meet in her aspect[2)] and her eyes:
Thus mellowed[3)] to that tender light
Which heaven to gaudy[4)] day denies.

One shade the more, one ray the less[5)],
Had half impaired the nameless grace[6)]
Which waves in every raven tress[7)],
Or softly lightens o'er her face;
Where thoughts serenely sweet express
How pure, how dear their dwelling place[8)].

And on that cheek, and o'er that brow,
So soft, so calm, yet eloquent,
The smiles that win, the tints that glow,
But tell of days in goodness spent,
A mind at peace with all below,
A heart whose love is innocent!

(From *Hebrew Melodies*, 1815)

---

* 바이런은 1814년 6월 11일 Lady Sitwell의 집에서 열린 무도회에 참석하였고, 거기서 상복을 입은 처사촌 Lady Wilmot Horton을 만났다. 그는 그녀의 미모와 그 아름다움을 감싸고 있는 검은 옷에 감동되어 집으로 돌아오자마자 밤 새워 이 시를 지었다.

1) *dark and bright*: 어둠과 광명; *bright*: (n) brightness, light
2) *aspect*: 얼굴, 용모 (countenance)
3) *mellow*: 무르익다 (ripen)
4) *gaudy*: 야한 (vulgarly colourful), 화려한 (splendid)
5) *One shade the more, one ray the less*: 그늘이 한 가닥 더 많거나, 빛이 한 줄기 더했더라면
6) *the nameless grace*: 이루 형언할 수 없는 아름다움: *grace*: attractiveness, elegance or refinement
7) *raven tress*: 검은 머리카락; *raven*: 새까만 (glossy black); *tress*: a long lock of human (esp. female) hair
8) *their dwelling place*: 생각의 보금자리

My Soul Is Dark

My soul is dark—Oh! quickly string
  The harp I yet can brook to hear;
And let thy gentle fingers fling
  Its melting murmur o'er mine ear.
If in this heart a hope be dear,
  That sound shall charm it forth again:
If in these eyes there lurk a tear,
  'Twill flow, and cease to burn my brain.

But bid the strain be wild and deep,
  Nor let thy notes of joy be first:
I tell thee, minstrel, I must weep,
  Or else this heavy heart will burst;
For it had been by sorrow nursed,
  And ached in sleepless silence long;
And now 'tis doomed to know the worst,
  And break at once—or yield to song.

(From *Hebrew Melodies*, 1815)

When we two are parted

When we two parted
In silence and tears,
Half broken-hearted,
To sever for years,
Pale grew thy cheek and cold,
Colder thy kiss;
Truly that hour foretold
Sorrow to this.

The dew of the morning
Sank chill on my brow
It felt like the warning
Of what I feel now.
Thy vows are all broken,
And light is thy fame:
I hear thy name spoken,
And share in its shame.

They name thee before me,
A knell to mine ear;
A shudder comes o'er me
Why wert thou so dear?
They know not I knew thee,
Who knew thee too well:
Long, long shall I rue thee
Too deeply to tell.

In secret we met
In silence I grieve
That thy heart could forget,
Thy spirit deceive.
If I should meet thee
After long years,
How should I greet thee?
With silence and tears.

1813 (1816)

So We'll Go No More a-Roving

So we'll go no more a-roving[1)]
    So late into the night,
Though the heart be still as loving,
    And the moon be still as bright.

For the sword outwears its sheath[2)],
    And the soul outwears the breast,
And the heart must pause to breathe,
    And love itself have rest.

Though the night was made for loving,
    And the day returns too soon,
Yet we'll go no more a-roving
    By the light of the moon.

February 28, 1817 (1830)

---

* 이 시에는 독특한 아이러니가 담겨 있다. 표면적으로는 인생무상에 대한 우울한 명상인 것 같으면서, 실은 베니스에서 사육제 마지막 날(Mardi gras) 술잔치 후의 숙취를 묘사한 것이다.

1) *a-roving*: roving

2) *sheath*: 칼집 (a close-fitting case for the blade of a sword)

From *Childe Harold's Pilgrimage*

A Romaunt[1])

From Canto the First

I

Oh, thou! in Hellas[2)] deem'd of heavenly birth,
Muse! form'd or fabled at the minstrel's will[3)]!
Since shamed full oft by later lyres on earth,
Mine[4)] dares not call thee from thy sacred hill:
Yet there I've wander'd by thy vaunted rill;
Yes! sigh'd o'er Delphi's[5)] long deserted shrine,
Where, save that feeble fountain fell is still;
Nor mote[6)] my shell[7)] awake the weary Nine[8)]
To grace so plain a tale—this lowly lay of mine.

---

* 이 시는 여행기(旅行記)이며, 화자는 우울하고, 열정적이며, 박식하고 화술이 뛰어난 여행자이다. 바이런은 1809년부터 2년간 스페인, 포르투갈, 알바니아, 그리스 등지를 여행하는 동안 제1편과 제2편을 썼고, 1812년에 이 두 편을 발표하고 나서 그는 일약 런던 사교계의 명사가 되었다. 그 후 1816년에 아내 밀뱅크(Milbanke)와 이혼하고 나서 영국을 영원히 떠나 유럽을 여행하면서 다시 쓰기 시작하여 그 해에 제3편을 발표했다. 제3편에는 벨기에에서 라인 강을 경유하여 스위스와 알프스를 여행한 경험이 기록되어 있다. 그리고 1818년에 발표된 제4편에는 이탈리아의 도시와 유적이 기록되어 있다. 이 시의 형식은 스펜서 시체(詩體)로 되어 있다. 스펜서 시체는 처음 8행은 약강5보격, 마지막 행은 약강6보격으로 이루어지며, ababbcbcc의 압운을 가진 9행시이다. 바이런은 제1편에서 스펜서 시풍을 따라 고어 체를 사용하였으나 제2편부터는 고어 체를 더 이상 사용하지 않았다. 첫 두 편의 서문에서 화자인 해롤드 공자(Childe Harold)가 상상력으로 창조한 가상적 인물임을 강조하였으나, 그의 원고에는 "Childe Burun"("Burun"은 그의 성인 Byron의 초기 형태)으로 되어 있었고 특히 제4편은 1인칭 화자로 되어 있어 세인들이 화자를 시인과 동일시하는 경향을 보인다.

1) Romaunt: a romance, or narrative of adventure
2) *Hellas*: Greece
3) *formed or fabled at the minstrel's will*: 시인들이 마음대로 지어낸; *fable*: 꾸며낸 이야기를 하다(tell fictitious tales).
4) mine: 나의 수금 (my lyre)
5) *Delphi*: 시신(詩神) 아폴로의 신전
6) *mote*: might
7) *shell*: 서사시인의 수금(竪琴)
8) *Nine*: the nine Muses

II

Whilome[1] in Albion's[2] isle there dwelt a youth,
Who ne[3] in virtue's ways did take delight;
But spent his days in riot most uncouth[4],
And vex'd[5] with mirth the drowsy ear of Night.
Oh, me! in sooth[6] he was a shameless wight[7],
Sore given to revel[8] and ungodly[9] glee;
Few earthly things found favour in his sight[10]
Save concubines and carnal companie[11],
And flaunting wassailers[12] of high and low degree.

III

Childe Harold[13] was he hight[14]:—but whence his name
And lineage long, it suits me not to say;
Suffice it, that perchance they were of fame,
And had been glorious in another day;
But one sad losel[15] soils[16] a name for aye,
However mighty in the olden time;

---

1) *whilome*: once upon a time
2) *Albion's*: England's
3) *ne*: never
4) *riot most uncouth*: 매우 천박한 환락; *riot*: 환락(loud revelry); uncouth: lacking refinement or grace, uncultured
5) *vex'd with mirth the drowsy ear of Night*: 야밤에 시끌벅적하게 소란을 피워 자는 사람을 깨웠다; *vex*: 괴롭히다 (trouble, irritate);
6) *in sooth*: in truth
7) *wight*: a person, a human being
8) *revel*: 환락, 주연 (riotous or noisy merrymaking)
9) *ungodly*: 불경한, 신앙심이 없는 (impious), 사악한
10) *Few earthly things found favour in his sight*: 그는 세상사에 별로 흥미를 느끼지 못했다 (He liked few earthly things)
11) *concubines and carnal companie*: 축첩과 육체적 교제; *concubine*: 내연의 처; *carnal*: fleshly, sexual
12) *flaunting wassailer*: 뽐내는 난봉꾼; *wassailer*: 술 마시고 떠드는 사람, 난봉꾼 (reveller)
13) *Childe Harold*: 해롤드 공자(公子); *childe*: (古) 기사 작위를 기다리는 귀족의 자제(貴公子)
14) *hight*: called
15) *losel*: 방탕아, 난봉꾼(profligate); 불량배(rascal), 악당 (wretch); Byron의 종조부(제5대 남작)는 술에 취해 결투를 하다가 친척을 죽인 일이 있었다.
16) *soil*: 더럽히다 (make dirty; defile or pollute with sin)

Nor all that heralds rake from coffin'd clay,
Nor florid prose, nor honied lies of rhyme,
Can blazon[1] evil deeds or consecrate[2] a crime.

IV

Childe Harold basked him in the noontide sun,
Disporting[3] there like any other fly,
Nor deemed before his little day was done
One blast might chill him into misery.
But long ere scarce a third of his passed by.
Worse than adversity the Childe befell;
He felt the fullness of satiety:
Then loathed he in his native land to dwell,
Which seemed to him more lone than eremite's[4] sad cell.

V

For he through Sin's long labyrinth had run,
Nor made atonement[5] when he did amiss,
Had sighed to many though he loved but one,
And that loved one, alas! could ne'er be his.
Ah, happy she! to 'scape from him whose kiss
Had been pollution unto aught so chaste;
Who soon had left her charms for vulgar bliss[6],
And spoiled her goodly lands to gild his waste[7],
Nor calm domestic peace had ever deigned[8] to taste.

---

1) *blazon*: 장식하다 (describe fitly or vividly)
2) *consecrate*: 죄를 씻다(sanctify), 정당화하다(justify)
3) *disport*: 장난 치며 놀다 (frolic, gambol, amuse oneself)
4) *Eremite's*: 은자의 (Hermit's)
5) *atonement*: 속죄 (reparation for injury or wrong)
6) *vulgar bliss*: vulgar: 저속한 기쁨(만족); *vulgar*: 저속한, 비천한 (coarse in manners; low)
7) *spoiled her goodly lands to gild his waste*: 꽤 많은 그녀의 땅을 빼앗아 자신의 낭비벽을 채웠다; *spoil*: 약탈하다 (plunder, deprive by force or stealth); *goodly*: 꽤 많은 (of considerable size); gild: 돈을 대주다 (supply with gold or money)
8) *deign (to do):* (자존심을 버리고)...하다 (think it worthy of oneself to do)

VI

And now Childe Harold was sore sick at heart,
And from his fellow bacchanals[1] would flee;
'Tis said, at times the sullen tear would start,
But Pride congealed the drop within his ee[2];
Apart he stalked in joyless reverie[3],
And from his native land resolved to go,
And visit scorching climes beyond the sea;
With pleasure drugged[4], he almost longed for woe,
And e'en for change of scene would seek the shades below[5].

VII

The Childe departed from his father's hall[6]:
It was a vast and venerable pile[7];
So old, it seemed only not to fall,
Yet strength was pillared[8] in each massy aisle.
Monastic dome! condemned to uses vile[9]!
Where Superstition once had made her den
Now Paphian girls[10] were known to sing and smile;
And monks might deem their time was come agen[11],
If ancient tales[12] say true, nor wrong these holy men.

VIII

Yet oft-times in his maddest mirthful mood

---

1) *bacchanals*: 박카스의 신도들 (worshippers of Bacchus); a noisy or drunken reveller
2) *Pride congealed the drop within his ee*: 자존심 때문에 눈물을 참았다; *congeal*: freeze; *ee*: eye
3) *joyless reverie*: 재미없는 몽상; *reverie*: 몽상(abstracted musing), 백일몽(a daydream)
4) *with pleasure drugged*: 쾌락에 신물이 나서; *drug*: cloy
5) *the shades below*: 세상의 은둔처; *shades*: a secluded spot or corner; *below*: on earth
6) *hall*: 저택 (a mansion, a large residence)
7) *venerable pile*: 거룩한 건축물, 즉 바이런가의 종가인 Newstead Abbey
8) *pillar*: embody in the form of a pillar
9) *uses vile*: 나쁜 용도, 사악한 관행(풍습)
10) *Paphian girls*: 창녀들 (prostitutes); 사랑과 미의 여신 Aphrodite의 신전이 있던 파포스 섬(Paphos)에서 유래
11) *agen*: again (운을 맞추기 위해 철자를 바꾸었음)
12) *ancient tales*: 예날 이야기; 바이런은 수도원에 숨어서 음탕한 행위를 해온 오랜 전통에 관해 언급하고 있다.

Strange pangs would flash along Childe Harold's brow,
As if the memory of some deadly feud[1]
Or disappointed passion lurked below:
But this none knew, nor haply cared to know;
For his was not that open, artless soul
That feels relief by bidding sorrow flow,
Nor sought he friend to counsel or condole[2],
Whate'er this grief mote be, which he could not control.

IX

And none did love him—though to hall and bower
He gather'd revellers from far and near,
He knew them flatterers of the festal hour;
The heartless parasites[3] of present cheer[4].
Yea! none did love him—not his lemans[5] dear—
But pomp[6] and power alone are woman's care,
And where these are light Eros finds a feere;
Maidens, like moths, are ever caught by glare[7],
And Mammon[8] wins his way where Seraphs might despair.

X

Childe Harold had a mother—not forgot,
Though parting from that mother he did shun;
A sister whom he loved, but saw her not
Before his weary pilgrimage begun:
If friends he had, he bade adieu to none.
Yet deem not thence his breast a breast of steel:
Ye, who have known what 'tis to dote upon[9]

---

1) *deadly feud*: 불구대천의 원한; *deadly*: implacable; *feud*: (여러 대에 걸친 가문 간의) 숙원(宿怨) 또는 불화 (lasting mutual hostility, esp. between two tribes, families, etc.)
2) *condole*: 위로하다 (express sympathy with)
3) *heartless parasites*: 냉혹한 기생충들
4) *cheer*: joy, cheerfulness, mirth
5) *lemans*: lovers
6) *pomp*: 허세, 겉치레 (splendid display, magnificent show)
7) *glare*: 화려한 겉치레 (showy appearance, gaudiness)
8) *Mammon*: 물질적 부와 탐욕의 신
9) *dote upon*: 맹목적으로 사랑하다 (be expressively fond of)

A few dear objects, will in sadness feel
Such partings break the heart they fondly hope to heal.

XI

His house, his home, his heritage, his lands,
The laughing dames in whom he did delight,
Whose large blue eyes, fair locks and snowy hands,
Might shake the saintship[1] of an anchorite[2],
And long had fed his youthful appetite:
His goblets brimmed with every costly wine,
And all that mote to luxury invite,
Without a sigh he left[3], to cross the brine[4],
And traverse[5] Paynim[6] shores, and pass Earth's central line.

XII

The sails were fill'd, and fair the light winds blew,
As glad to waft[7] him from his native home;
And fast the white rocks[8] faded from his view,
And soon were lost in circumambient[9] foam:
And then, it may be, of his wish to roam
Repented he, but in his bosom slept
The silent thought, nor from his lips did come
One word of wail, whilst others sate and wept,
And to the reckless gales unmanly moaning kept.

XIII

But when the sun was sinking in the sea

---

1) *saintship*: 성인다움 (saintliness)
2) *Anchorite*: religious hermit
3) *leave*: 버리고 떠나다 (depart without taking); 목적어는 "His goblets"와 "all"
4) *the brine*: 바다 (the sea)
5) *traverse*: travel across
6) *Paynim*: pagan을 의미하는 중세영어
7) *waft*: convey easily through air or over water
8) *white rocks*: Dover의 흰색 절벽; 영국을 떠날 때 마지막으로 보이는 것
9) *circumambient*: surrounding

He seized his harp, which he at times could string,
And strike, albeit with untaught melody,
When deem'd he no strange ear was listening:
And now his fingers o'er it he did fling,
And tuned his farewell in the dim twilight.
While flew the vessel on her snowy wing,
And fleeting shores receded from his sight,
Thus to the elements he pour'd his last 'Good Night.'

Childe Harold's Good Night

1

'Adieu, adieu! my native shore
  Fades o'er the waters blue;
The Night-winds sigh, the breakers roar,
  And shrieks the wild sea-mew[1].
Yon Sun that sets upon the sea
  We follow in his flight;
Farewell awhile to him and thee,
  My native Land—Good Night!

2

'A few short hours and He[2] will rise
  To give the morrow birth;
And I shall hail the main[3] and skies,
  But not my mother earth.
Deserted is my own good hall,
  Its hearth is desolate;
Wild weeds are gathering on the wall;
  My dog howls at the gate.

3

'Come hither, hither, my little page[4]!
  Why dost thou weep and wail?
Or dost thou dread the billows' rage,
  Or tremble at the gale?
But dash the tear-drop from thine eye;
  Our ship is swift and strong:
Our fleetest falcon scarce can fly
  More merrily along.'

---

1) *sea-mew*: 갈매기 (a gull)
2) *He*: i. e. the Sun
3) *main*: 큰 바다 (high seas)
4) *page*: a boy employed as personal attendant

4

'Let winds be shrill[1], let waves roll high,
  I fear not wave nor wind;
Yet marvel[2] not, Sir Childe, that I
  Am sorrowful in mind;
For I have from my father gone,
  A mother whom I love,
And have no friend, save these alone,
  But thee—and one above.

5

'My father bless'd me fervently,
  Yet did not much complain;
But sorely will my mother sigh
  Till I come back again.'
'Enough, enough, my little lad!
  Such tears become thine eye;
If I they guileless[3] bosom had,
  Mine own would not be dry.

6

'Come hither, hither, my staunch[4] yeoman,
  Why dost thou look so pale?
Or dost thou dread a French foeman?
  Or shiver at the gale?'
'Deem'st thou I tremble for my life?
  Sir Childe, I'm not so weak:
But thinking on an absent wife
  Will blanch[5] a faithful cheek.

---

1) *shrill*: high-pitched and piercing; keen or sharp to the senses
2) *marvel*: be surprised
3) guileless: 정직한, 순진한
4) *staunch yeoman*: 충실한 시종; 충실한 (loyal, trustworthy)
5) *blanch*: make white

7

My spouse and boys dwell near thy hall,
Along the bordering lake,
And when they on their father call,
What answer shall she make?'
'Enough, enough, my yeoman good,
Thy grief let none gainsay[1];
But I, who am of lighter mood,
Will laugh to flee away.

8

'For who would trust the seeming sighs
Of wife or paramour[2]?
Fresh feres[3] will dry the bright blue eyes
We late saw streaming o'er.
For pleasures past I do not grieve
Nor perils gathering near;
My greatest grief is that I leave
No thing that claims a tear.

9

'And now I'm in the world alone,
Upon the wide, wide sea:
But why should I for others groan,
When none will sigh for me?
Perchance my dog will whine in vain,
Till fed by stranger hands;
But long ere I come back again
He'd tear me where he stands.

10

'With thee, my bark, I'll swiftly go

---

1) *gainsay:* deny, contradict
2) paramour: 정부(情婦) (an illicit lover of a married man or woman)
3) *fere*: 친구 (a friend)

Athwart the foaming brine;
Nor care what land thou bearest me to,
So not again to mine.
Welcome, welcome, ye dark-blue waves!
And when you fail my sight,
Welcome, ye deserts, and ye caves!
My native Land—Good Night!'

From Canto the Third

I

Is thy face like thy mother's, my fair child!
Ada![1] sole daughter of my house and heart?
When last I saw thy young blue eyes they smil'd,
And then we parted—not as now we part,
But with a hope[2]—Awaking with a start,
The waters heave around me; and on high
The winds lift up their voices: I depart[3],
Whither I know not; but the hour's gone by,
When Albion's lessening shores could grieve or glad[4] mine eye.

II

Once more upon the waters! yet once more!
And the waves bound beneath me as a steed
That knows his rider. Welcome to their roar!
Swift be their guidance, wheresoe'er it lead!
Though the strain'd mast should quiver as a reed,
And the rent canvas fluttering strew the gale,
Still must I on; for I am as a weed,
Flung from the rock, on Ocean's foam to sail
Where'er the surge may sweep, the tempest's breath prevail.

III

In my youth's summer I did sing of One[5],
The wandering outlaw of his own dark mind;
Again I seize the theme, then but begun,
And bear it with me, as the rushing wind
Bears the cloud onwards: in that Tale I find

---

1) *Ada*: 바이런 부부 사이에 태어난 딸 Augusta Ada Byron, 1815년 12월 10일 생
2) *with hope*: (아내와 화해할) 희망을 가지고; 그들 부부는 끝내 화해하지 못하고 이혼했다.
3) *I depart*: 나는 떠난다; 바이런은 1816년 4월 25일 영국을 떠나 돌아가지 않았다.
4) *glad*: 기쁘게 하다 (gladden, make glad)
5) *One*: Harold

The furrows of long thought[1], and dried-up tears,
Which, ebbing, leave a sterile track behind,
O'er which all heavily the journeying years
Plod the last sands of life—where not a flower appears.

IV

Since my young days of passion—joy, or pain—
Perchance my heart and harp have lost a string,
And both may jar[2]: it may be, that in vain
I would essay as I have sung to sing[3].
Yet, though a dreary strain, to this I cling;
So that it wean me from the weary dream
Of selfish grief or gladness—so it fling
Forgetfulness around me—it shall seem
To me, though to none else, a not ungrateful[4] theme.

V

He, who grown aged in this world of woe,
In deeds, not years, piercing the depths of life,
So that no wonder waits him; nor below
Can love or sorrow, fame, ambition, strife,
Cut to his heart again with the keen knife
Of silent, sharp endurance: he can tell
Why thought seeks refuge in lone caves, yet rife[5]
With airy images, and shapes which dwell
Still unimpair'd, though old, in the soul's haunted cell.

VI

'Tis to create, and in creating live
A being more intense, that we endow
With form our fancy, gaining as we give

---

1) *The furrows of long thought*: 오랜 생각의 자취;
2) *jar*: 삐걱거리다, 불협화음을 내다
3) *essay to sing*: make an attempt to sing
4) *ungrateful*: unpleasant, disagreeable
5) *rife (with)*: full of

He would not yield dominion of his mind
To spirits against whom his own rebell'd;
Proud though in desolation; which could find
A life within itself, to breathe without mankind.

XIII

Where rose the mountains, there to him were friends;
Where roll'd the ocean, thereon was his home;
Where a blue sky, and glowing clime, extends,
He had the passion and the power to roam;
The desert, forest, cavern, breaker's foam,
Were unto him companionship; they spake
A mutual language, clearer than the tome
Of his land's tongue, which he would oft forsake
For Nature's pages glass'd by sunbeams on the lake.

XIV

Like the Chaldean[1]), he could watch the stars,
Till he had peopled them with beings bright
As their own beams; and earth, and earthborn jars,
And human frailties, were forgotten quite:
Could he have kept his spirit to that flight
He had been happy; but this clay will sink
Its spark immortal, envying it the light
To which it mounts, as if to break the link
That keeps us from yon heaven which woos us to its brink.

XV

But in Man's dwellings he became a thing
Restless and worn, and stern and wearisome,
Droop'd as a wild-born falcon with clipp'd wing,
To whom the boundless air alone were home:
Then came his fit again, which to o'ercome,

---

1) *Chaldean*: 칼데아 인; 티그리스와 유프라테스 강 유역에 고대 도시 바빌로니아를 세운 셈 인종; 천문학과 점성술로 유명.

As eagerly the barr'd-up bird will beat
His breast and beak against his wiry dome
Till the blood tinge his plumage, so the heat
Of his impeded soul would through his bosom eat.

XVI

Self-exil'd Harold wanders forth again,
With nought of hope left, but with less of gloom;
The very knowledge that he lived in vain,
That all was over on this side the tomb,
Had made Despair a smilingness assume,
Which, though 'twere wild—as on the plunder'd wreck
When mariners would madly meet their doom
With draughts intemperate on the sinking deck—,
Did yet inspire a cheer, which he forbore to check.

*　　*　　*

LII

Thus Harold inly said, and pass'd along,
Yet not insensible to all which here
Awoke the jocund birds to early song
In glens which might have made even exile dear:
Though on his brow were graven lines austere,
And tranquil sternness, which had ta'en the place
Of feelings fierier far but less severe,
Joy was not always absent from his face,
But o'er it in such scenes would steal with transient trace.

LIII

Nor was all love shut from him, though his days
Of passion had consumed themselves to dust.
It is vain that we would coldly gaze
On such as smile upon us; the heart must
Leap kindly back to kindness, though disgust
Hath wean'd it from all worldlings: thus he felt,

Percy Bysshe Shelley

(1792~1822)

Edward Onslow Ford's sculpture in the Shelley Memorial at University College, Oxford

For there was soft remembrance, and sweet trust
In one fond breast[1]), to which his own would melt,
And in its tenderer hour on that his bosom dwelt.

LIV

And he had learn'd to love,—I know not why,
For this in such as him seems strange of mood,—
The helpless looks of blooming infancy,
Even in its earliest nurture; what subdued,
To change like this, a mind so far imbued
With scorn of man, it little boots to know;
But thus it was; and though in solitude
Small power the nipp'd affections have to grow,
In him this glow'd when all beside had ceased to glow.

LV

And there was one soft breast, as hath been said,
Which unto his was bound by stronger ties
Than the church links withal; and, though unwed,
That love was pure, and, far above disguise,
Had stood the test of mortal enmities
Still undivided, and cemented more
By peril, dreaded most in female eyes;
But this was firm, and from a foreign shore
Well to that heart might his these absent greeting pour!

---

1) *one fond breast*: 바이런의 이복누이 Augusta

Selected Bibliography

1. Primary Sources

More, Paul Elmer (ed.). *The Complete Poetical Works of Lord Byron*. Cambridge Edition of the Poets, Boston, 1905.

McConnell, Frank D. Byron's Poetry (A Norton Critical Edition). New York: Norton, 1978.

2. Secondary Sources:

Cooke, Michael G. *The Blind Man Traces the Circle: On the Patterns and Philosophy of Byron's Poetry*. Princeton, N. J.: Princeton UP, 1969.

Gleckner, Robert F. *Byron and the Ruins of Paradise*. Baltimore, 1967.

Joseph, M. K. *Byron the Poet*. London, 1964.

Lovell, Ernest J. Byron: *The Record of a Quest*. Austin, 1950.

Marchand, Leslie A. *Byron's Poetry: A Critical Introduction*. Cambridge, Mass., 1968.

Marshall, William H. *The Structure of Byron's Major Poems*. Philadelphia, 1962.

McGann, Jerome J. *Fiery Dust: Byron's Poetic Development*. Chicago, 1968.

Ridenour, George M. *The Style of Don Juan*. New Haven, 1960.

Rutherford, Andrew. *Byron: A Critical Study*. Palo Alto, 1961.

Steffan, Truman Guy. *Don Juan: The Making of a Masterpiece*. Austin, 1957.

Thorslev, Peter L. *The Byronic Hero: Types and Prototypes*. Minneapolis, 1962.

West, Paul (ed.). Byron: *A Collection of Critical Essays*. Englewood Cliffs, 1963.

한 플라톤의 우주관에 공감하였다. 셸리를 철두철미한 플라톤적 이상주의자로 본 초기의 해석은 최근에 대폭 수정되었다. 그는 영국의 경험주의 전통 속에서 데이비드 흄(David Hume)의 급진적 회의론에도 관심을 보였다. 셸리는 분명 이상주의자이지만, 그의 이상주의는 제한적 이상주의이다. 그는 경험을 초월하는 상상력에 의해 그려진 이데아의 세계를 잠정적으로 받아들이지만, 이데아의 세계를 순수한 가능성 이상의 것으로 보지는 않았다. 셸리의 회의적 이상주의에 의하면, 사랑과 상상력에 의한 인간의 궁극적 구원에 대한 희망은 확신이 아니라 도덕적 의무이다. 우리는 누구나 희망을 버리지 말아야 한다. 희망이 곧 성취를 보장하지는 않지만, 성취의 가능성을 열어주며, 그렇게 함으로써 희망의 성취를 위한 유일한 수단인 상상력과 창조력을 발현시킬 수 있게 된다.

셸리는 1820년에 Pisa에 정착하여 좋은 친구들과 교제하면서 비교적 평탄한 나날을 보냈다. 그의 종말은 돌연히 찾아왔다. 「아도네이스」의 마지막 연에서 셸리의 영혼이 맹렬한 폭풍에 휩싸여 미지의 암흑 속으로 밀려가는 배의 묘사는 마치 자신의 죽음을 예견한 것처럼 보인다. 그는 1822년 7월 8일 친구 에드워드 윌리엄즈(Edward Williams)와 함께 작은 배 돈 주안(Don Juan) 호에 몸을 싣고 레리치 근처의 여름 별장으로 항해하고 있었다. 그런데 사나운 스콜이 몰아쳐 그 배를 침몰시켜 버렸다. 며칠이 지나 그들의 시체가 해안에 밀려 왔고, 그의 시체는 화장되어 키츠와 그의 아들 윌리엄 셸리의 무덤이 있는 로마의 신교도 묘지에 묻혔다.

Ozymandias

I met a traveller from an antique land[1)]
Who said:—Two vast and trunkless[2)] legs of stone
Stand in the desert. Near them on the sand,
Half sunk, a shatter'd visage[3)] lies, whose frown
And wrinkled lip and sneer of cold command
Tell that its sculptor well those passions read
Which yet survive, stamp'd on these lifeless things,
The hand that mock'd[4)] them and the heart that fed[5)].
And on the pedestal[6)] these words appear:
"My name is Ozymandias, king of kings:
Look on my works, ye Mighty, and despair!"
Nothing beside remains: round the decay
Of that colossal wreck[7)], boundless and bare,
The lone and level sands stretch far away.

1817(1818)

---

* Ozymandias는 기원전 13세기 이집트 왕 람세스 2세(Ramses Ⅱ) (1292-1225 B.C.)의 그리스 이름이다. 기원전 1세기 그리스 역사가 Diodorus Siculus에 의하면, 이집트의 조상에 다음과 같은 글이 새겨져 있었다고 한다: "나는 왕 중의 왕 오지만디어스다. 누구든지 내가 누구인지 그리고 내가 어디에 있는지를 알고자 한다면, 나보다 더 위대한 업적을 쌓게 하라."

1) *antique land*: 고대의 나라; *antique*: ancient, having existed since old times
2) *trunkless*: 동체(胴體) 없는 (having no trunk, without a body)
3) *shattered visage*: 부서진 얼굴; *visage*: the face of a person
4) *mock*: ① 모방하다 (imitate) ② 조롱하다, 비웃다 (deride with scornful words or gestures); *the hand that mock'd them*: 그 정열을 모방한(비웃은) 손
5) *the heart that fed (them)*: (정열을) 기른 가슴
6) *pedestal*: 대좌(臺座) (the base on which the statue is erected)
7) *colossal wreck*: 거대한 잔해; *colossal*: 거대한 (gigantic, tremendous)

To Wordsworth

Poet of Nature, thou hast wept to know
That things depart which never may return:
Childhood and youth, friendship and love's first glow,
Have fled like sweet dreams, leaving thee to mourn.
These common woes I feel. One loss is mine
Which thou too feel'st, yet I alone deplore.
Thou wert as a lone star, whose light did shine
On some frail bark in winter's midnight roar:
Thou hast like to a rock-built refuge stood
Above the blind and battling multitude:
In honoured poverty thy voice did weave
Songs consecrate[1]) to truth and liberty,—
Deserting these, thou leavest me to grieve,
Thus having been, that thou shouldst cease to be.

1816

---

* 이 시에서 셸리는 워즈워스와 Robert Southey가 정치적으로나 종교적으로 점차 보수주의로 기울어진 것을 비판하고 있다. 셸리는 작품을 통해서 워즈워스를 알았고, 1812년 11월부터 1813년 1월까지 Cumberland의 Keswick에 머무는 동안 Southey와 알고 지냈다. Mary Shelley는 1814년 9월 14일자 일기에서 "셸리가...워즈워스의 *The Excursion*을 집에 가지고 와서, 우리는 그 일부를 읽고 매우 실망했다. 그는 노예이다"라고 적었다. (Reiman & Powers 88n)

1) *Songs consecrate to truth and liberty*: 진리와 자유에 바친 노래; *consecrate*: consecrated

Hymn to Intellectual Beauty[1]

I

The awful shadow of some unseen Power
Floats though unseen among us,—visiting
This various[2] world with as inconstant[3] wing
As summer winds that creep from flower to flower,—
Like moonbeams that behind some piny mountain shower,
It visits with inconstant glance[4]
Each human heart and countenance;
Like hues and harmonies of evening,—
Like clouds in starlight widely spread,—
Like memory of music fled,—
Like aught that for its grace[5] may be
Dear, and yet dearer for its mystery.

II

Spirit[6] of Beauty, that dost consecrate[7]
With thine own hues all thou dost shine upon
Of[8] human thought or form,—where art thou gone?
Why dost thou pass away and leave our state,
This dim vast vale of tears[9], vacant and desolate?

---

* 1816년 여름에 Byron과 함께 Geneva 호반에 머무는 동안 지은 시이다. 1817년 1월 19일 Leigh Hunt의 주간지 *Examiner*에 처음 발표되었다. 셸리는 이 시에서 영원불변의 진리는 이데아요 현상계는 이데아의 그림자에 불과하다는 플라톤의 관념론을 표현하고 있다. "이상미"는 실체가 보이지 않는 그림자이며 잠깐 나타났다가 금방 사라져 버린다. 이 "이상미"의 성격은 워즈워스의 「불멸송」("Ode: Intimations of Immortality")에 묘사된 "천국의 빛"과 매우 유사하다.

1) *Intellectual*: nonmaterial, spiritual; *Intellectual Beauty*: 이상미(理想美), 관념미(觀念美).

2) *various*: 변하는, 변화가 많은 (subject to variation or change, changing, variable)

3) *inconstant*: not steadfast or faithful, changeable, variable

4) *glance*: 섬광 (a flash, a gleam)

5) *grace*: 매력 (attractiveness, charm), 아름다움 (an attractive or pleasing quality or feature)

6) *Spirit*: 정령(精靈) (a creature without a physical body that some people believe exists, such as an angel, who has returned to this world and has strange or magical powers)

7) *consecrate*: 신성하게 하다 (set apart as holy, sanctify)

8) 전치사 "of"는 앞줄의 "All"에 연결된다; *all thou dost shine upon / Of human thought or form*: 그대가 비추는 모든 인간의 사상과 형태

9) *This dim vast vale of tears*: 이 희미하고 거대한 눈물의 골짜기; 앞줄의 "our state"와 동격.

Ask why the sunlight not for ever
Weaves rainbows o'er yon mountain-river,
Why aught should fail and fade[1] that once is shown[2],
Why fear and dream and death and birth
Cast on the daylight of this earth
Such gloom,—why man has such a scope[3]
For love and hate, despondency and hope?

III

No voice from some sublimer world[4] hath ever
To sage or poet these responses given—
Therefore the names of God, ghosts, and Heaven,
Remain the records of their[5] vain endeavour,
Frail spells[6]—whose uttered charm might not avail to sever,
From all we hear and all we see,
Doubt, chance[7], and mutability[8].
Thy light alone—like mist o'er mountains driven[9],
Or music by the night-wind sent
Through strings of some still instrument[10],
Or moonlight on a midnight stream,
Gives grace and truth to life's unquiet dream.

---

1) *fail and fade*: 점점 희미해져 보이지 않게 되다; *fail*: grow dim and faint; *fade*: disappear gradually.
2) *that once is shewn*: 한때 보이던; "that"의 선행사는 "aught".
3) *scope*: (활동의) 영역, 여지 (the reach or range of a person's mental activity or perception)
4) *some sublimer world*: (현세보다) 더 숭고한 어떤 세계; 즉 초월의 세계 또는 영혼의 세계
5) *their*: 현자와 시인의.
6) *frail spells*: 힘없는 주문(呪文); 앞줄의 "the records of their vain endeavour"와 동격임; "신, 유령 그리고 천국"을 추구하는 종교나 미신이 "이상미" 또는 "미의 정령"의 덧없음을 설명하려는 시도는 헛된 노력이며, "회의와 운명과 무상"을 해소할 수 없는 "힘없는 주문"일 뿐이다.
7) *chance*: 운명 (fortune, fate); the course of events regarded as a power
8) mutability: 무상(無常)
9) *like mist o'er mountains driven*: 산위로 몰려오는 안개처럼; 어순은 "like mist driven o'er mountains임.
10) *some still instrument*: 어느 조용하게 울리는 악기: Aeolian harp

IV

Love, Hope, and Self-esteem[1]), like clouds depart
And come, for some uncertain moments lent[2]).
Man were immortal, and omnipotent,
Didst thou, unknown and awful as thou art,
Keep with thy glorious train[3]) firm state within his heart.[4])
Thou messenger[5]) of sympathies,
That wax and wane in lovers' eyes—
Thou—that to human thought art nourishment,
Like darkness to a dying flame![6])
Depart not as thy shadow came,
Depart not—lest the grave should be,
Like life and fear, a dark reality.

V

While yet a boy I sought for ghosts, and sped
Through many a listening chamber[7]), cave and ruin,
And starlight wood, with fearful steps pursuing
Hopes of high talk with the departed dead.
I called on poisonous names[8]) with which our youth is fed;
I was not heard—I saw them not—
When musing deeply on the lot
Of life, at that sweet time when winds are wooing

---

1) *Love, Hope, and Self-esteem*: 사랑과 소망과 자존; 이것은 기독교의 3가지 미덕인 "믿음, 소망, 사랑" 중에서 "믿음"을 "자존"으로 바꾼 것이다. "자존"은 우리 내부에서 도덕적 선을 행하는 위대한 힘인 상상력에 대한 존중을 의미한다. 이 세 가지 미덕은 상상력 또는 이상미가 찾아올 때 우리에게 주어진다(Bloom 284).

2) *lent*: given; "for some uncertain moments lent": 불확실한 순간 동안만 주어진다.

3) *thy glorious train*: 그대의 영광스런 무리들, 즉 "사랑, 소망, 자존"을 가리킨다.

4) 39-41행은 가정법 구문이다. *were*: would be; *Didst thou...*: If thou didst...: 비록 그대가 미지의 존재이고 두렵기는 하나, 만약 그대가 그대의 영광스런 무리들과 함께 인간의 마음속에 확고한 상태를 유지한다면, 인간은 죽지 않고 전능하게 될 것이다. *train*: a long line of moving people, animals or vehicles

5) *messenger*: 사자(使者) (a person who carries a message or goes on an errand for another); *Thou messenger...lover's eyes*: 그대 연인들의 눈에서 차고 기우는 공감의 사자여.

6) *Like darkness to a dying flame*: 마치 어둠이 꺼져가는 불꽃을 더 밝게 보이게 만들듯이.

7) *listening chamber*: 조용한 방;

8) *poisonous names*: 해로운 이름들, 즉 "God, ghosts, and Heaven"을 가리킨다.

All vital things[1] that wake to bring
News of birds and blossoming,—
Sudden, thy shadow fell on me;
I shrieked, and clasped my hands in ecstasy!

VI

I vowed that I would dedicate my powers
To thee and thine[2]—have I not kept the vow?
With beating heart and streaming eyes, even now
I call the phantoms of a thousand hours[3]
Each from his voiceless grave: they have in visioned bowers[4]
Of studious zeal[5] or love's delight
Outwatched[6] with me the envious night—
They know that never joy illumed my brow
Unlinked[7] with hope that thou wouldst free
This world from its dark slavery,
That thou—O awful Loveliness,
Wouldst give whate'er these words cannot express.

VII

The day becomes more solemn and serene
When noon is past—there is a harmony
In autumn, and a lustre in its sky,
Which through the summer is not heard or seen,
As if it could not be, as if it had not been!
Thus let thy power, which like the truth
Of nature on my passive youth

---

1) *All vital things*: 살아있는 만물; *vital*: full of life and energy
2) *I vowed...thine*: 나는 그대와 그대의 것에게 내 힘을 바치기로 약속했다. 여기서 화자는 이상미에 헌신하기로 맹세한다.
3) *the phantoms of a thousand hours*: 천 년 전의 유령들; *hours*: years
4) visioned bowers: 유령의 방, 상상의 방 (abodes peopled with phantoms)
5) *studious zeal*: 학구적인 정열, 진리에의 열정
6) *outwatch*: (밤을) 지새다; 밤 새워 망을 보다
7) *unlinked with hope*: (그대가 이 세상을 암울한 예속에서 해방시켜 줄 것이라는) 희망과 무관한 (기쁨); 이것은 앞줄의 "joy"를 수식하는 형용사구이다.

Descended, to my onward life[1] supply
    Its calm—to one who worships thee,
    And every form containing thee[2],
    Whom[3], Spirit fair, thy spells did bind
To fear himself, and love all human kind.

1816(1817)

---

1) *my onward life*: 내 미래의 삶

2) *one who worships thee, / And every form containing thee*: 그대(이상미)와 그대를 내포하고 있는 모든 형상을 숭배하는 사람; 즉 화자 자신을 가리킨다.

3) *Whom*: 선행사는 앞에 나온 "one"이다; 아름다운 정령이여, 그대 마력에 자신을 경외하고 온 인류를 사랑하게 된 (사람)

The Indian Serenade[1)]

1

I arise from dreams of thee
In the first sweet sleep of night,
When the winds are breathing low,
And the stars are shining bright
I arise from dreams of thee,
And a spirit in my feet
Hath led me—who knows how?
To thy chamber window, Sweet!

2

The wandering airs they faint
On the dark, the silent stream—
The champak[2)] odors fail
Like sweet thoughts in a dream;
The nightingale's complaint,
It dies upon her heart—
As I must on thine,
Oh, beloved as thou art!

3

O lift me from the grass!
I die! I faint! I fail!
Let thy love in kisses rain
On my lips and eyelids pale.
My cheek is cold and white, alas!
My heart beats loud and fast—
Oh! press it to thine own again,
Where it will break at last.

1819 (1822)

---

1) *serenade*: 소야곡(小夜曲), 세레나데 (밤에 애인의 집 창 밑에서 남자가 부르던 사랑의 노래)
2) *champak*: 황목련 (동인도 산 목련과의 상록 교목)

Ode to the West Wind

I

O wild West Wind, thou breath of Autumn's being
Thou from whose unseen presence the leaves dead
Are driven like ghosts from an enchanter fleeing,

Yellow, and black, and pale, and hectic red[1],
Pestilence-stricken multitudes![2] O thou
Who chariotest to their dark wintry bed

The wingèd seeds, where they lie cold and low,
Each like a corpse within its grave, until
Thine azure sister of the Spring shall blow

Her clarion[3] o'er the dreaming earth, and fill
(Driving sweet buds like flocks to feed in air)
With living hues and odours plain and hill[4];

Wild Spirit, which art moving everywhere;
Destroyer and preserver[5]; hear, O hear!

II

Thou on whose stream, 'mid the steep sky's commotion[6],

---

* "This poem was conceived and chiefly written in a wood that skirts the Arno, near Florence, and on a day when that tempestuous wind, whose temperature is at once mild and animating, was collecting the vapors which pour down the autumnal rains." (Shelley's note) 이 시의 중심 심상은 바람이다. 자연의 바람은 시인의 내부에서 영적 활력을 소생시키고 시적 영감을 불러일으킨다. 라틴어 "spiritus"는 바람(wind), 숨결(breath), 영혼(soul), 영감(inspiration) 등의 의미를 갖는다. "서풍"은 가을의 숨결이며, 대지와 하늘과 바다에서 봄의 소생을 위해 파괴한다. 시인은 이 시에서 바람의 심상을 중심으로 죽음과 재생의 주제를 다루고 있다.

1) *hectic red*: 열병에 걸린 듯 한 붉은 색; 소모성 열(hectic fever)은 흔히 홍조를 수반한다.

2) *pestilence-stricken multitudes*: 역병에 걸린 군중들

3) *clarion*: 낭랑하게 울려 퍼지는 나팔 (a high shrill trumpet); Cf. "the trumpet of prophecy"

4) *plain and hill*: 들판과 산; 10행의 동사 "fill"의 목적어.

5) *destroyer and preserver*: 파괴자요 보존자; 서풍은 낙엽을 떨어뜨리기 때문에 "파괴자"이고 봄에 싹이 틀 씨앗을 땅 속에 보존하기 때문에 "보존자"이다.

6) *steep sky's commotion*: 가파른 하늘의 소란

Loose clouds like earth's decaying leaves are shed,
Shook[1] from the tangled boughs of heaven and ocean[2],

Angels[3] of rain and lightning! there are spread
On the blue surface of thine airy surge,
Like the bright hair uplifted from the head

Of some fierce Mænad[4], even from the dim verge
Of the horizon to the zenith's height[5],
The locks of the approaching storm. Thou dirge

Of the dying year, to which this closing night
Will be the dome of a vast sepulchre,
Vaulted with all thy congregated[6] might

Of vapours, from whose solid[7] atmosphere
Black rain, and fire, and hail, will burst: O hear!

III

Thou who didst waken from his summer dreams
The blue Mediterranean, where he lay,
Lull'd by the coil of his crystàlline streams,

Beside a pumice isle[8] in Baiæ's bay[9],
And saw in sleep old palaces and towers

---

1) *shook*: shaken
2) *the tangled boughs of Heaven and Ocean*: 대지와 하늘의 뒤엉킨 가지들; 바다에서 수증기가 하늘로 뻗어 올라 있는 모습을 거대한 나무에 비유한 표현.
3) *angel*: 사자(使者) (messenger, harbinger)
4) Maenad: 주신(酒神) Bacchus의 여사제; 흔히 미친 듯이 춤을 추는 여인들의 모습으로 그려진다.
5) *zenith's height*: 천정의 높이; *zenith*: the highest point
6) *congregate*: 모으다 (collect or gather together into a mass)
7) *solid*: 짙은 (dense, thick, compact)
8) *pumice isle*: 경석 섬; *pumice*: 경석(輕石), 다공성의 화산암(a porous volcanic stone)
9) *Baiae's bay*: 바이아 만; Baiae는 이탈리아 서남부 나폴리 부근의 고대 도시. 옛 휴양지로 Caesar, Nero, Pompey 등의 별장이 있었다.

Quivering within the wave's intenser day[1],
All overgrown with azure moss, and flowers
So sweet, the sense faints picturing them! Thou
For whose path the Atlantic's level powers[2]

Cleave themselves into chasms, while far below
The sea-blooms and the oozy[3] woods which wear
The sapless foliage of the ocean, know

Thy voice, and suddenly grow gray with fear,
And tremble and despoil themselves[4]: O hear!

Ⅳ

If I were a dead leaf thou mightest bear;
If I were a swift cloud to fly with thee;
A wave to pant beneath thy power, and share

The impulse of thy strength, only less free
Than thou, O uncontrollable! if even
I were as in my boyhood, and could be

The comrade of thy wanderings over heaven,
As then, when to outstrip[5] thy skiey speed
Scarce seem'd a vision[6]—I would ne'er have striven

As thus with thee in prayer in my sore need.

---

1) *the wave's intenser day*: 파도의 더 강한 햇빛;
2) *level powers*: 평평한 파도
3) *oozy*: 습한 (full of moisture)
4) *despoil*: undress, strip of clothes or armour; 여기서는 "잎을 떨어뜨리다"는 의미이다. 39-42행에 관해서는 다음과 같은 시인의 주석이 붙어 있다. "The phenomenon alluded to at the conclusion of the third stanza is well known to naturalists. The vegetation at the botton of the sea, of rivers, and of lakes, sympathizes with that of the land in the change of seasons, and is consequently influenced by the winds which announce it." (Shelley's note);
5) *outstrip*: 능가하다 (excel, surpass)
6) *vision*: 환상, 환영 (a person or thing seen in a dream or trance)

Oh, lift me as a wave, a leaf, a cloud![1]
I fall upon the thorns of life! I bleed!

A heavy weight of hours has chain'd and bow'd
One too like thee—tameless, and swift, and proud.

V

Make me thy lyre[2], even as the forest is:
What if my leaves are falling like its own?
The tumult of thy mighty harmonies

Will take from both[3] a deep autumnal tone,
Sweet though in sadness. Be thou, Spirit fierce,
My spirit! Be thou me[4], impetuous one!

Drive my dead thoughts over the universe,
Like wither'd leaves, to quicken a new birth;
And, by the incantation of this verse,

Scatter, as from an unextinguish'd hearth
Ashes and sparks, my words among mankind![5]

---

1) *Lift me as a wave, a leaf, a cloud!*: 나를 파도처럼, 낙엽처럼, 구름처럼 들어 올려 다오! 이 첫 번째 기도에서, 화자는 자신을 서풍에 실려 가는 파도, 낙엽, 구름과 동일화한다. 그의 소원은 바람의 힘에 굴복하는 것이다. 그는 패배와 좌절에 직면한 시인(예언자)으로서 자신의 정체성이 소멸되는 죽음을 받아들인다.

2) *Make me thy lyre:* 나를 너의 수금(竪琴)으로 만들어 다오, 이 두 번째의 기도에서 화자는 바람에 잎을 떨어뜨리며 "슬프지만 감미로운" 가을의 "화음"을 내는 숲이나, 바람이 불면 소리를 낸다는 에올루스의 수금이 되고자 한다. 여기서도 행위자는 서풍이고, 화자 자신은 서풍이 "거대한 화음"을 연주하는 악기이다. 비록 수동적이기는 하지만, 서풍의 힘을 빌어 예언의 메시지를 전할 수 있는 가능성을 열어두고 있다는 점에서 첫째 기도와는 차이를 보인다.

3) *both:* "나(me)"와 "숲(the forest)"

4) *Be thou.../ My spirit! Be thou me*: 그대...내 정신이 되어 다오! 그대 내가 되어 다오; 화자는 이 세 번째와 네 번째의 기도에서 점진적으로 자신을 서풍과 동일화한다. 그는 서풍이 되어 예언의 말을 인류에게 전하고자 한다. 이것은 그 다음에 나오는 다섯 번째 기도에서 구체화된다.

5) *Drive dead thoughts...And scatter...Ashes and sparks, my words among mankind!*: 내 죽은 사상을 몰아가서 재와 불씨를, 내 말을 인류에게 뿌려다오! 이 다섯 번째 기도에서 화자는 자신이 서풍이 되어 예언의 말을 인류에게 전하고자 한다. "죽은 사상"에는, 마치 낙엽 속에 새로운 생명의 씨가 포함되어 있듯이, "재와 불씨"가 포함되어 있다. "재와 불씨"는 낙엽과 "날개

Be through my lips to unawaken'd earth

The trumpet of a prophecy![1] O Wind,
If Winter comes, can Spring be far behind?[2]

1819 (1820)

달린 종자들"처럼 끝과 시작, 즉 죽음과 재생을 의미한다. 이것은 다시 낡은 질서의 소멸과 새 질서의 도래를 알리는 "나의 말" 즉 시인의 예언의 말로 치환된다.

1) *Be through my lips to unawakened earth / The trumpet of a prophecy!*: 내 입술을 통해 잠 깨지 않는 대지에게 예언의 나팔이 되어 다오! 다섯째 기도에서 서풍과 동일화되었던 화자는 여기서 서풍을 자신의 예언을 위한 수단으로 삼는 행위자로 전환된다. 화자는 바람의 힘에 복종하던 상태를 벗어나서 바람을 지배한다. 즉 서풍은 나팔이 되고 하자는 나팔수가 되어 있다. 이와 같은 어조의 변화는 Reiman and Powers (eds.), *Shelley's Poetry and Prose* (New York and London: Norton, 1977), pp. 620-625에 실린 Irene H. Chayes의 논문에 자세히 설명되어 있다.

2) *If Winter comes, can Spring be far behind?*: 겨울이 오면, 봄이 그리 멀겠는가? 이것은 화자가 인류에게 전하고자 하는 예언의 말이다. 접속사가 "When"이라면, 필연적인 계절의 순환을 의미하지만, "If"는 자연의 순환과 인간사의 변화가 반드시 일치하지 않는다는 의미를 함축하고 있다. 인간사의 순환은 중단될 수도 있으며, 인간의 의식적 노력에 의해 달라질 수도 있기 때문이다. (Reiman, *Percy Bysshe Shelley*, pp. 78-79 참조)

The Cloud

I bring fresh showers for the thirsting flowers,
　From the seas and the streams;
I bear light shade for the leaves when laid
　In their noonday dreams.
From my wings are shaken the dews that waken
　The sweet buds every one,
When rocked to rest on their mother's[1] breast,
　As she dances about the sun.
I wield the flail of the lashing hail,
　And whiten the green plains under,
And then again I dissolve it in rain,
　And laugh as I pass in thunder.

I sift the snow on the mountains below,
　And their great pines groan aghast;
And all the night 'tis my pillow white,
　While I sleep in the arms of the blast.
Sublime on the towers of my skyey bowers,
　Lightning my pilot[2] sits;
In a cavern under is fettered the thunder,
　It struggles and howls at fits[3];
Over earth and ocean, with gentle motion,
　This pilot is guiding me,

---

* 이 작품은 셸리가 1820년에 써서 *Prometheus Unbound*와 함께 발표하였다. 이 시는 실제로 이탈리아에서 있었던 사건이나 풍경에 영감을 얻어 쓴 것이 아니라, Leigh Hunt의 시 "The Nymphs"의 제2부에 나오는 구름 요정(Nepheliads)의 노래에서 영감을 받은 것이다. 셸리는 *Foliage* (1818)에 수록된 Hunt의 작품을 칭찬했다. Desmond King-Hele가 *Shelley: His Thought and Work*에서 (pp. 219-227) 지적한 바와 같이, Luke Howard는 그의 저서 *Essay on Clouds*에서 구름의 현대적 분류방법을 확립했고, 그름을 묘사하는 데 대한 관심을 불러일으켰다. Reiman은 *Percy Bysshe Shelley*에서 셸리가 구름에 대한 신화형성적 자서전을 만들었을 뿐만 아니라, 여러 작품에서 구름을 인간 정신의 상사물(analogue)로 사용하였으며, 이 시는 인간 영혼의 life-cycle을 묘사한 것이라고 주장했다(pp. 116-117).

1) *their mother*: 그들(꽃봉오리들)의 어머니, 즉 대지(the earth)

2) *lightning my pilot*: 내 안내자인 번개

3) *at fits*: 이따금 (at times)

Lured by the love of the genii[1]) that move
    In the depths of the purple sea;
Over the rills, and the crags, and the hills,
    Over the lakes and the plains,
Wherever he dream, under mountain or stream,
    The Spirit he loves remains;
And I all the while bask in Heaven's blue smile,
    Whilst he is dissolving in rains.

The sanguine[2]) Sunrise, with his meteor eyes,
    And his burning plumes[3]) outspread,
Leaps on the back of my sailing rack[4]),
    When the morning star shines dead;
As on the jag[5]) of a mountain crag,
    Which an earthquake rocks and swings,
An eagle alit one moment may sit
    In the light of its golden wings.
And when Sunset may breathe, from the lit sea beneath,
    Its ardors of rest and of love,
And the crimson pall[6]) of eve may fall
    From the depth of Heaven above,
With wings folded I rest, on mine aery nest,
    As still as a brooding dove.

That orbed maiden[7]) with white fire laden
    Whom mortals call the Moon,
Glides glimmering o'er my fleece-like floor,
    By the midnight breezes strewn;
And wherever the beat of her unseen feet,
    Which only the angels hear,

1) *genii*: 수호신들
2) *sanguine*: 붉은, 피처럼 붉은 (blood-red)
3) *burning plumes*: 불타는 깃털; 태양의 광륜(光輪)을 시적으로 표현한 것.
4) *rack*: 조각구름 (a high thick fast-moving cloud)
5) *jag*: 뾰족한 끝 (a sharp or rugged point of rock)
6) *the crimson pall*: 진홍색 덮개; pall: a rich cloth spread over something
7) *orbed maiden*: 둥근 처녀

May have broken the woof[1] of my tent's thin roof,
The stars peep behind her, and peer;
And I laugh to see them whirl and flee,
Like a swarm of golden bees,
When I widen the rent in my wind-built tent,
Till the calm rivers, lakes, and seas,
Like strips of the sky fallen through me on high,[2]
Are each paved with the moon and these[3].

I bind the Sun's throne with a burning zone,
And the Moon's with a girdle of pearl[4];
The volcanoes are dim, and the stars reel and swim
When the whirlwinds my banner unfurl.
From cape to cape, with a bridge-like shape,
Over a torrent sea,
Sunbeam-proof, I hang like a roof,— [5]
The mountains its columns be!
The triumphal arch, through which I march
With hurricane, fire, and snow,
When the Powers of the Air are chained to my chair,
Is the million-colored Bow;[6]
The sphere-fire above its soft colors wove,
While the moist Earth was laughing below.

I am the daughter of Earth and Water,
And the nursling of the Sky;[7]

---

1) *woof*: 천 (a woven fabric)

2) *Like strips...on high*: 마치 저 높은 곳에서 나를 뚫고 떨어져 내린 하늘 조각들처럼; 56-58행은 땅위의 "강과 호수와 바다"에 달과 별들이 비친 모습을 묘사한 것이다.

3) *these*: stars; 45-58행은 하늘의 중간 높이에 있는(中層雲) 방사상의 고적운(高積雲:altocumulus radiatus)의 모양을 묘사한 것이다.

4) 59-60행은 높고 투명한 흰 구름 장막이 하늘을 뒤덮고, 그 뒤에서 태양 또는 달이 비칠 때 생기는 달무리 또는 해무리를 묘사한 것이다.

5) *Sunbeam-proof, I hang like a roof*: 나는 햇빛을 차단한 채 지붕처럼 걸린다; 이 부분은 낮은 회색의 두꺼운 층적운(層積雲: stratocumulus opacus)을 묘사한 것이다.

6) 67-70행에 묘사된 무지개 빛 "개선문"을 지나가는 구름은 낮은 비구름(多毛雲: cumulonimbus capillatus: 위쪽이 심하게 흐트러진 머리털 덩어리처럼 발달된 積亂雲)이다.

7) *I am the daughter...the Sky*: 나는 대지와 바다의 딸이며, / 하늘의 젖먹이이다: 이것은 형이상

I pass through the pores, of the ocean and shores;
    I change, but I cannot die—
For after the rain, when with never a stain
    The pavilion of Heaven is bare,
And the winds and sunbeams, with their convex gleams
    Build up the blue dome of Air—[1]
I silently laugh at my own cenotaph[2],
    And out of the caverns of rain,
Like a child from the womb, like a ghost from the tomb,
    I arise and unbuild it again.—

1820

학적인 존재의 척도 상에서, 구름은 대지와 하늘의 중간에 위치하고 있음을 의미한다.

1) *And the winds...the blue dome of Air*: 바람과 햇빛이, 휘어진 빛으로, / 공중에 푸른 원형지붕을 만들 때; 햇빛은 대기에 의해 굴절되어, 위에서 보면 지구 곡면을 따라 휘어져 보인다. 햇빛이 먼지와 습기로 이루어진 구름에 의해 가장 덜 휘어질 때, 가시광선 스펙트럼의 끝에는 자장 파장이 짧은 자주색과 청색이 두드러져 보인다.

2) *cenotaph*: 기념비 (시체가 다른 곳에 묻혀 있는 사망자를 위해 세운 비석)

To a Skylark

Hail to thee, blithe spirit!
  Bird thou never wert,
That from heaven, or near it,
  Pourest thy full heart
In profuse strains of unpremeditated art[1].

Higher still and higher
  From the earth thou springest,
Like a cloud of fire
  The blue deep[2] thou wingest,
And singing still dost soar, and soaring ever singest.

In the golden lightning
  Of the sunken sun,
O'er which clouds are bright'ning,
  Thou dost float and run,
Like an unbodied joy[3] whose race is just begun.

The pale purple even
  Melts around thy flight;
Like a star of Heaven[4]
  In the broad daylight,
Thou art unseen, but yet I hear thy shrill delight—

---

* 이 시는 1820년 늦은 6월에 Leghorn 근처에서 지었고, *Prometheus Unbound*와 함께 출판되었다. 이 시의 주제는 세 부분으로 이루어져 있다. 제1부(1-30행)는 종달새의 비상을 다룬다; 종달새는 날고 있을 때만 노래하는 작은 새이다. 보통 너무 높이 날아서 지상에서는 잘 보이지 않는다. 제2부(31-60)에서 시인은 종달새 및 종달새의 노래에 적합한 상사물(analogue)을 찾지만 실패한다. 제3부(61-105)는 인간에게 그 은밀한 기쁨을 가르쳐 달라고 부탁하는 내용으로 되어 있다. 이 시에서 종달새는 세상에 널리 영향을 떨치는 영적인 힘을 상징한다.

1) *unpremeditated art*: 즉흥적 기교; premeditate: 미리 생각하다 (think out beforehand), 사전에 계획을 세우다 (plan in advance)

2) *the blue deep*: 푸른 하늘, 창공(蒼空)

3) *unbodied joy*: 육체를 벗어난 기쁨; 영적인 기쁨

4) *a star of Heaven*: Venus as the evening star

Keen as are the arrows
  Of that silver sphere[1],
Whose intense lamp narrows[2]
  In the white dawn clear
Until we hardly see, we feel that it is there.

All the earth and air
  With thy voice is loud—
As, when night is bare,
  From one lonely cloud
The moon rains out her beams, and heaven is overflow'd.

What thou art we know not;
  What is most like thee?—
From rainbow clouds there flow not
  Drops so bright to see
As from thy presence showers a rain of melody:

Like a poet hidden
  In the light of thought,
Singing hymns unbidden,
  Till the world is wrought
To sympathy[3] with hopes and fears it heeded not[4]:

Like a high-born maiden[5]
  In a palace tower,
Soothing her love-laden[6]
  Soul in secret hour[7]
With music sweet as love, which overflows her bower:

---

1) *silver sphere*: 은빛 별, 즉 샛별 (Venus as the morning star)
2) *narrow*: 작아지다 (decrease in width or breadth, diminish)
3) *is wrought to sympathy*: 공감하게 되다
4) *it heeded not*: 세상이 관심을 갖지 않았던 (희망과 공포)
5) *high-born maiden*: 지체 높은 처녀, 즉 공주; *high-born*: 지체 높은, 명문가의 (of noble birth)
6) *love-laden*: 사랑에 번민(괴로워)하는; *laden*: loaded, burdened
7) *in secret hour*: 은밀한 시간에, 혼자 있을 때

Like a glow-worm golden
In a dell of dew,
Scattering unbeholden
Its aerial hue[1])
Among the flowers and grass, which screen it from the view:

Like a rose embower'd[2])
In its own green leaves,
By warm winds deflower'd[3]),
Till the scent it gives
Makes faint with too much sweet these heavy-wingèd thieves[4]).

Sound of vernal showers
On the twinkling grass,
Rain-awaken'd flowers—
All that ever was
Joyous, and clear, and fresh, thy music doth surpass.

Teach us, Sprite[5]) or Bird,
What sweet thoughts are thine:
I have never heard
Praise of love or wine
That panted forth a flood of rapture so divine.

Chorus Hymeneal[6]),
Or triumphal chaunt[7]),
Match'd with thine[8]) would be all
But an empty vaunt[9])—

---

1) *aerial hue*: 영묘한 색깔; *aerial*: ethereal, immaterial)
2) *embower*: 잎으로 에워싸다 (surround with foliage)
3) *deflower*: ① 꽃을 따다 (deprive or strip of flowers); 아름다움을 빼앗다 ② 수정시키다 (fertilize); 두 가지 의미로 사용됨.
4) *heavy-winged thieves*: 날개가 무거워진 도둑; 향기를 실어가는 바람("warm winds")
5) *Sprite*: 영혼 (a disembodied spirit), 귀신 (ghost), 요정
6) *Chorus Hymeneal*: 결혼 합창(찬가); *Hymen*: Greek god of marriage
7) *triumphal chant*: 개선의 노래; *triumphal*: 승리를 축하하는 (celebrating a victory)
8) *matched with thine*: 너의 노래와 비교하면
9) *vaunt*: 허풍, 호언장담 (a boast, a brag, boastful or vainglorious speech)

A thing wherein we feel there is some hidden want.

What objects are the fountains
Of thy happy strain?
What fields, or waves, or mountains?
What shapes of sky or plain?
What love of thine own kind[1]? what ignorance of pain?

With thy clear keen joyance[2]
Languor cannot be;
Shadow of annoyance[3]
Never came near thee:
Thou lovest; but ne'er knew love's sad satiety[4].

Waking or asleep,
Thou of death must deem
Things more true and deep
Than we mortals dream,
Or how could thy notes flow in such a crystal stream?

We look before and after[5],
And pine for what is not:
Our sincerest laughter
With some pain is fraught[6];
Our sweetest songs are those that tell of saddest thought.

Yet if we could scorn
Hate, and pride, and fear;
If we were things born
Not to shed a tear,
I know not how thy joy we ever should come near.

---

1) *of thine own kind*: 너 다운 방식의
2) *joyance*: feeling of joy, delight, enjoyment
3) *annoyance*: 고뇌, 번뇌 (the state of being annoyed, trouble, vexation)
4) *satiety*: 포만(飽滿), 물림(싫증남) (the condition of having any desire gratified to excess)
5) *We look before and after: Hamlet*, Ⅳ. iv. 38의 인유이다.
6) *fraught*: full of; attended with

Better than all measures[1]
  Of delightful sound,
Better than all treasures
  That in books are found,
Thy skill to poet were, thou scorner of the ground![2]

Teach me half the gladness
  That thy brain must know—
Such harmonious madness[3]
  From my lips would flow,
The world should listen then, as I am listening now!

1820 (1820)

---

1) *measure*: 선율, 곡조 (a tune, a melody)
2) *thou scorner of the ground*: 그대 지상의 것을 경멸하는 자여
3) *madness*: 황홀 (wild excitement, ecstasy)

To Night

Swiftly walk o'er the western wave,
            Spirit of Night!
Out of the misty eastern cave[1],
Where, all the long and lone daylight,
Thou wovest dreams of joy and fear,
Which make thee terrible and dear,-
            Swift be thy flight![2]

Wrap thy form in a mantle grey,
            Star-inwrought![3]
Blind with thine hair the eyes of Day,
Kiss her[4] until she be wearied out,
Then wander o'er city, and sea, and land,
Touching all with thine opiate wand[5]—
            Come, long-sought!

When I arose and saw the dawn,
            I sighed for thee;
When light rode high, and the dew was gone,
And noon lay heavy on flower and tree,

---

* 시인(또는 화자)이 밤을 동경하는 것은 밤의 형제인 "죽음"이나 밤의 자녀인 "잠"을 위해서가 아니라, 완전하게 깨어 있는 의식을 위한 것이다. 그에게는 깨어 있는 의식만이 진정한 삶이며, 영혼의 창조적 밤 속에서만 그의 내부에 있는 시적 기능인 상상력이 작용할 수 있다. Harold Bloom, *Shelley's Mythmaking* (Ithaca and New York: Cornell UP, 1959), p. 7 참조.

1) *Out of the misty eastern cave*: 안개 낀 동쪽 동굴로부터; 해가 질 때, 어둠의 핵은 동쪽에 있으므로 "동쪽 동굴"이라는 표현을 사용한 것이다. 밤은 "동쪽 동굴"에서 "환희와 공포의 꿈"을 준비한다.
2) *Swift be thy flight!*: 빨리 날아와 다오!
3) *star-inwrought*: 별을 수놓은
4) *her*: Day; 밤은 남성이고 창조적이며, 낮은 여성이고 수동적이다.
5) *opiate wand*: 아편 마봉(魔棒); 밤은 요술 지팡이로 만물을 아름답게 변화시키는 마술사에 비유되어 있다.

And the weary Day turned to his rest,
Lingering like an unloved guest[1]),
I sighed for thee.

Thy brother Death came, and cried
"Wouldst thou me?"[2])
Thy sweet child Sleep[3]), the filmy-eyed,
Murmured like a noontide bee
"Shall I nestle near thy side?
Wouldst thou me?"—And I replied
"No, not thee!"

Death will come when thou art dead[4]),
Soon, too soon—
Sleep will come when thou art fled[5]);
Of neither would I ask the boon[6])
I ask of thee, beloved Night—
Swift be thine approaching flight[7]),
Come soon, soon!

1821 (1824)

---

1) *unloved guest*: 환영받지 못하는 손님 (unwelcome guest)

2) *Wouldst thou me?*: 너는 날 원하는가? (Wouldst thou want me?)

3) *Thy sweet child Sleep*: 그대(밤)의 귀여운 아이인 잠; 시인은 죽음을 밤의 "brother"로, 그리고 잠을 밤의 "child"로 의인화하고 있다. 화자는 죽음이나 잠과 관계를 맺기를 거부한다.

4) *Death will come when thou art dead*: 그대가 죽을 때 죽음이 찾아오리라. 영혼이 깨가 죽는 창조적 밤은 진정한 "삶"이요, 영혼이 잠드는 낮은 "죽음"이라는 의미이다.

5) *Sleep will come when thou art fled*: 네(밤)가 달아나면 잠이 오리라. 시인은 창조적인 밤에 활동을 하고, 낮에 잠을 자기 때문에 이렇게 표현한 것이다.

6) *boon*: 호의 (favour), 은총 (grace)

7) *Swift be thy approaching flight*: 그대 내게로 빨리 날아와 다오

Music, When Soft Voices Die

Music, when soft voices die,
Vibrates in the memory,
Odours, when sweet violets sicken[1],
Live within the sense they quicken[2].

Rose leaves, when the rose is dead,
Are heaped for the beloved's bed;
And so thy thoughts, when thou art gone,
Love itself shall slumber on[3].

1821 (1824)

---

1) *sicken*: 병들다, 시들다 (grow pale or weak, fade)
2) *quicken*: 자극하다 (stimulate, inspire)
3) *slumber on*: (당신을) 생각하며 잠들다 (sleep). 전치사 "on"의 목적어는 "thy thoughts"

One Word Is Too Often Profaned

One word[1)] is too often profaned[2)]
For me to profane it,
One feeling too falsely disdain'd[3)]
For thee to disdain it.
One hope is too like despair
For prudence[4)] to smother[5)],
And pity from thee more dear
Than that from another.

I can give not what men call love;
But wilt thou accept not
The worship[6)] the heart lifts above
And the Heavens reject not:
The desire of the moth for the star,
Of the night for the morrow,
The devotion[7)] to something afar
From the sphere of our sorrow?

---

* 이 시는 시인이 작고한 후 미망인 Mary Shelley가 *Posthumous Poems*(1824)에 수록함으로써 처음으로 세상에 알려졌고, Shelley와 함께 익사한 Edward Williams의 부인 Jane Williams에게 바친 시라 여겨진다.

1) *one word*: 한 단어, 즉 "사랑"이라는 말
2) *profane*: 신성을 모독하다 (desecrate); 남용하다 (abuse or defile where respect is due),
3) *disdain*: 경멸하다, 멸시하다 (regard with contempt, scorn)
4) *prudence*: 신중(愼重) (the state of being careful to avoid undesired consequences)
5) *smother*: 질식시키다 (suffocate, stifle), 억누르다 (repress or refrain from expressing by self-control)
6) *worship*: 숭배 (reverence paid to God or god); 사모의 정
7) *devotion*: 헌신 (divine worship); 헌신적 사랑 (strong love; zealous attachment)

Lines: "When the lamp is shattered"

I

When the lamp is shattered
The light in the dust lies dead—
When the cloud is scattered
The rainbow's glory[1] is shed.
When the lute is broken,
Sweet tones are remembered not;
When the lips have spoken,
Loved accents[2] are soon forgot.

II

As music and splendour
Survive not the lamp and the lute.
The heart's echoes render[3]
No song when the spirit is mute—
No song but sad dirges[4],
Like the wind through a ruined cell[5],
Or the mournful surges
That ring the dead seaman's knell[6].

III

When hearts have once mingled[7]
Love first leaves the well-built nest.[8]

---

1) *glory*: 영광(榮光), 찬란한 아름다움 (resplendent beauty); 눈부신 빛 (an effulgence of light); 원광 (halo)

2) *loved accents*: 사랑의 밀어; *accents*: speech, language

3) *render*: give (back)

4) *dirge*: 만가(輓歌) (slow mournful song, lament)

5) *cell*: (수도원의) 방 (a small room for one person in a monastery), (은둔자의) 암자 (a single-chambered dwelling inhabited by a hermit)

6) *knell*: 조종(弔鐘) (the sound of a bell, esp. of one rung solemnly after a death or at a funeral)

7) *When hearts have once mingled*: 마음이 한 번 섞이고 나면 (마음을 섞는다는 말은 서로 사랑을 주고받는다는 의미임.)

8) *Love first leaves the well-built nest*: 사랑은 먼저 잘 지어진 둥지를 떠난다. 즉 "Love first flies away from the stronger heart."

The weak one is singled[1)]
To endure what it once possessed.
Oh Love! who bewailest[2)]
The frailty of all things here,
Why choose you the frailest
For your cradle, your home, and your bier?

IV

Its[3)] passions will rock[4)] thee
As the storms rock the ravens on high.
Bright reason will mock thee,
Like the sun from a wintry sky.
From thy nest every rafter[5)]
Will rot, and thine eagle home[6)]
Leave thee naked to laughter,
When leaves fall and cold winds come.

1822 (1824)

---

1) *The weak one is singled*: 약한 자는 홀로 남는다. (The weaker of the two lovers is left alone).
single: separate from a group, isolate
2) *bewail*: 슬퍼하다 (mourn, express great sorrow or regret for)
3) *Its*: the weak one's
4) *rock*: 흔들다 (sway from side to side, shake)
5) *rafter*: 서까래 (one of the sloping beams forming the framework of a roof)
6) *eagle home*: 독수리 집, 즉 thy heart

To Jane

I

The keen stars were twinkling,
And the fair moon was rising among them,
Dear Jane!
The guitar was tinkling,
But the notes were not sweet till you sung them
Again.

II

As the moon's soft splendor
O'er the faint cold starlight of Heaven
Is thrown,
So your voice most tender
To the strings without soul had then given
Its own[1].

III

The stars will awaken,
Though the moon sleep a full hour later,
Tonight;
No leaf will be shaken
Whilst the dews of your melody[2] scatter
Delight.

IV

Though the sound overpowers[3],

---

* 이 시는 셸리가 말년에 Lerici에서 지은 시이다. 달이 별빛 비친 하늘에 광채를 던지듯이, 제인의 음성은 현(絃)에 영혼을 부여한다. 이처럼 예기치 못한 영혼과 물질의 결합은 순간적인 기쁨을 창조한다.

1) *Its own*: your voice's own (soul); 문맥은 "So your voice had then given its own (soul) to the strings without soul"이다.

2) *the dews of your melody*: 당신의 멜로디의 이슬; Cf. "a rain of melody"(*To a Skylark*)

3) *Though the sound overpowers*: 비록 그 소리가 (나를) 압도할지라도 (Though I am overpowered by the sound of your voice).

Sing again, with your dear voice revealing
　A tone
 Of some world far from ours,
Where music and moonlight and feeling
　Are one.

1822 (1832)

Selected Bibliography

1. Primary Sources:

Reiman, Ronald H. and Sharon B. Powers (eds.). *Shelley's Poetry and Prose*. New York: Norton, 1977.

2. Secondary Sources:

Baker, Carlos. *Shelley's Major Poetry: The Fabric of a Vision*. Princeton: Princeton UP, 1948.

Blank, G. Kim. (ed.). *The New Shelley: Later Twentieth-Century Views*. New York: St. Martin's Press, 1991.

Bloom, Harold. *Shelley's Mythmaking*. New Haven: Yale UP, 1959.

Hall, Jean. *The Transforming Image: A Study of Shelley's Major Poetry*. U of Illinois P, 1980

Hodgart, Patricia. *A Preface to Shelley*. London and New York: Longman, 1985.

Leighton, Angela. *Shelley and the Sublime: An Interpretation of the Major Poems*. Cambridge: Cambridge UP, 1984.

Pirie, David B. *Shelley*. Milton Keynes, Phil.: Open University Press, 1988.

Reiman, Donald H. *Percy Bysshe Shelley*, Updated Edition. Boston: Twayne Publishers, 1990.

Scott, R. Pickett. *The Place of Shelley Among the English Poets of His Time*. New York: Haskell House, 1971.

Wasserman, Earl R. *The Subtler Language: Critical Readings of Neoclassic and Romantic Poems*. Baltimore: The Johns Hopkins P, 1959.

Wasserman, Earl. Shelley: *A Critical Reading*. Baltimore: Johns Hopkins UP, 1971.

Woodings, R. B. (ed.). *Shelley: Modern Judgements*. London: Aurora Publishers, Inc., 1970.

John Keats
(1795~1821)

Portrait, Keats's Grave in Rome

키츠의 생애와 작품

키츠(John Keats)는 1795년 10월 31일 런던에서 태어났다. 그의 부친은 전세마차 집 마부 장이었는데, 주인집 딸과 결혼하여 그 사업을 물려받았다. 그의 어머니는 관능적인 여성이었으나 자녀들에게는 자애로운 어머니였다. 그의 부친이 1804년 4월에 낙마하여 사망하자 모친은 곧바로 재혼했고, 그의 남매들은 조부모의 손에 맡겨졌다. 1805년 조부가 사망하고 1810년 모친마저 폐결핵으로 사망하자, 그의 조모는 손자들을 위해 8천 파운드의 기금을 신탁해주었다.

키츠는 1803년에 런던 교외의 엔필드(Enfield)에서 존 클라크(John Clarke) 목사가 운영하는 사립학교에 입학하였다. 그곳에서 교장의 아들 (Charles Cowden Clarke)을 만난 것은 행운이었다. 그는 키츠의 독서를 도와주었고, 음악과 연극에 입문시켜 주었다. 키츠의 후견인 Richard Abbey는 상상력이 없고 실리에 밝은 상인이었는데, 키츠가 15세 되던 해에 학교를 그만두게 하고 에드먼턴(Edmonton)의 외과의사 토마스 해몬드(Thomas Hammond)의 도제로 보냈다. 그 후 1815년에 Guy's Hospital에 입학하여 의학공부를 계속한 결과 약제사 면허까지 받았으나, 키츠는 후견인의 반대를 무릅쓰고 시를 쓰기 위해 의학을 포기했다. 이 결정은 클라크(Clarke)와 당시 *Examiner* 지의 편집자였던 헌트(Leigh Hunt)의 영향 덕택이었다. 헌트는 Hazlitt, Lamb, Shelley 등 당대의 훌륭한 작가들을 그에게 소개해 주었다. 이들은 오래 동안 그의 친구로서 그리고 독자로서 그가 시인으로 성장하는 데에 도움을 주었다.

키츠는 18세까지 시작에 손을 대지 않았으나, 1816년에 「채프만의 호머를 처음 읽고」라는 장중한 소네트를 발표하여 문단의 주목을 받게 되었고, 그해 말에는 「수면과 시」(Sleep and Poetry)를 창작했다. 그 후 그는 계속해서 *Examiner* 지에 소네트를 발표하였다. 그가 22세 되던 해인 1817년에 「엔디미언」(*Endymion*)을 쓰기 시작하여 4천 행 이상의 대작을 완성했고, 그 다음 해에 발표하고 나서 『쿼털리 리뷰』(*Quarterly Review*)로부터 혹평을 받았다. 그는 혹평에 굴하지 않고 밀턴의 『실낙원』을 모방하여 더욱 야심적인 작품 「하이피리언」(*Hyperion*)을 쓸 계획을 세웠다.

1818년에 들어서면서 그에게 일련의 재앙이 닥쳐왔다. 그해 봄과 여름에 키츠는 호수지방과 스코틀랜드 지방을 도보로 여행했다. 그리고 8월에 습하고 추운 날씨 속에서 감행된 스코틀랜드 여행에서 돌아왔을 때, 그에게도 어머니와 동생을 앗아간 폐병의 징후가 나타났다. 그의 병을 악화시킨 것은 『쿼털리 리뷰』에 대한 야만적인 혹평이었다. 셸리는 키츠의 죽음을 애도한 시 「아도네이스」(*Adonais*)에서 야만적인 비평이 키츠의 정신에 치명적인 영향을 준 것으로 묘사했다. 게다가 그 무렵 동생 조지는 켄터키로 이민 가서 무분별한 투자로 인하여 돈을 날리는 바람에 극심한 재정적 타격을 입고 있었다. 그 해에 동생 톰이 폐병에 걸렸고, 키츠는 그 해의 마지막 몇 달 동안 간호를 하면서 죽어가는 동생의 모습을 속수무책으로 지켜보아야 했다. 동생은 12월초에 숨을 거두었다. 그 와중에 그는 그해 11월 미모의 패니 브라운(Fanny Brawne)과 사랑에 빠졌다. 그들은 약혼까지 했으나, 키츠가 가난하고 병에 걸려 있으면서 시작에만 몰두하여 그 사랑은 결실을 맺지 못했다.

1819년 1월부터 9월까지의 기간은 그가 극심한 고통과 정서적 혼란을 겪고 있었음에도 불구하고 그의 시작 생활에서 가히 "경이의 해"였다. 「성 아그네스 전야」(The Eve of St. Agnes), 「무자비한 미녀」 (La Belle Dame Sans Merci), 6편의 송시(Odes), 「레이미어」(Lamia) 등의 걸작들이 이 기간에 창작되었다. 이들 작품에는 우아한 운율, 감각적 묘사, 명상의 대상과의 합일에서 오는 강한 쾌감, 압축된 언어, 등 원숙기의 특질이 모두 드러나 있다. 그리고 그 해 말에는 「하이피리언」을 꿈의 환상의 형태로 개작하여 「하이피리언의 몰락」(*The Fall of Hyperion*)이라는 제목을 붙였다. 키츠는 이 시에서 새로운 시도를 하려고 계획하였으나 죽음으로 인하여 좌절되고 말았다.

키츠의 시 못지않게 중요한 문학적 자료는 그의 편지이다. 그의 편지는 "Negative Capability"를 비롯한 시 이론과 아울러 그의 삶과 독서, 사색, 작품에 대한 논평을 담고 있다. 또한 그가 생의 마지막 순간까지 꿋꿋한 용기를 가지고 세상의 악과 모순에 맞서 싸우면서 쉽게 안락을 구하기를 거부하였으며, 인생과 예술에 대해 진지하고 집요하게 사색하였음을 보여준다.

키츠는 병세가 점점 악화되어 1820년 2월 3일 밤에는 각혈을 하였다. 키츠는 그해 가을에 이태리로 전지요양을 떠났다. 그는 1821년 2월 26세의 젊은 나이에 세상을 떠났고, 그의 유해는 로마의 교회묘지에 안장되었다. 병마의 고통, 위대한 시를 쓰고자 하는 희망의 좌절, 패니 브라운에 대한 절망적인 사랑, 등으로 인하여 비탄과 분노를 터뜨렸지만, 언제나 다시 용기를 회복하곤 했다. 그는 찰스 브라운에게 보낸 마지막 편지에서 "나는 안녕이라는 인사조차 할 수가 없네, 편지에서 조차 난 항상 어색하게 절을 하곤 했었지. 안녕히! 존 키츠"라는 말로 끝을 맺었다. 24세의 나이에 이룬 업적으로 불 때, 만약 키츠가 더 오래 살았더라면 셱스피어나 밀턴을 능가하는 시인이 되었을 것이라 미루어 짐작해 불 수 있다.

On first looking into Chapman's Homer

Much have I travell'd in the realms of gold[1],
And many goodly states and kingdoms seen;
Round many western islands[2] have I been
Which bards in fealty to Apollo hold[3].
Oft of one wide expanse[4] had I been told
That deep-brow'd[5] Homer ruled as his demesne[6];
Yet did I never breathe its pure serene[7]
Till I heard Chapman speak out loud and bold:
Then felt I like some watcher of the skies
When a new planet swims into his ken[8];
Or like stout Cortez[9] when with eagle eyes
He star'd at the Pacific—and all his men
Look'd at each other with a wild surmise[10]—
Silent, upon a peak in Darien.

October, 1816 (1816)

---

* 이 시는 키츠가 어느 날 그의 스승인 클라크(Charles Cowden Clarke)와 함께 밤 새워 채프먼이 번역한 호머의 작품을 읽고 감동하여 지은 시이다. George Chapman(1559-1634)은 엘리자베스 조 시인이며 극작가인데, Homer의 *Iliad*와 *Odyssey*를 영역했다.

1) *realms of gold*: 황금의 영토, 즉 문학의 세계
2) *western islands*: 서쪽의 섬들; 즉 영국(영시)을 가리킨다.
3) *Which bards in fealty to Apollo hold*: 시인들이 아폴로 신에게 충성을 바치는; *fealty*: loyalty
4) *expanse*: 넓은 땅(공간) (a very large area of water, sky, land etc.)
5) *deep-browed*: 이마에 깊은 주름이 잡힌, 즉 지혜로운
6) *denesne*: 영토 (realm, domain)
7) *pure serene*: 순수하고 맑은 공기 (pure and clear air); *serene*: n (폐) a condition of fine quiet weather
8) *ken*: 시계(視界), 시야 (range of sight or vision)
9) *Cortez*: 스페인의 군인 Hernan Cortez(1485-1547); 멕시코의 정복자. 이 시에서 키츠는 코르테스가 파나마의 다리엔(Darien) 정상에서 태평양을 처음 발견한 것으로 묘사하였으나. 실은 스페인의 탐험가 Vasco Nunez de Balboa(1475-1517)가 1513년에 태평양을 발견하였다.
10) *with a wild surmise*: 멋대로 추측을 하며

La Belle Dame Sans Merci

O what can ail thee, Knight-at-arms,
  Alone and palely loitering?
The sedge[1] has wither'd from the Lake,
  And no birds sing.

O what can ail thee, Knight-at-arms!
  So haggard and so woe-begone[2]?
The squirrel's granary[3] is full,
  And the harvest's done.

I see a lily on thy brow
  With anguish moist and fever dew[4],
And on thy cheeks a fading rose
  Fast withereth too.

I met a Lady in the Meads,
  Full beautiful—a faery's child,
Her hair was long, her foot was light,
  And her eyes were wild.

I made a Garland for her head,
  And bracelets too, and fragrant Zone[5];
She look'd at me as she did love,
  And made sweet moan.

---

* 이 시의 제목은 중세 프랑스의 궁정시인 Alain Chartier(1385-1430)의 시 제목에서 따온 것이다. 그 의미는 "The Beautiful Lady Without Pity"이다. 초자연적 요부에 대한 사랑 때문에 망한 남자의 이야기는 신화, 동요, 민요시 등에 흔히 나온다. 키츠는 대화 형태로 된 민요시 형식을 자주 모방하였는데, 이 시의 첫 3연은 기사에게 던지는 질문이고 나머지는 그 질문에 대한 대답으로 이루어져 있다.

1) *sedge*: 사초(莎草)
2) *woe-begone*: 슬픔에 잠긴
3) *squirrel's granary*: 다람쥐의 곡간
4) *With anguish moist and fever dew*: 고뇌와 열병의 이슬에 젖은
5) *fragrant Zone*: 향기로운 허리띠

I set her on my pacing steed,
  And nothing else saw all day long,
For sidelong would she bend, and sing
  A faery's song.

She found me roots of relish sweet[1],
  And honey wild, and manna dew[2],
And sure in language strange she said—
  "I love thee true."

She took me to her elfin grot[3],
  And there she wept, and sigh'd fill sore,
And there I shut her wild wild eyes
  With kisses four.

And there she lulled me asleep,
  And there I dream'd—Ah! Woe betide![4]
The latest[5] dream I ever dream'd
  On the cold hill's side.

  I saw pale kings and princes too,
  Pale warriors[6], death-pale[7] were they all;
They cried—"La belle dame sans merci
  Hath thee in thrall![8]"

I saw their starved lips in the gloam[9],
  With horrid warning gaped wide[10],

---

1) *roots of relish sweet*: 달콤한 맛이 나는 뿌리
2) *manna dew*: 감로(甘露); manna: 만나(옛날 이스라엘 사람들이 광야를 헤맬 때 신이 내려준 음식; Exodus 16:14-36)
3) *grot*: grotto: 동굴 (a cave or cavern, esp. one which forms a pleasant retreat)
4) *Ah Woe betide!*: 아 슬프도다!
5) *latest*: last
6) *pale warrior*: 창백한 무사
7) *death-pale*: 죽음(시체)처럼 창백한
8) *Thee hath in thrall*: 그대를 홀렸구나. (has enthralled you).
9) *gloam*: 어둠 (twilight, dusk)
10) *With horrid warning gaped wide*: 무서운 경고로 입을 벌린 채

And I awoke and found me here,
  On the cold hill's side.

And this is why I sojourn here,
  Alone and palely loitering,
Though the sedge is wither'd from the lake,
  And no birds sing.

1819 (1820)

Ode to Psyche

O Goddess![1] hear these tuneless numbers[2], wrung
By sweet enforcement and remembrance dear[3],
And pardon that thy secrets should be sung
Even into thine own soft-conched ear[4]:
Surely I dreamt to-day, or did I see
The winged Psyche with awaken'd eyes?
I wander'd in a forest thoughtlessly[5],
And, on the sudden, fainting with surprise,
Saw two fair creatures, couched[6] side by side
In deepest grass, beneath the whisp'ring roof
Of leaves and trembled blossoms, where there ran
A brooklet, scarce espied[7]:
'Mid hush'd, cool-rooted flowers, fragrant-eyed,
Blue, silver-white, and budded Tyrian[8],

They lay calm-breathing on the bedded grass[9];

---

* 이 시는 키츠가 1819년 4월 하순에서 5월에 걸쳐 쓴 여섯 편의 송시들 중 첫 작품이다. 키츠는 소네트 형식을 실험하면서 얻은 경험으로 송시의 복잡하고 다양한 구조를 발전시킬 수 있었다. 그는 1819년 4월 30일에 동생 George Keats에게 보낸 편지에서 이 시가 그때까지 쓴 작품 중에서 가장 공들인 작품이라 말했다. "[Psyche] is the first and the only one with which I have taken even moderate pains. I have for the most part dashed off my lines in a hurry. This I have done leisurely—I think it reads the more richly for it and will I hope encourage me to write other things in even a more peaceable an healthy spirit."

1) *Goddess*: 여신; 큐피드(Cupid)와 프시케(Psyche) 이야기는 기원 2세기 로마의 풍자작가 아풀레이우스(Lucius Apuleius)의 『황금 당나귀』(*The Golden Ass*)에 나온다. 프시케는 큐피드가 사랑한 미소녀인데, 비너스(Venus)의 질투 때문에 온갖 고초를 겪고 나서 큐피드와 결혼하여 여신이 되었다. 그 이전에는 여신이 아니라 인간이어서 신전이 없었다.

2) *tuneless numbers*: 소리 없는 노래; tuneless: 운율이 아름답지 못한 (untuneful, harsh- sounding); 소리 없는 (having no song or sound)

3) *wrung / By sweet enforcement and remembrance dear*: 달콤한 강제(强制)와 그리운 추억이 만들어낸; *wring*: squeeze and twist; obtain with effort or difficulty

4) *soft-conched ear*: 부드럽고 소라껍질 같이 생긴 귀 (soft and shaped like a seashell)

5) *thoughtlessly*: 생각 없이, 분별없이(heedlessly)

6) *couched*: 누워 있는; *couch*: cause to lie down, lay down

7) *scarce espied*: 거의 눈에 띄지 않는

8) *budded Tyrian*: 보라빛 꽃봉오리; *Tyrian*: purple (고대 페니키아의 항구도시인 Tyre에 자주색 염료가 많이 생산되는 데서 유래)

9) *bedded grass*: 풀 침대; *bed*: (v) prepare a bed

Their arms embraced, and their pinions too[1];
Their lips touch'd not, but had not bade adieu,
As if disjoined by soft-handed slumber[2],
And ready still past kisses to outnumber[3]
At tender eye-dawn of aurorean love[4]:
The winged boy I knew;
But who wast thou, O happy, happy dove?
His Psyche true!

O latest born[5] and loveliest vision far
Of all Olympus' faded hierarchy[6]!
Fairer than Phoebe's sapphire-region'd star[7],
Or Vesper[8], amorous glow-worm of the sky;
Fairer than these, though temple thou hast none,
Nor altar heap'd with flowers;
Nor virgin-choir to make delicious moan
Upon the midnight hours;
No voice, no lute, no pipe, no incense sweet
From chain-swung censer teeming[9];
No shrine, no grove, no oracle, no heat[10]
Of pale-mouth'd prophet dreaming[11].

---

1) *their pinions too*: 날개로도 껴안고서
2) *As if disjoined by soft-handed slumber*: 고이 잠든 동안 떨어져 있듯이 (잠이 부드러운 손으로 입술을 떼어놓은 듯이)
3) *ready still past kisses to outnumber*: 간밤의 입맞춤보다 더 많은 입맞춤을 할 준비를 하고서; 어순은 "ready still to outnumber past kisses"이다.
4) *At tender eye-dawn of aurorean love*: 새벽의 사랑이 부드럽게 눈 뜰 적에; *Aurora*: the goddess of the dawn
5) *latest born*: 가장 늦게 태어난; 프시케는 올림포스의 신들 중에서 가장 나이 어린 신이다.
6) *faded hierarchy*: 퇴색한 계보(系譜); 사람들의 숭배를 받지 못하기 때문에 "퇴색한" 계보라 말한다. *hierarchy*: the ranks of the classic gods
7) *Phoebe's sapphire-regioned star*: 맑은 밤하늘에 뜬 달 (포이베의 별은 달을 의미한다); *Phoebe*: 달의 여신(Diana); *sapphire-regioned*: 청옥색 하늘의
8) *Vesper*: 저녁별(evening star: Venus); 그 다음의 "사랑스런 반딧불"은 동격
9) *From chain-swung censer teeming*: 사슬에 매달려 흔들리는 향로에서 흘러나오는; *teem*: pour out, flow in a stream
10) *heat*: 열정 (passion)
11) *pale-mouthed prophet dreaming*: 창백한 입술의 꿈꾸는 예언자

O brightest! though too late for antique vows[1],
Too, too late for the fond believing lyre[2],
When holy were the haunted forest boughs,
Holy the air, the water, and the fire;
Yet even in these days so far retir'd
From happy pieties[3], thy lucent fans[4],
Fluttering among the faint Olympians[5],
I see, and sing, by my own eyes inspired.
So let me be thy choir, and make a moan
Upon the midnight hours;
Thy voice, thy lute, thy pipe, thy incense sweet
From swinged censer teeming;
Thy shrine, thy grove, thy oracle, thy heat
Of pale-mouth'd prophet dreaming.

Yes, I will be thy priest, and build a fane[6]
In some untrodden region[7] of my mind,
Where branched thoughts, new grown with pleasant pain[8],
Instead of pines shall murmur in the wind:
Far, far around shall those dark-cluster'd trees[9]
Fledge[10] the wild-ridged mountains steep by steep[11];
And there by zephyrs[12], streams, and birds, and bees,
The moss-lain Dryads[13] shall be lull'd to sleep;

---

1) *though too late for antique vows*: 비록 옛날의 맹세를 받기엔 너무 늦었지만 (신에게 경건하게 맹세를 하던 시대는 이미 지나갔지만)
2) *too late for fond believing lyre*: 어리석게 믿는 수금(竪琴)을 구하기엔 너무 늦었지만 (만물이 신성하다고 믿음으로 시를 지었던 시대는 지나갔지만)
3) *so far retir'd / From happy pieties*: 행복한 믿음(신앙)과는 거리가 먼 (오늘날)
4) *lucent fans*: 빛나는 날개 (shining wings)
5) *the faint Olympians*: 맥 빠진 올림포스의 신들;
6) *fane*: 신전 (temple)
7) *untrodden region*: 조용한(한적한) 곳
8) *branched thoughts, new grown with pleasant pain*: 즐거운 고통으로 새로 자란 생각의 가지
9) *those dark-clustered trees*: 저 울창한 나무들
10) fledge: (깃털로) 덮다 (cover as with feathers or down)
11) *steep by steep*: 겹겹이
12) *zephyr*: 산들바람 (a soft gentle breeze)
13) *moss-lain Dryads*: 이끼 위에 누운 나무의 요정들

And in the midst of this wide quietness
A rosy sanctuary[1] will I dress[2]
With the wreath'd trellis[3] of a working brain,
  With buds, and bells[4], and stars[5] without a name,
With all the gardener Fancy e'er could feign[6],
  Who breeding flowers, will never breed the same:
And there shall be for thee all soft delight
  That shadowy thought can win,
A bright torch, and a casement ope[7] at night,
  To let the warm Love[8] in!

April, 1819 (1820)

---

1) *sanctuary*: 성당, 신전 (a place set apart for the worship of a god or gods, a temple)
2) *dress*: 꾸미다, 장식하다 (adorn)
3) *wreath'd trellis*: 꽃들이 엉킨 격자 울타리; *trellis*: 격자 울타리, 덩굴시렁; *wreathe*: 감아올리다 (entwine)
4) *bells*: 초롱꽃 (bluebells), 종 모양의 꽃
5) *stars*: 별 모양의 꽃들 (star-shaped flowers)
6) *feign*: invent
7) ope: 열려 있는 (open)
8) *Love*: 사랑의 신 (Cupid)

Ode to a Nightingale

I

MY heart aches, and a drowsy numbness pains
My sense, as though of hemlock[1] I had drunk,
Or emptied some dull opiate to the drains[2]
One minute past, and Lethe-wards[3] had sunk:
'Tis[4] not through envy of thy happy lot,
But being too happy in thine happiness,—
That thou, light-winged Dryad[5] of the trees,
In some melodious plot
Of beechen green[6], and shadows numberless,
Singest of summer in full-throated ease[7].

II

O, for a draught of vintage[8]! that hath been
Cool'd a long age in the deep-delved earth,
Tasting of Flora[9] and the country green,

---

* 1819년 봄에 지은 시이다. 그 때 키츠는 친구 Charles Brown과 함께 Hampstead에 살고 있었다. Brown은 이 시의 창작 경위에 대해 다음과 같이 적었다. "In the spring of 1819 a nightingale had built her nest near my house. Keats felt a tranquil and continual joy in her song; and one morning he took his chair from the breakfast table to the gras plot under a plum tree, where he sat for two or three hours. When he came into the house, I perceived he had some scraps of paper in his hand, and these he was quietly thrusting behind the books. On inquiry, I found those scraps, four or five in number, contained his poetic feeling on the song of our nightingale."

1) *hemlock*: 독당근 (a poisonous herb)
2) *empty...to the drains*: 찌꺼기까지 마시다
3) *Lethe-wards*: 망각의 강 쪽으로 (toward Lethe); Lethe는 저승(Hades)의 강인데 그 강물을 마시면 일체의 과거를 잊어버린다고 한다.
4) *'Tis*: It is; 여기서 "It"는 앞의 내용, 즉 "내가 가슴이 아프고 고통을 느끼는 것"을 의미한다.
5) *Dryad*: 나무의 요정; 나이팅게일을 가벼운 날개로 날아다니는 나무의 요정에 비유하고 있다.
6) *melodious plot / Of beechen green*: 푸른 너도밤나무의 선율적인 장소; 즉 나이팅게일이 노래하는 너도밤나무 숲을 의미한다.
7) *in full-throated ease*: 마음 놓고 목청껏
8) *vintage*: 고급 포도주 (a wine of high quality made from the crop of a single identified district in a good year)
9) *Flora*: 꽃의 여신 (Roman goddess of flowers); 꽃

Dance, and Provencal song[1]), and sunburnt mirth[2])!
O for a beaker full of the warm South[3]),
Full of the true, the blushful Hippocrene[4]),
With beaded bubbles winking at the brim,
And purple-stained mouth;
That I might drink, and leave the world unseen,
And with thee fade away into the forest dim:

III

Fade far away, dissolve, and quite forget
What thou among the leaves hast never known,
The weariness, the fever, and the fret
Here[5]), where men sit and hear each other groan;
Where palsy shakes a few, sad, last gray hairs,
Where youth grows pale, and spectre-thin[6]), and dies;
Where but to think is to be full of sorrow
And leaden-eyed despairs[7]),
Where Beauty cannot keep her lustrous eyes,
Or new Love pine at them[8]) beyond to-morrow.

IV

Away![9]) away! for I will fly to thee,
Not charioted by Bacchus and his pards[10]),
But on the viewless[11]) wings of Poesy,
Though the dull brain perplexes and retards[12]):

---

1) *Provencal song*: 프로방스의 노래; Provence는 중세기에 연시를 읊었던 서정시인들(troubadours)로 유명한 프랑스 남부의 옛 주 이름이다.
2) *sunburnt mirth*: 햇볕에 그을린 남국(사람들)의 환희
3) *full of the warm South*: 따뜻한 남불(南佛)의 포도주로 가득 찬
4) *Hippocrene*: 헬리콘 산(Mt. Helicon)에 있는 시신(詩神)의 샘; 이 샘물을 마시면 영감을 얻는다고 한다.
5) *Here*: 이 세상에서는 (In this world)
6) *spectre-thin*: 유령처럼 야윈 (thin as a spectre)
7) *leaden-eyed despair*: 졸린 눈의 절망; *leaden*: 납빛의, 회색의; 납처럼 무거운
8) *pine at them*: 그(빛나는) 눈을 그리워하다;
9) *Away!*: Go away!
10) *Not charioted by Bacchus and his pards*: 표범이 끄는 박카스의 전차를 타지 않고;
11) *viewless*: 보이지 않는 (invisible)
12) *perplexes and retards*: 갈팡질팡하다

Already with thee! tender is the night,

And haply the Queen-Moon is on her throne,
Cluster'd around by all her starry Fays[1];
But here there is no light,
Save what from heaven is with the breezes blown
Through verdurous glooms[2] and winding mossy ways.

V

I cannot see what flowers are at my feet,
Nor what soft incense hangs upon the boughs,
But, in embalmed darkness[3], guess each sweet
Wherewith the seasonable month[4] endows
The grass, the thicket[5], and the fruit-tree wild;
White hawthorn, and the pastoral eglantine[6];
Fast fading violets cover'd up in leaves;
And mid-May's eldest child[7],
The coming musk-rose, full of dewy wine,
The murmurous haunt of flies on summer eves[8].

VI

Darkling[9] I listen; and, for many a time
I have been half in love with easeful Death[10],
Call'd him soft names[11] in many a mused rhyme[12],

---

1) *starry Fays*: 별 요정들; *fay*: fairy
2) *verdurous glooms*: 푸른 나무그늘; *verdurous*: green-foliaged
3) *embalmed darkness*: 향기로운 어둠
4) *seasonable month*: 계절의 달, 즉 오월(May)
5) thicket: 잡목 숲
6) *pastoral eglantine*: 목장(pasture)의 들장미
7) *mid-May's eldest child*: 오월 중순의 맏아들, "꽃 피는 사향장미(The coming musk-rose)"와 동격임.
8) *The murmurous haunt of flies on summer eves*: 여름 저녁에 날벌레들이 윙윙대며 날아드는 곳; 앞의 "musk-rose"와 동격
9) *darkling*: in the dark
10) *easeful Death*: 편안(안락)한 죽음
11) *called him soft names*: 다정한 이름으로 그를 불렀다
12) *mused rhymes*: 명상적인 시; *mused*: meditated

To take into the air my quiet breath;
Now more than ever seems it rich to die,
To cease upon the midnight with no pain,
While thou art pouring forth thy soul abroad
In such an ecstasy!
Still wouldst thou sing, and I have ears in vain—
To thy high requiem become a sod[1].

VII

Thou wast not born for death, immortal Bird!
No hungry generations[2] tread thee down;
The voice I hear this passing night was heard
In ancient days by emperor and clown[3]:
Perhaps the self-same song that found a path
Through the sad heart of Ruth[4], when, sick for home,
She stood in tears amid the alien corn;
The same that oft-times hath
Charm'd magic casements[5], opening on the foam
Of perilous seas, in faery lands forlorn.

VIII

Forlorn![6] the very word is like a bell

---

1) *To thy high Requiem become a sod*: 네 높은 진혼곡에 나는 흙이 된다.

2) *hungry generations*: 굶주린 세대; 키츠는 이 연에서 상상력의 비상을 극대화한다. 그는 시간과 공간을 확대하여 나이팅게일을 "불멸의 새"로 승화시킨다. 그는 먼저 현재의 "굶주린 세대"에서 "황제와 농부"가 살았던 고대 세계를 거쳐서 룻(Ruth)이 살았던 구약성서의 세계로, 그 다음 역사적 시대를 넘어선 선경(仙境)의 세계로 거슬러 올라간다.

3) *clown*: 농부 (a rustic or peasant)

4) *Ruth*: 구약성서의 「룻기」(The Book of Ruth)에 나오는 Moab 족의 여인; 이스라엘 사람에게 시집가서 남편이 죽은 후에도 시어머니 Naomi를 섬기며 살았다. 그녀는 보리이삭을 주워 생계를 유지하며 착하게 살아서 하나님의 보상을 받는다. 키츠는 이 이야기를 수정하여 룻이 고향 생각이 날 때 나이팅게일 노래를 듣고 위안을 받은 것처럼 묘사하고 있다. *alien corn*: 이국의 보리밭(wheat)

5) *magic casement*: 마술의 창문; 중세 로맨스나 동화에 나오는 마법의 창을 가리킨다. 바닷가 어느 왕국에 마법사의 성이 있고, 그 성의 외로운 탑 속에 공주가 갇혀 있다. 공주는 나이팅게일의 노래를 듣고 바다로 향한 창문을 열고 자신을 구해줄 기사가 타고 올 배를 기다린다.

6) *Forlorn!*: 쓸쓸한! 이 말에 화자는 상상의 나래를 접고 현실세계로 되돌아온다. 키츠는 이 말을 마치 환상의 죽음을 알리는 조종(弔鐘)에 비유한다. 화자는 "잘 속이는 요정"(deceiving elf)인 환상에게 작별을 고한다. 새의 노래는 점점 멀어져 간다.

To toil me back from thee to my sole self!
Adieu! the fancy cannot cheat so well
As she is fam'd to do, deceiving elf.
Adieu! adieu! thy plaintive anthem[1] fades
Past the near meadows, over the still stream,
Up the hill-side; and now 'tis buried deep
In the next valley-glades[2]:
Was it a vision, or a waking dream?[3]
Fled is that music:—Do I wake or sleep?[4]

May, 1819 (1820)

---

1) *plaintive anthem*: 슬픈 노래; *plaintive*: mournful; *anthem*: any song of praise or gladness

2) *valley-glades*: 계곡의 숲속; *glade*: 숲 속 빈터 또는 오솔길 (a clear open space or passage between trees in a wood)

3) *Was it a vision, or a waking dream?*: 이게 환상인가 아니면 백일몽인가? 화자는 자신이 본 것이 어떤 초월적인 계시인가 아니면 헛된 공상인가 묻고 있다. 편의상 vision을 "환상"이라 번역했지만, 이 말은 잠이나 어떤 영적으로 고양된 의식 상태에서 신 또는 초자연적 존재가 나타남을 의미한다.

4) *Do I wake or sleep?*: 나는 깨었는가? 자는가? 이것은 화자가 환상 속에서 본 나이팅게일의 세계가 진실 또는 실재인가 아니면, 고통과 슬픔의 현실세계가 실재인가에 대한 물음이다.

Ode on a Grecian Urn

I

Thou still[1] unravish'd bride[2] of quietness,
  Thou foster-child of silence and slow time,
Sylvan historian[3], who canst thus express
  A flowery tale more sweetly than our rhyme:
What leaf-fring'd legend[4] haunts about thy shape
  Of deities or mortals, or of both,
    In Tempe[5] or the dales of Arcady[6]?
  What men or gods are these? What maidens loth[7]?
  What mad pursuit? What struggle to escape?
    What pipes and timbrels[8]? What wild ecstasy[9]?

II

Heard melodies are sweet, but those unheard
  Are sweeter; therefore, ye soft pipes, play on;
Not to the sensual[10] ear, but, more endear'd,
  Pipe to the spirit ditties of no tone[11]:
Fair youth, beneath the trees, thou canst not leave

---

* 이 시에 묘사된 그리스 고병(古甁)은 키츠가 본 여러 도자기와 조각과 그림에서 얻은 이미지들을 종합하여 만들어낸 것이다. 따라서 실제의 항아리가 아니라 키츠의 상상력에 의해 창조된 항아리이다. 여기에는 쫓고 쫓기는 젊은 남녀, 나무 아래서 피리 부는 목동, 그리고 어느 공동체의 제사 의식이 그려져 있다. 키츠는 이 시에서 그가 끈질기게 추구한 주제—즉 변하는 세계에서의 영원성의 주구—를 다루었다.

1) *still*: 아직도 (as yet); 조용한 (motionless); 이 두 가지 의미가 모두 적용될 수 있다.

2) *unravish'd bride*: 겁탈 당하지 않은(순결을 보존하고 있는) 신부; 이 항아리는 정적과 결혼했지만 아직도 처녀성을 보존하고 있는 신부에 비유되어 있다; *ravish*: rape

3) *Sylvan historian*: 숲의 역사가;

4) *leaf-fring'd legend*: 잎으로 가장자리를 장식한 전설

5) *Tempe*: [témpi] 템페 계곡; 그리스 Thessaly에 있는 아름다운 계곡이다.

6) *the dales of Arcady*: 아르카디아(Arcadia)의 계곡; Arcadia는 Peloponnesus 반도에 있는 고원지대인데 흔히 목가적 이상향의 상징으로 사용된다.

7) *loth*: loath: 싫어하는, 마음이 내키지 않는 (reluctant, unwilling)

8) *timbrel*: 탬버린(tambourine)과 비슷한 악기; 작은 북

9) *wild ecstasy*: 열광적인 황홀

10) *sensual*: 육신의 (physical, bodily)

11) *pipe...ditties of no tone*: 소리 없는 노래를 연주하다; *ditty*: a short simple song

Thy song, nor ever can those trees be bare;
Bold Lover, never, never canst thou kiss,
Though winning near the goal—yet, do not grieve;
She cannot fade, though thou hast not thy bliss,
For ever wilt thou love, and she be fair!

III

Ah, happy, happy boughs! that cannot shed
Your leaves, nor ever bid the Spring adieu;
And, happy melodist[1], unwearied,
For ever piping[2] songs for ever new;
More happy love! more happy, happy love!
For ever warm and still to be enjoy'd,
For ever panting, and for ever young;
All breathing human passion far above[3],
That leaves a heart high-sorrowful and cloy'd[4],
A burning forehead, and a parching[5] tongue.

IV

Who are these coming to the sacrifice[6]?
To what green altar, O mysterious priest,
Lead'st thou that heifer[7] lowing[8] at the skies,
And all her silken flanks with garlands drest?
What little town by river or sea shore,
Or mountain-built with peaceful citadel[9],

---

1) *happy melodist*: 행복한 악사(樂士)
2) *pipe*: play on a pipe
3) *far above*: 훨씬 능가하는, 초월한; 어순은 "far above all breathing human passion"이다.
4) *cloy*: 싫증을 느끼게 하다, 물리게 하다 (satiate or weary by richness, sweetness, sameness, excess, of food or pleasure)
5) *parch*: 바싹 마르다, 타다 (become hot and dry)
6) *sacrifice*: 제사(祭祀); 신에게 제물을 바치는 의식 (the ritual killing: the practice of offering a material possession to a god)
7) *heifer*: 송아지 (a young cow)
8) *low*: (소가) 음매 울다 (moo, utter cry as of cattle)
9) *mountain-built with peaceful citadel*: 평화로운 성채(城砦)로 산 위에 지어진; *citadel*: a fortress guarding or dominating a city; a stronghold

Is emptied of this folk[1], this pious morn?
And, little town, thy streets for evermore
Will silent be; and not a soul to tell
Why thou art desolate, can e'er return.

V

O Attic shape[2]! Fair attitude![3] with brede[4]
Of marble men and maidens overwrought[5],
With forest branches and the trodden weed;
Thou, silent form, dost tease us out of thought[6]
As doth eternity: Cold Pastoral![7]
When old age shall this generation waste,
Thou shalt remain, in midst of other woe
Than ours, a friend to man, to whom thou say'st,
"Beauty is truth, truth beauty,"[8]—that is all
Ye know on earth, and all ye need to know.

May, 1819 (1820)

---

1) *What little town...Is emptied of this folk?*: 이 사람들은...어느 작은 마을을 비우고 떠나왔는가? *empty*: 비우다 (make empty, remove the contents of)

2) *Attic shape!*: 희랍의 형상이여!; *Attic*: Greek

3) *Fair attitude!*: 아름다운 자태(姿態)여! *attitude*: the disposition of a figure, the posture of a body

4) *brede*: 땋은 머리 (braid), 자수(刺繡) (embroidery); interwoven pattern

5) *overwrought*: 표면에 새긴; *overwork*: decorate the surface of

6) *tease us out of thought*: 생각이 미칠 수 없게 우리를 괴롭히다; *tease*: 애태우다, 괴롭히다 (irritate or bother persistently in a playful way)

7) *Cold Pastoral!*: 차가운 목가(牧歌)여! (목가적 풍경이 새겨진 항아리를 가리킨다.)

8) *"Beauty is truth, truth beauty"*: "美는 眞理요, 眞理는 美다"; 이 말은 항아리가 인간에게 하는 말이다. 키츠는 *Endymion*에서 "아름다운 것은 영원한 기쁨이다"(A thing of beauty is a joy for ever.—I. 1)라 말했고, Bailey에게 보낸 편지(1819년 9월 22일자)에서도 "What the imagination seizes as beauty must be truth—whether it existed before or not"라고 말한 바 있다. 이 말은 상상력으로 창조한 미는 곧 진리이며 영원하다는 것을 의미한다. 이 부분은 판본에 따라 인용부호가 없는 경우도 있다. 인용부호가 없을 경우 항아리가 말한 내용은 마지막 두 줄 모두가 된다. 이 부분은 인용부호 유무에 따라 다양한 해석이 가능해진다.

Ode on Melancholy

I

No, no, go not to Lethe, neither twist
  Wolfs-bane[1)], tight-rooted, for its poisonous wine[2)];
Nor suffer thy pale forehead to be kiss'd
  By nightshade[3)], ruby grape of Proserpine[4)];
Make not your rosary of yew-berries[5)],
  Nor let the beetle[6)], nor the death-moth[7)] be
    Your mournful Psyche[8)], nor the downy owl
A partner in your sorrow's mysteries[9)];
  For shade to shade will come too drowsily,
    And drown the wakeful anguish of the soul[10)].

II

But when the melancholy fit[11)] shall fall
  Sudden from heaven like a weeping cloud,

---

* 키츠는 1819년 4월에 Robert Burton(1577-1640)이 쓴 『우수의 해부』(*The Anatomy of Melancholy*)(1621)를 읽었다. 18세기 중엽부터 키츠 당대에 이르기까지 소위 "묘지 파"(The Graveyard School)이라 불린 일군의 시인들이 죽음, 숙명, 우수 등의 주제를 다룬 시를 발표했다. 키츠는 이 작품에서 우수 신봉자에게 이들이 즐겨 사용하는 장치들—망각의 강, 주목, 딱정벌레, 올빼미, 해골나방, 등—에서 슬픔을 구하지 말고, 아름답고 무상한 것을 응시함으로써 기분을 강화하라고 말한다.

1) *wolfs-bane*: 바곳 (독초의 일종)

2) *poisonous wine*: 독즙; *wine*: juice

3) *nightshade*: 까마종이 (독초의 일종)

4) *ruby grape of Proserpine*: 저승의 붉은 열매; "nightshade"와 동격. *Proserpine*: 저승의 왕 Pluto에게 유괴되어 그의 아내가 되었다.

5) *Make not your rosary of yew-berries*: 주목 열매로 염주를 만들지 말라; 주목(yew)은 묘지에 심는 나무이며, 그 열매는 죽음을 상징하니까, 우울한 기도를 드리지 말라는 뜻이다. *rosary*: a string of beads used by Roman Catholics for counting prayers

6) *beetle*: 딱정벌레; 고대 이집트 사람들이 부활의 상징으로 무덤에 놓았던 검은 풍뎅이(scarab) 상(像)을 가리킨다.

7) *death-moth*: death's head moth; 해골나방 (등에 해골 무늬가 있음)

8) *mournful Psyche*: 슬퍼하는 영혼(프시케); 옛날에는 나비나 나방을 영혼의 상징으로 보았다. 프시케는 때때로 죽어가는 사람의 입에서 날아 나오는 나비나 나방으로 그려진다.

9) *mystery*: 비의(祕儀), 비밀 종교의식 (secret religious rites)

10) *the wakeful anguish of the soul*: 깨어있는 영혼의 고뇌

11) melancholy fit: 우수의 발작; *fit*: a short sudden attack (of illness)

That fosters[1] the droop-headed flowers all,
  And hides the green hill in an April shroud[2];
Then glut thy sorrow[3] on a morning rose,
  Or on the rainbow of the salt sand-wave[4],
    Or on the wealth of globed peonies[5];
Or if thy mistress some rich anger shows,
  Imprison her soft hand, and let her rave[6],
    And feed deep, deep upon her peerless[7] eyes.

III

She dwells with Beauty[8]—Beauty that must die;
  And Joy, whose hand is ever at his lips
Bidding adieu; and aching Pleasure nigh,
  Turning to poison while the bee-mouth sips:
Ay, in the very temple of Delight
  Veil'd Melancholy has her sovran shrine[9],
    Though seen of none save him whose strenuous tongue
  Can burst Joy's grape against his palate fine;
  His soul shall taste the sadness of her might,
    And be among her cloudy trophies hung[10].

May, 1819 (1820)

---

1) *foster*: 키우다, 기르다 (nourish, feed; raise)
2) *April shroud*: 사월의 수의
3) *glut thy sorrow*: 네 슬픔을 만끽하라; *glut*:; 포식하다 (feed to repletion), 만끽하다 ((indulge to the utmost)
4) *the rainbow of the salt sand-wave*: 짠 모래 물결의 무지개 (바닷가 모래 위에 뜬 무지개)
5) *the wealth of globed peonies*: 둥근 작약의 무리
6) *rave*: 미친 듯이 울부짖다 (talk wildly as if mad, roar furiously)
7) *peerless*: 견줄 데 없는 (matchless), 더할 나위 없이 아름다운
8) *She dwells with Beauty*: 우수는 미와 함께 산다. 키츠는 우수를 신격화하고 있다. 우수는 쾌락의 신전에 성단(shrine)을 갖고 있다.
9) *sovran shrine*: 지고의 사당; *sovran*: sovereign: supreme; *shrine*: 성당, 사당(祠堂) (a place of worship or devotion to a saint or deity, a temple)
10) *her cloudy trophies*: 우수의 어두운 전리품들; 영혼이 우수의 전리품이 되어 우수의 신전에 매달리게 될 것이라는 의미이다. (그리스와 로마 사람들이 전리품을 신전에 매달았던 관습에 관해 언급한 것이다.)

To Autumn

I

Season of mists and mellow fruitfulness[1),
  Close bosom-friend[2) of the maturing sun;
Conspiring[3) with him how to load and bless
  With fruit the vines that round the thatch-eaves[4) run;
To bend with apples the moss'd cottage-trees[5),
  And fill all fruit with ripeness to the core[6);
    To swell the gourd, and plump[7) the hazel shells
With a sweet kernel[8); to set budding[9) more,
  And still more, later flowers for the bees,
  Until they think warm days will never cease,
    For Summer has o'er-brimm'd[10) their clammy cells[11).

II

Who hath not seen thee oft amid thy store[12)?
  Sometimes whoever seeks abroad[13) may find

---

* 이 시를 짓고 나서 이틀 뒤에 키츠는 J. H. Reynolds에게 보낸 편지에서 다음과 같이 적었다. "How beautiful the season is now—How fine the air is. A temperate sharpness about it. Really, without joking, chaste weather—Dian skies—I never liked stubble fields so much as now—Aye, better than the chilly green of the spring. Somehow a stubble plain looks warm, in the same way that some pictures look warm. This struck me so much in my Sunday walk that I composed upon it." (September 21, 1819)

1) *mellow fruitfulness*: 무르익은 결실; *fruitful*: bearing abundant fruit
2) *bosom-friend*: 절친한 친구 (a very close friend)
3) *conspire*: 공모하다 (secretly plan with someone else to do something illegal); 협력하다 (cooperate by intention)
4) *thatch-eaves*: 초가집 처마
5) *cottage trees*: 시골집 (사과)나무
6) *to the core*: 속속들이; *core*: the hard central part of a fruit
7) *plump*: 살찌게 하다 (make plump); Cf. *plump*: (a) having a full rounded shape
8) *kernel*: 인(仁), 속살 (the softer part contained within the hard shell of a nut or fruit stone)
9) *set budding*: 꽃이 피게 하다; *bud*: sent out buds(=leaves or flowers not yet fully open)
10) *overbrim*: 넘쳐흐르게 하다, 넘칠 정도로 가득 채우다 (brim over, overflow)
11) *clammy cells*: 끈적끈적한 벌집; *clammy*: moist, cold, and sticky
12) *amid thy store*: 가을의 곡물창고에서 (in the midst of Autumn's granary); *store*: 창고(a storehouse)
13) *abroad*: 집 밖에서 (out of one's house or abode)

Thee sitting careless[1] on a granary floor[2],
  Thy hair soft-lifted by the winnowing[3] wind;
Or on a half-reap'd furrow sound asleep,
  Drows'd[4] with the fume of poppies[5], while thy hook[6]
    Spares the next swath[7] and all its twined flowers:
And sometimes like a gleaner[8] thou dost keep
  Steady thy laden head across a brook[9];
  Or by a cyder-press[10], with patient look,
    Thou watchest the last oozings[11] hours by hours[12].

III

Where are the songs of Spring? Ay, where are they?
  Think not of them, thou hast thy music too,—
While barred clouds bloom the soft-dying day[13],
  And touch the stubble plains[14] with rosy hue;
Then in a wailful choir[15] the small gnats[16] mourn
  Among the river sallows[17], borne aloft
    Or sinking as the light wind lives or dies[18];

---

1) *careless*: 속 편하게, 태평하게 (carelessly); Cf. *careless*: free from care or anxiety
2) *granary floor*: 곡물창고 바닥; *granary*: 곡물창고 (a storehouse for threshed grain)
3) *winnow*: 키질하다 (fan with a breeze, fan the chaff from the grain)
4) *drowse*: make drowsy
5) *the fume of poppies*: 양귀비 향기; *fume*: 향기 (an odour emitted from an object)
6) *hook*: 낫 (a scythe)
7) *spare the next swath*: 다음 벨 줄을 남겨 놓다; *swath*: 한 번 벤 면적 (a row or line of grass, corn, etc. as it falls when mown or reaped)
8) *gleaner*: 이삭 줍는 사람; *glean*: gather ears of corn left by reapers
9) *keep / Steady thy laden head across a brook*: 짐을 머리에 이고 개울을 건너다
10) *cider-press*: 사과 착즙기(搾汁機); 사과즙 짜는 기계(압착기)
11) *the last oozings*: 마지막 방울; *ooze*: 스며 나오다 (pass slowly through small openings)
12) *hours by hours*: 여러 시간 동안
13) *barred clouds bloom the soft-dying day*: 줄무늬 구름들이 조용히 저무는 하늘을 석양으로 물들이다; bloom: colour with a soft warm tint
14) *stubble plain*: 그루터기만 남은 들판
15) *in a wailful choir*: 구슬픈 합창으로
16) *gnat*: 각다귀 (a small two-winged biting fly)
17) *river sallow*: 강가의 버드나무; *sallow*: willow
18) *borne aloft / Or sinking as the light wind lives or dies*: 바람이 일거나 잦아듦에 따라 떠올랐다 가라앉았다 하는

And full-grown lambs loud bleat from hilly bourn[1];
Hedge-crickets sing; and now with treble soft[2]
The red-breast whistles from a garden-croft[3];
And gathering swallows twitter in the skies.

September 19, 1819 (1820)

---

1) *hilly bourn*: 언덕 가, 언덕 언저리; *bourn*: a boundary between fields, etc.

2) *treble soft*: 부드러운 고음

3) *garden croft*: 채원(菜園), 남새밭; croft: a plot of arable land attached to a house)

The Eve of St. Agnes

I

St. Agnes' Eve—Ah, bitter chill it was!
The owl, for all his feathers, was a-cold[1];
The hare limp'd trembling through the frozen grass,
And silent was the flock in woolly fold[2]:
Numb were the Beadsman's[3] fingers, while he told
His rosary[4], and while his frosted breath,
Like pious incense from a censer old,
Seem'd taking flight for heaven, without a death,
Past the sweet Virgin's picture, while his prayer he saith.

II

His prayer he saith, this patient, holy man;
Then takes his lamp, and riseth from his knees,
And back returneth, meagre[5], barefoot, wan,
Along the chapel aisle by slow degrees[6]:
The sculptur'd dead[7], on each side, seem to freeze,
Emprison'd in black, purgatorial rails[8]:
Knights, ladies, praying in dumb orat'ries[9],

---

* 성녀 아그네스제 전야(St. Agnes' Eve)는 처녀 수호성녀 아그네스 제일(祭日)인 1월 21일의 전야이다. 아그네스는 303년경 13세의 나이에 순교한 로마의 처녀다. 이날 밤에 처녀가 정해진 의식을 행하면 미래의 남편이 될 사람의 모습을 꿈에서 보게 된다고 전해진다. 키츠는 이 전설에 가문의 원한 때문에 사랑이 좌절된 로미오와 줄리엣의 주제를 결합시켜 이 작품을 썼다. 이 시는 더위와 추위, 진홍색과 은백색, 청춘과 노령, 환락과 고행, 관능과 순결, 생과 사, 천국과 지옥 등의 대조를 통하여 첫 사랑의 경험의 양면성을 상징적으로 묘사하고 있다.

1) *a-cold*: cold, chilled; 동사 "acool(=cool)"의 과거분사 형으로 추정됨

2) *wooly fold*: 양 우리, 양사(羊舍) (a sheepfold)

3) *beadsman*: 기도승 (돈을 받고 죽은 이의 명복을 빌어주는 사람) (a person paid to pray for others)

4) *told / His rosary*: 묵주(默珠)를 세었다; 기도승은 기도 횟수를 기억하기 위해 염주 알을 센다.

5) *meagre*: 야윈 (lean, thin)

6) *by slow degrees*: 천천히, 느린 걸음으로

7) *the sculptur'd dead*: (예배당 통로 양편에 세워져 있는) 사자(死者)들의 조상(彫像)

8) *purgatorial rails*: 연옥의 난간 (彫像을 에워싸고 있는 난간이 연옥을 연상시킨다)

9) *dumb orat'ries*: 조용한 기도실 (silent chapels); *oratory*: 작은 예배당, 기도실 (a small chapel,

He passeth by; and his weak spirit fails
To think how they may ache in icy hoods and mails[1].

III

Northward he turneth through a little door,
And scarce three steps, ere Music's golden tongue
Flatter'd to tears[2] this aged man and poor;
But no—already had his deathbell rung[3];
The joys of all his life were said and sung:
His was harsh penance[4] on St. Agnes' Eve:
Another way he went, and soon among
Rough ashes sat he for his soul's reprieve[5],
And all night kept awake, for sinners' sake to grieve.

IV

That ancient Beadsman heard the prelude soft;
And so it chanc'd[6], for many a door was wide,
From hurry to and fro. Soon, up aloft,
The silver, snarling[7] trumpets 'gan to chide[8]:
The level chambers, ready with their pride[9],
Were glowing[10] to receive a thousand guests:

---

a place for private worship); 기도실이 조용한 이유는 기도하는 기사와 귀부인들이 조상(彫像)들이기 때문이다.

1) *hoods and mails*: 두건과 갑옷; *mail*: armour composed of interlaced rings and chains
2) *flatter to tears*: 매혹시켜 눈물짓게 하다(charm to tears)
3) *already had his deathbell rung*: 이미 그의 조종은 울렸다 (이미 죽은 사람이나 마찬가지다)
4) *His was harsh penance*: 혹독한 참회를 하는 것이 그의 일이었다. *penance*: 참회, 고행 (죄의 고백, 회개, 사면 등을 포함하는 일련의 성사)
5) *among / Rough ashes sat he for his soul's reprieve*: 그는 영혼의 사면(赦免)을 위해 거친 재 속에 앉았다. Cf. *in sackcloth and ashes*: 깊이 뉘우치며 (거친 베를 걸치고 머리에 재를 뿌리는 것은 구약 성서 시대의 회개 또는 슬픔의 표시였다—Matthew 11:21; Esther 4:1; 2 Samuel 3:31 참조) *reprieve*: 집행 연기(respite), 일시적 구원
6) *so it chanc'd*: 우연히 (전주곡이) 들려왔다
7) *snarling*: 요란한; *snarl*: 으르렁거리다 (make a low angry sound, showing teeth)
8) *chide*: 꾸짖다(scold), 꾸짖는 소리로 울리다 (give loud and angry expression)
9) *The level chambers, ready with their pride*: 화려하게 치장한 평지(같은 층)의 방들; *pride*: 화려, 장려, 장엄한 장식 (pomp, magnificent or ostentatious adornment)
10) *glow*: 빛나다 (shine), 달아오르다 (burn with the fervor of emotion)

The carved angels, ever eager-eyed,
Star'd, where upon their heads the cornice[1] rests,
With hair blown back, and wings put cross-wise on their breasts.

V

At length burst in the argent revelry[2],
With plume, tiara[3], and all rich array[4],
Numerous as shadows haunting fairily[5]
The brain, new stuff d, in youth, with triumphs gay[6]
Of old romance. These let us wish away[7],
And turn, sole-thoughted[8], to one Lady there,
Whose heart had brooded, all that wintry day,
On love, and wing'd St. Agnes' saintly care[9],
As she had heard old dames full many times declare.

VI

They told her how, upon St. Agnes' Eve,
Young virgins might have visions of delight[10],
And soft adorings[11] from their loves receive
Upon the honey'd middle of the night,
If ceremonies due they did aright[12];
As, supperless to bed they must retire,
And couch supine their beauties[13], lily white;

---

1) cornice: 배내기, 처마 돌림띠 (천정과 벽이 만나는 곳에 띠 모양으로 두른 장식)
2) *argent revelry*: 은빛 옷을 입은 환락 객들(silver-clad revelers); *revelry*: revellers
3) *tiara*: 보석관(寶石冠) (보석이 박힌 여성용 머리 장식)
4) *rich array*: 화려한 성장(옷차림); *array*: attire, dress
5) shadows haunting fairily: 요정처럼 출몰하는 환영(幻影)들; *shadow*: phantom, ghost
6) *triumphs gay*: 화려한 축제(행렬); triumph: 축제(행렬) (public festivity, esp. one involving a procession)
7) *These let us wish away*: 이것들은 그만 생각하자; *wish away*: 없었으면 좋겠다고 생각하다
8) *sole-thoughtd*: 일념으로, 한 가지 생각으로
9) *wing'd St. Agnes' saintly care*: 날개 달린 성녀 아그네스의 성스러운 보살핌
10) *visions of delight*: 즐거운 환상
11) *adorings*: 연모(戀慕) (deep respect and affection)
12) *If ceremonies due they did aright*: 적당한 의식(儀式)을 바르게 행한다면
13) *couch supine their beauties*: 아름다운 육체(beauties)를 반듯이 눕다; *couch*: 침대에 눕다(lay on bed); *supine*: 반듯이 (lying face upwards)

Nor look behind, nor sideways, but require
Of Heaven with upward eyes for all that they desire.

VII

Full of this whim[1] was thoughtful Madeline:
The music, yearning like a God in pain,
She scarcely heard: her maiden eyes divine,
Fix'd on the floor, saw many a sweeping train[2]
Pass by—she heeded not at all: in vain
Came many a tiptoe[3], amorous cavalier[4],
And back retired[5]; not cool'd by high disdain,
But she saw not[6]: her heart was otherwhere:
She sigh'd for Agnes' dreams, the sweetest of the year.

VIII

She danc'd along with vague, regardless eyes[7],
Anxious her lips[8], her breathing quick and short:
The hallowed hour was near at hand: she sighs
Amid the timbrels, and the throng'd resort
Of whisperers[9] in anger, or in sport;
'Mid looks of love, defiance, hate, and scorn,
Hoodwink'd with faery fancy[10]; all amort[11],

---

1) *whim*: 변덕스러운 생각 (freakish idea), 환상 (a sudden fancy)
2) *sweeping train*: 휩쓸고 지나가는 행렬; *train*: succession of persons or things
3) *tiptoe*: (a) 들뜬 (excited), 기대에 부푼 (with eager expectation)
4) *amorous cavalier*: 사랑에 빠진 기사; *cavalier*: 기사 (knight), 예의 바른 신사(courtly gentleman)
5) *back retired*: 물러갔다
6) *not cool'd by high disdain, / But she saw not*: 그녀의 오만한 경멸에 열정이 식었기 때문이 아니라, 그녀가 보지 않았기 때문에 (not because they were cooled by Madeline's high disdain, but because she saw not); *cool*: make less ardent; *high*: haughty, arrogant
7) *vague, regardless eyes*: 멍하고 무관심한 눈; *regardless*: heedless, indifferent
8) *anxious her lips*: 입술은 불안에 떨리고 (her lips quivering with anxiety)
9) *the thronged resort / Of whisperers in anger, or in sport*: 화내거나 장난치며 속삭이는 사람들의 혼잡한 왕래; *resort*: a crowd, a person's frequenting of a place
10) *Hoodwinked with faery fancy*: 선경(仙境)의 환상에 눈이 가려진 채; *hoodwink*:cover the eyes of a person with a hood, delude; *faery*: enchanted, beautiful but unreal
11) *all amort*: 죽은 듯이 (as though dead); (성녀 아그네스와 털을 깎지 않은 양들과 내일 아침이 오기 전에 있을 모든 축복을 제외하고는) 모두 잊은 채

Save to St. Agnes and her lambs unshorn[1]),
And all the bliss to be before to-morrow morn.

IX

So, purposing each moment to retire,
She linger'd still. Meantime, across the moors,
Had come young Porphyro, with heart on fire
For Madeline[2]). Beside the portal doors,
Buttress'd from moonlight[3]), stands he, and implores
All saints to give him sight of Madeline,
But for one moment in the tedious hours,
That he might gaze and worship all unseen;
Perchance speak, kneel, touch, kiss—in sooth[4]) such things have been.

X

He ventures in: let no buzz'd whisper tell:
All eyes be muffled[5]), or a hundred swords
Will storm[6]) his heart, Love's fev'rous citadel[7]):
For him, those chambers held barbarian hordes[8]),
Hyena foemen[9]), and hot-blooded lords,
Whose very dogs would execrations[10]) howl
Against his lineage[11]): not one breast affords
Him any mercy, in that mansion foul,

---

1) *her lambs unshorn*: 털을 깎지 않은 아그네스의 양들 (성녀 아그네스 제일에 양털을 깎아 제단에 바치고 수녀들이 그 양모로 천을 짜는 것이 관습이었다.)
2) *with heart on fire / For Madeline*: 메디라인에 대한 사랑에 불타는 마음으로
3) *Buttressed from moonlight*: 버팀벽에 달빛이 가려진 채 (sheltered from the moonlight by buttresses)
4) *in sooth*: 실제로, 사실 (in fact, in truth)
5) *All eyes be muffled*: 모든 눈을 가려 못 보게 하라 (Let all eyes be muffled); *muffle*: cover up, wrap
6) *storm*: attack suddenly
7) *Love's fervorous citadel*: 뜨거운 사랑의 (신의) 성채 ("his heart"와 동격); *fervorous*: full of passion
8) *barbarian hordes*: 야만적인 무리들; *horde*: a troop, a gang
9) *Hyena foemen*: 하이에나 같은 적(敵)들
10) *execrations*: 저주 (curses)
11) *lineage*: 혈통, 계보 (lineal descent from an ancestor); 혈족들 (a tribe, a clan)

Save one old beldame[1], weak in body and in soul.

XI

Ah, happy chance! the aged creature came,
Shuffling along with ivory-headed wand[2],
To where he stood, hid from the torch's flame,
Behind a broad hall-pillar, far beyond
The sound of merriment and chorus bland[3]:
He startled her; but soon she knew his face,
And grasp'd his fingers in her palsied hand,
Saying, "Mercy, Porphyro! hie thee from this place[4];
They are all here to-night, the whole blood-thirsty race!

XII

"Get hence! get hence! there's dwarfish Hildebrand[5];
He had a fever late, and in the fit
He cursed thee and thine, both house and land:
Then there's that old Lord Maurice, not a whit
More tame for his gray hairs—Alas me! flit!
Flit like a ghost away."—"Ah, Gossip[6] dear,
We're safe enough; here in this arm-chair sit,
And tell me how"—"Good Saints![7] not here, not here;
Follow me, child, or else these stones will be thy bier."

XIII

He follow'd through a lowly arched way,
Brushing the cobwebs with his lofty plume;
And as she mutter'd "Well-a—well-a-day!"
He found him[8] in a little moonlight room,

---

1) *beldame*: 노파 (an old woman); "lovely lade"의 의미를 가진 프랑스어에서 유래
2) *ivory-headed wand*: 상아 손잡이 달린 지팡이
3) *bland*: 부드러운 (soft)
4) *Mercy, Porphyro! hie thee from this place*: 포피로, 제발 여기서 도망쳐요
5) *dwarfish Hildebrand*: 난장이 힐데브란드
6) *Gossip*: 할머니 (고어로 代母, 또는 옛 친구의 의미)
7) *Good saints!*: 제발!
8) *him*: himself

Pale, latticed, chill, and silent as a tomb.
"Now tell me where is Madeline," said he,
"O tell me, Angela, by the holy loom[1)]
Which none but secret sisterhood[2)] may see,
When they St. Agnes' wool are weaving piously."

XIV

"St. Agnes! Ah! it is St. Agnes' Eve—
Yet men will murder upon holy days:
Thou must hold water in a witch's sieve[3)],
And be liege-lord[4)] of all the Elves and Fays,
To venture so: it fills me with amaze
To see thee, Porphyro!—St. Agnes' Eve!
God's help! my lady fair the conjuror plays[5)]
This very night: good angels her deceive!
But let me laugh awhile, I've mickle[6)] time to grieve."

XV

Feebly she laugheth in the languid moon,
While Porphyro upon her face doth look,
Like puzzled urchin on an aged crone[7)]
Who keepeth clos'd a wond'rous riddle-book,
As spectacled she sits in chimney nook.
But soon his eyes grew brilliant, when she told
His lady's purpose; and he scarce could brook[8)]
Tears, at the thought of those enchantments cold,
And Madeline asleep in lap of legends old.

---

1) *loom*: 베틀; *by the holy loom*: 성스러운 베틀에 맹세코
2) *secret sisterhood*: 수녀 (nuns)
3) *Thou must hold water in a witch's sieve*: 당신은 마녀의 채에 물을 담아야 한다(마술의 힘을 빌리지 않고선 불가능하다); 채에 물을 담는 것은 마녀들의 상투적인 재주이다.
4) *liege-lord*: (봉건) 영주(領主) (a feudal superior, a sovereign)
5) *the conjuror plays*: 마술사 노릇을 하고 있다 (미래의 남편의 환상을 불러일으키려고)
6) *mickle*: much
7) *crone*: 쪼그랑 할머니 (withered old woman)
8) *brook*: 참다 (tolerate)

XVI

Sudden a thought came like a full-blown rose,
Flushing his brow, and in his pained heart
Made purple riot[1]: then doth he propose
A stratagem, that makes the beldame start:
"A cruel man and impious thou art:
Sweet lady, let her pray, and sleep, and dream
Alone with her good angels, far apart
From wicked men like thee. Go, go!—I deem
Thou canst not surely be the same that thou didst seem."

XVII

"I will not harm her, by all saints I swear,"
Quoth Porphyro: "O may I ne'er find grace
When my weak voice shall whisper its last prayer,
If one of her soft ringlets I displace,
Or look with ruffian passion[2] in her face:
Good Angela, believe me by these tears;
Or I will, even in a moment's space,
Awake, with horrid shout, my foemen's ears,
And beard[3] them, though they be more fang'd than wolves and bears."

XVIII

"Ah! why wilt thou affright a feeble soul?
A poor, weak, palsy-stricken, churchyard thing[4],
Whose passing-bell[5] may ere the midnight toll;
Whose prayers for thee, each morn and evening,
Were never miss'd."—Thus plaining, doth she bring
A gentler speech from burning Porphyro;
So woful, and of such deep sorrowing,
That Angela gives promise she will do
Whatever he shall wish, betide her weal or woe[6].

---

1) *made purple riot*: 피 끓는 반란을 일으켰다; purple: bloodstained, brilliant, striking
2) *ruffian passion*: 흉악한 욕정
3) *beard*: 맞서 싸우다 (oppose openly, defy)
4) *churchyard thing*: 무덤에 ane힐 사람
5) *passing bell*: 조종 (death knell)
6) *betide her weal or woe*: 그녀에게 행운이 오든 불행이 닥치든 간에; *betide*: happen to

XIX

Which[1] was, to lead him, in close secrecy,
Even to Madeline's chamber, and there hide
Him in a closet, of such privacy
That he might see her beauty unespied,
And win perhaps that night a peerless bride,
While legioned fairies[2] pac'd the coverlet,
And pale enchantment held her sleepy-eyed.
Never on such a night have lovers met,
Since Merlin paid his Demon all the monstrous debt[3].

XX

"It shall be as thou wishest," said the Dame:
"All cates and dainties[4] shall be stored there
Quickly on this feast-night: by the tambour frame[5]
Her own lute thou wilt see: no time to spare,
For I am slow and feeble, and scarce dare
On such a catering[6] trust my dizzy head.
Wait here, my child, with patience; kneel in prayer
The while: Ah! thou must needs the lady wed,
Or may I never leave my grave[7] among the dead."

XXI

So saying, she hobbled off[8] with busy fear.
The lover's endless minutes slowly pass'd;
The dame return'd, and whisper'd in his ear
To follow her; with aged eyes aghast

---

1) *Which*: 안젤라의 약속 (선행사는 앞 연에 있음)
2) *legioned fairies*: 수많은 요정들
3) *Since Merlin paid his Demon all the monstrous debt*: 멀린이 그의 악마에게 엄청난 빚을 갚은 이래로 (Merlin은 아서왕 전설에 나오는 마법사인데, 여 마법사 Vivien이 그가 가르쳐준 마법을 써서 그를 죽인다.)
4) *All cates and dainties*: 온갖 산해진미; *cate*: choice food; *dainty*: (delicacy
5) *tambour frame*: 북틀; *tambour*: drum
6) *On such a catering*: 이런 음식을 장만하는 일에; *cater*: provide meals
7) *leave my grave*: 내 무덤을 떠나다 (즉 부활을 의미한다)
8) *hobble off*: 절뚝거리며 걸어가다; *hobble*: walk lamely, limp

From fright of dim espial[1]. Safe at last,
Through many a dusky gallery, they gain
The maiden's chamber, silken, hush'd, and chaste;
Where Porphyro took covert[2], pleas'd amain.
His poor guide hurried back with agues in her brain.

XXII

Her falt'ring hand upon the balustrade,
Old Angela was feeling for the stair,
When Madeline, St. Agnes' charmed maid[3],
Rose, like a missioned spirit[4], unaware:
With silver taper's light, and pious care,
She turn'd, and down the aged gossip led
To a safe level matting[5]. Now prepare,
Young Porphyro, for gazing on that bed;
She comes, she comes again, like ring-dove fray'd and fled[6].

XXIII

Out went the taper as she hurried in;
Its little smoke, in pallid moonshine, died:
She clos'd the door, she panted, all akin
To spirits of the air, and visions wide[7]:

No uttered syllable, or, woe betide![8]
But to her heart, her heart was voluble[9],
Paining with eloquence her balmy side[10];

---

1) *From fright of dim espial*: 들킬까 봐 두려워서
2) *take covert*: 숨다; *covert*: shelter
3) *St. Agnes' charmed maid*: 성녀 아그네스에 매혹된 처녀
4) *missioned spirit*: 사명을 받은 천사
5) *matting*: 돗자리, 깔개
6) *like a ring-dove frayed and fled*: 겁에 질려 도망쳤던 산비둘기처럼; *fray*: frighten
7) *all akin / To spirits of the air, and visions wide*: 마치 공기의 요정들과 먼 환영들처럼
8) *No uttered syllable, or, woe betide!*: 한 마디도 말하지 마라, 그렇지 않으면 재앙이 닥치리라!
9) *But to her heart, her heart was voluble*: 그러나 그녀는 자신의 가슴에 말을 했다 (즉 혼자 말했다) 왜냐하면 그녀의 가슴은 달변(達辯)이었으니까 (But she uttered to her heart, for her heart was fluent.)
10) *her balmy side*: 향기로운 옆구리(를 아프게 했다)

As though a tongueless nightingale should swell
Her throat in vain, and die, heart-stifled, in her dell.

XXIV

A casement high and triple-arched[1] there was,
All garlanded with carven imag'ries
Of fruits, and flowers, and bunches of knot-grass[2],
And diamonded[3] with panes of quaint device[4],
Innumerable of stains and splendid dyes[5],
As are the tiger-moth's[6] deep-damasked[7] wings;
And in the midst, 'mong thousand heraldries[8],
And twilight saints[9], and dim emblazonings[10],
A shielded scutcheon blush'd with blood of queens and kings[11].

XXV

Full on this casement shone the wintry moon,
And threw warm gules[12] on Madeline's fair breast,
As down she knelt for heaven's grace and boon[13];
Rose-bloom fell on her hands, together prest[14],
And on her silver cross soft amethyst[15],

---

1) *a casement high and triple-arched*: 삼중(三重)의 아치를 이룬 높은 창문
2) *knot-grass*: 마디풀 (줄기에 마디가 있는 여뀌 속의 일년초)
3) *diamond*: (v) 다이아몬드처럼 박아 넣다 (furnish or adorn as with diamonds)
4) *quaint device*: 절묘한 무늬; *device*: 도안, 의장, 무늬 (design, figure)
5) *Innumerable of stains and splendid dyes*: 화려한 물감으로 물들인 수많은 유리 (전치사 "of" 앞에 "panes"를 보충할 것)
6) *tiger-moth*: 불나방 (날개에 반점이 있음)
7) *deep-damasked wings*: 짙은 분홍색 무늬가 있는 날개; damask: (양면에 화려한 무늬가 새겨진) 능직천 (a richly-figured woven silk with a pattern visible on either side, produced at Damascus)
8) *heraldry*: 문장(紋章)(가문을 표시하는 도형)
9) *twilight saints*: 어두운 성인상(聖人像)
10) *emblazonings*: 문장(紋章) 장식; *emblazon*: 문장을 새기다 (inscribe on a heraldic shield)
11) *A shielded scutcheon blushed with blood of queens and kings*: 여왕과 왕의 혈통으로 붉어진 문장(紋章)이 새겨진 방패; scutcheon: 가문(家紋)이 새겨진 방패 (*escutcheon*, the shield or shield-shaped surface on which a coat of arms is depicted)
12) *gules*: (紋章의) 붉은 빛 (the heraldic tincture red)
13) *boon*: 축복 (gift, blessing)
14) *hands, together prest*: 합장한 손
15) *amethyst*: 자수정 (a purple quartz)

And on her hair a glory[1], like a saint:
She seem'd a splendid angel, newly drest,
Save wings, for heaven:—Porphyro grew faint[2]:
She knelt, so pure a thing, so free from mortal taint[3].

XXVI

Anon his heart revives: her vespers[4] done,
Of all its wreathed pearls her hair she frees;
Unclasps her warmed jewels one by one;
Loosens her fragrant boddice[5]; by degrees
Her rich attire creeps rustling to her knees:
Half-hidden, like a mermaid in sea-weed,
Pensive awhile[6] she dreams awake, and sees,
In fancy, fair St. Agnes in her bed,
But dares not look behind, or all the charm is fled.

XXVII

Soon, trembling in her soft and chilly nest,
In sort of wakeful swoon, perplex'd[7] she lay,
Until the poppied warmth of sleep oppress'd
Her soothed limbs, and soul fatigued away;
Flown, like a thought, until the morrow-day;
Blissfully havened[8] both from joy and pain;
Clasp'd like a missal[9] where swart Paynims[10] pray;
Blinded alike from sunshine and from rain,

---

1) *a glory*: 원광(圓光), 후광(後光) (a circle of light, esp. as depicted around the head of Jesus or a saint)
2) *grew faint*: 기절했다
3) *free from mortal taint:* 속세의 때가 묻지 않은
4) *vespers*: 저녁기도 (evening prayers or devotions)
5) *fragrant bodice*: 향기로운 동의(胴衣); bodice: 동의, 코르셋 (a sleeveless undergarment for the upper body)
6) *pensive awhile*: 잠시 생각에 잠겨
7) *in a soft of wakeful swoon, perplexed she lay*: 잠과 깨어있음의 중간인 혼미한 상태로 그녀는 누워있었다.
8) *haven*: 피난시키다 (put into a haven, shelter in a haven)
9) *missal*: (삽화가 있는) 기도서 (a Roman Catholic book of prayers, esp. when illuminated)
10) *swart Paynims*: 피부색이 검은 이교도들; paynim: pagan, non-Christian, esp. Muslim)

As though a rose should shut, and be a bud again.

XXVIII

Stol'n to this paradise, and so entranced,
Porphyro gazed upon her empty dress,
And listen'd to her breathing, if it[1] chanced
To wake into a slumberous tenderness;
Which when he heard[2], that minute did he bless,
And breath'd himself: then from the closet crept,
Noiseless as fear in a wide wilderness,
And over the hush'd carpet, silent, stept,
And 'tween the curtains peep'd, where, lo!—how fast she slept.

XXIX

Then by the bed-side, where the faded moon
Made a dim, silver twilight, soft he set
A table, and, half anguish'd, threw thereon
A cloth of woven crimson, gold, and jet[3]:—
O for some drowsy Morphean amulet![4]
The boisterous, midnight, festive clarion,
The kettle-drum, and far-heard clarionet,
Affray[5] his ears, though but in dying tone:—
The hall door shuts again, and all the noise is gone.

XXX

And still she slept an azure-lidded sleep,
In blanched linen, smooth, and lavendered[6],
While he from forth the closet brought a heap

---

1) *it*: her breathing

2) *which when he heard*: 숨소리를 들었을 때 (which의 선행사는 "her breathing"이고, which는 heard의 목적어)

3) *jet*: 검은색 (deep glossy black)

4) *O for some drowsy Morphean amulet!*: 아 졸음이 오게 하는 잠의 신(Morpheus)의 부적(amulet)이 있었으면!

5) *affray*: 겁주다 (frighten)

6) *In blanched linen, smooth, and lavendered:* 매끄럽고 라벤다 향기가 나는 표백된 린네르 옷을 입고

Of candied apple, quince[1], and plum, and gourd[2];
With jellies soother than the creamy curd[3],
And lucent syrups, tinct with cinnamon[4];
Manna and dates, in argosy transferred[5]
From Fez[6]; and spiced dainties[7], every one,
From silken Samarcand to cedared Lebanon[8].

XXXI

These delicates[9] he heaped with glowing hand
On golden dishes and in baskets bright
Of wreathed[10] silver: sumptuous[11] they stand
In the retired quiet of the night[12],
Filling the chilly room with perfume light.—
"And now, my love, my seraph fair, awake!
Thou art my heaven, and I thine eremite[13]:
Open thine eyes, for meek St. Agnes' sake,
Or I shall drowse[14] beside thee, so my soul doth ache."

XXXII

Thus whispering, his warm, unnerved[15] arm
Sank in her pillow. Shaded was her dream

---

1) *quince*: 마르멜로
2) *gourd*: 참외 (melon)
3) *creamy curd*: 크림 응유(凝乳)
4) tinct with cinnamon: 시나몬 맛이 나는; tinct: coloured, tinted
5) *in argosy transferred*: 큰 배로 실어온; argosy: 큰 상선 (large merchant-vessel)
6) *Fez*: 아프리카 북서부 모로코의 도시
7) *spiced dainties*: 향료를 가미한 산해진미들
8) *From silken Samarcand to cedared Lebanon*: 비단의 사마르칸드(우즈베크 공화국 동부, 아프가니스탄 북쪽에 있는 도시)에서 삼목 우거진 레바논까지
9) *delicates*: 맛있는 음식, 진미(珍味) (choice or dainty items of food)
10) *wreathe*: intertwine to form a single structure, adorn with a wreath; *baskets bright / Of wreathed silver*: 꽃 장식이 있는 빛나는 은 바구니
11) *sumptuous*: 화려한 호화로운 (rich and costly)
12) *In the retired quiet of the night*: (사람들이 잠든) 한적하고 고요한 밤에; *retire*: go to bed, withdraw to seek shelter
13) *eremite*: 은자(隱者) (hermit)
14) *drowse*: be drowsy or half asleep, doze
15) *unnerved*: 나른한, 힘없는 (physically weak)

By the dusk curtains:—'twas a midnight charm
Impossible to melt as iced stream:
The lustrous salvers[1] in the moonlight gleam;
Broad golden fringe[2] upon the carpet lies:
It seem'd he never, never could redeem[3]
From such a stedfast spell his lady's eyes;
So mused awhile, entoiled in woofed phantasies[4].

XXXIII

Awakening up, he took her hollow lute[5],—
Tumultuous[6],—and, in chords that tenderest be[7],
He play'd an ancient ditty, long since mute,
In Provence call'd, "La belle dame sans mercy:"[8]
Close to her ear touching the melody;—
Wherewith disturbed[9], she utter'd a soft moan:
He ceased—she panted quick—and suddenly
Her blue affrayed[10] eyes wide open shone:
Upon his knees he sank, pale as smooth-sculptured stone.

XXXIV

Her eyes were open, but she still beheld,
Now wide awake, the vision of her sleep:
There was a painful change, that nigh[11] expelled

---

1) *salver*: 접시, 쟁반 (a tray or flat dish of metal)
2) *fringe*: 가장자리, (숄, 스카프 따위의 가장자리에 달린) 술장식 (ornamental bordering of threads left loose or formed into tassels or twists
3) *redeem*: 되찾다 (recover); 목적어는 "his lady's eyes"
4) entoiled in woofed phantasies: 복잡하게 얽힌 환상에 사로잡혀 (entangled in a weave of fantasies); *entoil*: 사로잡다, 덫에 걸리게 하다 (ensnare); *woof*: 천을 짜다(weave)
5) *lute*: 류트 (17세기의 기타 같이 생긴 현악기)
6) *tumultuous*: disturbed, confused
7) *in chords that tenderest be*: 가장 부드러운 화음으로; *chord*: 가락, 화음(和音) (a group of notes sounded together)
8) *"La belle dame sans mercy"*: "무자비한 미녀"; 15세기 프랑스 시인 Alain Chartier의 시 제목인데 키츠가 같은 제목으로 시를 지었다.
9) Wherewith disturbed: 그 선율에 잠이 깨어 (Disturbed by the melody)
10) *affrayed*: 놀란 (frightened)
11) *nigh*: almost

The blisses of her dream so pure and deep
At which[1] fair Madeline began to weep,
And moan forth witless words[2] with many a sigh;
While still her gaze on Porphyro would keep;
Who knelt, with joined hands and piteous eye,
Fearing to move or speak, she looked so dreamingly.

XXXV

"Ah, Porphyro!" said she, "but even now
Thy voice was at sweet tremble in mine ear,
Made tuneable with every sweetest vow;
And those sad eyes were spiritual and clear:
How changed thou art! how pallid, chill, and drear!
Give me that voice again, my Porphyro,
Those looks immortal, those complainings dear[3]!
Oh leave me not in this eternal woe,
For if thou diest, my Love, I know not where to go."

XXXVI

Beyond a mortal man[4] impassioned far
At these voluptuous accents[5], he arose,
Ethereal[6], flush'd, and like a throbbing star
Seen mid the sapphire heaven's deep repose;
Into her dream he melted, as the rose
Blendeth its odour with the violet,—
Solution sweet[7]: meantime the frost-wind blows
Like Love's alarum[8] pattering[9] the sharp sleet

---

1) *At which*: 그 변화에; which의 선행사는 "a painful change"
2) *witless words*: 분별없는 말; *witless*: lacking wisdom or sense, foolish
3) *complainings dear*: 사랑스런 하소연
4) *Beyond a mortal man impassioned far*: 이 세상 사람이 경험할 수 있는 것 이상으로 감명을 받아; 어순은 "Impassioned far beyond a mortal man"이다. *impassioned*: deeply moved
5) *voluptuous accents*: 요염한 말(투); *voluptuous*: 육감적인, 관능적인, 요염한 (suggestive of sensuous or sensual pleasure); *accents*: (mode of) speech
6) *ethereal*: (공기처럼) 가벼운 (light, airy), 천상의 (celestial), 영묘한
7) *solution sweet*: 감미로운 융합; solution: 용해(溶解) (the state of dissolving or being dissolved)
8) *Like Love's alarum*: 사랑의 신의 경보(警報)처럼
9) *patter*: 두드리다, 부딪치게 하다 (cause to strike with a rapid succession of short soft strokes)

Against the window-panes; St. Agnes' moon hath set.

XXXVII

'Tis dark: quick pattereth the flaw-blown sleet[1]:
"This is no dream, my bride, my Madeline!"
'Tis dark: the iced gusts still rave and beat:
"No dream, alas! alas! and woe is mine!
Porphyro will leave me here to fade and pine.—
Cruel! what traitor could thee hither bring?
I curse not, for my heart is lost in thine,
Though thou forsakest a deceived thing[2];—
A dove forlorn and lost with sick unpruned[3] wing."

XXXVIII

"My Madeline! sweet dreamer! lovely bride!
Say, may I be for aye thy vassal blest[4]?
Thy beauty's shield, heart-shap'd and vermeil dyed?
Ah, silver shrine, here will I take my rest
After so man2y hours of toil and quest,
A famished pilgrim[5],—saved by miracle.
Though I have found, I will not rob thy nest
Saving of thy sweet self[6]; if thou think'st well
To trust, fair Madeline, to no rude infidel[7]."

XXXIX

"Hark! 'tis an elfin-storm from faery land[8],
Of haggard seeming[9], but a boon indeed:

---

1) *the flaw-blown sleet*: 질풍에 날리는 진눈깨비; *flaw*: 돌풍. (a sudden blast or gust of wind)
2) *a deceived thing*: 속아 넘어간 사람 (즉 Madeline 자신)
3) *unpruned*: 다듬지 않은, 헝클어진; *prune*: (새가) 부리로 깃털을 다듬다 (preen the feathers)
4) *vassal blest*: 행복한 신하; *vassal*: 신하 (a humble servant), 봉신(封臣)
5) *famished pilgrim*: 베고픈 순례자: *famish*: reduce to extreme hunger
6) *Saving of thy sweet self*: 귀여운 당신을 제외하고는
7) *if thou think'st well / To trust...to no rude infidel*: 만약 당신이 무례하지 않은 이교도인 나를 신뢰하겠다고 생각한다면
8) *faery land*: 요정의 나라, 선경(仙境)
9) *haggard seeming*: 난폭해 보이는; haggard: wild-looking, untamed

Arise—arise! the morning is at hand;—
The bloated wassaillers[1] will never heed:—
Let us away, my love, with happy speed;
There are no ears to hear, or eyes to see,—
Drown'd all in Rhenish and the sleepy mead[2]:
Awake! arise! my love, and fearless be,
For o'er the southern moors I have a home for thee."

XL

She hurried at his words, beset with fears,
For there were sleeping dragons all around,
At glaring[3] watch, perhaps, with ready spears—
Down the wide stairs a darkling way they found.—
In all the house was heard no human sound.
A chain-droop'd lamp[4] was flickering by each door;
The arras[5], rich with horseman, hawk, and hound,
Flutter'd in the besieging wind's uproar[6];
And the long carpets rose along the gusty floor.

XLI

They glide, like phantoms, into the wide hall;
Like phantoms, to the iron porch, they glide;
Where lay the Porter, in uneasy sprawl[7],
With a huge empty flaggon[8] by his side;
The wakeful bloodhound[9] rose, and shook his hide,
But his sagacious eye an inmate owns[10]:

---

1) *bloated wassailers*: 오만한 주객(酒客)들: *bloated*: swollen with pride;
2) *Rhenish and the sleepy mead*: 라인 산 포도주와 졸리게 하는 꿀술; *Rhenish*: Rhine wine
3) *glaring watch*: 노려보는 감시; *glare*: stare fiercely
4) *chain-drooped lamp*: 사슬에 매달린 등불
5) *arras*: (아름다운 그림무늬를 짜 넣은) 벽걸이, 커튼
6) *the besieging wind's uproar*: 몰려오는 바람의 소란
7) *in uneasy sprawl*: 불편하게 사지를 뻗고 누워; *sprawl*: (v) spread one's limbs in a careless way, (n) sprawling attitude
8) *flaggon*: 큰 술병 (a large vessel, with handle, spout, and lid)
9) *bloodhound*: 맹견 (a large keen-scented dog)
10) *an inmate owns*: 집안사람을 알아본다; *own*: recognize as an acquaintance

By one, and one, the bolts full easy slide[1]:—
The chains lie silent on the footworn stones[2];—
The key turns, and the door upon its hinges groan.

XLII

And they are gone: ay, ages long ago
These lovers fled away into the storm.
That night the Baron[3] dreamt of many a woe,
And all his warrior-guests, with shade and form
Of witch, and demon, and large coffin-worm[4],
Were long be-nightmared[5]. Angela the old
Died palsy-twitch'd[6], with meagre face deform[7];
The Beadsman, after thousand aves told[8],
For aye unsought for[9] slept among his ashes cold.

1819 (1820)

---

1) *By one, and one, the bolts full easy slide*: 하나씩 하나씩 빗장이 쉽게 벗겨진다.
2) *footworn stones*: 발길에 닳은 돌
3) *the Baron*: 남작 (그 성의 성주)
4) *coffin-worm*: 관(棺) 벌레
5) *were be-nightmared*: 악몽을 꾸었다
6) *died palsy-twitched*: 중풍 경련으로 죽었다; *twitch*: 경련을 일으키다 (give a sudden sharp pull)
7) *with meagre face deform*: 일그러진 수척한 얼굴로; *deform*: (a) deformed
8) after thousand aves told: 아베마리아를 천 번 외우고 나서 (after telling thousand aves): *ave*: 성모송 (Ave Maria: "Hail Mary"); "Hail, thou that art highly favored, the Lord is with thee: blessed art thou among women." (Luke 1:28, 42 참조)
9) *For aye unsought for*: 영원히 찾는 이 없이 (기도 요청을 받지 못하고)

Selected Bibliography

1. Primary Sources:

Allott, Miriam (ed.). *The Poems of John Keats*. London and New York: Longman, 1970.

Barnard, John (ed.). *John Keats, the Complete Poems*. Harmondsworth, 1973.

Bullett, Gerald. *John Keats's Poems*. London: Dent & Sons, 1957.

Keats, John. *The Letters of John Keats, 1814-1821*, ed. by Hyder E. Rollins, 2 vols. Cambridge, 1958.

2. Secondary Sources:

Baker, Jeffrey. *John Keats and Symbolism*. Sussex: The Harvester Press, 1986.

Bloom, Harold. *John Keats* (Modern Critical Views 52). New York: Chelsea House Publishers, 1985.

D'Vanzo, Mario L. *Keats's Metaphors for the Poetic Imagination*. Durham, N.C.: Duke UP, 1967.

Evert, Walter H. *Aesthetic and Myth in the Poetry of Keats*. Princeton, NJ.: Princeton UP, 1965.

Garrod, H. W. *Keats*. Oxford, 1926.

Ghent, Dorothy Van. *Keats: The Myth of the Hero*. Princeton UP, 1983.

Gittings, Robert. *John Keats: The Living Year*. London: Heinemann, 1954, 1978.

Hirst, Wolf Z. *John Keats* (Twayne's English Authors Series). Boston: Twayne Publishers, 1981.

Jones, John. *John Keats's Dream of Truth*. London: Chatto & Windus, 1969.

Pollard, David. *The Poetry of Keats: Language & Experience*. Sussex: The Harvester Press, 1984.

Ridley, M. R. *Keats' Craftmanship*. London, 1933.

Rollins, Hyder Edward (ed.). *The Letters of John Keats: 1814-1821*. Cambridge, Mass.: Harvard UP, 1958.

Sperry. Stuart M. *Keats: the Poet*. Princeton, N. J.: Princeton UP, 1973.

Vendler, Helen. *The Odes of John Keats*. Harvard UP, 1983.

Waldoff, Leon. *Keats and the Silent Work of Imagination*. Urbana and Chicago: University of Illinois P, 1985.

Watts, Cedric. *A Preface to Keats*. London and New York: Longman, 1985.